The
Electronic
Marketing
Manual

The Electronic Marketing Manual

Cecil C. Hoge, Sr.

McGraw-Hill, Inc.

New York   San Francisco   Washington, D.C.   Auckland   Bogotá
Caracas   Lisbon   London   Madrid   Mexico City   Milan
Montreal   New Delhi   San Juan   Singapore
Sydney   Tokyo   Toronto

Library of Congress Cataloging-in-Publication Data

Hoge, Cecil C.
    The electronic marketing manual : integrating electronic media into
your marketing campaign / Cecil C. Hoge, Sr.
        p.   cm.
    Includes index.
    ISBN 0-07-029365-1
    1. Telemarketing—Handbooks, manuals, etc.
I. Title.   HF5415.1265.H64 1993
    658.8'4–dc20   92-44804
                                                                            CIP

    2 3 4 5 6 7 8 9 0   DOC/DOC   9 9 8 7 6 5 4

ISBN   0-07-029365-1

*The sponsoring editor for this book was Betsy N. Brown, the editing supervisor
was Caroline Levine, and the production supervisor was Donald Schmidt. It was
set in Palatino by McGraw-Hill's Professional Book Group composition unit.*

Printed and bound by R. R. Donnelley & Sons Company.

To Fritzi
Partner, Wife, and
Always There

Contents

Preface   xix
Acknowledgments   xxv

1. What Is Electronic Marketing?   1

Whom Does EM Most Concern?   2
Each New Medium Affects Others   3
EM Is No Panacea   3
What Failures Teach   4
Dramatic and Frequent Failures but Overall Success   5
Electronic Marketing—Your Business from Home   5
Electronic Moonlighting   6
Why EM Succeeds   7
Picture Yourself Sitting in My Office   7
Help Source Guide   9

2. Getting Started   11

The Internal EM Team   12
Outside Help versus Do-It-Yourself   12
    Production Houses   13
    Produce-It-Yourself Projects   13
    Service Bureaus   15
    Serve Yourself   16
    Consultants   16

Advertising Agencies 17
  Selecting the Right Agency 17
  Setting Up a House Agency 19
Market Research Companies 19
  Report Forms 21
  Free Research 21
  Do-It-Yourself Research 21
  How Your Firm Services Customers 22
  The Marketing Plan 23
  Target Marketing 23
  Market Testing 24
Creating the Right EM Message 24
Help Source Guide 25

3. **Audience Research and Measurement for Broadcast
   TV, Cable, and Radio**   27

Who Measures...and How 28
The People Meter 28
Ratings 29
  Rating Reports 29
  Detailed Data Provided 29
  Sample Sufficiency Varies 31
Sales, Audience Measurement, and Advertising 31
  Traced Sales Get More Promotion Dollars 32
  Combining Audience and Sales Measurement 32
  Better Measurement of Sales 33
Marketing Research Data and Target Marketing 33
  Single-Source Data 34
  How a Single-Source Study Works 34
  Many Constraints 36
Research Priorities 37
  Computer Help Increasing 37
  Calculating Geographical Coverage 38
  Free Media Research Help 39
  The Terms 39
  Before Media Selection 40
  Can Research Experts Help You? 41
  Selecting and Negotiating Other EM Media 41
  Electronic Direct Marketing Media 41
  Electronic Co-Media and Support Media 42
Help Source Guide 43

4. **Broadcast TV**   45

Broadcast TV Still Reigns 46
  How to Get More from Less 47
  Getting Started 48
  How to Test Market BTV 50

Some BTV Viewing Trends   51
Network BTV   52
    Big Network Targets   52
    Giant Audience Limits Targeting   53
    Specialized Networks   53
Spot TV   54
    More Kinds of Winning Shows   54
    Audience Research Is Vital   55
    Computer Programs Help   55
How to Buy Spot TV   56
    Bargaining Begins   57
    Small Markets   57
    If You're a Local Advertiser   59
Help Source Guide   62

5. Cable TV: For Biggest National and Smallest Local
   Advertisers   65

Should You Use Cable?   66
    Where Other Media Might Be Better   67
    Why Cable Works for So Many   67
The Cable Networks   68
    How Top Marketers Buy Network Cable   68
    How to Analyze a Cable Network Buy   68
    The Biggest-Audience Cable Networks   70
    Winning Formats   70
    Cable Networks Start and Change   72
    Competition Creates Opportunity   72
    Investigate Network Cable Carefully   73
National Spot and Local Cable   73
    Locally Programmed Cable   74
    Spot Cable   75
    A Better Way to Analyze Local Cable   75
    Spot and Local Cable Cost   76
    Local Entrepreneurs Benefit   76
    Many Local Success Stories   78
    Cable Classifieds   79
Help Source Guide   81

6. How to Make a TV Commercial That Sells   83

Do Your Homework   84
    Study Classic TV Commercials   84
    Zap Programs—Watch Commercials   85
    Analyze Each Commercial's Purpose   85
Production Decisions   86
    How Much Do-It-Yourself?   86
    Software-Made Commercials   88

Lowest-Cost TV Studio Commercials   88
Crude Productions   89
The Next Rung on the Quality Ladder   90
A Successful Commercial   91
Copy Writing as a Start   91
Storyboards   92
Do-It-Yourself TV Copy   92
Increasing Quality in Commercials   94
How Much Should You Spend?   96
How to Select a TV Production Firm   97
Last Chance for the Least-Cost Change   99
Cost Self-Control   99
A Final Caution   100
Help Source Guide   100

7. Radio: How to Benefit Most from What It Does Best   101

What Companies Use Radio Most?   102
How to Start   104
Organize a Team   104
Creating the Best Radio Copy   105
Producing Your Radio Commercial   106
How to Buy Radio Time   107
Test-Marketing Costs   109
Programming Creates the Audience   110
Look for the Right Format Combination   111
Quality before Quantity   112
How Frequently and How Long Should You Run?   113
Further Suggestions   117
Help Source Guide   118

8. In-Bound Telemarketing   119

How to Prepare   122
What to Do If You Succeed   122
Gear Up Gradually   123
Should You Use an 800 Number?   123
Should You Use a Telemarketing Service Bureau?   126
How a Phone Service Bureau Works   127
Growing Bureau Flexibility   128
Two Ways to Overcome Bureau Disadvantages   128
What Are Your Needs?   129
How to Avoid the Biggest In-Bound Telemarketing Disasters   130
Don't Waste Your Advertising   130
A College Dropout's Lesson   131
Some Other Ideas That Have Worked   134
Help Source Guide   135

9. Organized Out-Bound Telemarketing   137

Avoiding Failure   138
Telemarketing and the Smallest Business   139
  Try First What Is Easiest   139
  Tell Them What They Want to Know   140
  Next Easiest Calls   141
Database Marketing   142
Cold Calls   144
  Cold Calling's First Problem   145
  Calling Someone You Don't Know   145
  Revolutionize Your Business by Phone   146
Growing by Out-Bound Phone   148
Telemarketing Scripts   149
  Creating a Script   150
  Staffing and Training   150
The Role of Telemarketing Specialists   151
Out-Bound Phone Service Bureaus or In-House?   152
Help Source Guide   154

10. Audiotext: Voice Mail, Talking Ads, and Telemedia   155

What Is a Voice System?   156
  A Technological Revolution   157
  Voice Systems and Marketing   157
Voice Mail Transforms the Business Phone   158
  Increased Sales at Little Cost   158
  Instant, Automated, Interactive Ordering   159
  Start Simple   159
Talking Ads   159
Sponsored Telemedia   161
  How Sponsored Telemedia Works   162
  Telemedia: Simple, Cheap, Sometimes Risky   163
  Creating Your Telemedia   164
Marketing via 900 Numbers   166
  Advertising   167
  Big Companies Dominate   168
  Self-Liquidating Response Medium   168
  Sponsored Pay Dial-It   169
Local Market Tests   170
900 Numbers   171
Dial-It Service Bureaus   171
Parting Cautions   171
Help Source Guide   172

11. Fax Marketing 175

Should You Use Fax Marketing? 175
How Fax Works 176
Computers Turn Fax into Medium 177
Fax and Faxmail Marketing 178
  Fax Break-Throughs 180
  Trends to Watch 184
Help Source Guide 186

12. Video Brochures 189

How Do You Start? 191
  Your Company Concept on Video 192
  Do You Advertise on TV? 192
  Do You Direct Market? 193
Video Response Success 193
Video as Public Relations 196
Video Brochures and Other Media 197
Retail Videos 197
Avoid Video Failure 199
Make Your Video a Profit Center 201
Help Source Guide 203

13. Video Catalogs 205

Education and the Video Cocatalog 207
Guidelines for Success 208
  Marco Polo 208
  Common Questions about Video Catalogs 209
  Timing and Tone 209
  Video Brochures Combined into a Catalog: Wood Mizer 210
  The Spiegel VC Analysis 211
How to Test-Market a VC 213
  Important Packaging Reminders 214
  Phone Follow-up and Multiple Use 214
  Rolling Out Your VC-Test Success 215
Proceed with Promotions Step by Step 216
Judging Success at Each Stage 218
Last Suggestions on Tests and Roll-Outs 218
Help Source Guide 219

14. Making a Video According to Your Needs 221

The Right Spokesperson 222
Previous Footage 222
How Others Succeed 222
  International Business Exchange 223
  Apple Computer 224

Wood Mizer   225
Doug Miles   228
Marco Polo Ltd.   229
Video Consultants   231
Help Source Guide   231

15. Video Media   **233**

Ads in Movies on Videocassettes   233
  New Possibilities   235
  Considering Video Sponsorship   235
  The Self-Help Profit Center   237
Videos as Premiums   238
  Big Marketers   239
  Small Successes   240
Lessons from the Master Marketer   241
Video Magazines   242
Movie Theater Commercials   244
Help Source Guide   245

16. Interative Computer Disks   **247**

Considering Disk Marketing   249
Researching Disk Marketing   250
Getting Started   251
ID Promotion Costs   252
Sales Applications   253
  Sales for One-Twentieth of Former Cost!   253
  Chase Manhattan's ID   255
  Other ID Applications   255
Can ID Marketing Expand?   257
Help Source Guide   258

17. Interactive Catalogs on Computer Disk   **261**

Considering IDcats   262
  Car IDcats   263
  Other Consumer IDcat Markets   267
Business-to-Business IDcats   267
IDs versus IDcats   269
Do-It-Yourself IDcats   270
HC IDcat Sold to the Fortune 1000   271
Help Source Guide   273

18. Modem Marketing: E-Mail, EDI, Bulletin Boards   **275**

Basic Modem Applications   275
Communications Tool to Marketing   277
EDI Networks   278

EDI Preparation   280
How EDI Works   281
Considering EDI   282
Marketing Information Online   283
Online PR   283
Shareware   284
Product-Support BBSs   286
Service and Cross-Selling   286
BBS Take-Off under Way   287
Help Source Guide   288

**19. Information and Entertainment Networks: Videotex
and the Super Bulletin Boards**   **289**

CompuServe   290
Marketing via CompuServe   291
Electronic Mail Promotions   291
CompuServe's Disadvantages   292
CompuServe Improvements   292
Prodigy   293
An Electronic Magazine   293
Prodigy Providers and Advertisers Succeed   294
Prodigy Costs, Requirements, Benefits   298
Other I & E Networks   299
GEnie   299
Byte Created BIX   299
Two Other I & E Networks to Watch   300
Check and Compare Networks   301
Help Source Guide   301

**20. Online Catalogs: Consumer, Trade, and Special-
Purpose Markets**   **303**

Considering an Online Catalog   305
I & E Networks for Online Catalogs   305
Leveraging Your Online Experience   306
Low-Cost Phone and Promotions   307
Other Promotion Ideas   307
Online Catalog Items   308
Tips for Success   310
BBS Catalogs   312
Buying Online Catalog Software   313
Help Source Guide   315

21. Online Marketplaces   **317**

Finding Online Marketplaces That Fit   318
The Salvage Marketplace Network   319
The Online Yacht Marketplace   320

Bargain Ad Marketplace   321
PUBNET   321
Other Online Marketplaces   322
Results   323
Marketplace Tour de Force   324
Independent Travel Marketplace   325
Starting a Marketplace   326
Help Source Guide   327

22. CD-ROM: Catalogs and Marketplaces   329

Should You Market via CD-ROM?   330
Marketing Uses   331
Auto Parts Catalogs on CD-ROM   333
Jet Parts Catalog   332
CAD/CAM Catalogs   332
New CD-ROM Sales Method   333
Creating a CD-ROM Catalog   335
Should You Use a Service Bureau?   336
In-House CD-ROM Production   336
What Should CD-ROM Catalogs Cost?   337
CD-ROM Marketplaces: Sharing Costs   338
The Mannequin Marketplace   339
Furniture Marketplace   340
The Spread of CD-ROM Marketplaces   340
CD-ROM Off-Shoots   341
Help Source Guide   342

23. Electronic Marketing Machines   345

ATMs   345
Multimedia Kiosks   346
What a High-Tech Electronic Kiosk Contains   347
Much Promise, Many Failures   347
Effective Uses of Multimedia Kiosks   351
Big Changes Expected   353
Digital Video Interactive Technology (DVI)   355
Compact Disc Interactive Technology (CD-I)   356
DVI versus CD-I   356
Creating Kiosk Programs   357
Help Source Guide   358

24. Retail Marketing Machines   361

Considering In-Store Kiosk Marketing   363
Researching In-Store Kiosks   363
The ATM Model   364
ATMs Go Network   364
ATM Habit Took 20 Years   365

ATMs Keep Improving   365
How Kiosks Can Succeed   366
  Salesperson Upgrade   369
  Study Kiosk Methods   370
  Ingenious In-Store Kiosk Services   372
  Do-It-Yourself Design Kiosks   372
Kiosk Market Research   373
Help Source Guide   375

25. Mass Outlet In-Store Electronic Media   **377**

Considering In-Store Electronic Media   379
On Shelf Computer Kiosks   379
  National Rollout   381
  Variations of Shelf Kiosks   381
Fun Kiosks   382
  Microkiosk Games   382
  Single-Media Electronic Sales Help   383
  VCR Demonstrations   383
  In-Store VCR Networks   383
  Talking Displays and Products   384
  Computer Disk Displays   384
In-Store Electronic Ad Media   385
In-Store TV and Radio Broadcasting   385
Health Information and Ad Network   386
Video Preview Kiosks   387
In-Store Animated Sign Networks and Direction Kiosks   387
The Advertising Video-Wall   387
The Couponing Kiosk   388
  Combining Media and Couponing   389
  Coupon Targeting and Tracking   389
  Three-in-One Kiosk   390
Keeping Up with Change   391
Help Source Guide   392

26. Electronic Marketing Machines in Public Places and Trade Shows   **393**

Direct-Marketing Public Kiosks   394
  In-Bank ATMs Go Public   395
  Fax Kiosks   396
  Other Unstaffed Transactional Kiosks   396
  Unstaffed Inquiry Kiosks   398
Staffing Public Kiosks   398
Big Mall Traffic   399
Kiosk Lead-Getting   400
Test-Market First   401
Expand with Caution and Trace Results   401
Kiosks in Trade Shows   402

Kiosk Market Research   403
Other Kiosk Uses   403
Help Source Guide   405

27. Direct Broadcast Satellite Business Television Marketing   407

How Business TV Works   408
Business TV Costs   409
Considering Business TV   410
Different Kinds of Business TV   411
DBS Creates a New Industry   417
Satellite Real Estate Auctions   419
Sharing the Cost   419
New Strategies for Ads on DBS Programs   420
Another Business TV Network   420
The Evolution of Business TV   421
Help Source Guide   421

28. Other Profitable Forms of Electronic Marketing   423

Audio Marketing   423
    Success Can Be Natural   425
    Considering Audio   426
Vending Becomes Marketing   426
    Audioconferencing   429
    Audioconferencing as a Free Service   431
    AC Marketing Applications   432
Videoconferencing   433
    The Videoconference Facilities Room   433
    Public Videoconference Rooms   434
    Considering Videoconferencing   435
Electronic Targeted Magazines   435
Other Innovations in Electronic Marketing   436
Help Source Guide   437

29. Electronic Customer Service   439

Customers Lost by Phone   439
The General Electric Model   441
    Selecting and Training Staff   441
    Answering the Right Questions   443
    Turning Complaints into Profits   443
Other Customer Service Models   445
Many Service Possibilities   452
Help Source Guide   454

30. The Integration of EM into All Marketing   457

The Electronically Enhanced Sales Force   461
Integrating Sales and Advertising, Telemarketers, and
   the Salesforce   463
Integrating All Direct Marketing   464
   IDM-Enhanced TV   465
   Catalog and Phone Combined   466
   Multimedia Integration   467
   Enhanced, Integrated PR   468
Judging EM Enhancement   470
   Which EM Enhancement Fits?   470
   The Spectrum of EM Forms   471
   Integrating EM Most Profitably   473
Help Source Guide   473

Index   474

Preface

Electronic marketing is not new. Telegraph marketing began over 150 years ago. Telephone marketing is now over 100 years old, radio over 70 years, broadcast TV almost half a century, and cable over 25 years old. The power of electronic marketing to sell is not new; neither is its dominant role in all marketing and its ability to mesh with and make more effective other forms of marketing.

The change and evolution of each electronic marketing medium into newer, more effective media is well known. Telegraphed sales proposals, the first interactive form of electronic marketing, led to proposals by telex, then by fax, and most recently by electronic mail (E-mail). Likewise, commercials on gramophone records led to those on film, on audiotape, and then, videotape.

What is new is the accelerated pace of change of present electronic media and methods and the much bigger increase and creation of quite new electronic marketing. Let's discuss the forces behind this.

A Response to the Economy

There is no profit protection for industries or businesses, or job security for middle or top executives or trainees. If the competition offers better products and quality control, better service and customer satisfaction, or more effective financial controls and marketing, the livelihood of these professionals can be threatened. There is no solution but to rise to such challenges, catch up, equal, and surpass the competition. To every action there is a reaction, any problem can lead to a solution.

The biggest cost in retailing—labor—keeps rising. People costs, including benefits, are rising for most companies. More companies are cutting staff. More employees are becoming harried and overworked, underinformed, and undermotivated as employee turnover increases. Travel costs and the cost of each personal sales call keep rising. More manufacturers are building new, unique uses into their products, but the knowledge gap in how to use them is widening. Electronic marketing in one form or another has become a cost-effective solution.

Three Powerful Factors

1. *The customers*. They have less time to read, view, or hear, and less time for leisure, hobbies, and travel. More time is spent in commuting. There's more media fatigue and less viewer and listener attention. Customers are becoming more frustrated. For most, obligations are greater and disposable income, less. Their use of credit cards is becoming more cautious while their use of debit cards grows.

2. *The media*. Print and traditional electronic media are increasingly *aging* and *changing*. There is now more choice and more sell to smaller audiences, with higher cost per thousand. There's greater ability to target desired special groups but usually less effective measuring of the smallest audiences. New publications, networks, outlets, programs, formats, and stars compete. Audience preferences change quickly and make yesterday's marketing successes obsolete.

3. *New technology*. Easier-to-use personal computers, peripherals, and software offer more power and capability at lower prices, *and* new abilities to combine functions. New ways keep evolving to communicate from hand-helds to PCs to mainframes. New compression technology keeps increasing data storage. The ability to transmit better quality text, graphics, and pictures faster keeps increasing.

Interaction Accelerates EM Growth

Higher costs force increases in advertising CPMs for established media, which drive advertisers into newer media, often electronic. New lower cost and greater capability make various forms of electronic media profitable where they had been unprofitable. The success of any new medium rarely replaces established media, but rather forces them to change and modify via electronic enhancement.

Smarter marketers are changing and updating the traditional electronic marketing they now use. They are employing new kinds of electronic marketing that do (often interactively) what could not be done before by other means. They are enhancing electronically the effectiveness of their salespeople, direct mail, publication advertising, and their other electronic media. They are integrating, electronically, entire marketing, sales, and advertising campaigns.

Electronic marketing is the way more and more big and sound businesses are being started and it is the way many of these businesses have increased profits and expanded sales safely on a controlled basis. Many businesses keep updating their know-how and effective use of the latest electronic marketing technology and have gone on to use electronic marketing to integrate and enhance their entire sales, distribution, and marketing programs, passing by competitors who don't have the know-how.

Smarter marketers who have mastered one or more of the electronic marketing disciplines in one area after another have already dramatically outcompeted those who have not. How about you?

My electronic marketing method helps those starting in electronic marketing to be successful at it.

My method is fundamental and based on the methods of sound, conservative, and successful electronic marketers. It eliminates one of the greatest threats to success, lack of basic know-how in the latest electronic marketing technology. It reduces other risks as well. In my own case, it has helped our family business to survive and prosper and has given us much of what we now own.

My method is not a panacea, but it *will* help you analyze whether your company, your product, your organization, and you, are getting what you can out of electronic marketing. It will help you determine whether your firm is now ready for electronic marketing and whether you should "do-it-yourself" or combine your strengths with outside specialists. Should you decide to go outside, we'll help you select the right associates and negotiate the right deal.

Safer and Entirely Practical

I tell it like it is in the real electronic marketing world—its difficulties as well as its opportunities. My method comes from what our family advertising agency learned while pioneering for clients new ways to use radio, then broadcast TV, then cable, and what our family product company learned in electronically marketing its own products. I'll tell you what I learned as a telephone marketer and what I learned as an electronic marketing cosultant for my clients. I'll share with you what we have all learned in updating our know-how in ever-changing traditional electronic marketing and in ever-increasing new forms.

You'll read what I learned from over 2000 electronic marketers, large and small entrepreneurs, top specialists, media executives, and experts in many different electronic media forms, including the 1200 who participated in one-on-one interviews about what really worked and what failed for them.

And my method is what I learned from intensive research of the hard facts, the tough statistics, the record of what succeeded and what failed year by year up to the present in electronic marketing.

We Tell What Works

My method derives from my own experience with clients of our family advertising agency and with our own products. Top consultants and media heads of the biggest ad agencies answer specific questions I've asked *for* you. Learn state-of-the-art methods employed by the smarter, big advertisers. The combined expertise in this book tells you how each EM form works best: with other EM forms, with print advertising, with salespeople and in stores. Learn how each form fits best into an overall marketing plan.

We tell new ways to profit more from existing media, which traditional media have changed most, and the new ways to use successfully each of the most important new media that are emerging. We describe the key new electronic marketing media that are profitable now for small firms, big companies, and many in-between, often in unexpectedly different ways.

A Versatile Learning Tool

The manual can quickly update experts who feel their know-how rusting. Often a brief scan of the chapter or chapters and Help Source Guides on their specialty, including references to where to go for a stream of the latest information, is all that is needed. It can easily and rapidly broaden the know-how of specialists who've gotten behind in some closely related specialties because new developments occur in so many different areas and subareas of electronic marketing.

Even a quick look through the manual can provide some new and valuable information to advanced electronic marketing specialists or generalists. For any marketers who have not kept up with electronic marketing, a more thorough reading can quickly and easily give a thorough brush-up of basics as well as update them. Any department head can provide through the manual a beginning to more advanced training in needed areas.

Let Hoge Help

The manual is surprisingly simple and fast to consult for anyone investigating or just starting to use electronic marketing—even if you now have a minimum of (or no) marketing experience. I cut out MBA jargon, use the fewest possible hi-tech words, and explain in plain words what each term means. I simply spell out step-by-step how today's smartest marketers succeed, whatever their size or field, by enhancing their marketing electronically and then adding the new synergy made possible by integrating their marketing electronically. I enumerate possible dangers in every chapter, and advise how to avoid or overcome them.

I have helped others to improve profits by more effective use of electronic marketing—(from big-name firms to start-ups and even moonlighters)—and many have profited greatly. It is my hope that my *Electronic Marketing Manual* can help far more companies and executives than I could personally. So join me. Good fortune in your electronic marketing! And let me know how you do with EM.

Cecil C. Hoge, Sr.,
Setauket, New York

President, Huber Hoge and Sons Advertising, Inc.
200 Wilson St.
Port Jefferson Station, NY 11776.
(516) 473-7308

Acknowledgments

Thanks...

To Barbara Obolensky, my editorial assistant on each book I have written, including *Mail Order Moonlighting, Mail Order Know-How, The First Hundred Years Are the Toughest*, and this one.

To Ray Roel, who for over a year spent many evenings and weekends editing every word of the final draft of this book for me before it went to McGraw-Hill. Ray was editor of *Direct Marketing* magazine for 5 years and edited each article I wrote for it. He now heads public relations for Ogilvy & Mather Direct.

To the three McGraw-Hill Senior Editors who worked so hard with me at each stage: Martha Jewett, who got the project well under way; then Elisa Adams, who, whenever I got off track, gave invaluable advice to help me get back on, and to Betsy Brown, who then took over and with her quiet certainty, chapter by chapter, steered the book to completion. To Bill Sabin who was Publisher for most of the time I worked on the book and who gave me a crucial change of approach at just the right time.

To the over 2000 marketing and media executives and entrepreneurs who answered my questions, including the 1200 who participated in one-on-one interviews to make this book possible. Each patiently answered my many questions, often in several lengthy sessions. They gave me a lot of case histories and much insight into why each use of electronic marketing failed or succeeded. These people and the constant study of sources too numerous to list here resulted in several thousand pages of research notes in my computer, which were condensed finally into this book.

A man may as well attempt to
carry on a successful trade by
means of the old flatboat and keel
against a steamboat...as to
transact business by use of the
mails against the telegraph.

THE ST. LOUIS REPUBLICAN, 1847

1

What Is Electronic Marketing?

Any transfer of goods or services from seller to buyer (the broadest definition of *marketing*) that involves one or more electronic methods or media can be considered *electronic marketing* (EM).

Electronic buying and selling started by telegraph in the nineteenth century. With the advent and mass acceptance of the telephone, radio, TV, and then cable, electronic media have become the dominant marketing force. New permutations of these four electronic methods—as well as the microcomputer explosion—continue to create many new forms of electronic media.

Marketing through an electronic medium ranges from the familiar to the cutting edge of technology. This book covers the gamut. Which of these electronic marketing forms are you familiar with or do you now use?

Broadcast or cable TV	Radio
In-bound or out-bound telemarketing	Audiotape
Audiotext	Voice mail
Talking ads	Sponsored telemedia
In-bound or out-bound faxmail	Fax-aided ads
Video brochures	Video catalogs
Video media ads in videocassettes	Video premiums

Movie ads on planes and in theaters	Interactive ads on computer disks
Interactive computer disk catalogs	
EDI	E-mail
Information and entertainment computer networks	Computer bulletin boards
Online marketplaces	Online catalogs
Electronic multimedia kiosks in retail businesses	CD-ROM catalogs and marketplaces
Electronic kiosks in public places and trade shows	Other in-store electronic media
TV shopping networks	Direct-by-satellite business
Audio- and teleconferencing	TV marketing
	Electronic vending machines

Although this book devotes many chapters to individual electronic media and how they are successfully used, the larger context is also essential. Final chapters devoted to electronic customer service; electronic aid for your salesforce; electronic public relations; and the integration and enhancement of EM into all marketing give you a guide to making EM a powerful force in your successful company.

Which kinds of electronic marketing now impact your business most? Which will most affect your career? How soon? Nothing that I or you make, import or sell, no service we offer, no job that you can hold or aspire to will not be very soon significantly affected by electronic marketing, perhaps more than by any other force in your business life. And EM change is accelerating.

Whom Does EM Most Concern?

Electronic media and their marketing applications will soon touch virtually every aspect of business. EM knowledge is critical for those who hold the following jobs in big firms: CEO, CFO, VP of marketing, director of sales, advertising manager, direct marketing manager, head of PR, promotion manager, market research manager, telemarketing manager, product brand and category managers.

EM know-how is now vital for any new college graduate, even an MBA who is marketing-oriented, computer-trained, and innovative. But any trainee concerned with marketing, sales, advertising, display, promotion, PR, research, or service, will advance more quickly by demonstrating an understanding of EM. In addition, EM can be a life saver for career changers seeking a growth field in marketing.

Marketing specialists without EM know-how are becoming outmoded in many areas, including: advertising agency CEOs, account executives, creative heads, media buyers, research directors, or ambitious trainees in advertising agencies; catalog managers, creative heads, phone marketers, list brokers; marketing consultants in direct marketing; or principals, account executives; senior writers, and beginners in public relations.

Advancement or even getting hired in any field is becoming difficult without EM know-how, particularly in the areas of broadcast and cable TV, radio; new electronic media; mass and targeted print media; electronic information providers; trade magazines and newsletters; and trade associations.

Small businesses without EM facilities and expertise face a bleak future. EM know-how can save jobs and mean survival for a small firm. EM can make the difference between firing or advancement for an executive. And for home office business and other start-ups—whether you're a rep, consultant, or other type of one-person operation—electronic marketing know-how can make the difference between success and failure.

Each New Medium Affects Others

Any change in media affects the marketing mix. For sophisticated marketers, electronic media provoke these questions:

1. Is it too early to use new forms of EM?

2. Which work? Which fail? Which are too small to matter?

3. Can older EM forms still work as new ones surge ahead?

4. Does electronic media take away enough audience from print media to make print a poor buy as their rates go up?

EM Is No Panacea

No form of EM is a shortcut to success for failing ventures or people. If your company is unprofitable, or if your products are failing or are not responsive to promotion despite spending as big a percentage of sales as your competitors, your chances of getting help from EM are slim. Most businesses, products, and people who succeed via EM are already successful. Those who previously failed in business are more apt to fail using EM. However, some start-ups, "retread" products, and failed entrepreneurs do subsequently succeed in EM for reasons specific to individual cases.

What Failures Teach

Big organizations with highly promoted products and ample capital have sometimes failed in their use of EM. Some big companies acted like "King Canutes," ordering the public to use a new, untried medium, even expecting people to buy expensive equipment to do it. Huge sums have been squandered in misguided EM ventures. Other big companies start in EM more to keep others out than to truly succeed; some enter EM markets just to be able to proceed in earnest if it proves necessary. Most failures come from the following:

1. A lack of understanding of, interest in, and commitment to the EM project of all those concerned within the company.
2. Lack of flexibility, or a failure to change the original plan as constraints and opportunities change.
3. Starving EM efforts through the fear of cannibalizing old income source by new EM forms.
4. Halfhearted efforts. EM advocates in management get undermined by others who are dubious and resistant.

Small companies often fail in EM for the same reasons they suffer high mortality rates overall: underfinancing, poor management, lack of research, know-how, control, and planning. Small companies tend to underinvestigate and to dive in too fast. They fail sometimes by choosing a form of EM that's mismatched to their products, presentation and market. But some companies can be marketing bumblebees—who, according to scientific principles, can't fly—but by trial and error find a way to succeed.

Both large and small companies often fail with electronic marketing because they fall in love with the technology but lack the know-how to use it. Many companies have failed because the technology they used cost too much at that time. The irony is that based on today's improved technology cost, many of the same tests would succeed.

Dramatic and Frequent Failures but Overall Success

However great the total losses in all electronic experiments to date, the overall profits by electronic marketers are already many times more. Big losses are easy, but profits can be obtained only by someone with the right products, profit margins, offers, and presentation making the right decisions, usually made possible by study and know-how. Winners are the most competent and entrepreneurial, the most adventurous and scientific, the most practical and realistic marketers who accept and select and use EM most effectively. My job is to help you become such a winner. Regardless of every EM disaster, plenty of bright and brilliant people have demonstrated the vision, courage and the practicality necessary to create EM successes.

In Chapter 21, I describe how American Airlines transformed itself when it created SABRE—the first PC-based airline reservation network and the basis for its revolutionary frequent flyer program. American Airlines' travel agent business went way up, it air freight zoomed up, and its profits leaped. American Airlines became the number-one airline and made over a billion dollars in additional profit from just this one form of electronic marketing.

Plenty of other big companies have been surprisingly flexible in setting up decentralized, profitable EM operations run like small companies. Often they have backed innovative, small EM firms. Chapter 22 describes how Greg Kolodziejzyk, a commercial artist from Calgary, Canada, first created a new business and then started a new industry through electronic marketing. He bought a Mac and a laser printer and founded Image Club Graphics, with a mail-order ad which sold clip art and type fonts on floppy disk. But then he created a whole new way to market his art on a CD-ROM disc. This new electronic marketing technique is responsible for driving many companies today.

Electronic Marketing—Your Business from Home

With electronic tools, sales reps and consultants can now market themselves so well from home that they sometimes double and triple their incomes. Telephones and fax machines, personal computers and modems, copiers and printers, and other new technologies are helping to proliferate electronic home businesses. Writers can become desktop publishers.

EM is rewarding and fulfilling and can give you a lifestyle you may prefer; it may make you rich. Many software companies start this way. But EM also could cause you to go broke. Success takes the following:

- Self-sufficiency to plan, start, and finish yourself
- The initiative and curiosity to find and master each electronic tool
- Entrepreneurial ideas on how to use each electronic tool
- The ability to match the right electronic tool to the right product
- Creative flair for an electronic presentation
- The financial ability to estimate costs accurately at each step
- Practicality, frugality, confidence, and judgment
- The right product, right cost, right market, and right timing
- The ability to persuade and a willingness to work very hard

Electronic Moonlighting

Starting a business after hours is safer than quitting your job to launch a business. Overall, start-up business mortality is lower, and, often, firms started this way are sounder. In addition, EM is a great husband-and-wife business. First, both can work at jobs full time and moonlight evenings and weekends. Then, the lower earner can work half-time at a job and half for the new business. Finally, both can work full time for the new business. In bad times, the process can be reversed. Here are some of the many ways to start an electronic marketing business:

- Outbound telephone marketing to businesses, hospitals, schools, and individuals with mail follow-up
- Answer phone inquiries from low-cost ads, first yourself, and then via a low-cost voice system
- Using a computer bulletin board ($2000 or less) to provide an online catalog that you advertise with small ads to your trade
- Use of $500 worth of computer add-ons and programs to target prospects, produce personalized letters and labels
- With a fax board (under $400), send explanatory ads and catalog sheets to inquiries from small ads in trade and business publications
- Any other low-cost electronic tool or method described in this book that is most suited to you

Why EM Succeeds

Electronic marketing succeeds for a wide variety of purposes and kinds of companies because each EM form has special advantages. But there are two advantages common to most EM:

1. Electronic "friend-making," via a seen and/or heard spokesperson, can be more compelling than a printed message. Sights and sound can start a relationship between seller and prospect—and secure the loyalty of a customer. The same spokesperson can give a short message by TV or radio and a far longer explanation in a video. Different spokespeople can talk to distinct audiences on separate different audiocassettes, even in different languages. Electronic testimonials from real people are more personal. Entirely new uses for a product, new benefits, and new reasons for using it come across on EM as news, in a very personal way. Electronic service information help is also more personal as well as faster, and can lower your cost of doing business. With a caller-paid 900 number, customer service can even become a profit center.

2. Many companies cannot have their complete range of product available everywhere. Retailers only handle certain brands, and they choose selectively from the brand's line of products. The greatest waste in advertising is a customer's inability to find the product advertised. EM, in many ways, can cut this waste through instant referral or by actually taking orders. Failure to integrate marketing into every available electronic system (especially inventory control) amounts to throwing away a percentage of each dollar you make from your advertising.

Other general and specific advantages of each of the major and most promising forms of electronic marketing media are detailed in subsequent chapters, including how each medium is used by big, middle-sized, and small marketers. The electronic marketing Help Source Guide then refers you to far more detailed source material.

Picture Yourself Sitting in My Office

Imagine that you are asking me how to start in electronic marketing. You want to know what form best suits your business and what can be experimented with in the least-risk, least-expensive way. But you also want the maximum chance of success.

I've just met you. I want to raise questions that stimulate you to ask yourself more, to get answers, and to make a sound decision. If you are with a big firm, and it already uses some EM, I would ask: What kinds of EM mentioned in this chapter has your company already attempted? Why were they chosen? What was the objective of each type of electronic marketing in your overall marketing plan? How did that type of EM enhance and integrate other media? Did it ask for action? Were specific results measured? If so, did your EM fail or succeed? Why?

How *organized* is your firm for doing business via EM? Ask yourself questions like these:

- How much does it cost you to process an order from a salesperson? By mail? On the phone?
- Does your salesforce or dealer network follow up leads you send them? Do you know your cost per sales versus your lead cost?
- Is the "people cost" too high for your firm to distribute information as it now does?

If your firm is small, I would ask you to confirm with your accountant your profit margins and determine the following:

- What are your successful products?
- Are they now responsive to any form of promotion?
- How much money do you have to spend on marketing?
- What percentage of sales can you afford for advertising?
- Is that percentage comparable to that of your competitors?
- What can you afford to lose in a failed market test?

Whether your firm is large or small, you need to hold off on any one form of EM until you get an overview of the field. This will raise a lot more questions for you to answer. Read through this book first and then turn back to the chapters that concern you most.

Now refer to the Help Source Guide and follow up on the sources suggested for more detailed information. These Help Source Guides also will help you select equipment, plus refer you to the directories, associations, magazines, and newsletters for more information and the latest lists of sources.

Most big firms can use EM profitably to a far greater extent than they currently do. Even a small company with a very limited budget has a choice of inexpensive ways to use electronic marketing. Later chapters will discuss how others have overcome problems and money constraints and succeeded. Let's go on to Chapter 2 on "How to Get Started."

Help Source Guide

1. Ask for special issues, lead articles on electronic marketing in the following periodicals: *Advertising Age*, 220 E. 42d St., NY, NY 10017. (212) 210-0100; and *Business Marketing*, 740 Rush St., Chicago, IL 60611. (312) 649-5200. *Adweek* and *Media Week* at 49 East 21st St., NY, NY 10010. (212) 529-5500. *Inside Media* at 911 Hope St., Six River Bend Center, Stamford, CT 06907. (203) 358-9900.

2. For the newest computer-based electronic marketing technology, look for occasional articles in *PC World*—(415) 243-0500; *PC Mag*—(212) 503-5255; *MacUser*—(415) 378-5600; *MacWorld*—(415) 243-0505; *Byte*—(603) 924-9281; *Computer World*—(508) 879-0700; they can be found at your library or newsstand.

3. *American Management Association* provide *free* catalog of excellent books, *free* catalog of videotapes and audiotapes on management skills, and *free* catalog on seminars: Amacom Publications, P.O. Box 1026, Saranac Lake, NY 12983. (518) 891-1500.

4. *Arlen Communications,* a pioneer analyst of the field, provides a *free* electronic marketing study: 7315 Wisconsin Ave. (Suite 600), Bethesda, MD 20814. (301) 656-7940.

5. *"BizPlan Builder"* is a strategic business and marketing plan on diskette—how to launch a new product, service, or company. JIAN Tools for Sales, Inc., 127 2d St., Lost Altos, CA 94022. (800) 346-5426.

6. *Digital Media, a Seybold Report,* provides latest news on various EM forms based on digital technology: Seybold Publications Inc., P.O. Box 644, Media, PA 19063. (215) 565-2480.

7. *Interactive World* covers interactive TV, newspaper, magazine, radio, phone, and fax. The *Journal* sponsors enhanced information services conference and expo: Virgo Publishing, Inc., 4141 N. Scottsdale Rd., Suite 316, Scottsdale, AZ 85251. (602) 990-1101.

8. *Home Office Computing,* provides many articles, case histories on computer-based electronic marketing: P.O. Box 53561, Boulder, CO 80322-3561. (800) 544-2917.

9. *Multimedia & Video Disc Monitor* is a newsletter with sound advice on various EM areas; *free* sample issue: P.O. Box 26, Falls Church, VA 22040. (703) 241-1799.

10. *NTC Publishing Group* provides catalog of business books; latest on electronic marketing areas, media, and marketing research: 4255 West Touhy Ave.,

Lincolnwood, IL 60646-1975. (800) 323-4900.

11. *Strategies in Interactive Video Company* provides electronic marketing, launch advice from John J. Pollack, CEO, a top expert; includes information on cable, laserdisc, videotext: 207 Bridge St., Dedham, MA 02026. (617) 329-5273.

12. *Telecom Library Inc.* provides book catalogs. One features telecommunications bestsellers, another the most important books on business and technology in the field. Both cover various areas of electronic media: 12 West 21st St., NY, NY 10010. 800-LIBRARY.

2
Getting Started

Here are two electronic marketing fundamentals:

1. Your company's marketing budget probably can't (nor should it) include every form of electronic marketing. But studying each form can help you choose the best ones for you.

2. Marketing via an electronic medium is seldom used on a stand alone basis. It is therefore vital to enhance and integrate the use of each electronic media with other EM forms and/or with print and other promotional media.

Other basic requirements for EM success mirror what experienced marketers do in any marketing campaign:

- Research your customers, products, and competition.
- Target your market and pick the media ideal to reach it.
- Create and produce the most effective message for the medium.
- Study the available research that measures a medium's audience.
- Negotiate the best buy.

Ask for action and measure results. Then compare these results with other media results based on the same budget. This book will show you how to measure EM response and how to adapt these methods to your business.

Let's start by discussing some procedures common to most forms of EM. First, you must choose how you will approach each form of EM, at each major step. Your options include the following approaches:

1. First class—hire and buy the best
2. Budget class—seek new, talented, low-cost expertise
3. Do it yourself—get some low-budget help

Some big firms only go first class. Other companies mix a first-class approach to most important projects with a budget-class orientation on smaller projects to niche markets. Middle-sized firms often try to succeed with lower budgets, and small companies tend to gravitate to the lowest cost, do-it-yourself budget. Each choice contains a wide range of alternatives. Throughout this book, I will describe how large companies economize, which shortcuts smaller companies take, and how start-up outfits improvise.

At each phase of the alternatives described above, in whatever EM project you undertake, you must make another basic choice: whether to use outside specialists and services or buy equipment and acquire in-house expertise. Your choices must be governed by what is sensible and affordable for your situation.

The Internal EM Team

The size and internal politics of your company shall determine how you create an EM team. If your company is large, you need to get each appropriate department head to buy into the EM mission. Whatever size your firm, you must win over these people: the CEO, the chief financial officer, whoever heads sales, your advertising creative head, and the decision maker for media. If you are small, the decision makers could be your accountant, partner, ad agency person, and you—or only you.

In a big organization, reach out for help from other departments or divisions. You may be able to find and use the exact expertise you need on a part-time basis for nothing or at modest cost, depending on company policy. Whatever your firm's size, look for competent electronic expertise at hand in your ad agency, media buying service, accountant, consultant, or your trade association. I'll soon suggest how.

Outside Help versus Do-It-Yourself

In most forms of EM, there is almost no function—whether creating a message or program, producing it, or negotiating with EM media—that you cannot pay someone else to do. But for many of these areas of expertise, you can acquire the know-how and buy the equipment to do the task yourself. Plenty of advice is available as to when it is practical for you to do it yourself. The Help Source Guide at the end of each chapter helps direct you to sources of advice.

No company, no matter how large, has the expertise and equipment to be totally self-sufficient for every phase of each EM campaign. The following sections discuss your choices for outside help.

Production Houses

Many companies that service business marketing needs can produce a range of EM commercial messages and programs, including audiotape; TV; audiotext messages and interactive phone calls to free 800 and pay-per-call 900 numbers; voice mail; videos; interactive computer disk ads and catalogs; software programs in text, audiotext bulletin boards, on-line catalogs; CD-ROM catalogs; and interactive electronic kiosks and other computer multimedia forms.

Some production houses come up with the concept, create the copy, and carry through to full production. Others work from your concept and often your ad copy or script. Production houses tend to specialize in one or a few EM forms and produce on a high-, middle-, or low-budget range. Others specialize by industry or type of client such as medical, toys, or travel.

Every production firm will supply you with samples of its work. Look at samples done within your budget. Phone customers and find out their experiences. Here are three cautions:

1. Check how a production firm has performed in the past. Specifically, find out how practical it has been, how competent, whether it was on time, and if it performed within budget.

2. Beware of low quotes from inexperienced firms. The firms may go bankrupt, perform badly, or append extra charges.

3. Any agreed-upon cost is only enforceable if you stick to your quoted requirements. Each change adds more cost and a complex alteration can cost far more.

Chapters 6 and 14 on producing TV commercials and videos are useful guides to selecting and getting the most per dollar spent from a production house in other EM fields. Chapter 23 describes the production of multimedia commercial messages and programs. Multimedia productions are complex and shouldn't be produced as if they were radio or TV commercials.

Produce-It-Yourself Projects

Within certain simple limits, you can perform in house many of the key activities of production houses. You can rent equipment, often by the job or hour. You can learn the know-how needed, pay to be taught, hire the expertise to guide you, or combine your own production with the use of freelancers.

In nearly every EM field, one or more specialized magazines publish a yearly equipment issue. (See the Help Source Guide. The Help Source Guide also lists training sources such as books, seminars, audio and videotapes, computer demo disks as well as newsletters and magazines.)

Audit Your Equipment. Big companies often have plenty of both the equipment and know-how necessary for producing some forms of EM in house. Yet many small companies also have successfully started EM ventures with just a PC and a little know-how. For small companies, the in-house equipment and know-how available may help determine not only whether to produce the project in house but whether to test a particular electronic marketing medium.

List all available electronic equipment from the main frame or minicomputer system to your voice messaging system to even your tape recorder, VCR, PC (and its software and peripherals), camcorder, and audiovisual projector. Also include all company literature, catalogs, and manuals you have on computer disk; all advertising art in any form; and your radio commercial tapes and videotapes of TV commercials. Also explore what you can borrow from vendors, customers, or outlets you sell or deal with—including your trade association or the government.

Audit Your Know-How. Next, write down the names of any electronic media experts in your organization, whether the person is or has been a radio commercial copywriter, a telephone marketer, or a TV art director. Also audit for in-house performing talent—whether the talent is proven demonstration, inspiration, or teaching skills. Gather the names of your camera bugs, computer bugs, artists, photographers, and camcorder users. If you're a moonlighter, write down the names of friends or relatives who have any of these abilities and might help.

For Dedicated Do-It-Yourselfers, Three Provisos. Use what you have and do what you're good at, but here are three cautions:

1. Equipment you own that is slow and limited may prove to be overly expensive to use and yield inadequate results.

2. If your firm is big, letting electronic media amateurs loose on company time may cost more (and produce far worse results) than hiring professionals.

3. Poor electronic productions usually fail and are embarrassing.

State-of-the-art electronic equipment is improving so dramatically and so quickly that EM production companies are constantly replacing existing equipment with newer models. Competition makes them automate. But this book is full of case histories of small firms who successfully produce initial electronic marketing tests partially or entirely in house. If your subject matter is interesting and exciting, low-cost home equipment often can get across much of what you wish at a fraction of the cost of a big-time production.

Service Bureaus

Different kinds of specialized electronic service bureaus perform various aspects of the following EM activities:

- Take all your inbound phone orders or inquiries.
- Conduct outbound telemarketing.
- Take virtually any volume of calls on their own voice system for your toll-free 800 phone number or pay-per-call 900 sweepstakes or any other similar promotion.
- Take your inbound fax or phone requests and fax back replies for you.
- Duplicate, package, process, and ship orders (or requests) for audiotapes or videotapes.
- Store voice mail messages for you and send voice mail messages to your customer list.
- Reproduce interactive ads, catalogs, and programs on computer disks; package and mail to your list of customers and/or prospects.
- Reproduce CD-ROM disc catalogs and marketplaces and package and mail them to your lists.

Some service bureaus are also production houses for the same forms of EM. By working with a number of clients, these service bureaus gain experience, keep up with the latest changes, and provide invaluable advice. As fast as a new EM form develops, service bureaus for that form are organized. Service bureaus often allow companies to develop electronic marketing media without much expertise in house. Sometimes companies grow their business via EM into sales of many millions of dollars with very few employees. Occasionally, you can grow with less overhead risk and less investment by using outside EM facilities. Where service bureaus are available, each chapter's Help Source Guide lists where to get their names and addresses.

Serve Yourself

The more individually you service your customers, the more advantageous it is to deliver this service yourself rather than to use a service bureau. You may already have the facilities to do some of or all the work. You get more control and may be able to save money. You can give yourself priority service and, in some cases, set up a test more quickly. A service bureau may require start-up charges and a minimum volume and ask for security deposits. A bureau might also make a simple test more complicated and expensive and tie up more money. Under certain circumstances, you may want to conduct a simple test yourself and then use a service bureau.

To be your own service bureau requires enough volume to support activity on a regular basis. Attaining that volume often forces even big companies to go into the service bureau business themselves and to service other firms in their off periods. If you have no EM facilities, it's usually best to start with a service bureau. You can learn what equipment and expertise you need and later switch to handling the same functions in house. The service bureau often will help you select equipment and train personnel for you.

Consultants

Companies often supplement their in-house EM expertise with outside EM consultants. In new fields, this can sometimes be invaluable and save mistakes caused by trial and error. There are top consultants for every form and facet of EM. The best often give seminars, make audiotapes and videotapes, and write books. The consultants promote themselves by speaking at trade meetings and by writing articles for trade magazines. The Help Source Guide lists some of them.

A consultant is not licensed and often starts out by being unemployed. A "bargain" consulting fee may be a case of the blind leading the blind. The best consultants earn more than what many of them earned when they worked at a major company. Their fees can range from $100 to $1000 an hour plus travel expenses, but these costs can save you or make you far more. If the desired consultant also writes books and articles and gives talks at trade meetings, read his or her book and articles first. Listen to her or his audiotapes. Then write down questions specific to your business. For most value per hour, stick to your specific points and limit the consultant's time.

Advertising Agencies

Ad agencies range from huge worldwide organizations to one-person shops, sometimes launched from a home. If your firm has an advertising agency that you have confidence in and that has experience in the form of EM media you are interested in, you can get considerable help in deciding whether to use that medium, how to use it, and how to profit from it. If you are considering using an agency for electronic media marketing but know little about them, two publications should be helpful. *Advertising Age* and *Adweek* magazines are both weekly trade magazines that cover the activities of agencies and their clients. Besides giving you a quick education on current advertising trends and personalities, both annually list the largest advertising agencies and direct marketing ad agencies in the United States. There are thousands of advertising agencies. *McKittrick's* and the *Standard Advertising Register* are annual two-volume directories that list most of the advertising agencies with their accounts and advertisers and their agencies. Often they will list the principal media used by an advertiser. The American Association of Advertising Agencies (The Four A's) offers a booklet listing its members by area and specialty. The Help Source Guide at the end of this chapter refers you to each of these resources and to a book to aid you in the selection of an agency.

Traditionally, ad agencies received 15 percent of the billing from the media used. So for every $1000 in media placed by the agency for the advertiser, the agency received $150 with 1 percent to 2 percent cash discount and passed this along to its clients. Now, advertising agency compensation formulae range all over the lot, from reduced media percentage to large upfront fees and retainers. An increasing trend is to bill the client directly based on people's time and the assignment, much as a lawyer or any accountant. Big agencies have big minimum charges, and even middle-sized agencies often require a minimum of $150,000 for the first year of serving a client.

Selecting the Right Agency

Big agencies often are cautious in recommending the newest kinds of electronic media to their clients and in setting up a department to handle these media. Most agencies specializing in niche electronic media are small with young principals. Sometimes these agencies also act as consultants to larger advertisers whose agency of record is not yet interested in a particular, specialized electronic medium. SoftAd, a San

Francisco agency run by Paula George which specializes in ads on interactive disks for PCs, is one example which I'll describe in Chapter 16.
Again, the Help Source Guide refers you to specialized media magazines and newsletters which list such agencies. Also, consult the associations and ask consultants, production houses, and service bureaus in a
specific EM field for their recommendations.

Consider a direct marketing ad agency. Because many forms of electronic marketing are instantly measurable and very effective in securing
direct response, direct marketing agencies often have more interest in
electronic media than general agencies. And because they are smaller,
with less overhead, the agencies' minimum fees are often less. The
Electronic Marketing Division of Ogilvy & Mather Direct (the biggest
direct marketing agency in the world) operates independently and has
experience in many forms of EM.

Make a list of the agencies which seem best suited to you. A large
agency has a vice president in charge of new business. Ask to talk to him
or her. For a small agency, ask for the president, general manager, or
one of the partners specializing in the electronic medium you are interested in. Ask what the minimum fee is and whether the agency is interested in and if it has facilities for the kind of electronic media in which
you are interested. Next find out if the agency

- Understands your product and your business.
- Is competently staffed with able talent.
- Will give you its top EM talent rather than less experienced staff.
- Has the latest knowledge of electronic marketing that is ideal for you.
- Is not more expensive than you can afford.
- Has the right chemistry for you.

The biggest agencies are often the most sophisticated in the most universal electronic media—radio, TV, and cable. And the largest marketers often appear to have a near monopoly on the biggest agencies
with the top talent. But advertising is a fiercely competitive business.
You may get the best talent in a small agency versus the worst in a big
one. New, small, talented agencies constantly start up, often founded by
the alumni of the big. Don't rush into an agency marriage. Phone several clients first. Ask about their experience regarding the points in the
above list; ask about the success of work done; and ask about any excessive production charges.

Setting Up a House Agency

Any ad medium will usually grant a 15 percent agency commission to any entity that states it is an advertising agency. Any company can set up such an agency, usually with a piece of stationery. No license or government permission is required. However, the medium will only grant a new house agency credit if a satisfactory financial statement is produced or if a guarantee by the parent company is given, provided it has a satisfactory statement. If not, cash is usually required in advance.

If you purchase a lot of advertising in one transaction from one electronic media company, a house agency may save money. Having an agency can also give you the flexibility to use mainly freelancers and consultants. But a house agency arrangement usually does not save you money from the 15 percent commission, because you immediately take on expenses and administrative duties which are normally part of an outside agency's overhead. You will need the right staff to create and produce effective commercials, attain the desired electronic marketing effectiveness, and negotiate the most favorable rates with electronic media. You may need at least an EM consultant and a freelance writer-producer to start and do your own EM media buying.

If your firm already has top advertising talent in house and prefers to add more talent and control from within, a house agency may result in better EM advertising. If your firm can't afford a competent agency, forming a house agency may be the only viable way to start. Many small ventures have succeeded in this way. Sometimes you can combine a house agency with outside help for part of the commission—perhaps a talented writer-producer in a specialized EM form or a time-buying service for broadcast TV, cable, or radio.

Market Research Companies

Before the birth of a product, service, store, or catalog, market research companies are often hired to find out what you need to know to market more effectively. Their work often precedes every important step of the smartest marketers, from the product concept, market determination, advertising development, and marketing rollout, from developing a product line to meeting and overcoming competition and anticipating economic change. The scope of what marketing research companies do keeps expanding.

Some marketing research companies only do custom research. Others publish and sell research findings aimed at one or more industries.

Chapter 3 describes market research companies which measure the audience of broadcast TV, cable, and radio—in total and by various categories—to different programs and events. Some firms gather (from existing public sources and through their own investigation) various kinds of demographic information based on useful facts for a specific marketing situation. Typical, credible secondary sources include the U.S. Census, automobile and other state and local license bureaus, summaries of credit reports, and IRS data. These sources plus privately collected information that's available to other marketers (i.e., warranty cards) form a rich mosaic of quantitative data that includes the following:

- Ownership of homes, cars, appliances, anything
- Net worth of people and companies
- Income of people and profits of companies
- Market-share leaders by industry

Market research companies also conduct qualitative surveys to get answers to questions about opinions, habits, and choices of any target audience. How surveys are conducted, questions asked, answers solicited, and results summarized are often audited by a recognized research organization. The methods include

- Phone interviews
- Mall intercept or short interviews with shoppers
- Focus group interviews guided by a moderator
- In-home, one-on-one interviews
- Mail questionnaires

Qualitative data can help you understand how people spend time, why they buy what, what their planned purchases are—even suggestions for product improvements. Data are collected for everything from customer profiling to trend analysis. The summaries of answers supply soft psychographic information, useful for a wide range of marketing situations.

Quantitative and qualitative data may be national in scope or broken down by area (zip codes, census tracts, or even city blocks), sex, age, parents versus single or income groups, or any combination of these groups. Data may include tabulations of other major studies and marketing research extracts, combining what is most relevant. The effort to integrate into media selection use of more kinds of marketing research is increasing.

Report Forms

Market research findings and presentation formats range from a customer penetration map of an area to purchase diaries. Every year, Simmons Market Research Bureau publishes its study of media and markets, disclosing which kinds of programs older viewers spend more time watching than other viewers and what kinds of products viewers buy more of by mail than others. MediaMark publishes a product preference report which predicts the growth and decline in usage of many types of products throughout the 1990s by age and sex. A wide variety of research is also available via online computer (see Chapter 19).

To find market research assistance, this chapter's Help Source Guide lists books, magazines, and newsletters. They will provide more detail and give you an idea of the costs of specific research services and custom assignments.

Free Research

If your firm is big, you may have available useful market research already bought for another purpose. Consult with your research director about what kinds of research you need most. Ask about pertinent research other divisions of your company may now have, about research your customers or vendors or trade association may have, and about any other research services your company or an associated one subscribes to that may be available to you in print or online. Throughout this book are examples of free and low-cost market research as a derivative of EM.

However small your firm is, you can get research help. If you're a dealer, ask your manufacturer for the marketing research on the key products you sell. Check the sources in the Help Source Guide at the end of each chapter. Ask your association and your trade magazine editor for more. Big or small, your best sources of free marketing research are the pertinent various branches of the U.S. government, states, and municipalities and all types of media. But remember that research supplied free to you is often designed to persuade you to buy a service. Careful analysis by your research director is needed.

Do-It-Yourself Research

If you are concerned with the use and selection of electronic media, know your company's history thoroughly, its marketing successes and failures, and its policies. Know the line of products you are associated with, the competitive advantages and sales objectives of each, and the attitudes of your customers and prospects. Examine research about your company and products. If you have a store or service, research your customers every day. If you sell through stores, talk to your sales reps, store buyers, and the end users of your products—and those of your competitors. Find out from your sales reps what competition you must overcome, including rumored new entries. Create your own questionnaire about your business to ask yourself, your colleagues, and your boss. For starters, try these questions:

1. How have you attracted past customers?
2. How does your top competition market its products?
3. Why do your customers buy your products from your firm?

Make your own customer profile. Find out about customers' lifestyles, habits, and preferences, including radio listening, TV watching, shopping, and other product purchase selections. You can then create a tailored electronic sales message, seek prospects similar to your customers, and skillfully select and use electronic media.

How Your Firm Services Customers

Each customer who phones you or comes to your place of business is a rich source of research. I'll later describe how GE developed profitable new products from customers who called for information or even to complain. The following are some questions to answer:

- Do you have resentful prospects and unhappy customers? What do they say about your firm?
- How many rings does it take before your phone is answered?
- How much business do you lose because prospects can't find your products?

If you're small, you and your employees can do in a simple way what expensive research companies do. If you can afford to pay for research, attempting to do it yourself is often a misuse of time. But doing some of your own research will teach you how to get more out of any research you get free or later buy.

The Help Source Guide refers you to excellent books, seminars, audiotapes and videotapes, and computer disks on market research. Some of these are very inexpensive. And check your business library for the latest marketing research books.

The Marketing Plan

For every profitable business, marketing success starts with strategic planning, with the right business plan and with a sound marketing plan. Any one form of EM is just a part (and sometimes a very small part) of the overall marketing plan.

Most large firms have a long-term marketing plan over a number of years. If your firm is small with no marketing plan, make one. Start by asking yourself these questions:

1. What are your company's objectives?

2. Who is your market?

3. What are the strengths and weaknesses of your firm and product line? What is your firm's history? Your firm's competition?

4. How do you plan to grow aggressively but with safety?

5. What are your alternative plans if conditions change?

Your cashflow projection is the first step to controlling your marketing budget. Constant correction of actual to estimated income and outlay, along with timely modification of marketing expenses, is the next step. The selection, customization, use, and upgrading of computer hardware and software can guide, stimulate, and speed this process. The Help Source Guide lists books on marketing which explain this in detail.

Target Marketing

People now make most of their purchases by selecting specialized products and services. Most products made even by the largest companies appeal to special population segments. Different models of the same car in the same company, for example, have different prospective customers.

Target marketing matches special products, product lines, services, stores, and catalogs with the special groups that want them most. Media and marketing research match viewers, readers, and listeners with targeted groups. All electronic media can be used to target markets. Even broadcast TV, with its range of programming, appeals to and reaches huge segments of relatively homogeneous groups of people by age, sex, education, income, tastes, and interests. Cable networks, each programmed with a distinct personality, reach big to small special niches. And radio reaches, via different station types, other distinctive niches. The Help Source Guide lists books on target and database marketing.

Market Testing

There is no single best way to test-market. The right choice depends on who you are and what you're selling, to whom, at what price, and via what electronic medium. Some tests work, but others have failed miserably. A test's function is to tell you whether to proceed or stop, expand or contract, go faster or more slowly. You want accurate information at the least cost. Sophisticated advertisers estimate how much achieving a specific market share in a test area will cost and how long it will take, and they determine whether an expansion regionally or nationally has the probability of sufficient profit to proceed.

Failure is highest for market tests that not only should not have been made but that certainly should never have been continued in the face of disappointing early returns. The smartest marketers investigate, but often rule out, many test campaigns by determining that an element(s) of the test is flawed—be it an inappropriate product or service, theme, offer, script, choice of talent, test area, station, or even the timing.

How do researchers rule out these test campaigns? They simply research much more at each step. They meet more, discuss more, and get more opinions. These opinions come from within their company and ad agency and by surveying for other opinions, including a portion of their potential customers. Often, what appears a novel idea has already failed elsewhere. However small you are—even if you are just launching your company—you can apply much of this same approach. The Help Source Guide lists books on market testing.

Creating the Right EM Message

Later chapters will discuss creating successful EM messages for each key electronic medium. Chapter 7, for example, provides considerable detail on how to create a radio commercial (much of the discussion also applies to other forms of EM). For some forms (such as outbound telephone marketing), one skilled writer-phone marketer can prepare an entire campaign. But for most forms, a creative team is best—a team which typically includes a writer, art director, and a computer person (not necessarily a programmer). The creative person usually starts with an idea. It is developed into a script and is then visualized by a storyboard. Chapter 6 can also serve as a rough guide to other electronic media.

The idea behind an electronic message is often stimulated by research. Ed McCabe, CEO of McCabe & Co. and a top creator of successful ad campaigns, says, "Without great research you can't make great advertising." Sometimes, surprisingly effective ad campaign ideas can come from the do-it-yourself variety of research. Talk to your partners, boss, assistants, sales manager, marketing manager, and director of research. Even if you're a one-person band, ask your customers, vendors, other marketers, and electronic media people. Then study your present advertising, that of your competitors, and ads in different fields that might be translated to your product. In Chapter 6, I suggest this for TV commercials.

Make up a creative research questionnaire to your team or yourself.

- What is our message? How are we unique?
- What image of our company does our present advertising create? What does the trade think?
- What image do we want to convey to the market?
- What are our ads trying to accomplish?
- What length commercial messages should we use?

Most important, ask yourself how the electronic medium you are about to use can uniquely present your product and integrate your message within your entire marketing campaign. Examine your audit of production materials for those you already have or can get free. For example, an audio conference may be created from an existing audiovisual presentation used in meetings. And any other marketing tool already being used successfully—from a glossy picture to an audiotape or videotape message by your corporate spokesperson—may be so useful as to affect how your electronic marketing message is created.

Of the many constraints on how your electronic marketing messages are produced, the chief one will be money. In the many chapters on each electronic medium, the Help Source Guide suggests where you can brush up on the basics of production, recent changes in technology and creative approaches in that medium. While I have tried to help you create an EM message yourself, most of us are better off hiring competent pros at the right price to help us achieve greater success in our present field rather than learning a new profession. In this light, your production house, ad agency, or consultant can also advise you.

Whether you decide that your electronic message will be created by your advertising agency, production house, consultant, your own creative staff, a freelance team, or by yourself, this book has many examples of how others have succeeded. Chapter 3 explains audience research and measurement issues for three of the broadcast forms of electronic media—broadcast TV, cable TV, and radio.

Help Source Guide

1. *American Association of Advertising Agencies* (AAAA) provides *free* roster of members (larger agencies) by areas. Publications Department, AAAA, 666 Third Ave., NY, NY 10017. (212) 682-2500.

2. *Adweek Agency Directory* is a directory of ad-related associations, clubs, networks, 5000 ad agencies, PR firms, media buying services alphabetically, geographically indexed; 35 service categories, account of each. To order, write or call: 1695 Oak St., Lakewood, NJ 08701. (800) 468-2395.

3. *American Demographics* is a magazine on latest consumer trends; find in library or subscribe: P.O. Box 68, Ithaca, NY 14851. (800) 828-1133.

4. *American Marketing Association* provides seminars, conferences, newsletter, *Journal*, catalog of latest books on marketing. For information, write: 250 S. Wacker Dr., Suite 200, Chicago, IL 60606. (312) 648-0536.

5. *Claritas/NPDC* (National Planning Data Corp.), a research organization, provides demographic and marketing information, including *free* information kit at 11 W. 42d St., 12th floor (11th for mail), NY, NY 10036. (212) 789-3580. Read, at your library, *The Clustering of America* by Michael J. Weiss (Harper Collins, 1989) the story of Claritas.

6. R. Shaw & M. Stone, *Database Marketing*, Wiley, 1990, is a clear, thorough, basic book. At libraries, bookstores, or direct: 1 Wiley Dr., Somerset, NJ 08875. (800) 225-5945.

7. *Direct Marketing Association* provides much expertise on direct response electronic marketing. Book catalog, videotapes and audiotapes, seminars, events, annual meetings, list of local direct marketing clubs can be ordered at 11 W. 42d St., NY, NY 10036-8096. (212) 768-7277.

8. *Impact Resources, Inc.*, provides a *free* information kit on single-source research, MART (Market Audience and Readership Traffic); write or call: 2681 Sawbury Drive, Columbus, OH 43235-9957. (614) 789-9797. (800) 234-6278.

9. *Lifestyle Market Analyst* is an annual provided by Standard Rate & Data Services, which collects demographic, lifestyle data for 212 areas of dominant influence (ADIs). For *free* info kit, write or call: 2000 Clearwater Dr., Oak Brook, IL 60521. (800) 232-0772.

10. *Look for* special issues, sections, and articles on electronic direct marketing, including the following magazines: *Direct Marketing*, 224 Seventh St., Garden City, NY 11530, (516) 746-6700; *DM News*, 19 W. 21st St., NY, NY 10010, (212) 741-2095; *Target Marketing*, 401 N. Broad St., Philadelphia, PA 19108, (215) 238-5300; *Direct*, 911 Hope St., 6 River Bend Center, Stamford, CT 06907, (203) 358-9900.

11. *Sales & Marketing Management* magazine provides the *Annual Survey of Buying Power*—population and retail sales by region, state, metropolitan area, county: 633 3d Ave., NY, NY. (212) 986-4800.

3

Audience Research and Measurement for Broadcast TV, Cable, and Radio

All electronic media must be measured in some way to become accountable marketing methods. Because radio, broadcast, and cable TV are so pervasive, their audience measurement systems will inevitably influence all electronic marketing. This chapter discusses these measurement systems, the research behind them, and how new audience reporting techniques are affecting this imperfect science.[1]

After a discussion of general media audience measurement methods, we'll look at the efforts being made to measure sales produced by specific electronic advertising. This chapter also provides an overview to research to help you to identify and target those who most want (and who can best afford) your specific products.

Media audience research measures the size of an audience by using the sampling method of asking a representative panel of people. Researchers measure nationally (and by areas) virtually all the different programs aired by the different networks, stations, and cable systems. Researchers also measure the total audience and the special groups of viewers and listeners (mostly by age groupings and by sex).

---

[1]Please note the caution each authority I interviewed advises on the use of research. I thank them all and Dr. William Cooke, editor of the *Journal of the Advertising Research Foundation,* who kindly read the completed chapter and made editing suggestions.

Who Measures...and How

Nielsen Media Research, Inc., is the oldest TV audience research firm that measures broadcast TV and cable, both nationally and locally. Arbitron is also highly respected for its audience rating reports in local markets for broadcast TV, cable, and radio. Birch Radio gives local radio audience ratings, and RADAR, owned by Statistical Research, Inc., provides radio network ratings.

Both Nielsen and Arbitron have used meters attached to sets in the homes of panel members (combined with diaries kept by panel members) to rate TV programs. This locally conducted system is used mostly in larger marketing areas, and the diary- only measurement is used solely in smaller markets. For TV, both companies use a mailed-in set diary in which one family member reports for every other family member as well. Arbitron rates radio by marketing area in the same way but uses a personal diary. Birch Radio uses a personal interview via the phone from a random sample in metropolitan areas to measure radio. The most sophisticated measuring means are being introduced for network TV.

The People Meter

It's about two-thirds the size of a videocassette and sits on each TV set in a sample household. The "people meter" automatically records each channel viewed, when it's changed, and when the set is off. A remote control unit allows more electronic entries to be made from anywhere in the room by each member of the sample household. Each people meter has a personal viewing button to press if watching. Buttons pushed indicate how many people are watching, their ages, for how long they watch, and what they watch. Other buttons are for visitors to press and indicate age and sex.

Nielsen uses a national panel of 4000 homes to measure network TV shows. It also derives information from it to measure syndicated TV shows nationally. People meter research also creates Nielsen ratings for cable network programs. Arbitron also uses people meters (in some areas) to rate local TV and cable programs. For both firms, answers are stored in the meter and transmitted each night to a mainframe computer. Program schedules from the networks that match information from the viewers are then fed in. Ideally, the sample is sufficiently balanced and randomly selected on a scientific basis to include all types of households: cities, towns, farms; rich and poor. Although the people meter is considered to be an accurate measurement, Arbitron and Nielsen are both working to attain still more accuracy with a "passive" people meter. Without button pushing, it will recognize how many and who are watching what on the tube when.

Ratings

The need for radio, TV, and cable audience measurement grew with the choices available for viewers and listeners—and for marketers. The job of audience measurement has expanded from prime-time hours to 24 hours a day, 7 days a week. At first, measurement involved counting everybody listening or viewing. Then advertisers asked for more information about the audience, for differentiation between men and women, children and adults, and then different age groups of each. As more media target special audiences, audience categories proliferate into more subdivisions.

Rating Reports

A "rating" measures audience quantity not quality. A network TV rating of 15 means that 15 percent of *U.S. television households* (*HUT*) tuned in. A network TV rating is based not on a count of all TV households but on the count of a sample of TV households selected from all U.S. television households. Some TV ratings are made based on *people using TV* (*PUT*). The same methods are used for individual areas. Radio ratings, however, usually count only people.

Every national TV network program with a rating over 0.1 at any time is reported. This includes almost all broadcast TV network and most cable network programs. Most national network and local radio programs are also rated. So are African-American and Hispanic programs on national network TV, cable, and radio.

Most local broadcast TV and radio programs are measured, but *low power TV* (*LPTV*) stations, described in Chapter 4, rarely are. Since most ratings for local cable systems are derived from national network cable ratings, much of local cable is not adequately measured.

Both national and local ratings for all three media are measured periodically, usually over a week or so. This period is called "sweeps week."

Detailed Data Provided

Reports are issued periodically and give ratings by time periods. A comparison of several different reports shows which programming, networks, and stations are gaining or losing audience, at what times and for which groups. A comparison of reports also indicates the effects of new competitive programs as well as changing seasonal activities, in total and by different groups.

Specialized research findings are available, from how many people zap which commercials to how many tape a program and see a commercial more than once. The four main audience measurement services offer a great deal of marketing information derived from their ratings. These include program and brand cumulative audiences and *cost per thousand* (CPM) audience estimates for program advertisers. Some advantages of current ratings are that they provide

- Time-tested quantitative guides to the selection of time, program, and/or medium
- Indispensable data for the negotiation process
- An accepted method for guaranteeing to the advertiser that the audience will be delivered
- A performance scorecard to the clients of agencies, or media buying experts

A disadvantage of the rating system is that sampling decreases in accuracy with the size of the audience, resulting in the following difficulties:

- Very large samples are needed to measure the smallest audiences.
- A multitude of program choices splinter audiences.
- Doubling of audience accuracy requires quadrupling the sample.
- The cost of equal accuracy for all program audience measurement is prohibitive.

A rating concerns the past. A media buy concerns the future under conditions that start to change the moment a rating is issued. Tim Brook was media research director at N.W. Ayer, a respected ad agency. Brook says that audience measurement information is fuzzy around the edges, that it is a smoky mirror; Tim points out that

- People resent surveys.
- People don't like to push buttons.
- All research is compromised by economics.
- Four thousand is still a small sample.

According to Brook, electronic media has fragmented considerably. This means there are more smaller pieces to target. Although some cable networks and programs go after mass audiences, cable is far more targeted than broadcast. Selection of fragmented media is a long way from being precise.

Sample Sufficiency Varies

The current size system is much more accurate for all types of viewers or listeners to the prime-time hit programs and much less accurate for fringe programming. There's more accuracy in the biggest cities and less in the smallest towns, more in broadcast TV and less in cable, more in top-hit, rock radio than for far less popular classical music. The usual sample size may not be big enough to accurately measure emerging but not yet dominant audience trends such as new forms of African-American, Hispanic, or other ethnic programming on broadcast TV, cable, or radio.

Each research methodology has its own drawbacks. Even the people meter combines a meter that can have bugs and people who sometimes forget to report, make mistakes, or lie. This happens so rarely that people meters are regarded by ad agencies as more accurate than phone polling or than the diaries of family's listening or viewing habits kept by a family member. Rating companies can scientifically sample and measure even a small sliver audience. But for the smallest slivers, the cost is prohibitive. The situation worsens as niche audiences multiply.

Sales, Audience Measurement, and Advertising

Mail-order sales have been traced to specific, keyed ads for more than a century. The sales made by the first demonstrator in a bazaar were known each day. The first retailer who ran an ad could easily see what it sold. For a hundred years, stores could count phone orders. Nielsen pioneered research on the movement of goods through mass outlets a half century ago. Marketers have long based their national rollouts on the careful measurement of total sales in their test markets versus their total ad cost.

Many stores can now trace sales from specific in-store promotions. Barcodes on packages can be electronically scanned at checkouts and each item subtracted from inventory and each item's price added to sales. In-store electronic media, point-of-sale electronic displays, and self-selling electronic demonstrators in stores often help measure sales.

Coupons can be printed in store and offered at the check-out counter and each sale thereby produced recorded, and a conversion percentage determined, all by computer. This kind of data is collated nationally by computer for every K-Mart store and for many other chains.

Traced Sales Get More Promotion Dollars

There has been a steady switch of dollars from ads to promotions partly because proof of specific results for each promotional dollar spent is easier. However, measurement of sales versus promotion cost is easiest in one store for one test for one product. For many big marketers, too much is happening too fast under many different conditions to prove precisely what caused what sales except under test controls.

Measurement of store promotions, using a variety of methods, leads the way. Research service auditors, for example, visit thousands of stores every week to gather information regarding sales versus ad cost of all in-store ads, promotions, and displays. Marketers and salespeople check inventory movement with hand-held computers and scanners and measure sales in detail right after store promotions. National chains provide results daily to co-op advertisers.

Combining Audience and Sales Measurement

Arbitron does it in a few markets with ScanAmerica, and Nielsen has experimented with ScanTrack. Arbitron combines people-meter ratings of programs and commercials with sample panel ratings of store sales. For both, panel members have used hand-held scanners to record their purchases, the prices they paid, and what caused them to make a purchase of groceries (such as a coupon offer or the impact of TV advertising). After shopping and coming home, Arbitron panel members waved electronic scanner-wands over barcodes on each item. This went daily into Arbitron's computer. Nielsen's ScanTrack traced media usage via passive household meters which indicate only the channel being watched. For both, inventory movement could be tracked daily and, via product usage ratings, in far more detail.

The marketing promise is to be able to test media and programs and to measure sales from tests and (where needed) make changes, even in the middle of an advertising campaign. Many media researchers caution that crediting sales movement to a specific promotion and media buy is not easy or presently practical and that attempts so far ask too much of respondents. Jon Swallen, director of media research at Ogilvy

& Mather, says, "Agencies have looked at [sales and audience measurement] and the role it plays in media planning and buying and feel it falls short of its promise. The complexity of what you ask people to do...push buttons, wave wands, hand in ID cards—is enormous. Cooperation rates are a serious issue."

Better Measurement of Sales

Marketers are combining the use of scanner wands and hand-held computers by a missionary staff with computer networks and special programs. These scanners and computers transmit up-to-the-minute vital information to top management who, in turn, deliver daily instructions back to their staff. With this method, Frito-Lay Inc., a Pepsico subsidiary, has developed what it calls "micromarketing," its way of tracking local promotions and gaining extra sales measurement control. Frito-Lay's micromarketing program has attained increases in sales while slashing its costs of acquiring information and its losses due to mistakes in oral reports and orders.

Big marketers are extending their sales reports from sales forces in specific outlets to many stores in a specific area where a brand promotion is run. Specific commercials are now rated and can be copy-tested by comparing ratings. Some marketers believe this will gradually (perhaps quickly) proliferate much more widely to encompass states, regions, and even countries. Some dream of making each ad dollar versus each sales dollar as traceable as mail order.

Marketing Research Data and Target Marketing

The effort to integrate into the media selection process the use of more kinds of marketing research is increasing. For example, 60,000 households in 24 markets record their supermarket product purchases through ID cards they present each time they shop through Information Research Inc.'s (IRI) InfoScan. IRI also collects demographic and magazine subscribership information through annual questionnaires, and IRI meters attached to TV sets in 10,000 households report which stations are tuned in when. Nielsen's ScanTrack has collected additional shopping data, such as the place of purchase, in-store promotions, and who came with the shopper.

Other market studies are underwritten by media companies which own media outlets that sell advertising appealing to the old, teenagers, working women, and singles. Zip-code demographic information can then add income, home ownership valuation, education, and much more. There are even studies (such as VAL) on different psychological types and how best to market to each and reports on inner-city and ethnic buying habits. Birch-Scarborough publishes *The Black Market Report* and *The Hispanic Market Report*.

Single-Source Data

When one service measures a consumer's preferences in all media and shopping preferences as well, the product is called "single-source data." Single-source data measure the same individual's reading, listening, viewing, and shopping behavior and their relationships to each other. In some studies, quantitative and qualitative data are combined. Some single-source advantages are

- All data are collected at one time.
- All data are from the same individual.
- Cross-media comparisons are based on actual behavior.

There is a growing list of single-source players. Nielsen offers single-source data and detailed information on the characteristics of TV viewers to specific programs. Its "National Audience Demographics Report" supplies estimates of audiences by person and categories within household demographics. Arbitron purchased other research firms, aiming to become a single-source research firm. Birch Radio combined with Scarborough, a market research service used by major newspapers, radio and TV stations, and retailers to create a single-source service for big metropolitan areas. Impact Resources of Columbus, Ohio, operates MA*RT (Market Audience Readership Traffic), which researches consumer preferences in buying, viewing, listening, and reading habits. MA*RT works not only with a database of more than 250,000 consumers in the biggest U.S. markets but also with local media to provide local research so that the sample in any one area can be small. Marshall Marketing and Lee Stowell both also survey individual markets, usually under contract, such as analyzing 40 markets for CBS. Simmons and Media Market Research, Inc. are doing national research surveys on product usage, primarily for magazines.

How a Single-Source Study Works

Birch-Scarborough offers the "Consumer, Media and Retail Report," a multistage study which combines measures of media, retail shopping, and product consumption gathered from individual respondents (over 18) in a household. Each respondent is questioned at length by phone and receives by mail a detailed questionnaire covering 450 points. There is continuing contact. A wide range of shopping information is collected which provides demographics of many kinds. Birch-Scarborough's CEO, Bill Livek, stated the following:

> Qualitative data...income, education, occupation, shopping and product purchase information...is rapidly becoming the weapon of choice in the broadcast sales arsenal.
>
> You can create customized data breakouts on your own PC, using single-source and multi-media data. On your PC, you can target unmarried women with individual incomes of $75,000+ who hold active health club memberships and reside within particular Zip Codes.
>
> You can then find out where they shop for groceries, where they dine, what their favorite vacation destinations are, as well as which credit cards they own, the types of cars they drive, and the number of movies they've attended in the last three months—and the radio stations they listen to.
>
> Market segmentation follows a four-step process: identifying the target, researching the target, delivering to the target, and promoting to the target. Select an optimal target audience. Consider where most of them live—the key counties, the key Zips; their income, education and occupational profile.

Livek then delineated some of the key attributes to look at to figure out "what really makes that audience tick":

- Life stage: Married? Divorced? Number of children in the Household? Ages of children? Own or rent?
- Lifestyle: Propensity for rock concerts, sports events, dining out, international travel?
- Consumption patterns: Retail shopping by store and mall? Auto owned by type? Own bank card? Department store credit card?
- Media use: Cume and AQH...by TV show? Average issue and one- and two-day newspaper cume readership?

> Single-source data helps you to calculate and compare the cost efficiency of advertising in a campaign in one medium vs. another or several. It helps analyze the reach and frequency advantages of each. It identifies for a retailer or service the profile of customers who shop there.

Overlays of different kinds of research using different methods can give far more detailed information. National research of the most specialized markets can be broken down to the smallest marketing areas. But most experts are cautious about what media measurement and marketing research can do together.

Quantitative research is measurement of facts, such as the number of people who report that they watched or heard a specific program. It is "hard" information whose percentage of error is predictable.

Qualitative research is often a survey of more general preferences and involves a more general memory of past or present actions. It may ask opinions and intentions. It is "soft" information whose percentage of accuracy is less predictable. Qualitative research may better stimulate ideas than be a foolproof guide.

Many Constraints

Despite advances, media measurement can't do it all. Ratings for local and national niche audiences are less accurate, and when researchers attempt to break down these niche audiences into smaller groupings, the ratings become proportionately less accurate.

Combining quantitative research and qualitative research to produce ratings is not acceptable to many media research statisticians. Parts of a mix of research may vary by date. Accuracy of the demographic data regarding customers, prospects, listeners, viewers, and readers may vary. Different ways of asking the same question can result in different answers.

The constraints continue. Tim Brook of Ayer says that accelerating fragmentation is driving up the cost of media research beyond the ability to pay. Research companies can be persuasive in selling new and unproven kinds of research. Media can skew ratings by running special programs when measurements are made. Media can be persuasive in using research to influence you to buy from them. Ad agencies and marketing heads can be tempted to use research to justify recommendations. In short, every form of research and audience measurement has its pitfalls, which can become magnified when combined with others.

Quantitative and qualitative research methods are useful tools which should be used as indicators, not as fixed guides. Research results do not make decisions—they aid you in making them. Research is not perfect, but it helps in many ways. Its effective use involves incessant detail, intensive study, and interpretation. Big firms know its shortcomings but rely on research at each marketing step. Tim Brook says: "With all its defects, most experts believe that you're a fool to fly by the seat of your pants. Research still rules."

One day, used together, in a perfect research world, media-rating measurement, sales results measurement, and marketing research may become a three-pronged troika driving all marketing. For now, you must use your common sense, practicality, and some skepticism to get the most out of each. The next several chapters will discuss how smart marketers use research to their best advantage as they investigate, select, and negotiate broadcast TV, cable, and radio time buys.

Research Priorities

Here's what applies to all three media: Understanding market research comes first, then media research, and finally the measurement of sales results. Studying your own company's market research is the best starting point. Again, make your own profile of your end-customer. More research than you'll ever use is available to you free from virtually every medium. In many cities, smart broadcast TV, cable, and radio executives believe strongly in research. They employ research as a selling tool, but research can help educate you too. The research may teach you to buy from them, from a competitor, or not at all.

Computer Help Increasing

Every year new and better software make it easier and faster to analyze marketing information—including media buys. Research services offer online computer analysis and PC software to perform time-consuming analyses such as rankings, trends, and cost comparisons. Networks, stations, and cable systems send research data and "availabilities" instantly by fax or modem to ad agencies and directly to clients.

Nielsen offers 38 "breaks," which become 380 breaks when used in a Nielsen computer program. Each break is a rating breakdown for a classification of viewers. Breaks start with age and sex and include income and other characteristics of viewers. Nielsen's online data systems provide a number of special analytical programs, including Nielsen Media Research's "Spotbuyer," "Radio Spotbuyer," and "Postbuy Reporter" software.

To help sell its medium, the Cable TV Advertising Bureau (CAB) developed the Cable Planning System, a computer program that sets rating points and estimates reach and frequency. CableCume, another computer program developed by CAB, provides comprehensive reach and frequency data across a range of age and sex demographics. The CAB Local Planning Kit program is yet another source of data for cable systems and "interconnects" between systems. And further, radio research software (RADAR-On-Line) can help clients get needed data and make calculations for a specific network radio buy. This software is released twice a year.

Agencies all over have PCs with inexpensive services and programs to instantly access needed research. Telmar Micronetwork II offers online data, reach, and frequency analysis, providing information from Nielsen and Arbitron, Birch, SRDS, MRI, and other services. Birch-Scarborough also offers online access to all its databases.

Calculating Geographical Coverage

For local electronic media buys in radio, cable, or broadcast TV, you should become familiar with each medium's way of selling its audience. A radio station or TV station usually can reach the most people in a metropolitan area or a suburb. Sometimes coverage includes parts of one or more metro areas. Cable systems very rarely cover entire metro areas, but cable "interconnects" (that join neighboring cable systems) sometimes allow you to buy coverage for most of or all a metro area (and often for parts of others). Research services have slightly different names and definitions for the area a station, system, or interconnect mainly covers.

Arbitron calls the broadcast TV station's principal market an *ADI* (area of dominant influence). Nielsen calls it a *DMA* (designated marketing area). Birch Radio follows (with some variations) the definitions of the U.S. government of three different-size metropolitan areas: an *MSA* (metropolitan statistical area), a *PMSA* (primary metropolitan statistical area), and a *CMSA* (consolidated metropolitan statistical area).

Suppose you are a retailer and you want to analyze your customer and prospect base within a tightly defined trading area around your store. A local TV or radio station most likely can analyze your base for you in minutes—for free. Using special PC-based software, station X can define a geography using zip codes and then analyze the demographics, socioeconomics, and buying patterns of viewers or listeners within the area.

Bonita Le Flore is director of Local Broadcast TV and Cable TV at Ayer. She says the following:

> Rather than using an area defined by over the air broadcast signals, advertisers can define their own geography. Local cable is able to target by geography. A national client with local outlets can define a trading area for their customer base. These retail accounts can now look at a market by zip code.
>
> Advertisers whose target fits a specific demographic, psychographic (lifestyle) or ethnic group can identify areas within a market where their customers are living. They then advertise to the most likely consumer rather than a market.

Local cable systems can be mapped across any geography and the correct system purchased. Nielsen and Arbitron are now able to generate cable network viewing in local markets that are metered. Although numbers are very small for the majority of networks, advertisers can now see the tremendous fragmentation that is occurring in viewing.

Free Media Research Help

Associations of broadcast TV, cable, and radio media all offer much free media measurement material, including the CAB, the TV Network Association, and the Radio Network Association. Each media research company also offers a variety of information kits. In addition network and local media subscribe to research services and make them available to smaller agencies and accounts which do not subscribe.

The most scientifically accurate media measurement quantifies the broadest audience. It's also the easiest to understand. Once learned, the principles of accurate measurement are easy to apply and to adapt to narrower audiences and to a campaign of messages as well as to a single commercial or program. Originally, electronic media measurement involved sets. Now, for TV and cable, measurement is usually available both for sets and people. For radio, it is usually for people only.

The Terms

SIU means total sets in use. People Using TV (*PUT*) and People Using Radio (*PUR*) refer to the totality of persons. *Share of audience* is the percentage of people using broadcast TV and cable or TV who see or hear a program. Audience measurement rates listening and viewing per average quarter hour (*AQH*) and calculates cumulative (*cume*) audience of a schedule of spots. The measurement calculates cume duplication and how many unduplicated listeners or viewers are reached. This is *reach.* The number of times the same listener or viewer is exposed to a message is *frequency.* Each can be calculated for different groups.

A little arithmetic helps, and a computer speeds the plow a lot more. Gross rating points (*GRP*) are the sum of all quarter hour ratings for a particular schedule. To calculate the GRPs of a schedule, simply add the AQH ratings. To evaluate reach and frequency quickly, simple formulas are used. Reach multiplied by frequency equals GRPs, whereas GRPs divided by frequency equals reach, and GRPs divided by reach equals frequency. Cost per thousand (*CPM*) is the cost for each 1000 impressions. Keep in mind that you want the viewers or listeners most prospective for your product at the lowest CPMs possible.

Before Media Selection

You've researched your company and products and identified the lifestyles, habits, and preferences of your customers and desired prospects; you've received the *latest* available rating and program information for times offered on each broadcast TV and radio station and cable system or interconnect. *Avoid* making decisions based on research quoted over the phone. Have it faxed to you and doggedly dig for more facts. Get competitive salespeople to supply research data. Each salesperson will tend to feature his or her media's favorable research and to point out the weaknesses of competitors. Often, you'll hear that a seeming bargain spot is now up against a very highly rated program.

Next, combine your prospective buys with audience demographic data by zip code, block group, and county, at the times offered, in the areas reached. Compute the CPM cost to reach your right prospects, for each spot each station offers. Pick a schedule within your budget. Compare the desired prospect CPM of your schedule with that of other stations and other media in the area. But be very skeptical. Take your time and use your common sense. The more narrow your niche group of prospects, the less accurate are the ratings. You must make some practical adjustments to compensate:

1. Look at the rating of a program over a number of rating periods. The average of six rating periods has six times the sample of viewers or listeners.

2. The cumulative rating for your schedule will be more accurate than for any one spot, for the same reason.

3. If you're considering a spot on a cable system within a cable network program, look at the national rating for the program. Then compare both the local and national competitive program ratings.

4. Look for a spot in a narrow-niche program that immediately follows a broader-appeal, higher-rating program and which airs opposite or against the least rated competition.

5. Rely more on ratings by age and sex only. For ratings of the same program by area demographics, seek supporting evidence such as a special survey (even if it's old) that is based on a bigger sample.

6. Use qualitative data to interest you in stations and programs, but do not rely on them as major factors in your decisions.

7. Combine the use of rating research with your own measurement and a quick-cancellation privilege. Make and measure a direct response offer, whether it's a premium, contest, inquiry, or sale. If you have a store or service or are in mail order, check your sales.

Can Research Experts Help You?

Research experts certainly can help you, as can the right advertising agency with a strong TV, cable, and radio research department. The biggest agencies have the most expertise. It's harder for smaller agencies. As a top executive of a very large agency said: "They don't have the tools. They don't have the training. They don't have the time." But small clients rarely can afford big agencies, and smaller agencies may have a big agency-trained research director or one from a top research firm. Look for one.

Selecting and Negotiating Other EM Media

Other chapters go into more detail for specific media, starting with Chapter 4 for broadcast TV, Chapter 5 for cable TV, and Chapter 7 for radio. Chapter 15 discusses the audience measurement and negotiating process for sponsorship of commercials in home video movies. Researchers are now using similar methods to measure the audience and determine the price of commercials in movies on planes and in theaters.

Chapter 25 describes how these audience measurement methods are beginning to spread to in-store TV and in-store radio. Companies probably will also apply these methods to national ad networks of multimedia kiosks in chain stores and public places; to direct-by-satellite business TV as described in Chapter 27; to sponsored TeleMedia described in Chapter 10; and to information and entertainment computer networks described in Chapter 19.

Electronic Direct Marketing Media

All the media discussed above can be used to direct market, but the following EM media are primarily used for direct marketing:

Outbound telemarketing

Voice mail

E-Mail

Outbound fax mail

Online catalogs (consumer, trade, or business-to-business)

Online marketplaces (multiple catalogs for consumer, trade, or business-to-business)

CD-ROM catalogs and marketplaces

Self-selling electronic kiosks in public places

Electronic vending machines

TV shopping networks

Audio- and teleconferencing

These electronic media are not yet touched by regular audience measurement series or studies. Researchers calculate the numbers of people to whom materials are sent or the number who access information, and then they calculate the cost per person reached. As with other direct response media, a great effort is made to determine how each of these media has pulled response for other direct marketers before any test is made.

Measurement of results and the cost per sale or per inquiry are usually far more important than calculating or estimating the cost per person reached. Tests can be made of item, price, offer, or copy approach and results tallied by actual sales or inquiries. Confirming tests become increasingly important in major campaigns to build in the least possible risk at any point.

Electronic Co-Media and Support Media

Much of electronic marketing is done to increase the sales from other media while producing sales on its own. But the following EM media are primarily used to enhance and support other media:

In-bound telemarketing

Fax-aided ads

Talking ads

Video catalogs

In-bound faxmail

Videos as premiums

Interactive ads on disks

EDI networks

Electronic aids for the salesforce

Electronic kiosks in retail businesses as sales assistants

Kiosks at trade shows

Interactive disk catalogs

Bulletin boards

Electronic servicing of customers

The object is to produce more added and traced benefit than added cost. Sometimes the electronic marketing is an auxiliary function, sometimes it's used in tandem with other media, and sometimes it's the dominant marketing form. Chapter 16 demonstrates the power of this synergy with a case study on how Citibank's Global Report eventually cut its lead cost from $800 to $80 and its selling cost by 95 percent.

Help Source Guide

1. *The Arbitron Co.* provides a *free* information kit that tells how ratings work, what they mean: 142 W. 57th St., NY, NY 10022. (212) 887-1300.

2. *Birch-Scarborough Research Corp.* Free info kit with full explanation of single-source media research. 12350. N.W. 39 St., Coral Springs, FL 33065. (305) 753-6043.

3. *CACI Marketing Systems* compiles reports that document significant demographic 10-year major changes; inexpensive, easy to use, based on 1990 census. Data available by zip code, block group, census tract, place, county, metropolitan area, ADI, DMA, state, any geometric area; by population age and number; by income, households, race. *Free* catalog of new reports: 1100 N. Glebe Rd., Arlington, VA 22201. (703) 841-7800.

4. *Bureau of the Census* provides a *free* brochure, "Census Bureau Programs and Products." Included are: how to get valuable market research info for small cost—printed reports, computer tapes, CD-ROM, floppy disks, microfiche, online—and addresses of state data centers, national clearinghouses of census data, and U.S. Government Printing Office bookstores: Bureau of the Census, Customer Services, Washington, DC 20233. (301) 763-4100.

5. *Donnelley Marketing Information Services* offers the Affluence Model PC program, which allows you to rank target households and/or geographies on 20 network breaks. *Free* information kit: 70 Seaview Ave., P.O. Box 10250, Stamford, CT 06904. (203) 353-7207.

6. *Electronic Media Rating Council, Inc.*, provides a *free* booklet called "Minimum Standards For electronic Media Rating Research," the rules to minimize distortion of ratings by efforts of individual media: 509 Madison ave., Suite 1112, NY, NY 10022. (212) 754-3343.

7. *Inside Media* is a biweekly magazine that includes media research developments: 911 Hope St., Six River Bend Center, Stamford, CT 06907. (203) 358-9900.

8. *Mediaweek* is a magazine that offers strong research coverage. For a subscription: P.O. Box 708, Brewster, NY 10509-9906. (800) 722-6658.

9. *The National Hispanic Market Trade Show & Media Expo* is held annually—a $180 billion market (1992) expected to reach 30 million consumers with the purchasing power of $330 billion by the year 2000. Videos available about annual best TV, print, radio advertising. Also available is a Hispanic Market Info-Pak—demographics, top 50 advertisers, spending power, growth companies, ad agencies: 360 S. Hope Ave., Suite 300C, Santa Barbara, CA 93105. (805) 682-5843.

10. For information from *Nielsen Media Research*, write or call: Communications Dept., 1290 Ave. of the Americas, NY, NY 10104-0061. (212) 708-7500.

11. The *Standard Directory of Advertising Agencies* provides detailed info about over 8100 U.S. ad agencies; lists clients, media, and sales promotional services, PR firms. Also available is the *Standard Directory of Advertisers:* Reed Reference Publications, P.O. Box 31, New Providence, NJ 07974. (800) 521-8110.

4

Broadcast TV

How to Benefit
as the Audience
Divides

TV is the most powerful method of advertising ever created. It is used successfully by many of the biggest national companies, particularly by manufacturers of cars, packaged foods, beverages, toiletries and proprietary medicines; fast-food and other restaurants; airlines; and many other businesses. TV succeeds locally for supermarkets, auto and truck dealers, drug stores, banks, and many other small and large enterprises.

In this chapter we will concentrate on broadcast TV (BTV) as well as low-power TV, a relatively new addition to the electronic media landscape. We will discuss cable TV separately in Chapter 5 and devote a whole chapter to how to make a TV commercial in Chapter 6.

First, let's summarize why both broadcast and cable TV have become such effective advertising media:

- TV combines sight, motion, sound, graphics, and, usually, color.

- This combination makes TV's power unrivaled in its ability to demonstrate, persuade, and create instant product recognition.

- TV reaches virtually everyone. More than 98 percent of U.S. homes have at least one TV set, most have more. The average home has two sets, and almost all TV homes have color sets.

However, people no longer watch TV as intently for long periods.

Sometimes screens turned on are unwatched; more often they are watched only intermittently or while the viewer is doing something else, from reading to cooking.

Audiences (the young most of all) resist the perception of commercial glut. They use hand tuners to eliminate or "zap" commercials and jump station to station. More than 75 percent of TV homes now have these remote-control capabilities. Moreover, studies suggest that viewers forget commercials faster than in the past.

These trends, coupled with the onslaught of viewer choices in more forms of TV and other video, have fragmented broadcast TV's formerly monolithic audience. For much of the 1980s, the audience for the three major BTV networks (ABC, CBS and NBC) declined as cable's programming and audience grew. The quality of BTV's audience also declined, as the more prosperous viewers pay for cable service, whereas the poorest do not. Furthermore, higher-income people spend less time watching TV, while the poor watch much more. Additional trends include the following:

- VCRs in most TV homes further reduce BTV's audience.
- Home satellite dish programming also reduces BTV.
- Multiset viewing is leveling out.
- TV audience groupings are growing smaller.
- Viewers exhibit less loyalty to keep watching any show.

And TV audience measurement research (due to splintering of the audience) is more difficult. Helen Johnston, vice president of Media Research at Grey Advertising, says, "TV research is woefully behind in many ways."

Broadcast TV Still Reigns

Shortly, we'll discuss how TV audience fragmentation has spawned new advantages (with opportunities for new kinds of advertisers) as well as new disadvantages to avoid. But we'll start with TV's first form, broadcast TV—which still commands more advertising dollars than any other medium. Here's why:

1. BTV still routinely delivers huger audiences than any other medium.

2. BTV reaches (and is regularly watched by) every cable and virtually every noncable home.

3. Mammoth broadcast network audiences still dominate all TV.

4. More top-rated syndicated shows are shown on broadcast TV.

5. Advertising negotiation (and competition) often keeps down the cost per thousand (CMP) rate paid for desired BTV station viewers.

Smart advertisers (from big to small) overcome BTV's disadvantages and profit from its change. First, investigate if broadcast TV fits *your* business and, if so, how you can use BTV most effectively.

If you sell very specialized or super-luxury products and services, BTV may not be for you. If you have a mass-appeal product or service many can afford, consider BTV. But its presentation must also be suited to TV's advantages while possessing enough profit margin for TV promotion.

How to Get More from Less

Take maximum advantage of the many forces changing broadcast TV. They can shrink or stretch every dollar you spend. Follow these guidelines:

1. Target better. Research your customers, prospects, and overall market.

2. Make BTV part of a comprehensive marketing plan.

3. Create TV commercials that: (a) cut through the clutter; (b) win credibility; (c) make long-term friends; and (d) ask for the desired action.

4. Test, measure, and modify both commercials and station placement before you roll out.

5. Analyze each BTV media choice. Bid aggressively for the best value for your best targeted purchases.

6. Keep measuring the effectiveness of each TV commercial, campaign, purchase, and time placement. Watch each campaign as if it were a cash-flow.

7. Be flexible. If results drop off, cut losses fast.

8. Keep up with the latest technology and analytical methods to use broadcast TV more effectively. Change methods accordingly.

Getting Started

Learn or brush up on BTV's basics, changes, and latest research, whether your firm is local, regional, or national, big or small, or whether you have sophisticated guidance or must rely on yourself. Reread Chapter 3 and refer to the Help Sources Guide at the end of this chapter. Investigate the creation of your TV commercial while you first consider BTV and cable time buys. Read Chapter 5 on cable and Chapter 6 on TV production before you buy TV time.

What Length Commercial? At What Cost?   BTV commercials can range from 10 seconds to 60 minutes. Length should depend on how you can most effectively present your product or service, with what frequency you can buy most advantageously, and what your pocketbook can stand.

BTV time can cost $20 or less for 30 seconds of the cheapest time in a small market, to $300,000 and more on a top-rated national network show. What matters more than the total cost is the *CPM*, or the cost per thousand (M) people reached. What matters most is the CPM of those you want most to reach. We'll soon discuss this in more detail.

How Many versus How Often.   Is your message short and your business concept and theme simple (such as a discounter)? Is your product easy to understand and low in cost? Is your distribution wide? If so, go for more repetition to the same people. You want *frequency*. In TV language, *frequency* does not mean the number of times your spots run but the average number of times a household or person is exposed to your ad.

Do you want to produce walk-ins for a sale of specific items? Do you want phone-call orders? Write-ins? To demonstrate an item? These needs usually require a longer message, and these messages do best when exposed to a variety of different audiences. You want *reach, cume, unduplicated,* or *net* audience. These are TV jargon meaning the number of different viewers your commercial is exposed to. In any situation, you need fewer spots if your spots run on high-rating shows rather than on lower-rating shows.

How Long Should Your Ad Run?   Should your commercial run year-round? If so, continuously or with different, but regular short schedules, (called *flights*)? But how long should each flight be? And how many flights a year? Or should you run only a portion of the year? And if so, when? A flight may be for 8 or 10 spots and a campaign of flights for a few months to most of or all the year.

The length of any BTV ad campaign varies by the type of product or service, by its seasonality, by the mission of the commercial, and by what has worked best in the past. Length can also be determined by rate considerations or by your budget.

If you want to create or change a perception about your price, quality, service, or product positioning, run a short commercial often, for as long as your budget allows.

When and How Intensively Should You Run Your Schedule? For a seasonal product or service, stick to the weeks and months that work best in print or other media. For special event promotions and sales run throughout the year, a concentrated flight of 10 days for each usually works best. For direct-response offers, run week to week. Measure response, stop when it drops. Take the offer off the air for several months, then come back.

Use "impact scheduling" to heighten impact and batter through TV ad clutter. The identical commercial is deliberately scheduled again and again as close as possible to the previous one run, sometimes only a minute apart. Many studies have shown that through impact scheduling, viewers are 25 to 50 percent more likely to remember the commercial's content. Ad persuasiveness studies show a 5 to 10 percent increase. Of course, fewer people are reached. Impact scheduling works best to sell to the same people more intensively. Use "scatter" campaigns to do the opposite of impact, by scheduling spots in shows reaching more people less often. Each does a different job.

One Commercial 240 Times Longer Than Another. As 15-second format commercials became popular, all-commercial programs also began. These are commercials and programs intertwined—a documentary history of America in photographs became a history of photography and also a one-hour commercial for Kodak. A "Showcase for Homes" became an hour of commercials for a residential realtor. A one-hour, documentary-style direct-response commercial for "stay young" cosmetics did over $90 million in phone and mail orders.

But don't rush in! The Kodak show was wonderful. House shopping shows are fine. But most products and services can only be dull when presented for half an hour or more. Many pseudodocumentaries are efforts to provide credibility for wild promises from which the public quickly turns away.

Interactive TV? Caution! There have been many attempts at interactive shows. Broadcast via TV, these are shows with which a viewer can interact electronically by pushing a button on a device provided, on a pushbutton phone, or even by holding up a device to the TV screen. John Flinn, a writer on the subjects of broadcast and cable TV, explains: "All interactive TV has been a disappointment. But the Interactive Video Trade Association grows. There is a search for more compelling interactive TV programs."

Study What Works for Others.   Jim Birschbach, sales manager of KMGH-TV Channel 7 of Denver, estimates that 5 percent of his station's advertisers run all 52 weeks, 40 percent run "occasionally," and 55 percent run regular flights throughout the year, usually 6 weeks out of each 13.

Every BTV salesperson, rep, and sales manager can tell you how businesses similar to yours have used TV advertising—and which campaigns have been most successful. If you are a retailer, what another, similar retailer does successfully in another city may work well for you. If your firm is big and has TV experience, ask associates. If your firm is small, ask your trade association for guidance. Again, use the Help Sources Guide at the end of this chapter.

What Should You Budget for TV?   Your company's ad budget may be based on a percentage of last year's sales volume or on this coming year's expected sales. Other companies budget based on what is considered enough advertising to gain a desired amount of competitive market share. A retailer's budget may depend on how much cooperative money from various vendors can be raised. For a manufacturer, advertising often depends on how many dealers agree to stock its products. The percentage spent on TV is based on how suitable TV is for the product and business.

How Much Should a Commercial Cost?   For local advertisers in Denver, recent costs to produce a 30-second TV spot ran from $500 to $8000. Typically, the cost ranged from $1000 to $2000 for one spot, plus about 15 percent more to produce a second spot at the same session. Local advertisers often make from one to five commercials at the same time for a series of flights. In New York and Los Angeles or in exotic location spots, a 30-second spot can cost $30,000 to more than $1 million for a major national advertiser.

However, in some markets, a TV station (if new or hungry enough) may produce your commercial for nothing, if you buy a modest schedule. Low-power TV stations, which we'll discuss, have been known to do this. Chapter 6 provides an in-depth discussion of commercial production costs.

How to Test-Market BTV

Test marketing depends on who you are and what you're selling. Retailers have begun with 20 spots over two weeks for one sale. Mail-order firms have tested 120-, 90-, or 60-second spots, which they've run three to six times on one station. Small marketers have tested ten 30-second spots a week, which they have run for 6 to 13 weeks in one to three small cities.

Sophisticated BTV advertisers want to find out how much it will cost and how long it will take to achieve a specific market share in a test area and whether an expansion regionally or nationally has the probability of sufficient profit to proceed. But also ask your customers, vendors, other marketers, and BTV station people what those most successful BTV advertisers do. Compare those answers until you gradually determine which approach seems most correct. At the same time, brush up on the basics of BTV production and creative approaches by viewing and noting the recent changes in audience preference. Reviewing the basics is the first step to buying the right kind of audience, in the right place, at the right price.

Some BTV Viewing Trends

BTV's audience rises during the course of the day, peaking between 8:00 and 10:00 p.m. (8:30 to 9:00 p.m. is the top viewing half-hour). BTV's late- afternoon and early-evening audiences are smaller in the summer than in winter, but the early-morning and late-night audience levels change little season to season. Younger children watch TV more than older ones. Women watch more than men; older adults watch more than younger ones. Sunday is the most popular viewing night.

Households that view TV most have three or more people, subscribe to pay cable, or have nonadults in the household. The lowest viewing group is the single-person household. Young, active, affluent, light viewers represent 20 percent of homes but only 3 percent of the viewing audience. These viewers are better educated and probably better customers for travel and financial services, but the CPM to reach them is too high for packaged goods advertisers.

TV viewing is a habit. Although audience fragmentation is increasing, broadcast networks still dominate new original serial programming, vital to major advertisers because of its measurable consistency. And this habit of viewing a serial persists even after its initial success. Many fans continue to watch the reruns on the network or as syndicated shows on independent stations or on cable. Local advertisers in small markets are often offered spots adjacent to older, winning shows. Each original BTV network program may be creating an opportunity for you, whether on a network, an independent, or a cable outlet.

The most watched BTV programs have been situation comedies, followed by feature films and general drama. But preferences can suddenly change to phone-in talk shows, etc. The following are categories of BTV programs:

Mystery/Suspense	Variety
Music	Sports
Dramatic shows	Religious programs
Adventure shows	Educational
Movies	Serial episodes
Children's shows	News programs
Light entertainment	Current events
	Talk shows

Network BTV

Most people regularly watch three to five TV stations—even those in cable homes with access to 85 stations. Although the average U.S. television household has a choice of close to 50 cable and BTV channels, each of the three or four BTV networks continues to hit the audience jackpot.

Over half of network ad dollars are still for packaged food and drug items. These and other universal, low-cost items need the giant audiences BTV networks still give, even after the network's audience share has dropped substantially.

Although the share of audience for ABC, CBS, and NBC keeps dropping, the networks still get huge, if reduced, audiences. A fourth BTV network, Fox Television, has had big audience growth among young families.

Big Network Targets

The networks try to group their shows to appeal to similar audiences by age and sex, in the hopes that they will tune in longer. Larry Giannino is vice president and director of Program Research for the ABC-TV network. He says, "We target to very broad areas. We go after the mass market. We leave it to cable to splinter and to counter-program." Helen Johnston, vice president of Media Research at Grey Advertising, confirms that this is how national advertisers buy network time: "Spots on

TV network shows are bought mainly aided by research of how much it costs to reach desired viewers based on age and sex."

Giant Audience Limits Targeting

Targeting your ad by viewer demographics and psychographics is usually not an economic way to buy broadcast network TV, so simple age and sex selection still predominate. Even so, the top 15 Nielsen-rated network TV shows reach everybody: women, men, children in different age groups and in different proportions.

Only a few of the top shows preferred by teens 12 to 17 years old are aimed just at them. The other preferred shows are in the top-rated overall. Teens usually join in family viewing. In deciding what the family will watch, teens often team up with their dads to select movies, instead of the sitcoms or nighttime soaps their moms may prefer. What shows are most watched by children age 2 to 11? Only a minority are children's programs. Most are among the top 15 rated shows overall and are viewed as part of the family group.

The action-adventure TV program category is strong among young males. Sitcoms also generally appeal to a younger audience, and sports programs attract men, including a lot of young men. Music award shows generally reach a much younger adult and teen audience, both male and female. Mysteries appeal to an older audience, as do adult soap operas in prime time, which have the strongest appeal among older females.

Specialized Networks

Hispanics are not only the fastest-growing ethnic group, they watch a third more TV than non-Hispanics on average. And because they view Hispanic TV far more than English-speaking TV, there already are two national BTV Hispanic networks.

These and other specialized networks are growing. INTV is an association of independent TV stations which function together. The association launched INTV news. Conus Satellite News Cooperative broadcasts "network" news programs which are mutually produced by its 81 affiliates. Stories are transmitted by satellite to the Conus master control in Minneapolis, which in turn feeds them back to subscribing stations.

Regional BTV networks and custom networks for special events are also proliferating, and more permutations of network BTV based on specialized programs are expected. Stay tuned in, because one or more of these new networks may be closely targeted to your prospects.

Spot TV

A viable alternative to buying network BTV airtime comes in the form of syndicated shows. In 10 years, ad sales on *syndicated* shows (SS) multiplied 20 times, to more than $1 billion a year. The total SS audience is larger than that of the biggest BTV network, and syndicated programs include some of the highest-rated shows on TV. SS's fast growth is the biggest reason that independent BTV stations are taking audience away from network stations.

Usually, you buy spots on SS through your TV station sales rep. If you do well on one in one area, you can buy spots on it all over. Nielsen provides the audience research, using its people meter to rate nationally the top 20 syndicated shows.

More Kinds of Winning Shows

You can target more on SS, with over twice as many daily and weekly series than on networks and over 300 movies and specials. Sitcom "reruns" compete for top ratings with big-prize audience participation shows. Next most popular are feature movies. Movie gossip masquerading as news is usually rated highly. Science fiction adventure does well. Exotic travel, near-documentary shows like those done by National Geographic rank high and offer prestige to advertisers. Regularly among the Top 10 rated syndicated shows is the World Wrestling Federation's weekly wrestling bouts. *People's Court,* with its simulated trial format, also has consistently been in the Top 20.

Caution! The types of syndicated shows that are hits rise and fall. The CPM offered for the same show can be twice as much in one city as in another. Varying SS ad pricing may be due to an arbitrary station policy, supply and demand, show competition, or placement following a better or worse show. The shows you want may only be available if you buy spots in shows you don't want. Investigate spot-time buying carefully.

The advantages of spot TV are

1. You have a greater choice of programs and sources. You can buy time on SS, a network show, or a local program. These choices provide more special-niche audiences, some of which are more upscale.

2. Spot TV offers maximum flexibility to start, stop, expand, or contract to bigger or smaller advertising schedules—and in more or fewer markets.

3. Spot TV provides an opportunity to take advantage of new, just-right time buys, a sudden audience leap, and other last-minute bargains.

Audience Research Is Vital

In larger BTV markets, researchers increasingly are using people meters to measure program viewing. But to measure every spot TV market via this, more accurate method is still too expensive; 100,000 people meters would be required for the 200 local markets.

In these smaller TV markets, BTV ratings are measured by the older "diary" methodology. (Review this discussion in Chapter 3.) To most accurately compare stations' rates and ratings, media time -buyers must be able to factor in how stations vary in the percentage of TV homes in an area each can physically reach. One station may be able to be seen by far more people than another in your marketing area. Note the following:

- UHF station signals (channels higher than 13) usually go about *half as far* as a VHF station (channels 2 to 13).

- Stations vary in power of their broadcast signal. More power goes further to *more* listeners.

- Station transmitters vary in height. More height allows the signal to go farther to reach *more* listeners.

- Station transmitters are often aimed differently.

- Direction can determine signal reception as well, as some stations must decide whether to aim toward *more homes* or to fewer, *more upscale* ones.

Computer Programs Help

Most larger advertising agencies recommend a TV schedule to a client based on reaching a quota of the desired audience. They set up a single system to police buying of TV time. To do the same yourself requires the know-how of a short, special vocabulary and several simple equations. A calculator helps. Special-services and PC computer software, mentioned below, speeds the analysis further and makes it possible to compare quickly station coverage with the demographics of the area covered.

Nielsen has developed programs to perform time-consuming analyses such as rankings, trends, and cost comparisons. *Spot and Postbuy Reporter* helps pinpoint the best schedules, evaluate results, and more. Arbitron offers similar services. There are other excellent PC software programs to help analyze and select the lowest CPMs for the kind of audience targeted. For BTV ad buys in big markets with the most stations, it's important.

How to Buy Spot TV

The biggest ad agencies have large staffs to buy spot TV; buying spot TV requires more computerization than buying network time. J. Walter Thompson, for example, has 135 local or spot TV media buyers. Each masters and buys for only one local market.

The complexity involved in buying spot BTV—especially in many markets simultaneously—requires more know-how, time, and tools than are available to many small firms (and some small agencies). But you learn much that is complex by mastering some each day and not proceeding too fast. Most big firms and agencies start small. First reread in Chapter 3 the explanation of TV research procedures and the meanings of the most commonly used nomenclature in network and spot BTV audience measurement. All this jargon simply defines precisely what you want to buy: enough audience of the type most likely to buy your product or service.

Spot TV buying requires the following:

1. The use of available scientific research analysis

2. Common sense to recognize and offset research limitations

3. Hard-headed negotiation to pay less for your desired audience

If you possess one of the above skills without the others, you will not be able to buy wisely, but you don't have to be equally strong in all three disciplines. The "science" to buying BTV time is like mastering the key ratios taught to lending officers as rules of thumb to analyze the ability to repay before loaning money. Learn your numbers thoroughly. Stations and networks use ratings as scorecards to justify the shows they run, move, or drop and the rates they charge.

But a rating for a show is what the audience *was* when the poll was taken. TV buys are made for the *future*, when conditions may change. A different time of year, a different show following or preceding, or different competitive shows at the same time may drive the rating up or down. A new show is far more of an unknown.

For the buyer, ratings ideally are a way to police the future. First, you must set an objective in terms of gross rating points (the total of all rated announcements bought). In any market there is an established guideline of X amount of gross rating points for the schedule cost. The desired *cost per rating point* (CPP) determined by the buyer is lowest for the widest mass audience and highest for a highly specialized niche audience.

Bargaining Begins

What are you looking for? The direct marketer wants to be "guaranteed" sales by any medium at a percentage of the sales produced. The retailer wants to be sure that enough store traffic and counter sales are produced above ad expense to show a profit. Big companies want to be guaranteed rating points for the desired audience. If the actual rating is less than guaranteed, the contract specifies that the network or station will then run enough extra commercials (make-goods) to deliver audience guaranteed. Everybody wants make-goods. Stations want business at a profit. It's a bazaar. Station promises may be precise or vague. There may be none.

But months later comes the postbuy analysis. This essential procedure might reveal that some of the most desirable spots did not clear (actually run), but the weakest rating spots did clear. Analysis might further show that for some reason the cost was as specified in the contract, but the number of rating points was fewer than aimed for. The hoped-for CPP was not achieved. Even if nothing was promised beforehand, presenting this information still may lead to some remedial action; this information at least can become a bargaining chip in negotiating a future schedule. If the desired CPP is for a specific audience by age or sex, the procedure is the same. However, the dynamics of bargaining can change dramatically if time is sold out or wide open.

Each station in each market has a range of programs reaching different audiences. Sample every channel from 2 to 13 and all the UHF channels you can get. Next, phone all the stations for media kits. From station sales reps, get the Nielsen, Arbitron and other single-source research to which the stations subscribe. Ask everyone for case histories of other advertisers who made up for lack of staff and equipment with time, effort, and common sense and who made BTV pay.

Small Markets

A smart retailer in a small market can be a role model for any new, small buyer of spot TV. Pete Vann is the owner of Vann's Audio-Video & Appliance Store, a small retail chain with five locations in Montana. The first store and headquarters is in Missoula, the largest market and one with three TV stations. The second store is in nearby Hamilton, covered by one of the Missoula TV stations. Another store is in Helena; the fourth one is in Butte. Pete's newest store is in Boise, a bigger market. All three markets are covered by one TV station in each market.

It's taken Pete almost 30 years to work out his way of budgeting, raising co-op money, selecting the right mix of media, and promoting his business most profitably. He has tried using advertising agencies but says he feels he has done better himself. He's never had time to master many TV research terms or a lot of the intricacies of detailed time-buy analyses as done by the big BTV advertisers. But he targets to different, special audiences for various products, plans carefully, buys astutely, and makes money.

What Pete Does, You Can.   Before each year begins, Pete Vann estimates the coming year's sales. He then sets up an ad budget based on 6 percent of total sales. When Pete launched his fifth store, he spent more than 6 percent of sales there in its first year, but he also received more co-op money from vendors—and a better break from the media. Pete raises about half of his advertising budget from vendor contributions. These co-op dollars actually average 75 percent, but Pete also advertises with no contribution from manufacturers. His budget breaks down roughly to 40 percent newspaper, 25 percent TV, 20 percent radio, and 15 percent direct mail. Pete feels that each helps the other.

In 1990, all production costs of a 30-second TV commercial averaged about $75 for Pete Vann. He makes three or four in one morning and then incorporates manufacturer's product-demo footage, such as a GE dishwasher action shot. He produces and is the on-screen talent for every TV commercial. He adlibs from a written outline, and each commercial is produced at his showroom, warehouse, or where he chooses.

Why Pete's Commercials Work.   Unending ideas pour out of Pete, like his "Surrender" sale, shot with white flags all around his showroom as a backdrop, as Pete sadly "surrenders his profit" on TV; or his "Free-Day" sale, where he takes off from his prices all the overhead he saves on Leap Year's extra day; or the "Ketch-Up" sale, which he runs the following year, and holds on screen the bottle of ketchup he gives away free to anyone who comes in, as his one hope of sales catching up to the year before; or the "Weed-Out" sale, where he offers garden equipment, shot with somebody's garden as a backdrop.

Pete's cash register tells him what works, and his experience tells him what to do. If sales are higher than expected, he increases his budget. If lower, he may cut or spend more, depending on his gut feeling. Pete is a low-key, high-credibility showman whose ideas never stop. He's constantly figuring out new ways to raise co-op money, get free, extra promotions from stations, and present his offers personally. He listens to every report from his vendors on what other dealers are doing.

Pete Likes and Studies People.   Pete knows which customers prefer each product and targets accordingly. He notices that mainly 40-plus women buy Kitchen Aid appliances. He therefore places Kitchen Aid spots on *Oprah Winfrey, Donahue,* soap operas, and daytime news. He sees mostly young men (but also young women) 18 to 25 years old buying his car stereos. For them, he does well with stereo spots on David Letterman and other late-night buys. He sees older, more prosperous men and women buying his giant-screen TVs. To attract more of them, he buys spots in evening news. And to reach the yuppies that go for his Camcorders, he advertises on evening and weekend news. The point is, Pete intuitively does much of what the most sophisticated media-buying methods are designed to do.

Pete Control.   Once a year, Pete buys TV time for the year for each station—his "upfront" buy. He's less concerned with a CPP guarantee than he is with dividing up his money into day-parts and getting a commitment for the number of spots he gets in prime time and on specific top-rated shows. He runs two flights a month to promote two stores in the Missoula market and one flight a month in every other market. Each flight is about 10 days. Pete selects the actual air times shortly before the flight and runs 10 to 20 commercials in a flight, depending on the product and season.

Despite the fact that 75 percent of the spot's cost often is being borne by the vendor, Pete retains control of content, presentation, and time selection. He runs a tight ship, spends close to $100,000 a year on TV, watches every penny, does more than $10 million a year in sales, and consistently makes money. He may be a model for you.

If You're a Local Advertiser

TV stations (new ones above all) need new revenue from local accounts and solicit many businesses which have never advertised on TV before. In more than 50 markets, one-hour (or longer) paid real estate TV "shows" now advertise homes. TV has turned many local business owners into spokespeople for their ventures and continues to offer many tie-in promotions.

But some local advertisers still buy "bargains" that are wrong for them. Many buy based on insufficient facts. Remember that whatever kind or size of local business you have, you can get a surprising amount of information free that can help you target, at the right CPM, the prospects most suited to you.

Smart Station People Can Help.   Henry Pappas is founder-president of KPTM-TV Omaha. His station primarily solicits retail accounts, many of which had only advertised in newspapers. Besides KPTM's researcher, the station subscribes to Arbitron and its Product Target-AID; to Nielsen's Conquest geo-psycho-demographic analysis tool; and to Simmons's single-source research service. Pappas says, "Each of my sales people is a real consultant to retailers. [Each] learns their businesses; their strengths, their weaknesses; how the station can help them most. Each puts in enough time with each account to do it. Each researches to dig up co-op dollars from national markets for local advertisers. We show our retail ad prospects who their prospects are and how to reach them with our station."

How do you find the Pappas in your town? Any TV station salesperson may provide real expertise, the sales manager or research director may know more, and the station manager should be the most knowledgeable. Ask in each meeting who are the smartest in town. Ask media buyers at ad agencies and marketing managers of advertisers. You may find several experts. Learn from them, and check stations against each other.

Computer-Controlled Ratecards. TV stations often sell time just as airlines now sell seats. Ratecards had been divided into day-parts, from early morning to all night, differing on weekends. But the same commercial length in the same day-part on the same station could cost several different prices, based on when you bought it. Prices are now routinely decided upon and changed by computer program—based on supply and demand. It's an unending electronic auction.

The computer responds to purchases or the lack of them. It does not foresee events. Sometimes station managers will anticipate demand and raise rates before an expected jump in orders.

Often you can take advantage of change before the computer raises rates—targeting prospects that are best for you. Although the biggest advertisers need to plan ahead, if you're small you can be more flexible, grabbing bigger, last-minute bargains and taking advantage of sudden change. Small but savvy advertisers buy BTV when rates are lowest, then switch to other media when they rise. Every schedule cancellation can be your opportunity, as can each new program that catches on and each rescheduling of a strong program to where the competition is less.

Even stormy weather in winter and rainy weather in summer can jump weekend viewing. Strong movies can create sudden audience surges for weak stations. A new affiliate of the number-1 network can get a big jump in viewing. Act before others.

If news programs work for you, look for a big, continuing news story to break—whether revolution, disaster, sweeping liberalization in a dictatorship, or a turn to dictatorship in a democracy. News ratings can jump 10 to 15 percent and sometimes more, carrying all ratings higher while the story lasts. ABC's *Nightline* has gone up as high as 41 percent. Cash in.

Investigate Unwired Networks. Once you find the type of niche program perfect for you, an "unwired" network may soon be a simple way to get maximum clearance nationwide in it, for a premium. Anyone can assemble a "network," securing commercial time in the same day-part on a number of often independent stations. One such unwired network is Premiere Announcement Network. It features national coverage of top-rate local news shows and says that "88 of our stations place #1 or #2 in early and late local news."

Before you buy commercials on such a network, however, check these points:

1. When will your spot run? In each city, in what program? Or between what programs?

2. What is the CPM? It's usually three-quarters that of spot TV and double that of network or barter.

3. What clearance will you get? The "network" may simply offer unsold time, if it's still available.

Low-Power TV (LPTV). LPTV is a way to start advertising on TV for many who otherwise could not—the smallest retailer or special service. The FCC allows an LPTV station to broadcast in areas where full power won't fit without causing interference. Some LPTV stations operate in or between major cities on VHF channels 2 through 13; others are on UHF channels 14 to 69. Most LPTV station signals reach out 15 to 25 miles versus 50 to 75 miles for full-power TV, and two-thirds of LPTV stations feed programs to cable systems. Remember, however, that in most areas, LPTV's share of audience is miniscule.

The following are some LPTV ad surprises:

- In Milwaukee, Kohl Grocers (an A&P subsidiary) used ethnic LPTV to reach blacks and Hispanics. Black walk-in sales jumped 1200 percent and Hispanic walk-in sales went up 600 percent.

- In Baton Rouge, a radio-TV school that owned part of an LPTV station advertised almost exclusively on it for students, for two years. Enrollment almost doubled.

- In Twin Falls, Idaho, LPTV pulled in traffic for an antique shop more profitably than any other medium used.

- On channels 54 and 44 in Brooklyn, New York, and Mineola, New York, programs in 15 languages are ethnic marketplaces.

Each LPTV station can be a laboratory for niche programs, providing specialized advertisers with new potential vehicles. Many LPTV stations carry syndicated shows; some are even network outlets. You may be able to test broader-appeal TV commercials at the smallest risk yet.

Proceed with caution, however. LPTV urban coverage is often inner city. And in smaller cities, LPTV often gives only chunks of coverage.

Summary

To summarize, more money is being spent on all forms of BTV than ever before. It delivers huge audiences instantly with a multisensory impact no other medium can match. Although BTV is still the preferred domain of many large national advertisers, there's now more choice, more tools, and more help easily available for advertisers with more modest budgets and markets.

Help Source Guide

1. *Advertiser Syndicated TV Association* provides *free ASTA Annual Programming Guide*—information on a large number of syndicated shows, ratings, projections, more. Also free is ASTA's 40-page magazine, *Guide to Advertiser Supported Syndication*, published with *Ad Age & Electronic Media:* ASTA, 1756 Broadway, NY, NY 10019. (212) 245-0840.

2. *The Arbitron Company* is a rating service for spot and local TV and provides these two fine *free* books: *Arbitron Television Book: Guide to Media Planning, Buying* (36 pages; easy, nontechnical, basic, sound) and *New TV Marketplace: Post Analysis and Buying* (expert method compares what you get with what you buy): 142 W. 57th St., NY, NY 10019. (212) 887-1300.

3. *Electronic Media* magazine provides the latest on broadcast TV, cable, radio. Ask for the most recent special issues with the latest updates on new electronic marketing media from Crain Publishing (also publishes *Advertising Age*): 740 Rush St., Chicago, IL 60611. (312) 649-5200. 220 East 42d St., NY, NY 10017. (212) 210-0100.

4. *Hispanic Media & Markets* is an annual Standard Rates and Data Service publication, providing comprehensive coverage of Spanish language U.S. media. Includes TV, radio rates, audience makeup, programming facts, contacts w/ numbers: 2000 Clearwater Dr., Oak Brook, IL 60521. (800) 232-0772.

5. *Network Television Association* provides a *free* information kit about why TV networks are still so desired by the biggest advertisers: 825 7th Ave., NY, NY 10019. (212) 887-1781.

6. For information from *Nielsen Media Research,* write or call: Communications Department, 1290 Avenue of the Americas, NY, NY 10104-0061. (212) 708-7548.

7. *The LPTV Report* is a monthly magazine which provides a good update. Get a *free* issue or subscribe. Includes the annual directory of LPTV program suppliers: P.O. Box 25510, Milwaukee, WI 52225. (414) 781-0188.

8. *Spot TV Rates & Data* is a monthly publication of SRDS (standard rate and data services). Local, national spot rates; audience profiles of TV stations. 2000 Clearwater Dr., Oak Brook, IL 60521. (800) 232-0772.

9. Ken Auletta's *Three Blind Mice: How the TV Networks Lost Their Way* (Random House, Inc., 1991) is a highly praised bestseller that explains what every TV time-buyer should know. At libraries, book stores: Order Service, 400 Hahn Rd., Westminster, MD 21157. (800) 733-3000.

10. *TV Bureau of Advertising Inc.* provides *free* booklets, brochures, and an annual, *TV Basics:* 477 Madison Ave., NY, NY 10022. (212) 486-1111.

11. *TV Dimensions* is an annual TV buyer's everything book—thorough, excellent in-depth analysis and latest trends: Bethlehem Publishing Company, Inc., 322 E. 50th St., NY, NY 10022. (212) 832-7172.

12. *Univision TV Network* reaches 90 percent of U.S. Hispanic households; cumes 83 percent of Hispanic TV in an average week. In 1992 that was nearly 25 million Hispanic-American viewers, growing 8 times faster than non-Hispanic. The 1990 purchasing power of Hispanic-Americans has shown a 103 percent increase over the 5 previous years. The network provides a *free* media kit; ask for case histories: 9405 N.W. 41st St., Miami, FL 33178. (305) 471-4062.

5
Cable TV

For Biggest
National and Smallest
Local Advertisers

- Over 60 percent of U.S. homes and over 70 percent of Canadian homes are wired for cable TV.
- Over 90 percent of homes wired for cable TV can be reached by local cable ads.
- Americans pay more yearly for cable service than for all movie tickets and video rentals combined.

As we noted in Chapter 4, people in cable homes watch cable more than broadcast TV (BTV). As cable's audience share grows, BTV's network share will probably continue to drop. Still, advertising on cable is not a sure thing. In many ways, cable advertising is much more difficult to master than BTV advertising. Let's examine the opportunities and dangers of this new, growing electronic medium. Five advantages of advertising on cable versus BTV are:

1. Cable offers many times as many national networks.
2. Each cable network provides more than *twice* as much programming. This greater volume of programming spawns greater diversity, competition, and choice.

3. Most successful cable channels provide advertisers with more *specialized* marketplaces. This specialization allows for more precise targeting of an advertiser's desired audience.

4. Because many cable channels air similar programming 20 to 24 hours each day, viewer demographics and psychographics are usually more consistent.

5. Cable's biggest audiences are considered "class mass" because, although most homes have cable, most poorer homes cannot afford it. Therefore, several cable channels attract far more upscale audiences than BTV. In fact, the average cable viewer when compared with the average BTV viewer

- Has more education, a better job, and higher income
- Travels more and rents more cars
- Has more credit and credit cards
- Consumes more of most products and services

For every category of goods, the portion of cable viewers per thousand who own them is as much as 35 to 50 percent higher. So if your firm is big, cable may be a fine buy for large, higher-quality circulation segments. And cable has created new opportunities for many niche advertisers, for most local advertisers, and for some very tiny advertisers.

However, cable has some significant disadvantages also, including the following:

1. Most big cable audiences are fractions of big BTV ones.
2. Many cable networks have holes in national coverage.
3. Obtaining wide local cable coverage is difficult in many markets.
4. Buying cable scientifically is very time-consuming.

In addition, in pay cable homes, viewing is split three ways between broadcast TV, basic cable, and pay cable. Of the three to five channels the average family viewer regularly sees, only two to three are cable, with frequent occasional viewing of others. TV shopping channels account for some of this viewership.

Should You Use Cable?

If your customers are few and extremely specialized and if your potential market is just as limited, cable is not suited to you. Cable is mostly a consumer medium and not suited to most nonconsumer products. Cable may succeed for others in your field who have a *broader* market, but not for your smaller customer and prospect base.

When Other Media Might Be Better

For most companies with mass distribution products, cable is still an *auxiliary* medium. Why? Despite its growth in audience, cable's cumulative network ratings for even its prime-time shows still may not be enough to give required saturation coverage, and the cost of running a broadcast TV national saturation campaign may leave you with no budget for cable.

Another difficulty of cable is its widely varying ad costs. In some markets, cable rates command higher cost per thousand viewers (CPM) for the kinds of audience desired than you should pay. Worse, just before you buy, the most successful cable networks may raise rates sharply and become more rigid in negotiations. To buy cable wisely just may take more work, time, and know-how than you can afford.

Why Cable Works for So Many

Despite these shortcomings, companies large and small routinely profit by advertising on cable. Your biggest asset to help make cable work for you is that most system and network top executives know their business, want yours, and constantly seek to improve the medium's power as an advertising vehicle. Recent trends confirm this:

- More money for programming increases cable's ratings.
- CPMs for local rates are becoming more stable.
- More new channels offer more choice, more targeting.
- New hungry channels are eager to negotiate.
- Better cable research and computer tools to analyze cable advertising are making it easier to buy cable time.

If cable advertising makes sense for you, how do you start? Essentially the procedure is the same as for broadcast TV, you just have more to investigate. Reread Chapter 3 on research and Chapter 4 on BTV. Read the next pages with care. Refer to the Help Source Guide at the end of this chapter, particularly the Cable Advertising Bureau (CAB). Phone CAB to request its pocket cable guide, which lists addresses and phone numbers to follow up much that this chapter covers.

The Cable Networks

How much does cable network advertising cost? The price range is dramatic. For example, the lowest-cost 60-second spot at the bargain direct-response rate for stand by advertisers, in the least desired time periods (1 a.m. to 4 a.m.), at the least desired time of year, for the least watched national cable networks, can cost under $100 if part of a package schedule. On the other end of the spectrum, a 60-second spot run in the highest-rating cable network programming (big-event sports) on ESPN, the cable network with biggest sports audience at the peak viewing of its most desired sports at most desired time of year (fourth quarter), costs over $220,000.

How Top Marketers Buy Network Cable

The largest national advertisers spend far less on cable than on BTV because the average major BTV network has over ten times more total viewers than the average cable network. These top advertisers require the bigger audience of BTV. Most buy spots in BTV network programs for most of their national TV budget and buy cable networks to supplement, often targeting precisely specific viewer segments most desired.

Large national advertisers are also cautious. As we detailed in Chapter 3, only a sample size ten times larger than what cable currently provides can be an accurate audience indicator. Yet advertisers' cable expenditures continue to climb as research methods improve. Sophisticated advertisers are developing their own research methods for cable, plus using those developed by other cable research organizations and the cable media themselves.

How to Analyze a Cable Network Buy

CableCume.   *CableCume* is a method to estimate more accurately and quickly reach and frequency. You remember that reach is the number of households (HH) which view a campaign and frequency is the average number of times during the campaign that a commercial will be viewed by the same HH. (For more details, reread Chapter 3.) Through the Cable Advertising Bureau (CAB), this system is available on a PC disk, free to any prospective user. For more information about the disk, please see entry 7 in the Help Source Guide at the end of this chapter.

CableCume software provides useful user prompts throughout all its functions. You are told what to do (usually one keystroke or two) to cause the system to apply automatically the kind of analysis the biggest agencies do to generate almost any cable-network buy or planning situation. For example, the software can help you determine how many spots you need to buy to reach a desired amount of total viewers, and to do so for each of 16 different breakdowns by age and sex of desired viewing groups. Each day-part from early morning to late night is included. Further, you are told how to update the CableCume data disk to reflect the latest population changes and cable penetration estimates and how to customize to most local planning situations.

Simpler Beginning Steps. Suppose your company is not yet advertising on cable. Even if other people in your firm and ad agency already have expertise in cable, you should orient yourself. Don't worry if you have no advertising background, no specialists to depend on, and little knowledge of TV research and cable-buying methods. Here's how to teach yourself some cable basics from scratch.

Read the TV listings in your newspaper or, better still, *TV Guide.* The biggest cities with the most broadcast stations have at least 50 percent more movies on basic cable and three times as many on pay cable. In smaller cities with fewer broadcast stations, cable offers a much bigger percentage of movies. Now check the reruns of broadcast shows. They run all over on cable. Check sports. You have found what people watch most on cable: Movies, reruns, and sports.

If you don't subscribe to basic cable, turn on the TV of a friend who does. Flick one by one to every cable channel. You are "grazing," as many people do when a commercial comes on. Stop only when the program interests you—make a note of it. Your cable program identifies each network show with initials. In a listing of initials, it gives full names. You will notice how these different types of basic cable networks compete:

- Big *variety* of mass appeal shows
- Far more of *one kind* of popular programs
- Programming all the time of what most people want some of the time and can tune to whenever they want
- *Wide* but *specialized* appeal
- *Narrow-niche* but *intense* appeal

You are watching how each cable network attempts to compete with BTV and with other cable networks. Any channel can get a huge audience by putting on what most people want to see most. But, whether broadcast or cable, most people, most of the time, watch only a few basic types of programs, plus movies, sports, and news. The bigger audience a cable network reaches for, the more it looks like a BTV network.

On a typical top-ten rating list for the cable-networks, eight shows will be reruns. But the many channels of cable let each mass-appeal channel specialize much as radio does. Everybody wants news some of the time, weather for less of the time, and TV program schedules some of the time. Special channels make each available all the time.

The Biggest-Audience Cable Networks

Let's first take a quick look at the formulae used by one of cable's most savvy program packagers, Ted Turner. The Atlanta-based SuperStation (WTBS) has Ted Turner's winning mix of movies, reruns of syndicated shows, and sports. WTBS attracts advertisers because of its cable viewer ratings. The Cable News Network (CNN) is Turner's 24-hour TV news network. As it has matured, it has gained stature—and audience—for in-depth news coverage (particularly during developing news stories), regular sports news, and plenty of business news. For travelers and others with time, Turner's Headline News Network (HNN) rotates lead news items every half hour.

Turner Network Television (TNT) is a virtually all-movie network made possible when Ted Turner bought MGM's vast movie library. By colorizing old black and white classic movies, Turner multiplied their worldwide television appeal. He also increased viewership on TNT and landed more advertisers faster than expected. TNT is positioned to give what pay TV does free (TNT has four-minute mini-intermissions for advertisements).

In combination, Turner's four networks appeal to a massive cross-section of middle America, from lower-middle-class rural folk to upper-middle-class urban business travelers. Turner's networks therefore appeal to advertisers who want to reach mass audiences as well as to those whose products are targeted to a finer segment. Turner further sweetens the pot by offering discounts to advertisers for combined use across several networks.

Winning Formats

Turner has plenty of competition, however, for cable advertising dollars. USA Network's formula also relies on some hit movies but it mostly airs reruns of the most successful broadcast network programs, new episodes of old shows, and new TV series. USA Network often has ratings of a third or more of the BTV networks and at an attractive CPM. USA also features special sports events and has even beaten in ratings the programs of two out of three BTV networks. A variety of other specialized formats are proving successful also.

ESPN. ESPN features sports programming exclusively, including an increasing number of mass-audience sporting events. When ESPN bought NFL Football, its ratings jumped. Then, ESPN agreed to pay $400 million to broadcast 700 major-league baseball games over four years starting in 1990.

Nashville Network. The Nashville Network draws a large audience with an all-country format. Besides *The Grand Old Opry Show* and big country sports like rodeos, the network's programming includes everything from country cooking to country sitcoms aimed at rural, small-town, and urban audiences.

Lifetime Television. Lifetime Television combines several program elements. It shows movies and family sitcoms that draw larger audiences, plus it features some specialized programming of a health and woman's network. For instance, its *Sunday PM* is a professional channel for doctors and health institutions.

Family Channel. The Family Channel runs entertainment appealing to family groups, from kids to grandparents. Its big winners are westerns such as *The Rifleman, Wagontrain, Gunsmoke,* and *Bonanza.*

Arts & Entertainment. Arts & Entertainment emphasizes quality programming that is "near-PBS" caliber but aimed to a larger audience. Shows range from popular classical music, drama, and ballet to prestigious, wide-interest movies.

Discovery Channel. The Discovery Channel is a surprise success, attracting a wide following by programming every kind of documentary 18 hours a day. Nature shows account for a third of its schedule. The Discovery Channel often gets nice ratings.

CNBC. CNBC or Consumer News and Business Channel (incorporating the Financial News Network) is another upscale 24-hour cable network. It's owned by NBC and Cablevision and covers consumer and business news on weekdays, plus sports on weekends.

Many Wide Special Interests.   The phenomenal success of MTV Music Television, which runs rock and pop music videos for teens and young adults, has spurred other special-interest cable programming. MTV's owners quickly launched a second, sister station, VH-1, aimed at MTV's alumni as their musical tastes change. Another music-based cable channel is The Country Music Channel. Then there's the Nostalgia Channel, which appeals to anyone over 45, with films and short subjects from the 1930s to 1950s. Comedy Central has a nonstop cable programming format of comedy movies and reruns of network TV sitcoms and comedy shows. The cable advertising special-interest list continues with The Weather Channel, two Spanish-language cable news networks, The Learning Channel, The Travel Channel, College Network Television, and Nickelodeon for children.

Cable Networks Start and Change

New specialized regional and national networks are being tested all the time. Some offer the potential of intensive viewing by narrow-niche audiences, from the Doctors' Network and Lawyers' Channel to the Hi-Sci Channel, The Asian Network, and The Silent Network cable service, which runs programming for the hearing-impaired.

Subscriber-paid or premium sports-TV cable networks on a local, regional, and national basis are increasingly carrying commercials. Some are becoming basic cable. Some are available to subscribers at little extra cost. And although movie pay-cable networks do not yet sell ads, some experts think they may, probably not within movies but between them.

Competition Creates Opportunity

Although it takes many cable networks to reach as many viewers as one of the big three BTV networks, several of the cable networks keep getting stronger. As the choice of cable network keeps increasing, cable networks' audiences and advertising effectiveness keep growing faster than the networks' ability to prove it. Caution on the part of certain advertisers leaves opportunities for the daring.

Rising entrepreneurs have different objectives than bigger marketers. A pragmatic direct marketer is not concerned with market share, the amount of gross rating points, or even the cost per point of a media buy. Cost per sale is more important than CPM. Many have made big fortunes on cable by simply making an effective commercial, testing it for 5 to 10 times for a week or so, and, if successful, spending more in gradually increased increments.

**Investigate Network Cable
Carefully**

Each new cable network creates unusual new opportunities for entirely new advertisers ideally suited to it, often starting in a small way. If your advertising succeeds in a specialized format on radio, or in a specialized magazine, look for a cable channel with the same appeal. Ask for a list of advertisers from each channel you consider. Phone and ask what proof of success each has and the rate each pays. Compare with the rate the network quotes.

Most successful cable networks recalculate rates frequently, going higher as less time is available and lower when more time opens up. Prices are typically lowest in winter, next lowest in summer, higher in spring, and highest in fall. Prices are always much lower for direct-response offers, but only for the time that's left over or "remnant." Each network obviously wants the best market price for its time.

The following are some tips for bargain hunters:

- Look for new networks and special rates or free spots.
- Investigate any network threatened by a new competitor.
- Give reasons for getting a bargain. These can include offering a higher-quality product, a prestige commercial, or being the first of a desired type of client.
- Look for big cancellations, then negotiate.
- Offer standby commercials for use in the event of cancellations.
- If rates seem firm, look for free, tie-in extras.
- Check all your advertising options, electronic or print. Take the best short-term deal, but be ready to buy long-term for the right deal.

National Spot and Local
Cable

Cable's biggest single advantage is its ability to target geographically far more narrowly than broadcast TV or radio can. This targeting offers opportunities for the smallest local firms and local dealers and branches of the biggest. You can select the zip code areas with your prospects' desired demographics and psychographics and then place spots in programs targeted to most-wanted viewers in these areas.

Many cable networks set aside a portion of commercial time for local purchase. Systems that comprise the network sell this time to advertisers. Cable ads can be bought on a "spot" basis for specific markets or for a local business in one entire market or for just the part of one market served by one cable system.

Locally Programmed Cable

Local talk shows are becoming more common and can be an inexpensive cable opportunity. One in Myrtle Beach, North Carolina, is called *Southern Style*. Leonard, Carl & Taylor (LC&T), a real estate brokerage firm, took 10 minutes twice a week in it. Doug LeVay, LC&T general manager, interviewed developers, brokers, and real estate entrepreneurs whom LC&T dealt with. Another 10 minutes of talk featured listings of a "parade of homes." In 3½ years, LC&T grew from $2.5 million in sales to $42 million.

Other popular, new local cable ventures include very local news and sports channels. They cover news and sports events too small for all but the tiniest of BTV stations—high school football, local crime, fires, and so on. These local events have remarkable audience appeal. The all-local news Channel 12, on Long Island's Cablevision system, for example, was watched by more of its subscribers in one recent 24-hour period than HBO, WTBS, or any of the 44 other channels on the system. Moreover, 76 percent of Cablevision's viewers watched 5 days a week or more. And local sponsors report good results.

Some Local-Cable Complexities.   Satellites orbiting the earth now beam more than 120 cable channels to over 10,000 U.S. cable systems. Almost all systems are owned by the 400-plus multiple-system operators (MSOs). Over 80 percent of cable homes are reached via systems owned by 20 MSOs. The average number of channels offered by each cable system is zooming past 50 and keeps growing.

When you subscribe to cable, one system provides all the cable channels you get. With more networks than channel positions, it cannot give you all the networks. Networks are like movie studios, cable systems like theaters, and MSOs like movie-theater chain owners. A system is the only "theater" for an area, unless a competitor "overbuilds" a second system.

Connections between Local Systems.   In almost no large metro area are all homes reached by one cable system. An "interconnect" exists where two or more cable systems link to distribute a commercial ad schedule simultaneously. An interconnect firm is required to join the cable systems in the area. In Los Angeles this involves over 100 systems. It's even possible in Chicago and Los Angeles to split-run two commercials for the same product at the same time, each reaching approximately the same number of homes. The interconnect has the equipment. The interconnect sells, forwards, and bills (with one contract for the area); it sets rates based on the sum of the system rates and the interconnect's own charges. Interconnects enable advertisers to make group buys in an area. But most interconnects do not deal with all systems in an area. Interconnect companies exist in more and more cities which cover an area with neighboring MSOs.

Spot Cable

Interconnects make possible spot cable, which allows regional and national advertisers to buy one or many markets just as they buy spot BTV. Some disadvantages of spot cable include the following:

- CPMs much higher than for BTV
- Spotty market coverage of some network programs
- Insufficient audience data
- Complexities of placing a local cable buy

As we have noted, big national advertisers often are frustrated by spot cable's disadvantages. Besides the wide price swings in spot cable CPMs, national advertisers often find that buying nationally on one cable network is cheaper than to buy just a minority of the country with spots on the same shows via spot cable.

   In addition to price, there is a question of more accurate audience data. Before spending more on spot cable, advertisers want the same information breakdowns provided by network cable and network TV: who watches when, by age and sex; how many view each commercial; and how often the average viewer sees that commercial. The problem is that most local TV research is diary-based, which understates cable viewing.

A Better Way to Analyze Local Cable

The J. Walter Thompson advertising agency recommends greater use of metered research audience data. Working with NCA (a leading local cable advertising buying firm), Thompson produced a handbook, *Local Market Ratings for National Cable Networks*. The handbook includes ratings for 7 cable networks in 23 metered markets. It tells how to analyze a cable buy for one cable system or one interconnect and how to determine the costs to reach all viewers or those of each of a number of demographic classifications. The handbook is simple and easy to use. For example, if CNN achieves a 0.9 rating in prime time in a people-meter-rated market of 100,000 homes, then a cable system of 20,000 HH is assumed to have the same rating and a fifth of the audience. Only bigger markets out of the over 210 rated are people-meter-rated. Thompson recommends using national people meter ratings for the smaller markets. In negotiations, an effort is made to agree with reps and systems on a cost per rating point of audience desired and abide by ratings worked out by these methods.

Spot and Local Cable Cost

In the smallest cable systems (covering only a small part of a small market), a 30-second spot may cost $1 to run once or about $10 for a series of 10 spots over a week or so. This compares with a 1-inch ad in the tiniest community weekly paper. A color-photo ad of 12 seconds in a city the size of San Diego might cost under 50 cents if part of 10 such ads each runs 84 times in one week. It's as cheap as a classified ad in the smallest weekly.

In Philadelphia, the cheapest availability of a 30-second cable spot might be somewhat over $1000 if run on both major interconnects covering almost all the marketing area (ADI). The most expensive spot would cost over $15,000. The good news is that local CMPs are coming down as cable viewing increases.

Local Entrepreneurs Benefit

Ron Kogut is secretary-treasurer of Kogut Florist & Nurseryman, Inc., of Meriden, Connecticut. He has never studied local cable viewing research. No salesperson came to him. He has no ad agency. When Ron first wanted to advertise on TV, he called the nearest broadcast TV station, asked for the rates, and decided they were too high.

He then called Dimension Cable, the cable system in town, just as it first offered spots locally. He recalls: "I bought ten 30-second spots for the price of one on the regular (BTV) station. I paid $12.50 each." He spent $50 for production for a spot, including announcer talent. When his $72.50 test got enough retail business to show a profit, he bought more.

Ron Kept Cable Simple.   Ron's cable ad offers are the same as he makes in newspaper and on radio. He negotiates in the same way. When he buys more, he offers less per spot. To get the best price he bought by the year. He got the price down to $8 to $9 a spot as Dimension soared past 160,000 subscribers. When Dimension asked for an increase, he answered that he was considering switching to other media.

Ron thinks that effective use of color has been responsible for much of his cable success. He pictures someone leisurely watching TV at home. Ron wants, with the system's help, to create spots which come across the screen with eye-catching scenes and color photos to stop and attract that person.

His commercials are simply produced, using voice-over techniques (see the next chapter on producing a TV commercial). The cable people come to Ron. He gives them his radio copy, his direct-mail pieces, each newspaper ad, and color pictures or actual flower arrangements for the station photographer to shoot. Then one excellent cable professional (not a professional photographer) takes an arrangement home, sets it up on a table, and photographs it.

Ron Knows His Customers.   A young woman spent $1000 with Ron on flowers to decorate a church, after spending $700 for all the other wedding costs. Ron's revenue for wedding decorations runs from $500 to $10,000. One totaled $25,000. Overall, 20 percent of his business comes from special orders for weddings, averaging about $1000 each. Another 30 percent comes from orders for funerals, averaging around $500 each. The other half of his business comes from corporate accounts and people buying for various personal occasions.

Ron realizes that the big majority of his customers have cable. He knows each kind of customer and forms his own opinions of the kinds of TV programming each group probably prefers and when they are most apt to watch TV.

When to Sell What to Whom.   Here's part of Ron's cable strategy:

> I buy a lot of prime-time spots. But not everyone watches at the same time. I sell older folks more funeral arrangements as they lose friends and relatives. I reach them with news. I sell young women wedding arrangements. Valentine's Day is a men's holiday. For anniversaries and births I also get men. I feature all this in commercials in games on ESPN.

Ron uses three channels: CNN for news, CNBC for business news, and ESPN for sports. He picks programs to reach each of his kinds of customers. Before gift-occasion holidays he runs eight to ten 30-second spots. For Easter he makes six special arrangements. Between Thanksgiving and Christmas, he runs 10 spots a day. He starts with one

or two early items. Next, he features trees, then poinsettias, then arrangements and centerpieces.

The Biggest Reason Cable Works for Ron.   Ron is an entrepreneur.
Once he found how effective cable was he kept coming up with new ways
to use it. Ron started as a florist. When he added decorating services with
flowers, he promoted by cable. When cable and other promotion worked, he
added more services. With profits from his business, he bought a huge road-
side stand in Long Island, New York, with 7½ acres of nurseries alongside
the Long Island Expressway.

Ron began to grow Christmas trees in big volume. Before Christmas,
he runs another special three-week campaign on Dimension and six to
eight other cable systems to sell Christmas trees. This campaign costs
$15,000 to $20,000. Ron runs trucks loaded with trees between
Springfield and Long Island to locations he advertises on TV. Each year
he sells out everything.

For 10 years Kogut Florist Nurseryman has grown 40 percent a year,
while Dimension in Meriden has grown from a few thousand to over
160,000 subscribers. Ron says,

> Two-thirds of our sales increases comes from cable. We don't have
> an 800 number, but I feature our phone number. When they call me
> they say they saw it on TV. Men often just see our commercial and
> pick up the phone; 50 percent of our business comes or starts by
> phone.
>   I stay with anything that works. I spend $25,000 to $30,000 on ca-
> ble. I use no broadcast TV. I cut out radio. I still use the newspaper
> for 60 percent of my budget.

Many Local Success Stories

Cable works so well for retailers because a bigger percentage of viewers
reached by a single system are much closer to their retail location than
via BTV. I have seen hundreds of testimonials demonstrating how cable
has become an important advertising medium for marketers large and
small. But be careful! Investigate, compare, decide. Use these guidelines:

1. Check with the Cable Ad Bureau for local success stories of an out-
    let, product, or service similar to yours, anywhere.

2. Call firms to get more details including copy, spot length, offer; per-
    sonality, production; times run, cost, and results.

3. Adapt successful copy. Design the right commercial.

4. Investigate local MSOs or interconnect firms. Get the schedules, rates, and names of any local successes in any field.

5. Call each MSO or interconnect firm. Ask for its results, how scientifically it was traced, and how results compare with those of any other advertising used. Ask if the firm will renew its cable contract. Ask how much the commercials cost, including talent and time. Compare with the quotes given you.

6. Using the CAB kit material, calculate the cost per viewer for local cable at specific times.

7. Investigate the advertising alternatives: local TV, LPTV, local radio, direct mail, local paper, and any other options.

8. Negotiate, while listening to all offers. Go with cable, if it's the best deal, but only after you lock in the right to cancel if your results are bad.

9. Start only after making the "right" commercial, one with an action offer you can measure, be it phone calls, walk-ins, whatever.

10. Cancel failure fast.

Cable Classifieds

Cable classifieds are a simple way for a small, local enterprise to advertise at a cost competitive to that of a newspaper classified ad. Consider color cable photo ads as cable classifieds. A patented process inexpensively digitizes color photos and art. This is converted to analog video and in that form put on cable. The result is the world's most beautiful classified ad, and an inexpensive way to advertise on cable. Cable classifieds combine text, line graphics, and photographic elements. Your ad appears on a colored background; you may choose a type style suitable to your business, use your logo within the ad screen format, and superimpose type over a photo.

The lowest-cost ads have one screen of text and no picture. More expensive ones include several screens, with one screen fading into another. Your ad is constantly rotated. The cost is usually competitive to newspaper classifieds in the area. Results often compare well.

What Works Best.   The biggest cable successes in most areas have been in real estate. The employment category has done well, as have unusual services. Response to cable classifieds in small, rural areas has often been quite good. And big suburban areas of large cities have proven effective when the classified channels have been advertised to subscribers consistently, aggressively, and effectively. Why? Viewers' incomes are often higher than those of readers of classifieds ads. Photo ads often work for higher-priced services and products.

Warning! Each classification is a marketplace. Each must be built by promotion to see the classified ads. Moreover, the channel itself must be promoted heavily to get a constant influx of advertisers offering a wide and interesting selection. Looking at and responding to classified ads is a habit that must be built. If a classified channel is treated like an orphan, it most likely won't pull.

Use these guidelines when using cable classifieds:

1. Cable classifieds are easy, simple, and fast to buy. Just give the words, logo, and color picture or art. But do it right.

2. Don't try a failing print classified ad. It will usually fail on TV. A successful one often makes it.

3. Don't run the wrong product, service, price, offer, headline, copy, picture, or art. Change your strategy before you lose money.

4. Ask for action, track the results, and modify them accordingly. Alternate ads and compare results.

5. Change ads for seasons, track responses, and modify them accordingly.

Failures and Potentials.   Be careful! The dropout rate of new advertisers on some classified channels has been 50 percent and more. But much of the mortality has been due to misunderstanding and misuse by advertisers. More advertisers are now reporting better results, with many of them using quite different methods, including the following:

- Longer photo ads do better.

- Single advertisers are succeeding with 10-minute and longer formats with more related products, services, and variations.

- Manufacturers are paying half the cost of photo ads, each featuring a local dealer.

- Combining pay-per-view technology with PhotoText for instant ordering of anything is planned. Don Mathison, vice president for marketing and programming, Media General Cables, says: "A catalog could easily go on a cable system in this manner. Eventually catalogers could not only use cable TV to send out messages like this but also to receive interactive responses by the same cable system. But now the response is by telephone."

Summary

With aggressive time-buying negotiation, cable can deliver the audience coverage big marketers want at a competitive CPM. At the same time, cable allows small advertisers to start small and build up, step by step. In fact, small firms can often measure sales results more accurately for specific cable expenditures than can large advertisers.

Whether your firm chooses to advertise via broadcast TV or cable, your advertising will only be as good as the quality of your commercial. The best selection of time and negotiation of rates can only succeed if your commercial works.

Help Source Guide

1. Ask your cable system to show you *Cable Target Aid* from the *Arbitron Company,* which is PC-based software that evaluates program, day-part viewing. Customized to your area, the software gives coverage statistics. See *Local Market TV Report:* 142 West 57th St., NY, NY 10019. (212) 887-1300.

2. R. B. Kaatz's *Cable Advertisers Handbook,* (NTC Publishing Group, 1990) is sound, detailed. Read at your business library or buy: 4255 W. Touhy Ave., Lincolnwood, IL 60646-1975. (800) 323-4900.

3. *Cable Networks Inc.* provides specialized software that simplifies cable media buying: 260 Madison Ave., NY, NY 10016. (212) 889-4670 (sales rep).

4. *Cable Avails* is a magazine that provides latest info for cable time buyers— both cable network and spot: 1905 Sherman St., Suite 800, Denver, CO 802030-9853. (303) 837-1215.

5. *Cable & Station Coverage Atlas* is an annual publication of maps of coverage of cable system or interconnect versus stations in each area: Warren Publishing, 2115 Ward Ct., N.W., Washington, DC 20037. (202) 872-9200.

6. *CTV Cable* is a national firm representing cable firms. It provides research information on every market: 667-B Lakeview Plaza Blvd., Worthington, OH 43085. (614) 848-5800.

7. Contact the *Cable TV Advertising Bureau* (CAB) to ask for *Cable TV Facts* booklet ($6); CAB provides local retail information *free* and *National Cable Planning System Guide* and *CAB CableCume Reach/Frequency System Guide* with CableCume computer disk *free* for advertisers and ad agencies. Also available are success case histories from your field, *free:* 757 3d Ave., NY, NY 10017. (212) 751-7770.

8. *National Cable Advertising* is a sales representative for cable systems using interconnects, provides *free* media kit: 137 Newbury St., Boston, MA 02116. (617) 267-8582.

6

How to Make
a TV Commercial
That Sells

What makes a TV spot great varies with your purpose and budget. Different approaches are warranted depending on your product or service, whether the spot advertises a store or a catalog. Moreover, a TV commercial can create an image, get an inquiry, or make an immediate sale. Will yours be integrated into a larger marketing campaign or stand alone? Is your product or service a trusted name or a business newcomer? Although this chapter will concentrate on producing a TV commercial, all these issues should influence your course of action. Before you start, you should consider whether to make *any* TV commercial for your company. Ask these questions:

- Do you now successfully use TV advertising?
- If not, do you have a product or service that's currently successful or worth testing?
- Is your product or service's offer, spokesperson, and presentation suited to TV?
- Of all the available media, should TV be part, most of, or all your advertising expenditures?
- Do you have enough money to advertise? Enough profit margin in your product? Enough control of your cashflow?
- Are the conditions right? Is the season right? Does your product or service outperform others?

- Are you set up to target TV advertising to your prospects and to buy it at a reasonable CPM?

- How does your company plan to get the full benefit from your TV advertising? In your own store? Via other companies' store distribution or by direct response?

Before answering these questions, you must also know your customers and prospects and their demographics and psychographics. Thoroughly research the features and benefits of your product or service and have a marketing plan. If you decide to go ahead, make a memo to yourself describing the job you want your commercial to do. In it, describe the desired mood and image of your product and firm.

Do Your Homework

Now do some no-cost homework. If you are a newcomer to TV advertising, orient yourself by reading some books from your business library. Some are recommended in this chapter's Help Source Guide. Ask the reference librarian for the newest books on TV copy and production which describe and picture great commercials. You may be able to borrow a videocassette or audiocassette of a seminar on TV copy and production. Ask for a tape of the all-time top TV commercials worldwide which you can borrow and run on your VCR. If you have to rent or buy the reel, do it.

Study Classic TV Commercials

The best TV commercials have the simplest concepts. Simple commercial themes made Federal Express the market leader in the United States and defended AT&T from fierce price competition. A TV campaign made one establishment the biggest tourist attraction in New York; not Broadway theaters, the museums, Chinatown, Harlem, or the Stock Exchange, but Bloomingdale's. The tagline repeated on TV commercials, "It's unlike any other store in the world," attracted a torrent of customers.

Four words, "I Love New York," became a national anthem for New Yorkers. The series of TV commercials showed an outpouring of New York's greatest talent that brought back the pride and glamour to the United States' greatest city. The slogan was a musical hit. Once heard, you hummed it, sang it, and talked about it. It became a PR campaign. It was picked up in print ads. "I Love New York" buttons became hit souvenir items. The slogan made friends, pulled visitors. The campaign produced one of the most successful commercials of all time.

Zap Programs—Watch Commercials

For a free course in TV advertising, switch from commercial to commercial. Study those that run most often which you consider to be the best made. Tape different commercials for the same product, service, or store until you get a series for a number of products. Analyze each. Notice how commercials are intertwined with programs. Note when a product becomes the basis for a program, such as kid shows built around character toys, such as the Nintendo computer games or game shows for adults.

Study different-length commercials. They are as short as 6 seconds and as long as 60 minutes. The "workhorses" are 15-second and 30-second spots, with the 60-second format used to introduce the campaign or for products and services where greater length is required. The same theme in a TV campaign often can be delivered in two or three of these lengths, with shorter versions largely being excerpts from the longer ones. Notice the frequently repeated short themes of national commercials and the longer action-offer copy of local commercials.

Analyze Each Commercial's Purpose

A commercial can provide a demonstration, announce a sale, or offer a premium. It can ask for response or refer viewers to the phone or a printed document for more details. A commercial can feature a spokesperson, a customer testimonial, or favorable quotes. A commercial can get across the simplest theme, sum up advantages, or make comparisons with specific competitors. It can gain attention with humor, stars, or through a news-bulletin style. Note how many commercials feature pets and babies.

Like the posters of a century ago, a commercial can be an art form, blending words, action, music, and color to create or change an image as each sells. A commercial can be designed to make future friends or primarily to bring in profitable business now. A commercial can make your package or your logo recognized anywhere.

Look at these issues when watching TV:

1. Watch TV clutter, but study the TV commercials that overcome it—particularly the simple ones.

2. Study more closely those that sell as they create an image, concept, or theme and hammer it home.

3. Study still more closely those that do best the kind of job you want your commercial to do.

4. Of those, study most closely the *simplest* commercials.

As you study other TV commercials, keep revising your memo. Describe in more detail what you wish your TV commercial to do. Whatever your business or budget, you probably can accomplish your TV commercial's purpose. Thousands of firms have made tens of thousands of TV commercials.

Production Decisions

Highly successful commercials of many kinds are constantly made within widely varying budgets. Pointers on how to proceed and where to get more detailed information largely depend on your company's size. Here are some guidelines:

1. If your company is small, start modestly in TV with a low-cost production.

2. If medium-sized, spend more, but find up-and-coming production talent. Do the best job simply. If necessary make fewer commercials better.

3. If your company is big, work with the top ad agencies, top consultants, top producers, top talent. Go first-class.

How Much Do-It-Yourself?

Let's start with the very small firm that is convinced it has a product TV can sell, but has little net worth, no ad agency, and no internal expertise in TV. Should you use a camcorder, your home as a studio, and your computer for the insertion of the desired special effects and for desktop editing? Not to make several short commercials! Even if you're expert and already have all the above material and software, you can probably get better equipment, lighting, and experience for very little. There are exceptions, of course. If you're in a small real estate firm and sponsor a home show, or if you have invented a line of seasonings and sponsor a home-cooking show, then you may be able to get away with recording and editing yourself. Chapter 14 explains how people in similar situations created videos that made money. These lessons can be applied to making simple TV programs that sell your product or service profitably. The rest of this chapter, particularly those parts detailing the steps bigger firms take to achieve top quality in dealing with top production people, is also instructive. It takes a lot of work to become sufficiently self-taught to proceed. Consider if you really want to do what will be necessary.

Learn as you go. There are books on every part of the process of TV commercial making-directing, budgeting, graphic design, writing, video techniques, lighting, and more. Read them *free* in a library. You can also rent or buy audiotapes and videotapes on these subjects. Plus, you can talk to seasoned TV pros and others starting out as you are. But be sure you want to make this effort.

Do you want to be both a creative and a "numbers" person? The talent, writer, and producer? Director and editor? Sound effects, music, lighting technician, and camera person? And be a perfectionist from beginning to end? And do your job? If so, here are some tips:

- Get a simple concept for your program. *Keep* it simple.
- Make the content useful, clear, and appealing.
- Make the offer tempting, credible, and friendly.
- Use simple production techniques to keep your costs down.
- Rent needed equipment by the hour.

Do-it-yourself perfection can be attained. All it needs is time, talent, the ability to learn, and perhaps the neglect of everything else in your business. There are alternatives. Concentrate on what you have a natural talent for and get a partner to do what you can't. Even without a partner, you can start with the most basic TV spots.

The simplest format is to use TV photo ads. Ask your cable company if it has a photo-ad cable channel. If it does, watch its TV classified photo ads. For the slide commercials, you should write your ad as if it were a newspaper classified ad. Follow the cable system's specifications. Get their ideas. Start with a small test, keep your cost under $300, and measure results. Stop if the test fails. If it succeeds, keep it running, but try new offers, copy, and layout. Then you're ready to go to the safest next step (if your cable system has no photo channel, it may be your first).

Software-Made Commercials

Even the new technology that can create desktop commercials requires more software, expertise, and time than most PC owners have. But many excellent freelance and other professional production specialists have this expertise—and the technology. They have the PCs, peripherals, and software needed to animate graphic and photographic images, transfer them to a VCR, and add a professionally recorded *voice-over* or offscreen voice. Without a camera or studio time setup, two simple 30-second commercials can cost under $500 and can then be tested on low-cost TV time.

Graphics software keep advancing rapidly. Some software can create movielike animations in millions of color variations and with fine resolution. Others can create scenes with realistic, multiple images moving independently. Or you can superimpose computer-generated graphics over a video picture. Some can cause graphics to seem to dance around the screen. And with computer-motion, graphics can move from left to right or up and down and fade and dissolve back onto the screen with superimpositions. Photos, logos, or artwork can be modified or made larger or smaller. Stills can be taken from videotapes and integrated with graphics using many fonts of text. Four images can be capsulated within each frame. You can get split screens and strobelike and other unusual effects. Music and sound effects can be added. New multimedia PCs can pull images, photos, and graphics from floppy disks and CD-ROM disks—even some action video.

PC software-based commercials are being used by more advertisers as the animation for them keeps improving. Top quality costs more, and, for a little extra, a studio commercial can be made. But the average quality keeps getting better and prices lower. Read magazines such as *PC Week* and *MacWeek* for the latest developments. Ask your cable system or TV station production manager to suggest freelance talent to produce it for you.

Lowest-Cost TV Studio Commercials

Most TV commercials which are profitable are not masterpieces and are not made by top professionals. Over 90 percent of all commercials produced are videotaped. Most are made not by a substantial production firm but by a TV station. The cheapest spots are those made by small stations, LPTV stations, and cable systems, in small areas. The simplest format involves the use of slides and/or footage with an offscreen voice. Cheap studio commercials are often made using half-inch (VHS) videotape. This smaller, lighter, and lower-cost format has become more common as VHS equipment quality has dramatically improved.

These commercials often feature the proprietors of small ventures. A commercial can be ad-libbed from rough notes in minutes at the local studio. The smallest advertisers in small markets, who want a cheap commercial, pay little for a 30-second spot on a local station or cable system. In small cities, production costs can be $100 to $300 for each session, during which over a dozen commercials are shot, sometimes in as little as two hours. Some LPTV stations make commercials for under $100 or even *free* for show sponsors.

Crude Productions

A new discount retailer often starts with a simple concept: Offer the lowest prices on wanted brand-name products. The resulting TV spots seek to grab attention; to make the retailer's bargains believed; and to get across the location, often including the driving directions. The retailer also wants to make each spot special—whether it's for cars or computers—urgent news of limited offers going fast. Each word, action, and body movement should convey the crackle of excitement. Prestige can come later.

These cheap commercials most often air on independent stations at off times, when low-power TV carries even lower-cost commercials. Watch late-night TV. Look for the retail and mail-order commercials. Zap the many that are badly made. Tape the good ones. I'll shortly describe how to write your own. To learn TV production by trial and error at the least cost, use LPTV. Try to get free production or the least-cost commercial to test for a total cost of under $1000. Or try your local cable system or the smallest TV station. Experiment. Be your own talent and producer. Measure results, and change your commercials accordingly. Succeed, project, upgrade, and keep succeeding.

Warning! The smallest stations may have less experienced help. An assembly-line rush approach runs the risk of creating a sloppy or incompetent production. Combining an overworked, underpaid producer under a tight deadline with a staff and talent who have never met can be a disaster. By simply paying for more studio time, a TV spot's quality can often be greatly improved. Sometimes, even the smallest station or system has a retired pro or a beginning top production talent. Look for either. Usually, the best protection is your own preparation (which I'll soon discuss).

The Next Rung on the Quality Ladder

In bigger cities, a spectrum of TV commercial production quality is yours to choose from. A small or medium-size firm can get a higher-quality commercial made at a TV station, which typically has better equipment than its small-town counterpart. As these commercial stations have largely switched from 2-inch videotape to 1-inch formats, their news departments have begun to switch from ¾-inch to ½-inch video format. A growing number of companies now make simple video commercials on ½-inch tape. This format benefits from smaller, lighter, lower-cost equipment whose quality has dramatically improved. Still, these commercial-grade video cameras are easier (and less expensive) to use in a studio than outside. Whereas most TV stations' studios offer little or no special lighting, these cameras now don't need as much light. Several other factors favor these larger station facilities. Their production people are more professional. Most stations have enough sophisticated equipment to allow for all sorts of computerized graphics in your commercial. Many have copywriters. Plus many of their sales executives know that a bad commercial will kill a good contract. They're smart enough to be able to help an advertiser considerably in creating or improving a commercial.

San Diego Law.   Sam Spital is one of 6000 lawyers in San Diego. Several years ago, Sam discovered that in various areas lawyers were successfully advertising on TV. He was introduced to Jim Birschbach, sales manager of KGTV, San Diego. In 1½ hours, Sam told Jim the essence of what he did best for his clients. Four days later, Jim came back with three 30-second scripts. With the common tagline or theme of "Let Sam Do It," each spot featured a different legal service and an 800 number. Jim then showed Sam time availabilities with the different audience characteristics for each.

Within three weeks, Sam was on TV testing his three services, each to a different audience. The test package cost $8000 for 10 days (including production). From then on, Sam and Jim experimented together, tracking and expanding their TV ads until Sam became the third biggest legal advertiser on TV in the United States, spending $400,000 yearly. Every sizable city has other dramatic case histories of small investment in and testing of TV commercials paying off big.

Gypsy TV Producers.   Many TV commercials are made by small production firms in relatively cheap studios with low-cost equipment and nonunion personnel. New cameras, peripherals, and other equipment keep bursting out. No one can own them all. A young producer may know a lot and rent anything that's needed, including studio time. The smallest free-lance producer with the lowest bid may be dangerous, but the right small one can be a bargain. Ask TV station production managers for some recommendations.

Look for that rare exception: the right kind of extraordinary talent in someone young and not yet successful. But he or she should still be experienced enough in TV production to do the job responsibly. Look hard for people who have succeeded with *simple,* low-cost commercials related to yours. Perhaps you'll find producers from a public TV station who like after-hours income. Get the names of their clients. Phone them and find out if customers are happy. See the commercials that these producers have produced. Go ahead only if you're convinced a particular producer can produce an excellent spot for you. If so, schedule your taping accordingly.

Short Commercials Are Often Simpler.   Time, study, and preparatory work help ensure quality and lower your cost. Dry-run rehearsals and painstaking attention to detail are your best answers. The shorter a commercial, the easier it is to prepare everything possible most perfectly in advance. Concentrate on simplicity, on achieving credibility, and on doing one spot right. Usually, a simple presentation by one spokesperson is all that's needed for a short commercial. But often slides coupled with PC computer animation and a voice-over can work even better. There's less to go wrong. But do not attempt a complex commercial, however short, with a very low budget.

A Successful Commercial

Copy Writing as a Start

A good TV commercial writer, with enough knowledge of your product, customers, and prospects and your marketing plan, can create a well-written commercial. There are many good freelance TV copywriters. The top TV copywriters in the largest agencies often will freelance. Ask TV station production managers, freelance producers, and production house executives to recommend good writers of simple-format TV commercials. Phone them, and get examples of their work.

TV copy makes an idea reality. It's used as the basis to get a quote on the cost of your TV commercial. It's also needed by your producer and director, each performer, artists, computer programmers, and technicians. On each page, visual video instructions with drawings or photographs (if available), are shown at left. Spoken words and other audio descriptions, including musical backgrounds and sound effects, are listed on the right.

Storyboards

The writer and art director work together to create a storyboard. A storyboard includes the script but shows in more detail what is happening visually. The art director sketches out in each frame the visual action or graphics for that scene. The visual depictions can be very rough sketches or detailed and far more finished depending on how much money you want to spend. Underneath each storyboard frame is the wording used by performers and/or offscreen voices. In parentheses, the sound, graphics, and visual effects to match are described. The sequence of panels shows each set of actions and every word of the entire video.

"Storyboarding" a TV commercial script serves a number of useful purposes. Storyboarding helps everyone involved grasp better what the commercial will be, beforehand. You may see a flaw that went undetected in script form. Your management may insist on a storyboard review before approving the TV spot. You're apt to get a more accurate quote from the production firm. And a storyboard offers better instruction for your talent to understand and perform their jobs quickly.

Do-It-Yourself TV Copy

Writing your own script is at least a bit more practical than a complete do-it-yourself TV production. But writing your own script is desirable only when you can't afford to pay a pro, are willing to subject your work to professional criticism, and accept that you will work on several rewrites. Any type of creative writing is a humbling experience. Very few first or second drafts cannot be improved upon, and settling for the mediocre can kill your TV advertising. Attempting any do-it-yourself project can quickly give you respect for the specialist and may help you understand and work better with him or her. Books on TV copy can help, but also try this approach: Let the great commercials you see on TV which do most closely what you want yours to do be your role models.

Play back a great commercial just taped. Study how it is broken into quick scenes. Play it again, one scene of a few seconds at a time. Write down the spoken words of each scene. Then draw (even in the crudest way) a sketch of the visual action of the scene. As you do this, you are reconstructing the rough storyboard. Every time you do this exercise, you are learning how great TV commercials are created and seeing more clearly which approaches suit your product.

Transposition. Some best-selling authors keep writing the same book with different characters and situations. Publishers seek new winners that are like the old ones. Agencies win a reputation for a certain style of ad or commercial. The biggest agencies have databanks of the latest successful ad campaigns (and classic ones) created for all kinds of products. Top copywriters recall old successes as they seek to create new hits. The most talented don't copy, but they often transpose a successful concept to a totally different field.

Suppose your firm imports from Estonia a fishing lure which, according to a letter just received from him, is the favorite of all the lures in the tackle box of an aging celebrity. Although you've never met, you offer him or her a royalty (because your firm lacks money) to become your spokesperson in TV commercials that will be based totally on his own words. He or she accepts. You tape the Angela Lansbury commercials for Bufferin, remake the storyboard, substitute the celebrity for Angela, ask questions as Angela is asked, and shorten the answers to fit the transposed storyboard. But don't plagiarize.

TV Copy Stimulation. The purpose behind transposing storyboards is not to steal words and phrases. It is to learn where to put what elements of your copy, graphics, sound effects, voice, and visual action scenes. It's a way to adapt successful TV selling methods that are far afield to products advertised by your role-model commercial. In short, it's a way to stimulate you to think in TV commercial terms.

Within a large advertising agency's creative team, a camcorder can be a TV copywriter's dream. It can create the equivalent of a copywriter's rough layout in video. Do the same. Write your TV commercial and make your storyboard. Now cast and record it with your wife or husband, children, and neighbors. Even better, create and insert a logo and other simple graphics. This can all be very rough and home made.

Pointing the Way. If it's a mishmash, forget it. But your own storyboard and then your own camcorder commercial may be the fastest way to dramatically show what you would like in a commercial. You can then hand it over to a professional to write, cast, and produce. It will definitely help you better understand the process. Plus, the further along you are with the concept, plan, script, and storyboard, the more accurate the quote will be.

A TV station in a middle-sized city or the right gypsy producer or a small production firm with modest equipment and a simple studio might produce three 30-second commercials with one or two performers for as little as $1800 to $2500. It will be done quickly, but not as a rush job. And the job will only stay on budget if you prepare meticulously for taping. But be ready to pay extra for some overtime and extra editing time.

Increasing Quality in Commercials

The TV commercial quality rungs from here on are in the good, better, and best categories.

Good Commercials.   The TV commercial production is usually supervised by an ad agency. A production house with its own studio may be used. A freelance producer may use facilities at a production house, a small studio, or a TV station. Wherever the facilities are, the outfit has made TV production a good profit center and has invested in excellent equipment and an experienced crew. The facility may be a public TV station. If it's a cable system, it's probably a major MSO. Still, the commercial is seldom made outside (also called "on-location" or "remote") or even with outside sequences. It is taped, not filmed.

The agency may frequently make commercials there for different clients. Sometimes, the facility is a house agency owned by a client. Otherwise, a representative of the client is seldom there. The atmosphere is businesslike, professional, and friendly. There may be two camera operators or just one. If there's only one cameraperson, he or she might be supplemented by one or two robotized cameras. The TV commercial may involve just an announcer talking offscreen, an on-camera performer, or both. There may be some product demonstration. There are usually product shots and a logo and other inserts ranging from slides to computer graphics. A director calls the shots.

The clock is always ticking. If three 30-second commercials are made, one-third to one-half of each may be identical. There may be just one commercial in several lengths of 60, 30, and 15 seconds. The studio has been rented for a specific time, usually for most of or a full day. Editing usually takes place the next day with the director, producer, and the agency reps present. There isn't a mad rush, but the pressure is on to meet the schedule. All must arrive on time and be completely prepared to produce the commercial as quoted on. If changes are made, major overtime charges can kick in.

The cost for the above TV production can range from $4000 to $10,000 with no overtime depending on the job and assuming that all concerned are competent. Cost can be less if modules that can be dropped into the commercial already exist. For example, a supermarket spot may feature vegetables with shots from the grower or growers' trade association. Any dealer may use some manufacturer footage. A department store or catalog may have previously taken still and TV shots at the same location and have many possible TV commercial inserts. A dealer may already have image commercials in the can and just need to add product shots and a new voice-over.

Better Commercials.   Within the first-class TV commercial production tier are a number of quality and price rungs. The bottom one starts with a price tag of $25,000 to $50,000 for several 30-second spots on a tight budget. This may include a name spokesperson whose cost is spread over many activities and a cast of several other people. Very likely, the production is supervised by a bigger agency. The copy may have been based on considerable focus group research. It may include segments shot outside of a studio. A campaign of six spots with more talent can cost more than $100,000. The director and producer work mainly on commercials in this price range. It's filmed first, but to save money, it's on 16-mm not 35-mm film.

These better-quality productions take twice as long to make and three times as long to edit as good-quality productions. They still proceed at a tight, fast pace. The commercial is probably produced away from New York City and Los Angeles because other large cities cost less for studios, directors, camera people, and union charges. But if you fly in and lodge enough out-of-town people, your travel and entertainment costs will escalate. The agency's client often sends someone and always studies the results along the way carefully. Sometimes, a top TV production consultant helps to guide the entire process (more likely for a national advertiser). If you spend $2 million on TV time for the spots, your production cost is only 5 percent of your time costs, and the right spot could be over 100 percent more effective.

The Top Tier.   The budget for a campaign of several sets of 60-, 30-, and 15-second commercials may run up to $1 million for a spectacular. The music rights alone for a popular tune can cost $250,000 to $500,000 and more. Each is filmed first on 35-mm film and transferred daily to videotape. The production is usually supervised by a large agency for a giant advertiser. The TV spots usually are not only based on the results of focus group interviews but also include revisions based on reactions by live sample audiences. The best TV productions are often made in a top facility in New York or Los Angeles and include on-location shots anywhere in the world. Production may take weeks or longer.

The presentation may feature a big-name personality and have a big cast. By piling on the excitement, pace, and complexity of a super movie and distilling it into a 30-second commercial, often a surprising amount of attention is obtained. A commercial may, however, involve seemingly far simpler production values in its attempt to break out of the ordinary. But it is in the attempt for perfection, regardless of its format, that the job of keeping the spots on budget will be a struggle. After all, the TV commercial will be integrated into, and probably become the centerpiece of, the entire advertising campaign that may run for years. Research surveys and sales analysis will decide whether the investment pays off.

How Much Should You Spend?

For those able to pay, the million-dollar commercial that sells is cheaper than the $75 commercial that fails. Bigger firms usually find it safer to spend more. Most tiny firms can only spend the least. Most of us try to be prudent by not attempting to spend like the giants but also by avoiding badly made cheap commercials that have no chance to succeed.

Money is invested in a TV commercial with the object of getting more viewers to see it, recall it, talk about it, and multiply its effect, and ultimately to get more people to buy the product. If your TV advertising works on these levels, it is often profitable to make much bigger time buys for it than for previous spots. So your higher production cost may result in an actual reduction in that cost's percentage of the total TV ad budget. In your decision on what to spend on TV production consider the following:

1. How much will you spend on your TV schedule?
2. If successful, how much are you expecting to spend to expand the campaign the first year?
3. How long do you expect to run your commercial?
4. How many commercials do you plan to make?
5. How often will your commercials run?
6. How often will one person see each?

Common sense can give you some answers: Rule out what you can't afford. Don't attempt to do in a budget commercial what only a blockbuster marketer can afford. Beware of the latest video technology that's hopelessly beyond your budget. Crawl *successfully* before you walk.

Make the right decisions for, and stay within, a small budget before you attempt a bigger one.

Always weigh your trade-offs. For example, if lighting is *free* for a commercial shot outdoors, why are TV commercials almost entirely taped in-studio? It's *faster*. There are fuller crews where they're needed and more readily available equipment. There's no bad weather. Making a commercial in a smaller city or in the Orient is much cheaper than the major production sites. But, the travel expenses (and the time away from the office) may add to more than any savings. Being your own consultant is cheap, but will you have a fool for a client? Trimming costs too closely may cause a TV disaster. Wise choices at every step are vital.

How to Select a TV Production Firm

In this book's Help Source Guides, you'll find the names of the appropriate trade publications, associations, trade shows, and newsletters to help you. Phone them, describe your needs, size, and financial constraints. Ask for the best TV production firms. Make a list of those that seem to be the most logical. If your firm is large, get suggestions from your ad agency and circulate a memo around your organization and to others who may help.

Phone production firms and ask a few key questions: Who are their clients? What kind of TV commercials do they make? Success stories? Range of costs for different-length commercials? And combinations? How busy are they now? When could they start and complete your commercial? Even before you have a finished script or storyboard, a knowledgeable inside-estimator (not a salesperson) can give you a surprisingly accurate "horseback quote" by phone, if you can describe your desired TV spot very accurately. Screen out those who don't fit, are too busy, or are too expensive.

Narrow the Choice Further.   Ask each firm you are considering for the names of their most successful TV clients, especially those with products or services that are most similar to yours. Ask each to send tapes of commercials it produced, including one or more made at your budget. View the tapes, particularly those done within your budget. Screen out the unsatisfactory producers. Phone customers of those tapes you like. Verify costs and find out their experiences. If it's bad, stay away.

Ask those firms that seem right for your purpose and budget to send you a specification sheet. This lists what you might need to spend money on, including items you won't need. Ask which items each firm recommends. A firm may call the same item a different name. Consolidate all the items into one list. If you're unsure of your next needs, get quotes on two or three versions from each firm. Give each production firm an identical kit. Include your script or storyboard and a memo with all the same information to help each make a proposal and quote for identical versions.

Compare More Than Price. You need a producer that's right for you, whose ability you respect, whom you trust, and who can advise you correctly. You must find someone you can get a lot of help from at the right price. A freelance producer can be flexible, go anywhere, subcontract with whoever is most suitable for any part of the project, and build a custom team for your needs. This will probably cost you more than going to a production studio.

Personally interview the best producers. Go to their facilities and meet their people. Don't select on the basis of the lowest price. Rather, choose the firm you feel can help you most to create the most profit from the commercial and the one which you are convinced is most reliable. Before you sign the contract, consider what could go wrong and what can be done about it, in time. Are you obligated to pay talent or anyone who works on your commercial according to union contracts? If so, how much are these residual fees and for how long? How about music? Voice-over talent? Multiply this by all the union performers in your commercial. Find out now how many future expenses you may have, beyond the original budget.

Make Each Conversation a Tutorial. You can learn from each production firm. Ask each production executive for the names of freelance copywriters. Also ask everyone to criticize your plan, script-casting ideas, or anything you've told them about your commercial, your budget, your studio and/or on-location shoots, and your production schedule dates. Do they recommend any changes in your concept, script, or storyboard, item by item?

Ask each for the names of advertisers with commercials that are similar to yours. Find out on what stations the commercials are being run. Phone the station or network, ask when the commercials air, and study them. Get the advertiser's and agency's phone numbers. Call and ask questions. Exchange information where it won't hurt you. You'll meet some bright people and learn a lot.

Pay for the Best Advice You Can Afford! The right ad agency can guide you at each step, save a lot of your time, and often give you the best chance of success. If your firm can't afford the best, a consultant can help you look before you leap.

Consider the Worst-Case Situations. Projects gone wrong can bring disaster. Equipment can break down, or the tape can be bad. A power loss, strike, fire, or hurricane can occur. Liability suits can follow these accidents. Producers, directors, or talent may not show or may arrive stoned or drunk. Or they might not be paid by the production firm (whom you've paid), and then your firm is sued. Advances can be given to a production firm that then folds with your commercial undone or half-done.

If you're big, your legal department may warn you and even protect you. To be safe, have a lawyer familiar with TV production check out the agreement. Your agency can help. Common sense, some advance negotiation, and caution regarding each move may avoid trouble. First, investigate thoroughly the production firm and its principals. Next, work closely with it.

Last Chance for the Least-Cost Change

Your production firm, after it's selected (but before it starts), may help you improve your chances of success dramatically. The firm may show you ways to save money or even persuade you to spend some more money. Meet with the firm's producers and get their final, candid opinion of your planning and concept of the project. Bring a list of questions on all matters that you have doubts about.

Young, creative TV copywriters rarely realize how much it costs to produce the effects their commercials call for. A production house can quickly determine what is too expensive, often suggesting visual alternatives that are more practical and sometimes more effective. The house may suggest revises, a new writer, or starting from scratch.

Cost Self-Control

Your final cost can only remain that which was originally quoted if you keep to your original specifications. If those ideas keep changing with "wonderful" improvements, each improvement often involves a new set of additional costs. Rarely will a new idea make a video simpler, better, and cheaper. For each improvement, go through the same cost procedure as for the original quote. Then compare the added cost to the benefit.

Forget changes when you get close to the deadline when everything must be completed; keep to that schedule. The more you get behind schedule, the more certain it is that you're going to pay a lot more than your quote.

A Final Caution

New breakthroughs keep slashing costs of production and editing but also offer exciting new capabilities which tempt you to spend more. To take advantage while avoiding mistakes, keep updating your TV commercial know-how. Or look for the latest state-of-the-art expertise and help. Start with the sources listed below.

Help Source Guide

1. *Adweek's* "Best Spots of the Year" is a videocassette available at a business library or *Adweek:* 49 E. 21st St., NY, NY 10010. (212) 460-5155.

2. *Bandelier, Inc.*, created cost-saving animated spot commercials for top national advertisers; for a demo, call or write Post-production & Creative Facilities: 3815 Osuna NE, Albuquerque, NM 87109. (505) 345-8021.

3. Request new books on TV production from *Broadcasting Magazine's* Book Division, Reed Reference Publishing: P.O. Box 31, New Providence, NJ 07974. (800) 638-7827.

4. *Millimeter* magazine, from Penton Publishing, provides special sections on the business of creating commercials: 826 Broadway (4th floor), NY, NY 10003. (212) 477-4700.

5. *NTC Publishing Group* publishes business books, including the latest on TV production and copy. Ask for the following two books at library or contact NTC [4255 W. Touhy Ave., Lincolnwood, IL 60646-1975. (800) 323-4900]: Huntley Baldwin, *How to Create Effective TV Commercials*—styles, formats, storyboard showmanship, production technques, copy testing, legal constraints—an indispensable guide (288 pages); Hooper White, *How to Produce Effective TV Commercials*—the entire process-step-by-step, using cost control and pre-production planning.

6. *Studio Center Broadcast Productions* provides a *free* information kit about TV commercials: 200 W. 22d St., Norfolk, VA 23517. (804) 622-2111.

7. A. Wurtzel and S.R. Acker's *Television Production (1993)* provides a basic course on video equipment, new technology, uses; cameras lights, audio, editing, graphics, professional procedures (660 pages). Can be found at library or contact McGraw-Hill:1334 Monterey Ave., Blue Ridge Summit, PA 17294. (800) 722-4726.

8. H. Zettl's *Television Production Handbook* (1991) is a fifth edition of a classic—over 900 photos and illustrations (624 pages): Wadsworth Publishing, 765 Empire Dr., Florence, KY 41042. (800) 842-3636.

9. M. Krupnick's *The Electronic Image, Examining Basic TV Technology (1990)*, provides fundamentals of broadcast and video TV, technology, production, electronics; also includes information about sound, light, waveforms, scanning, NTSC color, magnetic recording, video editing, audio sweetening, transmission, digital design: Knowledge Industry Publications, 701 Westchester Ave., White Plains, NY 10604. (800) 800-5474.

7
Radio

How to Benefit Most
from What It Does Best

More businesses advertise on AM and FM radio stations than buy broadcast or cable TV advertising. Let's consider why:

- Radio reaches 96 percent of all Americans each week, of whom almost 80 percent listen every day. Each day, most listen to radio for three hours. Almost all men and women over 18, plus those 12 years old to 17 listen to radio, but listeners tune in in different proportions, at different times, and in different places.

- Americans buy roughly 100 million radios a year, for a total of more than half a billion in active use. On average, the typical home has 5.5 radios. There's one in about half of the kitchens, more than two-thirds of the living rooms, about 60 percent of the bedrooms, in dens, dining rooms—even bathrooms.

- Radio goes everywhere; 95 percent of all cars have radios, as do a constantly increasing percentage of trucks, vans, and recreational vehicles. More than two-thirds of Americans listen to radio on each car trip they take. And more than 60 percent listen to radio at work. Radio is in stores, factories, offices—there are even 14 million walk-along radios.

Some advantages of radio are that

1. Radio is informal, friendly, persuasive, and highly targeted to big segments of the consumer market, including some upscale audiences.
2. Radio allows for more repetition and thus a larger cumulative audience, for a much smaller budget, than TV does.
3. For a national brand commercial, radio delivers close to the same listener "recall" levels as TV, at lower cost. Radio also often drives in more customer "store traffic" for a special sale or event than print.
4. Radio—for the right direct-response offer—often can produce high-quality phone inquiries for salesperson follow-up in the volume desired, and at low cost.
5. Radio can create a variety of moods or environments, from humor to romance. Moreover, radio can present a spokesperson as far more "real" than via print and can stimulate the mind to participate more than TV.
6. Commercials on radio often can be *timed* to within minutes of the buying decision. When heard in the car, radio can cause instant results; frequently, drivers immediately arrive at the place of purchase and buy.
7. Monthly levels of radio listening are almost equal year-round. In contrast, both TV viewing and reading print drops sharply in outdoor months. And every day from 8 a.m. to 5 p.m. more people listen to radio than watch TV.
8. Radio advertising production costs are a small fraction of those for TV.

In this chapter we will consider whether radio advertising is suited to *your* product or service and, if so, how best to use it.

What Companies Use Radio Most?

Over $8 billion a year, or more than 75 percent of all radio advertising, is placed by local marketers, a far bigger percentage of local advertising than for cable or broadcast TV. Recent spurts in local spending on radio have come from a wide number of retailers: banks, department and discount stores, building and hardware stores, supermarkets, auto dealers, real estate firms and furniture stores.

A host of regional and national radio advertisers spend another $2+ billion yearly, almost three-quarters via spot buys by individual markets. The biggest growth has been from manufacturers of cars, soft drinks, shoes and soap, oil companies, airlines, meat and phone companies, national chain stores, the U.S. government, and even TV networks.

Radio does have its disadvantages:

1. No picture

2. No color

3. No motion

4. Often heard just as background

5. No demonstration possible

6. Short message

7. Details rarely get across

8. Phone or mail response from car listener is usually difficult

Radio listening is more casual and more often combined with other activities than TV viewing. More attention is paid in car listening, but a driver can't write down an address, phone number, or product name. Radios in a busy home don't demand the attention of a TV show. Even less attention is paid in a place of business. Detailed explanations don't penetrate. The product can't be seen. How it works cannot be shown. The product's package remains unknown, and even the name is harder to remember, unless often repeated.

If your product or service is not aimed at a mass market, if it sells for a lot of money to small groups of specialized users, if the description needed is complex, forget radio. If your product must be seen, requires color, or must be demonstrated, if the product must be felt or touched to be appreciated, radio cannot be your sole medium. But radio advertising fails more often as a result of simple misuse than because radio is an inappropriate medium for the advertiser.

Some provisos follow. Don't buy radio

- With the wrong offer, at the wrong time

- Using methods that have already failed before

- For an untried offer, product, service, or store without the benefit of a sound concept, business plan, and research

- With careless, hasty, or poorly created spots

- With what seem like bargains of the wrong kind.

Obviously, the most profitable use comes from taking full advantage of all that radio can do for your business. The rest of this chapter discusses (often through example) how to apply radio's strengths to your product or service and to research your market to find the most cost-efficient stations. I suggest that you also take another look at Chapter 3 on media research.

How to Start

If your company is big, first consider radio as a supplement to your successful campaign in other media. Many companies use the same spokesperson or even some of or all their TV commercial sound tracks. You may decide to use radio to reach a group your TV has not covered enough or to get listeners to read ads or direct mail; or to phone an 800 or 900 number for a longer message. The point is that radio may become an important part of your advertising arsenal by reinforcing or extending your sales message to key customer and prospect segments. But keep in mind that, depending upon the complexity of your media spending, you may not always be able to measure separately actual sales produced by radio.

If your company is small and a new radio advertiser, you probably won't have the same in-house media expertise as the big firms. But you can use their strategy and approach research, copy, and production as they do. And you probably can measure actual sales from your radio dollars better and faster.

Organize a Team

Your radio campaign may require a company committee or just you. Before you start, make sure everyone agrees on the objective of your radio campaign and what sales are hoped for. Next organize an agenda. Include capsule theme ideas. Get opinions on the kind of commercial desired. Should it be funny? Have dialogue? A male or female announcer? What action should the listener take? Then assign the writing job.

Now narrow the focus to the one thing which must get across to the listener, including important facts, specifics about the offer made, essential information about company, product, or service. Discuss marketing strategy, demographic information you have on the target audience, suggested ways your commercial can stand out, how to "position" your firm based on a key benefit (make your benefit unique and credible). Consider any ideas. Try creative brainstorming. Start writing.

Creating the Best Radio Copy

Saturate yourself in all your company's available research, plus its successful marketing efforts in all media, before and as the writing process begins. Investigate radio station options at the same time. For although I'm presenting the task of understanding radio advertising in a linear fashion—first discussing creating and then buying—truly expert execution comes when you have an audience in mind as you write.

Radio copy is as natural as talking, the earliest form of persuading anyone to do anything. The short, simple, informal words you use are those of conversation. It's as colloquial as telephone calling. Think of an expensive long-distance call—how you condense to a minute really important points. That's radio.

Now think how differently you talk depending on whether you're trying to persuade a child or great aunt, sports fan or music lover, someone in business or retiree. In radio, you must speak the language of the audience you target.

Make friends. On radio, you want to attract and to persuade. You want to do business now with those you can and to keep friendly with (and make still more receptive) all others. These are the purposes of what you say in your commercial, how you produce it, and where you advertise.

Here are more suggestions for writing radio copy from a top-talent team of commercial writers and producers, The Commercial Works (a division of New City Communications, Inc., in Bridgeport, Connecticut, established by fourteen radio stations):

- *Never* talk down to the listener.

- *Empathize!* As you write, focus on the mind of the target consumer, not just on your desire to sell.

- *Focus* your copy on only one item, concept, or key benefit. Declare *one* clear, focused objective per message.

- Call for a *specific action*. Explain exactly what you want the listener to do, and how to do it. Ask for the order!

- Use a memorable *theme* or *"hook"* to get the listeners' attention, provoke thoughts, and weasel your way into their memory.

- Make *simple, truthful, and believable claims*. Chop out the hackneyed expressions and overused, discounted superlatives.

- *Remember that motivation* is first and foremost. Details are second and secondary. Motivated listeners search out the details.

- Employ *urgency* and *immediacy*. These natural qualities of radio can be critical to generating response.

- Make a *specific offer* and *price it* whenever possible.

- Use *"theater of the mind"*—prompt the listener to picture your message and put himself or herself into the picture.

- *Sell early, sell often, sell throughout!* Don't tag a 10-second "sell" on the end of a nonselling comedy routine.

- *Repeat* the product or firm name as often as you can. Use devices to make your listeners remember it.

- When promoting a *discount or other special offer*, make the offer powerful, simple, and prominent—with the right timing.

- Make any *slogan* unique, credible, and based on a key benefit perceived by your target audience.

- Include a *"tracing hook"* to find out if your radio schedule really is worth the money you are spending on it.

- Don't waste the *power of the last line*. The last few words have amazing potential.

- Humorous and "hard-sell" spots can wear out quickly. Your radio spot should build in recognition and persuasiveness with frequency.

- To decide on copy execution, always *listen* to a radio spot. Don't read it first. It should be written for the ears, not the eyes. If it looks as good as it sounds, it probably was not written for radio.

Producing Your Radio Commercial

For large companies, producing radio commercials simply becomes a matter of turning to your in-house facility, advertising agency, or a radio commercial production firm. Even an elaborate radio commercial will be far simpler than a TV commercial. But procedure is similar enough that I suggest you reread Chapter 6.

If your firm is small, you may decide to tape the commercial yourself or even let the on-air announcer read it each time. Other options include using the production facilities of a local radio station or those of a freelance producer or production house. Each can locate talent and select music and sound effects from a commercial production library. Each can help create a vocal "jingle." Ask each station's program manager to recommend outside producers and facilities. Listen to their commercials. Compare costs. Check results and satisfaction.

A man's voice usually is more clearly heard on radio. More single-voice commercials are delivered by men, often to sell to women. But for any product women usually know more about than men, a female voice may be more *trusted.*

Regardless of gender, the *most persuasive* voice to sell to any group is a known expert in the field of the product offered. Find a personality most looked up to and generally trusted by the targeted group, with the ideal being an expert from the group.

How to Buy Radio Time

The smartest radio station sales staffs prefer that you start your advertising on their station prudently and appropriately, to help ensure long-term success for both parties. Other will try to sell you as much time as possible, for as long a period of time as possible, starting as soon as possible.

Remember, you need the radio audiences that are right for your product, and to reach them at the right cost per person, at the right time, with a message of the right length and frequency.

You can get valuable free information and one-to-one advice from the smartest, most experienced local radio experts. But their time is limited. The trick is to "sell" the salesperson on your potential as an account and for the salesperson, in turn, to sell the boss and the specialists on the worthiness of giving you their time and counsel.

The following are some sound guidelines for buying radio time:

1. *Investigate each station thoroughly.* If you want to buy locally and don't have an advertising agency, just look in the yellow pages under "radio stations." Phone and ask for the sales department. You will be assigned a salesperson based on your location or your kind of business. The salesperson may be young, recently hired, briefly trained, and/or bright, eager, and helpful.

The salesperson will give you a media kit describing the station's program format, ad rate structure, plus a "coverage map" and other rating information, research data, and promotional success stories. The salesperson should inquire about you, your products or service, customers and prospects, present advertising, and plans and objectives. The good salesperson then will get help to advise you—usually from a sales manager, research manager, program manager, and often the station manager.

2. *Save their time and yours.* Prepare an information kit on your business comparable to the media kit each station gives you. Include a brief description of your business, brief history, sample commercials if any, ads, mailing pieces, catalog sheets, and photocopies of good press your company has received. Include any research data (or even your own opinion) of key characteristics of your customers and prospects.

On your first phone call to each station, suggest exchanging their media kit for your info kit before a visit. Study each media kit received: Compare its claimed primary coverage area with the entire metro area or the parts of it you want to reach. Note the program format description and audience age range and sex. If coverage and audience seems wrong for you, avoid a future meeting.

3. *Start the learning process.* Phone each station whose media kit indicates that it reaches your prospects. First, create a list of questions such as these:

- What rating and research services do you subscribe to?
- What stations with similar format do you compete with?
- What are the strengths and weaknesses of each?
- How does your audience differ?
- What accounts similar to mine have succeeded with you?
- How long a commercial does each run? How often? When?
- How will the rate I pay compare with the rates others pay?
- What rate protection against future increases do I get?

Ask your salesperson to confirm by fax the ratings and research information given by phone, including the name of the research service quoted and the date of the rating or survey. Note any rating difference for the same time period and station by the two main independent rating services, Birch and Arbitron. It has been due to different reporting methods. (Reread Chapter 3.)

4. *Visit stations.* It's most efficient to get information by phone, fax, and computer modem. But you can often persuade better in person. If the salesperson of an appropriate station comes to your office, a little time spent in a friendly tour of your place may sell your desirability as an account.

Make the next meeting at the station. Ask to meet the sales manager, promotion manager, research manager, and station manager. Each can teach. Answer their questions. Listen to their presentation. If their presentation isn't specifically tailored to you, ask why their format fits you, what are their recommendations, and how each will work with you as a client. Then ask them to describe in detail how their research and station promotions have worked for others. Finally, ask each if you can phone other advertisers with a specific question.

5. *Confer with other radio advertisers.* You can get their names from your trade association, from each station you talk to, and by listening to commercials. A retailer in one city will often advise a similar retailer in another city. A big firm may help a smaller one. A company in another field may use radio just as you plan to and inform and advise you. Ask by phone the following:

- How successful have you been in tangible terms?
- For how little money did you successfully test?
- To what degree are your radio spots targeted? Based on how much research? Of what kind?
- What time lengths are your spots or commercials? What frequency? During what time of day? Length of campaign, during which season?
- On what station or stations did you run spots? With what formats?
- Which agency did you use? Time-buying service? House agency?
- Which stations and formats pulled best?
- Type of spot? Who made it? What was the production cost?
- Of all the people you worked with, who were the smartest and helped you the most?

Don't just pick brains. Exchange information. Do business with stations that teach you the most while giving you good value. Listed at the end of this chapter are industry sources for more information on local, spot, and network buying. You can learn from research services how to use information provided by stations, and even receive it via computer modem.

Test-Marketing Costs

Several retailers in small markets have started advertising on radio with a two-week campaign of eight to ten 30-second spots a day. They used one station to promote a special sale, at a cost under $1000, and succeeded. Often, the retailers have continued radio advertising with more frequent campaigns on more stations. Other direct-response clients of ours have tested offers on three-minute commercials in one day on one station in New York City for under $500. The tests succeeded, and they subsequently spent $10,000 a week on radio, all very profitably.

Others started with much bigger commitments. When Montgomery Ward decided to try to change its image from that of a retail loser, it used radio intensively and spent millions of dollars nationally to convince listeners that Ward was now a revitalized winner. Research of buyer attitudes showed that it worked. Big companies use radio in a wide media mix coordinated in a test market or in an overall national campaign, even to reach special groups.

Programming Creates the Audience

Programs offered determine who listens when. Programmers are like chemists creating formulas, testing them, and then testing variations to reach a different audience mix. Different music and other types of formatting attract widely different audiences. Los Angeles has nearly a hundred radio stations with everything from jazz to business news to talk to rock music. The Top ten radio stations in LA are all practically tied for number one. But almost each one has a different audience mix.

The following lists different station formats:

All news	**Hispanic**
All sports	Nostalgia/big band
New age/jazz	News/talk
Classical	Soft rock
All business news	Album-oriented rock
Religious	Black news/talk
Adult contemporary	Country
Rock/contemporary hit radio	Nostalgia/big band
Easy listening	Black/R&B
Urban contemporary	Golden oldies
Soft contemporary (light)	Variety

Each of these has variations. Standard Rate & Data Service, a directory company that publishes advertising rates and other data for a variety of media, categorizes more than 100 radio program formats. Many more are constantly tried. To attract 18- to 34-year-olds, for example, a programmer uses contemporary hit radio (CHR). But some modify the CHR formula with more of today's hits that appeal most to younger females. Others try CHURB, which emphasizes dance music and rap hits, to appeal to more urban and often black audiences.

Most current album-oriented rock (AOR) music draws most heavily those between 18 and 24. But "classic AOR," which includes rock hits from the 1970s and 1960s, pulls in a wider audience, age 18 to 34 and older, as rock 'n' rollers get older. The adult contemporary (AC) music formula attempts to widen the audience even further, to embrace ages 18 to 49.

Oldies of 10 to 25 years tend to appeal to those aged 25 to 49. Older "oldies" can push the appeal to older people. The Country music format aims at ages 25 to 54, and the middle-of-the-road (MOR) format tries to appeal to those 35 to 55 by bringing them back to prerock days.

Classical music stations reach a more highly educated, older, higher-income audience. As such, they are more apt to be good prospects for better wines and more sophisticated magazines. Some classical stations modify the music selection to attract younger, trendier listeners.

Talk shows on many AM stations traditionally appeal to those older. But ABC radio network modified its content to appeal to younger audiences. Sports shows and all-sport-radio aim at younger men. All-news stations appeal more to men, especially business people with higher income. Business radio is after middle-aged, affluent men and women.

Ethnic radio reaches many groups. In Chicago, Detroit, New Orleans, and Philadelphia, black stations are usually rated first, second, and third. The fastest-growing U.S. ethnic market is Hispanic.

Look for the Right Format Combination

Suppose all-news stations reach a good share of your prospects, as do all-business stations and classical music stations. Then advertising adjacent to business news on classical radio stations may be a winner.

Companies with national advertising budgets have yet another way to buy radio time. More than 30 national radio networks offer many specialized audiences, with formats that enhance those that are the most successful locally, from music, talk, and business, to sports, ethnic, and whatever else proves topical. To survive, each network gives advertisers what they can't get locally—big-name hosts, famous guests, plus occasionally elaborate specials.

Although new radio trends constantly emerge, these trends of the last five years appear to be gaining strength and are apt to continue to shape the radio marketplace for the foreseeable future:

- More fragmentation of audience into special groups
- Changing formats for stations and networks

- Proliferation of new stations and networks
- Rapid growth of ethnic and other diverse audiences
- Big increase in (much more comprehensive) research
- Jump in computerization of research and time-buying
- Increased ability to target *your* prospects
- Faster change of latest format success

Change can be overnight. Station rankings are volatile. Any station with the right new format can become number one. Any variation can be number one in a format. A big bonanza for a radio advertiser is to buy time on a station just as its audience leaps up, before rates catch up. A new radio format successful anywhere tends to be successful everywhere. If you buy spot radio nationally, you may find a brand-new winning format before it becomes a national trend and ride a trend market by market, before rates jump.

Conversely, national advertising dollars go mostly to the two or three top-rated radio stations in each market. A hot new format trend eats up budgets and takes money away even from stations whose audience it does not reduce.

Quality before Quantity

Be less interested in which station is number one than in looking for additional information to better target your audience. Look for qualitative information as to how many listeners go to your kind of store and use your kind of product or service and how often. Classical music stations may have the lowest rating overall but may be the best choice to reach an audience who buys $2500 in travelers checks or spends the most on computer systems.

Your goal is to find the best format to reach *your* customer profile, and the lowest cost to reach customers. You'll need three kinds of research:

1. Detailed analysis of your customers: where they live, their income, age, sex; home and car ownership; are they working or retired; why do they buy from you? About your former customers, you need to know why they don't buy, what they do buy, and why. You should try to get the same information about your most logical prospects who are solicited but who do not buy. Plus you need to understand the listening, reading, viewing, and shopping habits of each group; the radio stations they prefer; when they listen, and how often.

2. Measurement of the number of radio listeners by age and sex and whether they're at home, in a car, or elsewhere at any time you might run your commercial on each station; and calculations of the cost per thousand (CPM) listeners in dollars to reach specific segments of them.

3. Both previous kinds of research to determine the various CPMs to reach those with the characteristics of your customers and desired prospects; at home, in the car, elsewhere, at the times when easiest to sell them.

How Frequently and How Long Should You Run?

Compare the advantages of reaching more prospects versus reaching fewer with more frequency. Products or services with relatively universal appeal and wide distribution which are meant for repeat use generally need their advertising to reach the same people frequently and continually. More expensive, specialized products usually require salespeople to follow up a qualified lead in order to make the sale. Thus, these higher-end products and services need fresh sources of inquiries from advertising. A "one low price" marketing position needs constant advertising repetition, whereas special sales need spurts of spots.

The length of your radio advertising campaign depends on your budget and ability to measure actual sales resulting from your campaign. Retailers advertising on only one station have their own research: Cash registers, barcode readers, and computers calculate sales daily and can be compared to periods before advertising. Direct-response advertisers often have no fixed budget except to constantly measure results and buy as much time for as long as it remains profitable.

Research and negotiate. When a new station starts or when any station changes its format, it may give significant price breaks for bigger, longer advertising schedules. But when a station's advertising time becomes virtually sold-out, it may prefer shorter schedules before it raises rates. Many of the most successful stations conduct a perpetual auction of their advertising time. Their computers raise prices when almost sold-out or lower them when time opens up.

When an important news story occurs—whether it be threat of war, scandal in high places, or a natural or human-made disaster—all-news stations get a big spurt in audience. Before the computers increase rates, a big, short schedule may be a bonanza. Likewise, a newspaper strike inflates radio's audience.

Weekend spots are sometimes underpriced because weekdays sell faster. Faced with little other prospect of its time being sold, a hungry station recently sold all its open spots for the weekend way below the rate card price on a Friday afternoon.

Media-buying services and barter firms acquire blocks of radio time on a variety of stations at wholesale rates to sell to advertisers, usually at off-rate. If the audience is right, negotiate.

Free Station Promotions Swell Sales.   WJLB-Detroit conducts a lot of promotions, from a $20,000 shopping spree to a ski night that filled four buses with skiers. WLIB-New York offers a "Family Card" that acts as a credit card and gets discounts of 10 to 15 percent or extra gifts when buying. In Los Angeles, FM station KOST 103 promoted a Supermarket Singles night for Pavilion Supermarkets.

Stations love to run contests, stage events, give things away, receive phone calls—anything to achieve excitement for their audience. They look for tie-ins with anybody who will contribute prizes or helps make things happen and to involve advertisers in ways to give them extra value. They're open to ideas. Cruise companies, Disneyland, record and movie companies, stars and fashion companies, and lots of small companies have helped and benefited. Maybe you can, for your company.

Get Someone Else to Pay Half.   Farmers & Builders Supply in Blackshear and Kingsland, Georgia, used radio exclusively for a Peachtree door and window special sale. What made the promotion work was cooperative advertising, 50 percent paid by Peachtree, the manufacturer, who also supplied a trailer loaded with doors and windows parked in front of the stores. Refreshments were served, a local radio station did a live remote. For two weeks before the special three-day sale, eight spots a day were run announcing the event. More than $60,000 of Peachtree doors and windows were sold in those three days.

For another promotion, Owens-Corning brought in a truckload of insulation for a one-day, Saturday sale. As much as would normally sell in two months sold out that day. That year Farmers & Builders spent $42,000 on radio alone, 99 percent co-op, all on three country music stations. If you manufacture, get the dealers to share. If you're a dealer, enlist a manufacturer. And always get a station to help.

Helping McDonald's Breakfast Business Burgeon.   In many markets, research showed that McDonald's customers were heavy radio listeners; most came by car; two-thirds made the decision to come within two hours before; and more than one-half decided within two minutes, while in a car, listening. Most of two target audiences, black and Hispanic car listeners, tuned to their own ethnic stations.

Armed with this information, McDonald's encourages local and regional franchise owners to run breakfast advertising schedules on radio—80 percent in AM drive time, when the in-car audience is biggest, both with spot and network buys. McDonald's became the top advertiser on both black and Hispanic radio. Heavy, frequent radio advertising caused 40 percent more consumers to hear McDonald's message over and above those who saw its TV commercials, for only 18 percent more than the original TV budget.

Much That McDonald's Does, You Can Do. Many McDonald's franchise owners started with one McDonald's in one town, as small businesses. They exchange information and create regional market and advertising plans. In very simplified form, each area group starts the year with a sales estimate for the year. An advertising budget for media is set, based on a percentage of sales targeted. A six-month plan is made, tied in with national advertising.

The plan adapts to local needs and competition. About half of McDonald's ads in any market are the responsibility of the franchise owners (locally and regionally) and their ad agencies. A local McDonald's promotion already successful elsewhere may be the safest route. However, McDonald's national headquarters is getting results from test markets all the time. It is not uncommon to change plans suddenly—they are flexible. Each owner and its agency continually get ideas and information from regional and national headquarters. McDonald's uses 55 local and regional ad agencies across the United States, each handling from three to hundreds of McDonald's locations.

In the three midwest and southeast regions, Hardee's is the big competitor; 40 to 50 percent of all Hardee business is breakfast. In a typical Hardee's market, about 60 percent of this is drive-through and 40 percent sit-down (but most come by car). For lunch and dinner about 40 percent of business is drive-through (nationally about 50 percent is drive-through). Breakfast attracts more men than women, and lunch is about even. And since dinner is more family-oriented, there are somewhat more women than men customers. This makes radio breakfast schedules important.

Obviously, there's less variety of radio programming in smaller markets. A good smaller market might have 60,000 people with an average age of 29, just right for McDonald's. It might have 10 commercial radio stations, four AM and six FM. Often, the AM talk station, whether business, general, sports, or combined (a format McDonald's stays away from), has the lowest rating. Two country stations often have good audience cross-sections. Overall, four or five stations may be suited to McDonald's needs.

The local or regional agency makes a suggested radio budget breakdown with an estimated cost per rating point (CPRP) of desired audience for its radio schedules for each market. If a spot schedule costs $10,000 and has a cumulative rating of 100, the CPRP is $100. The CPRP in a given market will vary, depending on the competitive situation, but the average CPRP in a market often remains about the same for years, aided by negotiation. Stations know the CPRP required to get and maintain McDonald's business.

Decisions to buy individual radio stations and what times to use are left more to local and regional franchisees and their agencies. The cash registers reveal quickly what is working. The local agency is often in touch by phone with each outlet on daily and weekly sales, product mix, and how business is going in other ways. Tracking results never stops. A failing promotion is killed quickly. Often, failure is averted before it starts because planned tests for local markets must be cleared with regional headquarters. If the idea has failed elsewhere, the owners and agency are told immediately.

Science, Gut Feeling, Negotiation.   Marketing and rating research narrow choices. CPRP calculations point the way. Gut feeling often determines the final selection of promotions, copy and time buys, and how best to match local plans with national promotions. Negotiation makes it a safer risk.

Many of the same research tools used by national advertisers are available to you, at no cost, via radio stations. Software used by many local and regional agencies for McDonald's is available at many other advertising agencies. You can plan, exchange information, discover new and better promotions, and then change your plan.

Number 4 Station May Be Number 1.   Research determined that almost half the customers of a downtown retailing center in a major city were professionals or managers. Almost half were college graduates. Almost 40 percent were in clerical or service jobs. Fewer than expected were students. For this shopping area, the fourth-ranked station in the city ranked number one in reaching men who shop downtown. Yet for women shopping this same downtown center, a different radio station was the best buy.

Research for Eldridge Fine Jewelry in Kansas City discovered that Eldridge had two main customer groups—those between the ages of 18 and 34 making smaller purchases and older, higher-income families making bigger ones. But each Eldridge branch in five different malls had a different customer mix—by age, sex, income, and tastes in radio listening. Eldridge's selected different stations and programs to promote each branch, ranging from country and western music for one mall to soft rock for another.

Media Buying for Chains. Cliff Shaluta handles a $600,000 radio budget for 325 Jr. Food convenience stores headquartered in Panama City, Florida. Before Cliff took over, Jr. Foods bought mostly bargain packages of lots of radio spots for very little each. Cliff's research showed that many of these "bargain buys" were on AM stations in locations with the least growth. Worse, most of these spots reached mainly older women, even though Jr. Foods primary customers were male, age 18 to 34, with 35- to 49-year-old men being the next most important customer category.

Cliff decided to concentrate his radio purchases in central Florida, Jr. Foods' most productive area. Here, AM stations largely had an older audience than he desired. Cliff switched to FM almost exclusively. He avoided "bargains" at the wrong times and paid more per spot at the right times, to achieve a big saving per real prospect. And in turn, he received more cooperative vendor money. If you are a retailer, get your share.

Further Suggestions

Don't make commercials first and then buy time, or vice versa. Do marketing and media research and make creative and media decisions as concurrently as possible. Only buy radio when

1. Your product, service, or store is successful.
2. Your offer or proposal works.
3. Your selling season is right.
4. Radio best fits into your marketing plan.
5. Radio best enhances your other media.
6. Your presentation is perfect for radio.
7. Radio reaches best the market you seek most.
8. Radio is priced lower than your best other option.
9. Scientific research indicates that radio is your best buy.
10. Traced results prove your ad's effectiveness.

Help Source Guide

1. *Billboard* magazine provides the latest music-format rankings nationally and by top markets: 1515 Broadway, NY, NY 10036. (212) 764-7300.

2. *Birch/Scarborough Research Corp.* provides a *free* information kit with full explanation of radio audience measurement research: 12350 N.W. 39th St., Coral Springs, FL 33065-2404. (305) 753-6043.

3. *Caballero Spanish Media Inc.* provides rates, facts, success stories: 261 Madison Ave., NY, NY 10016. (212) 697-4120.

4. *National Association of Black-Owned Broadcasters Inc.* (NABOB) lists black-owned radio & TV stations, call letters, addresses. Free information on NABOB and history of black radio available from 1730 M. St. N.W., Washington, DC 20036. (202) 463-8970.

5. *The Radio Advertising Bureau, Inc.* is a gold mine of facts, research, and success stories: 304 Park Ave. S., NY, NY 10010. (212) 243-4800.

6. *Standard Rate & Data Services* (SRDS) has a monthly publication that lists spot radio rates and audience information: 2000 Clearwater Drive, Oak Brook, IL 60521. (800) 232-0772.

7. *Statistical Research Inc.* publishes *RADAR,* the only national radio network rating service. Details on how it's done are available from: 111 Prospect St., Westfield, NY 07090. (908) 654-4000.

8. *Radio Expenditure Reports, Inc.* tracks who spends how much on what stations and networks. *Free* information kit available from: 740 W. Boston Post Rd., Mamaroneck, NY 10543. (914) 381-6277.

8
In-Bound
Telemarketing

Let's start with its simplest form. Have you ever put up a personal notice on a student or supermarket bulletin board to sell or rent anything? Or run a classified ad to do this? Did you include a phone number and get any phone response? If so, you were using in-bound telemarketing—and getting a lesson in how the smallest business can start in the simplest way and what in-bound telemarketing requires.

Your effort could succeed only if your copy mentioned the right phone number, got calls, and if your offer was desirable when effectively explained by phone. Your effort failed if no one answered the phone or if someone answered who

1. Didn't know what you wanted to sell or rent
2. Had the wrong or too little information
3. Didn't explain clearly enough
4. Had no interest and resented the interruption
5. Was not friendly, helpful, and persuasive
6. Did not ask for the desired action decision
7. Did not write down (or write correctly) the name and phone number of the person calling.

Seven vital rules of in-bound telemarketing success are to do the opposite of the above. Most important is to *always think like a customer ordering or inquiring by phone.*

When you try to buy anything by phone you may get no answer, a series of busy signals, or a succession of people who switch your call repeatedly. These are other common obstacles to avoid. For your firm's success, do the opposite of whatever irritated you most.

The key to successful in-bound telemarketing is that it must be organized. Unplanned, imperfect, and disorganized in-bound telemarketing may not seem that bad and may even succeed. But much potential profit may be lost. But much more than short-term money is involved. Your company's reputation is literally on the line. However big your company, a constant effort to correct these problems almost always pays off.

The telephone is a universal and personal device. It can be used as an electronic marketing medium and an integral part of advanced marketing. How your firm handles each in-bound call is key. This chapter will show you why answering of calls is key and help you to harness the telephone's incredible power.

Let's first list some of organized in-bound telemarketing's attributes. It can

- Be started with little risk (a small investment) by the smallest firm, start-up, or moonlighter
- Make any public relations effort—in print, TV, radio, or any other medium—instantly profitable
- Increase the value of any advertising in any form
- Qualify order inquiries, thereby often developing a higher percentage closing rate and a higher average sale than by most other means
- Upgrade your orders to higher-priced items or through additional sales (add-ons)
- Increase prospect goodwill and customer loyalty
- Give you a quicker reaction time in most forms of testing

Far more people routinely inquire or order by telephone than by filling out a coupon or order form. It's quicker and easier, and—in theory at least—it instantly answers any questions a prospective buyer might have. More than a half-million firms in the United States promote toll-free 800 numbers to receive almost 4 billion calls each year. Another 10 million companies without 800 ordering numbers get billions more inquiries and orders by phone. JC Penney's 9000 phone reps alone handle about 80 million in-bound calls a year.

Every year, more of this country's largest companies—along with most smaller retailers, service companies, wholesalers, manufacturers, and every catalog—get more of their sales completed by in-bound telephone. An amazing 97 percent of Sears catalog orders and 98.5 percent of JC Penney catalog orders come by phone.

But this is far from an easy medium to master. Some disadvantages of in-bound telephone marketing are:

1. A phone response only occurs if promotion makes it happen.
2. Too little response in proportion to your ad and overhead costs loses money.
3. There can be big fluctuations in the numbers of calls received. An irregular response rate that is handled by regular overhead creates significant operational inefficiencies and, often, losses.
4. Direct-response ads with phone numbers, placed without the staff to handle the ensuing phone calls, lose money and goodwill.
5. Mishandled calls cause ill will.
6. Expansion too quickly can turn your success to ruin.

Remember, every type of business gets customer and prospect in-bound calls, but fewer than 5 percent use organized in-bound telemarketing. This telemarketing can't work if your product is bad, your margins are wrong, your price is a bad value, your delivery is too slow, or your organizations is in chaos. But these disadvantages are self-created and can be self-corrected.

Success needs the right plan, promotion, and staff (trained and motivated). It requires integration with your company's entire marketing effort, effective logistical carry-through, and cost control. The basic guidelines for in-bound telemarketing are these:

- Only a combination of the right product, price, offer, copy, and timing works.
- Measuring phone response from each ad is key to maximizing sales from your ad cost.
- Only the right staff selection, training, motivation, and equipment can handle calls economically.
- Control is simplest for stable, small firms.

Effective in-bound telemarketing must be customized to your organization, whether you are a wholesaler, consultant, manufacturer, giant company, or a one-person start-up. Often, failure comes from the wrong use for your situation, typically by starting in a difficult way instead of employing the most natural process for you.

How should you start? If your firm is established and advertises in any way, you need only add a request to call for information or to order for any offer. If your firm is small, you can start in the simplest way for several hundred dollars, even for under $100, and sometimes for no cost. You can stop at once if response is poor. You may ask for calls in the yellow pages, with a 1-inch newspaper display ad or classified ad, with a tiny mailing, or just by adding an extra line in your present ad.

Free ways to start involve arranging for free public relations yourself. Just make sure that your interview on local radio or TV or the write-up in your city or community paper includes your phone number. Just one effort may be enough to test. Don't expect or even try to get a lot of calls. But, be ready for calls—and for more than you expect.

How to Prepare

Remember, never advertise or publicize a product or service you don't have ready to ship or one you know nothing about. And don't ask for inquiries for literature not yet written or printed.

First, write down all the important questions and answers about what you are selling. Research your competition. Write down every possible question about comparable claims, and your answers.

Next, get your friends and relatives to phone in as if they were prospects. It may sound silly or even prove to be a bit embarrassing, but this is the surest, simplest, and cheapest way to create and rehearse a selling script. And any embarrassment in involving friends in the development of your script should be viewed as minor compared to the potential damage done by unveiling a flawed script to critical and demanding customers and prospects.

For your small first test, don't worry about having an 800 number, getting a vanity number, using a telephone service bureau, buying elaborate equipment, or even using a PC with special software to help handle calls. But make sure that you or someone else that's trained is always by the phone. If that's absolutely impossible, get a telephone answering machine to take calls when you are out.

What To Do If You Succeed

If any condition of the first test changes, whether it be the season, competition, price, recommendation, or whatever else, make a new *small* test. If all the conditions are the same retest *exactly* what worked, but increase it by several times on the promotional scale. If this fails, stop.

Analyze why. Go back to square one and try again. It may take several false starts, but usually what works will continue to.

Few realize the full, step-by-step expansion possibilities of a very small, successful test. The trick is to stick exactly to what works. This is the control. But test from scratch ways to improve what you do. Always track and trace the number of calls and sales you get. When you beat the control, then replace it as the new control. Each improvement must earn its cost and produce profit. Cumulative improvements make expansion on a bigger scale safer. Advertise more and organize and equip your firm to handle more calls.

Gear Up Gradually

At the end of this chapter is a Help Source Guide listing books and periodicals on telemarketing. It's important to read them, because no single source can teach you all the ongoing nuances to in-bound telemarketing. Next, buy more products by phone. Call others just to inquire. One time call in a hurry. Another time, chat. Order for the first time from some, occasionally from others, and more regularly with one or two. Buy from a catalog, from an ad, from a mailing piece. Study how others handle you in each situation. Compare with how you and your people now handle calls.

If your firm is bigger and you do not now have an in-bound telemarketing department and want to start one, much of the above applies. But by virtue of your size, you're bound to have existing employees who handle orders and inquiries at least part of the time. First, listen in to hear how these employees now handle inquiries and orders. Time each call. Keep a record for each person in terms of speed, accuracy, dollar sales, conversion percentage to sale (the number of calls in which a phone salesperson closes a sale versus the number of calls he or she receives), appointment, or whatever action is desired. Then, with the help of your best in-bound "producers," write simple scripts to upgrade a phone order to a deluxe model or for multiple sales at additional savings. Test each.

Should You Use an 800 Number?

The giants do. 1-800-HOLIDAY brings over 20 million phone calls a year and over a billion dollars a year in Holiday Inns reservations. Hertz Rent-A-Car gets over 16 million calls a year; 80 percent of Spiegel catalog sales comes from over 15 million calls to its 800 number. The Sheraton Hotels' 800 number gets over 9 million calls a year worldwide, and one third of its reservations. The first Christmas season after L. L. Bean, Inc. installed an 800 number, its catalog phone orders doubled. So many people prefer to order this way that some advertisers use only an 800 number in ads, with no mailing address. Toll-free numbers have two big advantages: (1) They are much easier to remember. (2) Because they are free to the user, more people call. So for the same ad cost, many achieve a lower ad cost per call.

It's Not Magic.   Both L. L. Bean and Joseph A. Bank Clothiers of Baltimore tested an 800 number several times for their catalogs and did not get sales increases worth the cost. Both later found ways to make an 800 number profitable. Many companies are concerned about these disadvantages:

- You pay for each 800 call, which magnifies the loss from unnecessary time spent taking each inquiry and order.
- If answered by your regular office staff, an 800 number invites salespeople to call you at your expense.
- An 800 number may get more inquiries from fewer interested people, with fewer closures than from those who paid for their calls.
- More people tend to phone to complain, request customer service, to cancel, and/or to return something ordered.

Most firms find that these disadvantages of 800 numbers can be largely overcome by careful control. For most, the cost of an 800 number call is often a fraction of the total ad cost per inquiry or order and quite competitive with other handling costs. Such costs are reduced by careful control. Inquiry ad copy can be tightened to get better-quality response.

For quality products and services from efficient companies, a phone complaint often turns an angry, departing customer into a loyal repeater. Fast and satisfactory handling of a service call often gets an immediate tie-in purchase. A call to return is often converted into an exchange. Information given often enables the caller to use and keep the original purchase. In sum, most users of 800 numbers find that the advantages far outweigh drawbacks. AT&T surveyed customers about use of 800 numbers and got the following responses:

- 87 percent of consumers liked it.
- 800 numbers enhance company image.
- 86 percent of consumers preferred to call 800 numbers.

- Consumers found the average telephone customer-service person to be more knowledgeable than in-store personnel.
- 88 percent liked the 800 information lines; they even used them for in-store purchases.
- Consumers were more likely to buy if an 800 service was available, especially for technical or hi-ticket products.
- Those who purchased via an 800 number usually spent more than by mail.
- 50 percent wanted to be told about sale items or hear alternatives for out-of-stock items.

Know Your Phone Cost per Call. You can get an 800 number from AT&T, MCI, Sprint, your regional telephone company, and most phone service bureaus. The recent initial minimum cost has been as little as a few dollars a month. MCI, Sprint, and AT&T constantly compete. Rates constantly change. New rates schedules are designed to create a perception of being a greater bargain than those of competitors. Check all three.

Self-Selling Phone Numbers. Phone companies sell, for a small charge (usually under $200), telephone numbers that spell a name, business, sport, or some other word or phrase. They are called "vanity phone numbers." Marketers want them because the right self-selling number pulls more orders or inquiries. To create that number takes your ingenuity. To clear it takes time calling the business offices of different phone companies. It may clear on one and not on another. So have alternatives ready.

Sometimes, the entire name and business is built around an 800 self-selling number, such as 800 FLOWERS and 800 SPIRITS. Although a vanity number is easier to remember, it is harder to dial at least the first time, because people are not accustomed to dialing letters. A vanity number becomes more effective with more frequent use. Often advertising both spells out the "vanity" words and gives actual numbers.

A self-selling 800 vanity number is equivalent to a headline. One may be far superior to another. Test which is best and whether either is better than a regular number. In a split-run ad or mailing piece, use each different number for alternating copies of each ad or mailing printed. If one number is decidedly better, retest with an ad or a mailing of enough circulation to produce several hundred calls. Go with the winner.

How to Get More Calls. Ask for phone calls in every promotion. Emphasize how you ask for them. Test new methods to get more and better prospects to phone you. Project what works to the maximum circulation, and proliferate to more kinds of media. Most of the chapters in this book are concerned with how best to get orders and inquiries through various electronic media. The Help Source Guide at the end of this chapter recommends sources to get the latest direct marketing books, newsletters, and magazines for print and electronic media buying.

Here are some tips on 800 number emphasis in both print and electronic media:

- Repeat the 800 number every page or at least every 3 pages or so in a catalog.

- Keep your 800 number on screen through most of your TV commercial or video.

- Use your number in big print at the start of catalog, commercial, or video.

- Use bold type, state area served, hours open, and time zone.

- Include "1" before the 800. List any alternative numbers.

Should You Use a Telemarketing Service Bureau?

There are over 500 telemarketing service bureaus nationwide. Most are organized to handle calls for any firm anywhere in the United States as effectively as if the bureau were nearby. Bureaus handle hundreds of millions of incoming calls each year. Actors often work for service bureaus between jobs. They like to interact with people, are quick studies, easily read off the screen, and often are natural salespersons. Some advantages of using the best of the growing number of telemarketing service bureaus include the following:

- Bureaus have well-selected, trained, and closely supervised staff.

- Bureaus use latest technology equipment for fast, effective handling.

- Bureaus have ample experience with telemarketing situations like yours.

- Bureaus handle wide swings in volume of calls.

- Fixed costs are known to you for handling each call.

- Fast-growing companies can avoid the risks and investment involved in committing to internal additions to staff, space, and equipment.

The latest equipment of the biggest telephone service bureaus can handle over 100,000 calls in just minutes after one network TV broadcast. For irregular response, you escape overhead. And you avoid the huge management problems and risks of selecting, training, and controlling a fast-growing staff, or buying the wrong equipment.

But many in-bound service bureaus have these disadvantages:

- Many are set up to be order-takers, not sales-creators.
- Most can only offer simple alternatives to upgrade orders.
- Few can advise those asking for help in purchasing.
- Most cannot master and explain a complex line of items.
- Most need volume business, not tiny accounts.
- Many can take an inquiry name accurately and fast but not give lengthy information when needed to close.

Only as the same phone agents continue to answer calls for your offer do they become more familiar with it. This increases the risk of less than perfect handling for a first test of a small entrepreneur.

How a Phone Service Bureau Works

Matrixx Marketing Corp. of Cincinnati, Ohio, has a consumer division and a business division and offers more varied telemarketing services than many other service bureaus. But my family's company uses only the consumer division in Ogden, Utah, to handle our in-bound calls. It has taken over 350,000 orders by phone for our company for products selling for under $30. Over two-thirds of these orders were produced by TV commercials, many in big bursts from commercials reaching big audiences at one time, and the balance via print resulting in more scattered calls. For substantially higher-priced products we direct-market, Matrixx has taken tens of thousands of inquiries.

Matrixx has between 500 and 600 in-bound phone positions. For all its customers, it can receive and handle, with live operators, over 350,000 calls a day. For a big burst of calls typical from TV ads, it can handle over 10,000 calls in one hour for one client.

On the first ring, calls are immediately answered by the first available phone representative. Monitor screens provide Matrixx phone representatives with the number the caller dialed. Each number is the key. The same 800 phone number can be used for many TV stations, each 250 miles away from the next. The computer calls up on-screen information about the offer made featuring that number within that area. This keeps products, offers, and stations separated.

Matrixx ties its computer to our computer. It does the same for many clients. All names are then sent to us by computer. Every name processed by midnight reaches us before working hours the next morning. Matrixx sends, by FAX or modem, daily counts of what each phone number for that advertiser pulled each hour. This can be entered into computers of the client or advertising agency. Projections of future response can be estimated and modified daily. When urgently needed, Matrixx can update statistics hourly.

Growing Bureau Flexibility

We do not use Matrixx or any other service bureau to take orders for either of our catalogs. We have many items and accessories, and our own staff advises our customers to aid in the best selection. What is right for each business depends on many factors, and these factors keep changing. Key information can now be put on computer about any company, product, or line for instant flash-up on the screen to answer detailed questions. Hence, many more catalogers are now able to use service bureaus to take their in-bound phone orders.

Matrixx, and many service bureaus, will provide a special staff dedicated and specially trained to take orders for any of a variety of products for one client. The trend is to offer more services. Matrixx has an automated 800 and 900 in-bound call department. It has an out-bound telemarketing department, does market research by phone, manages databases, and has a fulfillment center. Matrixx will also stock products and literature for clients and fulfills orders and info requests.

Two Ways to Overcome Bureau Disadvantages

One approach is to bring a key phone representative from a bureau to your office to become completely indoctrinated in your business. The representative listens in as calls are handled and each day is taught more about products, offers, and your company background. The representative then handles calls alone, with a company expert and/or another salesperson listening in. Then, there is a "post-mortem" analysis with the representative. The phone representative returns to the bureau, puts all the needed information on computer so that a single key stroke can call up the right answers, and, finally, trains the other reps. The reverse is to send your own expert at handling in-house calls to the bureau to work as one of their phone representatives, supply all the needed information for their computer, and teach their people your business.

Use a telephone service bureau from the start for simple offers, provided that you give them thorough information. For any complex offer, or for those with many choices (and particularly for a catalog), start by taking calls within your own company. Then consider finding the right telemarketing service bureau that is oriented to complex offers.

What Are Your Needs?

To close an inquiry by phone is quite different from making an appointment for a salesperson, from referring the caller to a dealer, from qualifying and sending a mailing piece, or from phoning back later. To properly handle a phone inquiry from a customer is quite different from talking to a caller who has never dealt with your company.

The point is that your company may face varied in-bound phone situations. Select your staff or service bureau based on who is best suited to those most frequent, critical needs.

As your needs change, so must your operations. The biggest danger ironically comes when growth is sudden and big. An optimist responsible for marketing and handling the calls may keep expanding. Overcapacity can kill all your profits. If a pessimist is responsible for handling response, big trouble is also coming. Busy signals mean lost sales and added promotional costs never recouped. A realist must be vigilant and constantly check both capacity and promotional plans. How good is your present method?

Bureau Costs.   Bureau costs per call vary all over the lot—from as little as $1.15 to take an inquiry. In-bound pricing is usually based on a per-call rate, with price breaks upon reaching certain volume levels. But cost alone should not determine your bureau selection. As with any other service, check references. Look for clients with similar projected volume and types of products or services. Make sure you understand their reports and that they are forwarded in a timely fashion.

How Many Calls Do You Lose?   Phone your own 800 number. If busy, try every so often. AT&T will give you a printout which shows you each attempt to reach you, the area code, where the call originated, and the time of day made within the requested 24-hour time period. Find out how many orders you lose because you have too few phone representatives.

JC Penney gets over 200,000 calls every day on average. Yet in one week, JC Penney answered 78 percent more—or 2.5 million calls—with an average answering time of just two-and-a-half rings. How about your firm?

U.S. Monitor (USM) calls *Fortune 500* and other clients' offices to inquire, place an order, or complain and then makes a report as to how the matter was handled.

How to Avoid the Biggest In-Bound Telemarketing Disasters

To a big direct marketer, a breakdown of phone reception and handling by a service bureau can cause huge losses. If you're big, use two bureaus with each ready to take over from the other. Whatever your size, a phone breakdown in-house can be disastrous. Always have a service bureau ready to take over as needed.

Most phone-handling disasters come from failure to predict a flood of calls from a new promotion. Most efficient service bureaus have limits to their ability to handle larger jumps in calls than predetermined estimates. Unless you're JC Penney, AT&T, American Express, or a handful of other mammoth facilities, in-house facilities are even less flexible.

If your advertising asks for a phone order for a single item and volume is big and in bursts, train your people to get each order fast and jump off the line for the next one. If there's still a backlog, take the name and phone number and phone back. You can then often upgrade and cross-sell.

Don't Waste Your Advertising

Never, never buy advertising asking people to phone you unless you're equipped to handle the calls. Advertising costs per call can only be low if you answer every call possible. To predict, make tests to determine how many calls per thousand readers, viewers, or listeners you get and when and how fast they come after the advertising runs. You must then predict reasonably accurately how many calls will come in when placing new advertising.

Make a projection of the anticipated phone calls in the course of each day of your campaign. If you use broadcast radio and TV, be prepared for the "burst"—the calls received immediately after the message airs. Estimate how many calls will be in each burst and how much you will receive from each spot on each station, and be ready. It's very detailed but surprisingly possible.

A College Dropout's Lesson

A college dropout teaches best what organized in-bound telemarketing requires most—the product and service concepts that makes it possible. When he quit the University of Texas at Austin after one year, he was already getting over $50,000 of phone orders to his dormitory room a month. He had one assistant, and he was 18 years old.

His name is Michael Dell. He left to start Dell Computer Corp. When he was 26, Dell Computer's annual revenues were over three-quarters of a billion dollars, with almost 85 percent of sales coming in by phone. To start, Dell did not:

1. Have previous experience telemarketing anything

2. Learn from others anything about telemarketing

3. Hire highly experienced telephone sales persons

4. Create a phone sales script

5. Have any knowledge of phone marketing, direct response, phone technology, or how to get the lowest phone rates.

Many have called Michael Dell a genius. But the rest of us often need more guidance. And what Dell did is perhaps the best guidance of all: his notions of what is required to grow a business before anything else and his next priorities step by step.

Know-How Needed Most. Dell had been a computer bug since 12 and a kid entrepreneur since junior high. First, as a paper boy for the *Houston Post*, he recruited crews of students to sell and deliver papers and made tens of thousands of dollars.

At college, what Michael learned most was in Austin's new PC computer stores. Three years before, IBM had launched its PC, and PC clones began storming in. Peripherals of every kind were pouring out. Dell became a master at selecting and combining a computer chassis with peripherals and components. He could select a chassis here, hard drive there, and on and on until he had a better PC combo than most brands for less money. He sold one, then another, starting with an investment of under $1000.

New Concept. Michael did not sell any one computer make. His concept was never to sell anything to anyone unless it was the best buy for the buyer's purpose. He listened to each person's needs. He advised what computer combination fitted best. As a perfectionist purchasing agent for each customer, he bought first from dealers, often their overstocked items. He custom-assembled for each order.

Then Michael offered nationally what he did locally. He ran a half-page direct-response ad (prepared by a one-man Austin ad agency) in *PC Week.* The ad featured a PC clone but gave no address. No one could buy by mail; instead, the ad featured a big 800 number. Dell answered the phone himself from his dormitory room. He used a tape recorder as a back-up to take phone numbers when he was on the line.

Perfect Timing.   The first calls were from business people, often financially oriented professionals. The callers included small business owners, executives of big companies, and department managers in every kind of enterprise. They were more sophisticated in their know-how and often had technical knowledge. The callers wanted PCs to make money and to save money in specific ways. They had strong expectations. Direct-response ads were suspect. They wanted someone knowledgeable they trusted.

The new computer stores hired personnel that were often unfamiliar with business needs. And most salespeople who called on offices almost always worked for one manufacturer, rarely offered PCs, and were not applications-oriented. Programmers who talked to businesspeople knew one make best and usually worked with mainframes or minis.

Michael was an entrepreneur. He knew PCs. He thought in terms of how to best select, combine, and use PCs for specific business applications. He avoided orders from anyone whose needs he did not know. He was a free consultant.

A Trusted Phone Advisor.   Michael did not call anyone cold. He did not phone back a customer to sell more unless he had something new that was right for the customer's needs. To do this, he took careful notes and kept studying each new PC development. He became a phone advisor of what hardware to buy for the continuing computing needs that he could supply.

Almost from the beginning, customers reordered. They upgraded. They recommended Dell to others—all to a voice on a phone. Enough bought on the first call so that his advertising cost was paid for. He ran more ads to get more businesspeople to call him. With more orders, he bought at lower prices. Soon he teamed up with a dealer who could place a bigger manufacturer order. He then began to do the same with importers. Then he left college to found Dell Computer Corp., right in Austin.

Expanding In-Bound Phone Success.   He put an ad in the Austin paper and advertised for more Michaels—computer bugs who had a flair for business and who could also talk the language of serious PC buyers. Austin was a reservoir of them. It had computer plants, high-technology firms, big businesses with executive computer-users, and the University of Texas with 50,000 students and plenty of computer courses.

Michael interviewed and hired four recruits, made each a computer purchasing advisor, and advertised more. They could barely keep up. Calls came in so fast, representatives jumped from one call to another, often keeping the first call on hold. Customers who could not wait were lost. Each rep was on his or her own. There was no time to train or to measure, analyze, or compare performance. Within two years, volume had leaped up. By now, 20 phone representatives (each hired after a final interview by Dell) barely kept up, but most customers were happy.

Sales and Profits Jumping.   With more and more of the sales to repeat customers and with no more advertising expense, Dell could sell for less than stores and make more profit per dollar than most importers. Michael saw that growing businesses never stopped needing new, improved, and different PCs and more of them. But he also knew his telemarketing could only be corrected along with other changes.

Michael did not want just to catch up to orders. He wanted the best computer combination in the world for each purpose—quality at the best price, volume delivery on promised schedules and dependable customer support. But what he wanted was ahead of computer product design available to him. He did not want to import clones and be forever behind the latest models of the big, national manufacturers. He wanted Dell Computers to have the same advanced features as fast as and even before the biggest name brands. He wanted to control design, manufacture, quality control, and delivery for his customers.

In its third year, Dell Computer Corp. launched its own design computers and did almost $70 million in sales. Michael was 20 years old. His sales and profit rise was so meteoric that the next year, at 21, he raised $21 million privately. The year after, Dell Computer raised $30 million more, going public. He was 22. Almost all sales still came by phone.

Traveling First Class.   Michael still did not hire a telemarketing sales expert. Instead, he hired top talent from the biggest companies to design and build computers. He hired an expert on phone technology who also was a specialist in rates charged by each phone company for any purpose. He brought in one of the best direct-mail people in the country who began to mail the Dell list, on an organized basis.

Dell set up a human resources department to build leadership from within. A training program for phone representatives was headed by a top educator. Training was not devoted to selling but to how to be a "Dell Computer expert." Sessions taught representatives how to *listen* and what to ask in order to recommend the best choice.

By now, the Dell phone support system had solved 90 percent of product problems by phone. For any remaining problems, Xerox serviced every Dell computer at the customer's location.

In-Bound Phone Profit Machine.   In Dell's fourth year, the firm did $159,037,000 and in its fifth $257,810,000. After-tax profits jumped up to close to 10 percent. In the sixth year, sales leaped to $546,000,000. The seventh year sales soared to $889.9 million dollars. And profits kept rising even faster. The vast majority of the business was repeat.

At last count, Dell Computer Corp. employed over 200 in-bound phone representatives. Representatives do keep up with calls. But Dell now goes beyond its traditional computer magazines, testing step by step new ways that could multiply its in-bound calls and perhaps teach us far more.

Few of us can be a Michael Dell. But we can come up with a right new concept to make profitable Organized Inbound Telemarketing possible.

Some Other Ideas That Have Worked

The following are examples of in-bound telemarketing ideas that have succeeded:

Start international niche services.   Long & Foster, in Fairfax, Virginia, specializes in transfer real estate from overseas to Washington, D.C., and Baltimore. This service business targets people in the military or corporate world stationed in a new area. Long & Foster brokers conduct real estate and financial seminars at bases and embassies abroad, offering those who are interested 800 numbers in England, Germany, and the United States to phone when ready. When the phone call comes in, the representative finds out the kind of home wanted, the preferred type of community, plus the price range and down payment capabilities. Then their sales associates look for houses for the transferee. Houses are often found before the client leaves for home.

Deliver worldwide.   Arnold A. Kowalsky organized a service to deliver bottles or cases of liquor to 45 countries around the world. It's a division of 800 Spirits of which he is executive vice president of marketing. Just order by phone.

Give a unique phone service. TELEDAG is a D'Agostino Supermarket ordering service by phone. Everything costs the same as at the store (plus a modest delivery fee). Any day but Sunday, 8 a.m. to 8 p.m., an order-taker handles your call and can even discuss meal-planning and housekeeping. You get same-day delivery and can pay by credit card or cash.

Offer a new and widely needed service. If you need cash, call Telecash. Right after the call you can take your picture I.D. to the service desk at a listed supermarket and get $100. The phone company adds $16.50 to your bill. The $16.50 is your interest divided up between Telecash, the supermarket, and the phone company.

Refer clients to your clients. St. Luke's/Roosevelt Hospital Center advertised its New York DOCTOR Line. This was a referral phone service to match your specific needs with hundreds of New York's best doctors covering all specialties. It promised prompt referrals usually within minutes.

Use the phone to take repeat orders. Digital Equipment Corporation wants its direct sales force primarily to create new sales. DEC installed a toll-free in-bound number for customers. They then set up a policy to ship phone orders within 48 hours. This freed the sales force for new business.

All forms of telemarketing are growing so fast that *U.S. News & World Report* repeatedly has cited it as one of the fastest-growing industries in the United States through the end of this century and beyond.

Help Source Guide

1. *American Telemarketing Association* publishes a journal for members only. Nonmembers can order a video training package or a brochure; the Association also sponsors two annual conventions: 606 N. Larchmont Blvd., Suite 4B, Los Angeles, CA 90004. (800) 441-3335.

2. *Business by Phone, Inc.,* provides a *free* catalog about phone-training books, audios, videos, manuals, offering good buys. A *free* sample of the *Telephone Selling Report* newsletter is also available: 5301 S. 144th St., Omaha, NE 68137. (800) 326-7721.

3. The Telephone Marketing Council of the *Direct Marketing Association* sponsors the Annual Telephone Marketing Conference, seminars, video- and audiotapes: 11 W. 42d St., NY, NY 10036-8096. (212) 768-7277.

4. R. Bencin and D. Jonovic edited the *Encyclopedia of Telemarketing* (Prentice-Hall, 1989), with 32 experts contributing. Jampacked, this is a practical guide with over 700 pages and useful strategies. Available in libraries or direct: P.O. Box 11071, Des Moines, IA 50336.

5. *Free* information kits on in-bound 800/900 rates and features and a *free* booklet series, *Telecommunications Ideas to Grow On,* from AT&T: (800) 222-0400.

   Free information kits on in-bound 800/900: MCI (800) 444-3333; Sprint (800) 877-2000.

6. *Inbound/Outbound* magazine is available with special issues on training, equipment, software, service bureaus; find in a library or subscribe: 12 West 21st St., NY, NY 10010. (212) 206-6660.

7. *TeleProfessional* magazine addresses effective marketing via telecommunications. For a *free* sample or subscription: 209 W. 5th St., Suite N, Waterloo, IA 50701. (800) 338-8307.

8. *Telemarketing* magazine provides a combined conference and exhibit, "Telemarketing & Business Telecommunications" yearly in the East, Midwest, and West. Special issues include "50 Top Inbound Service Bureaus," "Buyers' Guide." "100 Do's and Don'ts." Catalogs available on books, video- and audiotapes; back-issue articles. Contact: Technology Marketing Corp., One Technology Plaza., Norwalk, CT 06854. (800) 243-6002. (203) 852-6800.

9. H. Newton, E. Leibowitz, and the *Teleconnect* magazine Research Group wrote *Which Phone System Should I Buy?, A Guide to Key Systems* (1991); Mini PBXs. In its eighth edition, the book addresses how to buy the right phone system for 2 to 200 people: Telecom Library Inc., 12 W. 21st St., NY, NY 10010. 800-LIBRARY.

9

Organized
Out-Bound
Telemarketing

Every salesperson uses the phone to prepare the way for a sale, to follow up, and, when possible, to save the time and expense of a face-to-face meeting by actually completing the sale. Out-bound telemarketing assists or replaces certain functions of a personal-visit sales force. In ever more ways, every kind of enterprise phones regularly to market almost anything.

For example, a packaged goods marketer phones retailers to set up a store promotion for a cents-off coupon, premium, or free goods offer. A retailer calls a customer or prospect to offer to open a credit account. A mortgage broker phones in search of home owners and buyers; seminar telephone sales representatives call to try to land more attenders. Each year, calls to members raise billions of dollars for labor unions, alumni associations, church groups, medical causes, and political organizations. *It's all out-bound telemarketing.*

Just about any kind of company as well as many nonprofit organizations use it. This includes most companies with a dedicated sales force; almost every politician; most publications and banks; and probably all public TV stations. Who else? Most nonprofit fundraising efforts, department stores, and almost all colleges and cable systems; more and more manufacturers, importers, specialty retailers, jobbers; and innumerable other services.

McGraw-Hill reported years ago that the average cost for a company to send a salesperson to a business prospect had *jumped* to well over $300 per sales call. Now, it's much higher. To close a sale, the typical salesperson averages 5.5 visits to a prospect. At the same time, long-distance phone rates have *dropped.* Plus *new technology* now helps telephone representatives call faster and more effectively. The result is a phone contact that can cost one-twentieth or even one-fortieth of a sales visit. Consider these advantages of out-bound telemarketing:

- You can reach virtually every home and business.
- A phone conversation is one to one: It's the closest thing to being there.
- Telephone conversations allow you to answer objections ads can't.
- Phoning gives you a fast, reliable, and acceptable vehicle for continuing and regular follow-up.
- Out-bound telemarketing offers an ever lower cost per contact compared to other methods.
- At a tiny cost to start, it can give you big, controlled growth.

But out-bound telemarketing is no "open sesame." A marketer must realize these disadvantages:

- It costs far more per person to call than to mail.
- Conversations can be misunderstood more than print.
- Telemarketing can be the most intrusive and thus the most resented form of marketing.
- Telemarketing is difficult to master and control.
- Telemarketing has a high percentage of failure.

The use of outbound telemarketing to sell a single item for under $20 with little or no follow-up sales potential usually fails. For these low-end sales items, a phone follow-up campaign to inquiries usually means a worse failure. And to phone for the same item "cold" (prospects that you've not had a prior relation with)—in order to try to qualify them for follow-up by any means—usually fails most of all. Quite simply, the cost of any of these methods is usually more than the profit margin in the sale.

Avoiding Failure

Out-bound telephone sales efforts fail most often due to poor organization or a flawed marketing concept, and out-bound telemarketing failures are often self-created. Listen to any of those who call you to sell you anything. Most will quickly teach you what not to do, usually with calls that should never have been made.

Richard L. Bencin, editor of *Encyclopedia of Telemarketing,* says, "Less than five percent of those who try to telemarket outbound do it in a properly planned way. And only a very small percentage of these, including many big companies, use it scientifically." Organized out-bound telemarketing done scientifically is a big endeavor. The right kind of program for you may involve one step or several. It may require a combination of other media and selling methods best suited to you. But the right formula can be determined and tested—often easily and quickly, for little money and risk.

Out-bound telemarketing plans can be expanded safely. If your program works with 5 telemarketers, it usually can successfully expand to 10 and perhaps 100 or even thousands. Your marketing effort can create big growth and profits, but only with planning, continued caution, and checking of results at each step.

Telemarketing and the Smallest Business

An out-bound phone representative always in the office can qualify inquiries for, assist and extend the value of each of these important sales functions. Vital answers needed by a customer on inventory, delivery dates, new product information, and how-to expertise can be communicated by trained telephone representatives.

Whatever your firm size or its field, out-bound telemarketing can be profitable in some way. It can be used *correctly* to some degree for almost any kind of item or service. Even if your company is small and you have done no organized out-bound telemarketing, starting is far simpler than you might guess. Before you buy any special equipment, get special phone rates, or investigate selection and training of staff, start with one person—perhaps yourself—and apply simple business logic.

Try First What Is Easiest

Customers prefer to buy more from a firm that has previously given them good products and service. Therefore, it's many times easier to sell by phone any product or service to a customer than to someone who's never done business with you. Common sense dictates that it's safest and the least risky to phone customers who *want* you to call—provided it's done in an organized way that's beneficial to all.

First, let all your commissioned sales people know what the plan is, after constructing one that will not hurt their commissions. Perhaps they will continue to receive commissions on phone sales for their accounts while they develop new accounts. Draw them into the process;

after all, you're both after the same thing—more sales, profits, and loyal customers.

Ask customers who order by phone, or those you visit personally, if they wish to be phoned back when specific items are on sale; an out-of-stock item arrives; a new, improved model comes; answers to customer questions are determined. Ask each customer when would it be most convenient to call. Build a small list of those who say yes to each category. Start with a few calls on one phone.

Before you start on any scale, be sure that you know your own product or service, what your competition offers at what price, and what your customers like about your products and firm. Study each customer's buying record. Decide what you want to propose and how.

Tell Them What They Want to Know

A retailer wants to know what is selling best where. All businesses want to know about a product that's applicable to their business and which has paid for itself, whether it be in labor saving or in extra sales. And virtually every customer badly wants pertinent information that can help his or her business or personal life.

What you advise is the key. Know your field and what your customers need, want, and can afford. Speak their language. Offer some special advantage that's right for each:

1. Phone and ask for reorder from the following:
   a. A regular customer—mention frequent buyer program
   b. An occasional customer—announce special sale coming up
   c. A new customer—say thanks, welcome, and give your name and extension
2. Call back to upgrade phone order just received to:
   a. Deluxe model
   b. Multiple sale at saving
   c. Longer subscription at saving
   d. Highly related add-on
   e. Less related add-on, but on sale.
3. Call back inactive customers to:
   a. Check if they're unhappy with the company. If so, try to correct the problem.
   b. Offer concession on first reorder.

Always ask if and when you can call back again. And always try to learn more about the future wants of each customer. Take notes to enable you during the next phone call to propose the right products needed then. Work in tandem with your sales force and your direct mail to follow up your calls. Win your customers' trust and build their desire to deal with your firm long-term. Get recommendations.

Vulcan Binder & Cover sends businesses its catalogs of loose-leaf binders and related items; 25 percent of the firm's sales comes from out-bound telemarketing, mostly by a series of follow-up calls to recent buyers to increase the amount of their order by informing them of special offers. Fidelity Products, an office supply cataloger, uses telemarketing to reactivate customers who hadn't ordered in one to three years. And Enterprise Publishing mainly uses out-bound telemarketing to call previous customers, adding about 10 percent to their total sales.

Next Easiest Calls

The next most promising candidates are your most seriously interested prospects, those who have contacted your firm recently, asking for more specific information. Few firms follow up inquiries properly. Yet these prospects want someone with expertise to tell them quickly and correctly exactly what they want to know in order to decide whether to buy and what to buy. Such prospects may include the following cases:

- Interest as a result of a customer recommendation
- Response to a company promotion or trade-in offer
- A call for a specific price quote
- An enthused inquiry to a product PR story
- An enthused inquiry after trade booth walk-in pitch
- A service support phone line caller, asking about an upgrade
- A qualified inquiry from advertising
- An answer to an 800 or 900 phone number description of a product offer
- A friend of a customer

Some call for themselves and some for their boss. Some want a personal visit at their office, some want to be called right back. Some want literature and then a call, and some want the information without a call. Some want to be called when back from a trip on a certain day or week. Each may prefer a different time to be called. An alert salesperson grabs any such promising lead and prepares special information suited to the call.

Classify the calls. When you call to find out how to help, you'll find that some are dreamers or have already bought from the competition. When you check, some have bad credit. Some will be marked NG and thrown out, or kept as part of your suppress list, not to be promoted to or responded to in the future. Mark those for further follow-up as *A*, *B*, or *C*, or however many categories you require.

Concentrate on your *A* list. Make a tickler file of when to call each on the list, with notes added from your first call. Each call adds more notes about each lead. Whether you ask for an order or arrange to send literature or make an appointment, you quickly find that inquiries from certain sources have a higher percentage of closure than others. Your time is money. Each minute costs dollars. By sampling calls to a small number of inquiries from the same source, you can soon concentrate on those from sources most responsive. Multiplying this process and applying it to more kinds of possible names to call makes out-bound telemarketing profitable.

Database Marketing

The science and art of gathering, organizing, and continually determining how best to market your products to prospects is the basis of database marketing. It starts with understanding and developing different selling approaches depending upon your customers' various needs and desires, then applying those and other marketing techniques to those who contact you in ways mentioned above. But database marketing goes far beyond these classifications. Only with the best possible database of whom to call (and with enough key facts about each) can your calls pay off. For more detailed information on database marketing, see Chapter 2's Help Source Guide.

For your database, beyond those listed above, there are others who have contacted your company who are worth calling for specific products, services, and offers most suited to them. These names may include the following:

- More restrained inquiries to product PR
- Casual trade show inquiries
- Magazine "bingo" card respondees
- Magazine 800-line bingo requests
- Information package requests
- Company 800-line information requests
- Service booklet recipients
- Mail-order purchasers from your firm
- Charge account holders
- Warranty card owners

- Purchasers of a premium from the company
- Survey responders

Before calling any such names, you must realize that

1. The total number of people on such lists can be very big.
2. These lists will vary a lot in responsiveness.
3. Most calls will probably fail.
4. The biggest classifications are often the least qualified.
5. The better segments of failed lists may still work.

Database marketing segments lists of people into groups in many ways: by recency, frequency, and/or dollars of orders for customers; by gender; or by kinds of products previously bought from your firm. Segmentation can be overlaid with more information, such as the average income and value of house in the zip code or even the financial rating of a business; its size, SIC code, whether it's a branch office or headquarters; and any other number of criteria that seems to be telling.

Start simply, with the newest names from sources that seem the most logical. Make 50 completed calls to each group. Before throwing out a classification or segment that proves unresponsive, mail a letter or postcard (at a fraction of the cost per name) asking them to phone you for the desired information.

For a borderline classification or segment, try a one-minute call to make a telephone appointment (TA) for yourself before going into a lengthier conversation. If any group responds, call a 100, then 500, then 1000 (as long as they continue to prove profitable). Or write first to five times as many. Experiment in your follow-up.

Use marketing synergy. Marketing tools used together in an organized way often create sales that would not otherwise occur or at a lower cost per sale than with one tool. A combination of media often yields better results faster. Ernan Roman, author of *Integrated Marketing,* cites many cases of increased sales and profits from combining outbound phone with other media. Try to integrate your cold calls with a follow-up information kit or other direct mail. Or if your product warrants the expense, send a video, audiotape, or computer disk. Or combine telemarketing with other electronic forms. Most chapters in this book have examples.

For bigger orders, the first call often qualifies and makes a telephone appointment to call back. Follow-up calls are often combined with literature, letters, and, for business calls, fax. Phone selling can be auxiliary to a sales force or replace a sales force for out-of-the-way locations, smaller accounts, or bread-and-butter repeat business.

Cold Calls

Now let's consider the phone selling most difficult to master, with the highest rate of mortality that, if suited to you and mastered, yields the most long-term sales. Cold calling is all these things and is also the most misused telemarketing tool.

Misuse includes stockbrokers using phones like shotguns to call cold, laying waste to the telemarketing landscape. Often several brokers or insurance agents from the same firm call the same person within days. More than a dozen people have called to sell a newspaper subscription to the same person, after being asked to stop.

Such cold calling drives people wild, causing antiphone legislation and creating stonewall phone resistance to the next person who calls. Such junk phoning comprises calls that should never be made. Nothing annoys me more than being called by someone I don't know about something I don't want or can't afford. Even worse are cold calls from robotlike machines. *Resistance to all cold calls is building tremendously.* Many firms, hugely successful at in-bound telemarketing, won't touch out-bound telemarketing because of its reputation as an overly intrusive and irritating sales method. Stay away from using it as a marketing "shotgun" to sell anybody anything.

In the spirit of database marketing, only call those most likely to be interested and avoid irritating others. Any cold-call telemarketing is only justified in narrow-niche marketing, reaching special groups with special needs. Cold calling to get an inquiry or to make a sale theoretically can be targeted to prospects most likely to want your product, when they are most likely to buy. But cold calling is not for the neophyte. Follow these cold-call commandments:

1. *Master database marketing* to call those who need you most and can best afford what you offer.

2. *Acquire expertise and know-how* about your products and services. Offer advice on your products' various uses and the best buy for the prospect's purpose.

3. *Phone others as you wish to be phoned!* Inform as you would like to be informed. Don't act like, really *be* a friend.

4. *Protect customers' time as if your own!* Don't destroy phone buying's biggest advantage—saving time.

5. *Find out fast if you've called a prospect*—now, later, or not at all. Then inform and advise, call back, or thank and get off.

Cold calling is the entrepreneur's friend. It is with ideas well suited to others that we persuade. Perhaps the idea is a way of saving or making money or a new answer to an old problem. How many times have entrepreneurs thought of applications of their products or services that were ideal for certain businesses, picked up the phones, called strangers, and arranged for appointments that benefited everybody? The ideal application saves or makes enough money for an entire classification of business firms, so that similar calls made to more strangers results in more mutual benefit.

Cold Calling's First Problem

If you call someone at home, often you get an answering machine. And when you call a business, it's common to reach an automated voice system. The message you leave can start or end your chances. Don't conceal or mislead. In your first words to anyone, or as a message, capsule why you are calling; that you have news, and why you should be talked to. If your prices are going up, if your firm has some special offer, if there is reason for urgency say so, *quietly*.

If your call is to someone logical and your message practical, you will likely get a call back. If he or she is out and you can reach a human voice, find out the best time to call back. At home, everyone's best time differs widely. At the office, it's surprisingly easy to get executives directly on the phone once you've learned the habits of each. With every call, update your database and tickler file.

Calling Someone You Don't Know

Even if your company is famous, you are a stranger. If your firm is unknown, you are more suspect. If you get your prospect on the phone, start your conversation with the same information you typically leave on the tape machine. If you get a call back, it's still wise to identify yourself by virtually repeating the same words as in the message. To make each word that you now say most effective, Richard Bencin suggests the following:

1. *Adapt to the prospect's pace* and way of talking, and let it determine how much you say and what you advise.

2. *Create a dialogue.* Ask his or her needs, problems, product-feature likes and dislikes. Get the person you call to talk 50 percent of the time.

3. *Guide to the close.* Listen, respond, converse, but work in each key point of your product's story—briefly and clearly.

4. *Ask for a yes* as soon as the reaction indicates it's plausible. Keep asking. Stop selling as soon as you hear "yes." But confirm.

5. *Learn from failures.* Ask people who said no why each did. Make a friend you can call again.

Revolutionize Your Business by Phone

You probably view your business as being "different," with its own peculiar sales problems, special kind of customers, and product story. Not the ideal telemarketing candidate, you might think. Consider how one businessman with no previous phone marketing background found phone success.

Nadji Tehrani started a magazine on polyurethane technology, one on radiation engineering, and then another on technology marketing. When he travelled to see the most logical specialized advertisers, he successfully sold ads—but at great travel expense. Moreover, he could not find enough area representatives who could sell ads as successfully. Then he tried to sell ads by phone from his office and succeeded. But when he tried to get others to sell by phone, again he failed. Nadji's situation and what he did about it may help you. He reports:

Getting started, we made every mistake in the book. I learned from each what not to do and most of all from my three biggest mistakes.

Mistake #1

When I asked outside reps to sell by phone this failed miserably. (Even if someone is capable of selling in person, he or she may fail on the phone). I put my best salesman on the phone. He had charisma and body language. He understood the art of persuasion—in the office with someone. But he failed on the phone.

Mistake #2

I interviewed, in person, many candidates for selling on the phone; a huge mistake. What you see isn't what anyone hears by phone. Interview potential phone sales reps by phone, never first in person. I suddenly realized that extroverts were good as outside salesmen but introverts were good as inside salesmen. The phone had to be intimate. It was best when you made calls from a bedroom, relaxed.

Mistake #3

I put all the new reps on the phone without training, product knowledge, industry knowledge or competitor knowledge (without which no one can sell anything). For these reasons, I continued to fail and nothing was working. I knew only that I could sell. It occurred to me that one reason was that I had adequate knowledge about all of our publications.

A Lucky, Common-Sense Solution

I sensed that one of the office secretaries, who had never been a salesperson, could be the answer. She had extensive knowledge of all our publications—plus an outstanding phone voice, a tremendous phone manner and "telephone personality." Above all, she sounded very honest and believable on the phone.

At first, she was very reluctant to have anything to do with sales. To encourage and motivate her, I told her that this could be a golden opportunity for her and all that she had to do was to have a positive, flexible, candid attitude toward the project.

I suggested that she go at it with 110 percent enthusiasm and positive thinking and know that she was offering the best product in the market and that she was the right person to do the job! I also added that if she was successful and really gave it 110 percent, she would get a *major* bonus by the end of the week.

In one week she sold 20 percent more advertising. In three months she got it up 55 percent. One by one, I found other reps like her, and trained each to sell the same way.

Nadji also recruited and trained in-bound phone sales reps to service advertisers. Now about 60 percent of Nadji Tehrani's phone selling staff does out-bound marketing, very successfully. Meanwhile, Nadji Tehrani began to share with others what he had learned. He now publishes *Telemarketing* magazine and operates a telemarketing trade show which runs once a year in the East, once in the Midwest, and once in the West. (See entry 6 in the Help Source Guide.) Thank you, Nadji.

Here are 10 tips for cold-call success:

1. *Target big-volume, new customers.* Northwest Orient Airlines created $3.1 million in new business with out-bound telemarketing to its most logical air freight prospects.

2. *Phone your customers with news.* R & R Direct, the computer supply catalog subsidiary of Reynolds & Reynolds, doubled its sales in three years. Via its out-bound telemarketing program, R & R Direct offered the latest, best-suited state-of-the-art peripherals and computer software.

3. *Sell by phone what others don't.* The New England Shrimp Company sells seafood items by phone to food brokers nationally. They "phone market" new products, plus reopen accounts and open new ones.

4. *Target special groups with unusual service.* Advanced Entertainment sells over $500,000 a year in Broadway and Off-Broadway tickets by phone. It offers credit card payment to identified theatergoers and uses the phone to sell them on seeing new products before they become box-office smashes.

5. *Third-party sponsorship.* Ally yourself with trust, strength, and credibility. A children's photo studio photographs each student in a class and then telemarkets to the parents of each. The studio operates with the blessing of the school and the parents and is a great success.

6. *Go after repeat customers.* When cold calls are so tough, why not sell something that leads to an easier sale of repeat orders every year? Learn from the child photographer.

7. *Cover accounts the sales force rarely will.* Signal Thread Company makes and distributes commercial sewing threads. Its nine field salespeople handle key accounts. Each of Signal's out-bound telemarketers handles 800 smaller accounts.

8. *Export sales by phone.* DenMat, in Santa Maria, California, has four phone representatives who just call Canada. They sell more each month than DenMat's Canadian distributor sold in a year.

9. *Tell what's newly available.* Delaware Valley Wholesale Florists calls on 600 florists each day across the nation. Its flowers may be cut in Holland on a Tuesday, shipped to florists in the United States by Wednesday, and delivered to customers by Wednesday night. It has to be able to tell the florists what's available and to take the orders as fast as they are available.

10. *Make the sales force more efficient.* General Foods Corporation's Food Service Product Division used a telemarketing campaign to get leads for their sales representatives. Ninety-five percent of the representatives were able to close sales on leads they were given, because telemarketers first determined whether a prospect was interested.

Growing by Out-bound Phone

Modest-size firms can start out-bound telemarketing in very small ways with almost no out-of-pocket expense. Small divisions of bigger companies also can start simply. But when the first tests succeed, growth problems of out-bound telemarketing start. To avoid the pitfalls of growth, follow these steps:

1. Expand your promotion and PR activity to create a "warmer" environment in which to call.

2. Build your database of other, likely prospects to call.

3. Increase your personal telemarketing effectiveness.

4. Multiply yourself by recruiting and training others.

5. Prune the unproductive telephone representatives and motivate the winners.

6. Increase your effectiveness and productivity by investing in telemarketing technology.

If you are successful on even a very small scale in any of the ways we've covered, you can expand—but don't go full-steam. If you are a one-person business with little money, you have only yourself to train and plenty of incentive. As you succeed, you must train others in how to sell your company's offerings by phone. Perfecting your own sales approach is the first step.

Analyze your phone selling effectiveness. Tape yourself in a practice call to a friend acting the part of a cold-call prospect. Talk in your own words. Listen and then transcribe your conversation. Read it carefully and analyze your impromptu "script." You probably spoke well in parts but left out some key elements of what you planned to say. Perhaps you didn't ask for action soon enough. Or your words were not always simple enough to grasp. More than likely, your call also took longer than it should.

Don't be discouraged. Each call is a lesson, teaching you new permutations of prospect reactions and the kind of advice each type may seek. As this experience grows and your expertise increases, your phone marketing effectiveness will increase. Correcting performance means more yes decisions from each ten calls, more calls per day, and more sales and profits per day, week, month, and year.

Telemarketing Scripts

Should you use a word-processed script? Yes, as a guide. Richard Bencin points out that a phone representative with no script will create a talk pattern anyway and say virtually the same thing to everyone. Unfortunately, this talk pattern is often the wrong thing, said in the wrong way. Besides missing many good points, an unscripted out-bound telemarketing representative can offend people and lose orders.

What should be in a script? Joel Linchitz, author of *The Complete Guide to Telemarketing Management*, thinks that the script should:

1. Get through to the decision maker.
2. Capture attention in 20 seconds or less.
3. Get the prospect to conduct at least half the conversation.
4. Ask effective questions at the right time.
5. Use words that create a visual selling image.
6. Offer features and benefits concisely and persuasively.
7. Give several options, in case the first answer is no.

Creating a Script

Tape yourself or whatever associate is most effective on the phone as you or he or she says naturally the words and phrases that make a sale. Now edit the transcription of a call to add what you forgot. Eliminate the unnecessary and improve with shorter, simpler, plainer words where needed—this may work as your basic script. Always look for ways to improve your script. Write down the ten interrupting objections you most often get, with a rebuttal for each. Put in a notebook with a flag tab for each. Then flick to each objection as needed.

Don't memorize or read your script. It will sound stilted, unnatural. The script is there as a guide. You may prefer an outline. But the discipline of scripting will help your out-bound calls become more profitable. And when you hire others to telemarket, sticking to a script is much more necessary—especially for beginners or if your offer is simple.

If you sell a complex product or line of goods, your telemarketing staff may require more detailed expertise (and may have to answer a very wide variety of questions) than a simple paper script or guide can accommodate. Although scripting is more difficult in these situations, computer screen prompting systems can prove to be invaluable.

Staffing and Training

Richard L. Bencin suggests the following steps for starting your program, hiring staff, and providing training:

1. Make a long-term telemarketing plan. Start with a research outline. Get the answers in order to determine your objectives.
2. Win the cooperation within your company, small or big. And submit your plan, before starting, to all who can make it work or block it.
3. Before you hire phone reps, select the right phone-sales boss. The choice will decide your outbound telemarketing success or failure.

4. Get a professional telemarketer that's suited to you—with proven aptitude within the business-to-business or consumer field, within a small or huge staff, and capable of handling one product or many.

5. Pay more to get more. Offer a bigger salary, incentives and good raises. If your company is lean, raise the commissions or consider partnership.

6. Seek reps who are curious, eager to learn, persuasive and who have the same experience and background of those reps who performed successfully in your tests.

7. Hire each cautiously, to your needs, only as needed, but in ample time. Train each carefully. Reward winners, and weed out non-performers fast.

8. Acting out the parts of prospect and salesperson is vital to give each rep the best chance. Never stop training.

9. Have frequent internal rep discussions. Let them analyze their performances and suggest to each other how to improve.

10. Look for training audio tapes. Create your own. Tape what the most successful telemarketers do, then get the input from the field sales force.

11. Give a star telemarketer, with a flair for teaching, an override to any added sales of a neophyte, after coaching.

12. Create more stars to train more neophytes. Track the sales of neophytes. Some will have startling increases.

13. Look for "burn-out" when good reps suddenly do worse. Find out their problems fast. Listen, analyze. Encourage them.

14. Create a successful team. Orient, enthuse, reward…with small incentives, simple social events, contests and prizes.

15. Give your sales team and each rep a "yes" quota for a test period, then for the selling season or year. Reward or fire based on these known quantitative goals.

The Role of Telemarketing Specialists

A highly informed phone representative in a niche specialty is invaluable to the customer and to you. Businesses will select a supplier simply for this reason. Often consumers will. Such representatives know their customers and become trusted. They get multiple-item sales per customer, more frequent repeat sales, and surprisingly big dollar orders. They are commonly classified as follows:

- Regular account specialists
- Major account specialists
- Tech representatives
- Bid specialists
- Spec specialists

Such representatives may mail, call, and sell, or they may give information by phone and then mail and then still later call back to sell.

Calculate profitability at each step. For every type of phone representative, your system should ideally be able to time and cost each call. Track the expense of each representative per minute plus add in the per-minute cost of representative and manager salaries, Social Security, and vacations. Also, amortize the cost per minute of equipment and the people assistance used. Include all ad and direct-mail costs to bring in inquiries. Include the credit card costs of sales, the share of rent or mortgage expenses. Add these costs to the cost of your product or service, plus the return of goods and the handling cost of return. Then compare the total cost to call each day with the phone sales for the day.

Make an out-bound telemarketing financial statement as though your phone sales operation were a separate firm. If it's a loser, stop. Go back to square one. Even if your test is successful, recalculate your profitability at each step of expansion. In short, measure everything—the profitability of each phone rep, of a new offer, a new script, a new list, and of new equipment you try on trial.

Out-Bound Phone Service Bureaus or in House?

Out-bound telemarketing is a complicated endeavor, fraught with potential management headaches as its scope increases. Depending upon your marketing application, it may prove far wiser to job the whole operation out to proven experts.

Out-bound service bureaus are hired like advertising agencies; many companies prefer to tap outside expertise rather than invest management resources in this specialized and competitive field. And when you consider that telemarketing representative turnover rates alone are commonly 200 percent and more annually, the task of building and managing an internal telemarketing department cannot be subordinated to less than excellent supervision without the risk of losing a lot of money.

The advantages of escaping investment, overhead, training, and equipment costs via a service bureau are as huge as for in-bound telemarketing. However, the difficulties of making an out-bound service bureau manageable mount with the complexity of your product, especially if you have a broad product line.

Linchitz estimates that you need a minimum of five or six phone representatives to start an internal out-bound telemarketing department, provided that you get a supervisor who is economical with four or five to boss. But Linchitz also figures that this small crew can make 4500 presentations a month to business firms (in two shifts of four hours each) or make 6000 presentations a month to homes (in one four-hour shift). Further, the same staff may be able to switch from in-bound to out-bound phone. Cost? $50,000 to set up, furnish, equip, and operate for a month.

Summary

To summarize, success at out-bound telemarketing requires the following:

1. Perception that the phone call is for the purpose of benefiting the buyer, not the seller

2. No "junk" phone methods in cold calls, that is, the use of misleading sweepstakes, heavy-handed "must have your answer today," or any other scripting ploys all too commonly used to close a sale but not build a relationship

3. Near-perfect targeting and timing

4. Thorough research of prospect and customer

5. More reliance on phone follow-up contacts of prospects who identify themselves

6. Higher average initial sale

7. Caring cultivation of customers

8. Well-trained telephone communicators with a good sales incentive structure

9. State-of-the-art equipment suitable for your purpose and size

10. Great script "tree" that answers all questions and objections and is continually tested for further improvements

11. Open and honest communication with the field sales force, including providing for continued commissions or other incentives for sales staff cooperation

12. Total integration into the overall marketing plan

Help Source Guide

1. *Richard L. Bencin & Associates* provides a *free* article, "Conducting a Telemarketing Operations Review" which tells how to check what's wrong about any telemarketing you do and how to fix it: 8553 Timber Trail, Brecksville, OH 44141. (216) 526-6726.

2. Joel Linchitz's *Complete Guide to Telemarketing Management* (1990) is an excellent resource from AMACOM, a division of American Management Association: P.O. Box 1026, Saranac Lake, NY 12983. (800) 538-8476.

3. *Free* info kits and detailed outbound rates and features are available from *AT&T* (800) 243-0900; *MCI* (800) 444-2222, or (800) 444-4444; *Sprint* (800) 366-0907.

4. The article *"How to Make Outbound Marketing Work for You: 33 Ideas That Will Increase Performance"* can be ordered from *Voice Processing* magazine: P.O. Box 42382, Houston, TX 77242-9901. (713) 974-6637.

5. S. Idelman and G. Dobbs's *How to Manage Growth and Maximize Profits in Outbound Telemarketing* (1990) provides case histories, mistakes, solutions. Available at libraries or from Prentice-Hall: P.O. Box 11071, Des Moines, IA 50336. (800) 288-4745.

6. Issues, articles, case histories on out-bound success, lists of out-bound service bureaus, software are available from two periodicals. *Inbound/Outbound* at 12 W. 21 St., NY, NY 10010, (212) 206-6660, and *Telemarketing* at One Technology Plaza, Norwalk, CT 06854, (800) 243-6002.

7. R. Self's book, *Long Distance for Less* (3d ed., 580 pages), can save most firms a lot on long-distance bills: 27 E. 22d St., NY, NY 10010. (212) 477-3221.

8. *Teleconnect* magazine provides a monthly source on telecommunications products, services. Annual publications include *The Year's Greatest Products* and *Annual Used & Refurbished Equipment Sources*: 12 W. 21st St., NY, NY 10010. (212) 691-8215.

10
Audiotext

Voice Mail,
Talking Ads, and
Telemedia

For our purposes, *audiotext* consists of any of the following:

Voice mail. When you leave a message or get a message on an answering machine or voice system

Talking ads. When you dial a number featured in an ad and hear a recorded message with more details of the offer

Telemedia. When you dial a number to hear the weather report or any other recorded information service and also hear a commercial message from the sponsor of the service.

Audiotext is the fastest growing area of telecommunications and one of the most versatile forms of telemarketing. Virtually every major business, in some way, uses audiotext. It is based on a technological revolution in telephone voice and switching systems. The many voice-system marketing capabilities and applications have some advantages in common. They are

- As user-friendly as the push-button phone
- As universal as the phone
- As persuasive as the human voice
- One-on-one, personal, and intimate
- Lower-cost than live telemarketing

However, each audiotext form is a tool suitable for marketing only certain types of products and services. And some of audiotext's common disadvantages include:

- Only the right use of audiotext for your marketing purpose has a chance.
- Finding appropriate audiotext choices takes time, effort, and research.
- Selecting the best audiotext choice requires an entrepreneurial feel.
- Refining and customizing systems involves creativity.
- Effective use demands a continuous marketing skill.
- Analysis of results involves a tracking regimen.

What is a possible, practical, and sufficiently profitable use for you? Your answer depends on your marketing problem and the type and size of your business. The wrong use is a waste of money. To benefit most from audiotext's advantages and overcome its disadvantages, let's start with the fundamentals.

What Is a Voice System?

Phone voice systems started with *passive playback* or *replay* such as your tape recorder. The local weather phone number is an example of passive playback. The local time phone number is also passive, but it's not taped. Instead, a voice response system records human speech, digitizes it, and stores it as a database in a computer. The system plays it back as a CD player plays back digitized music. Far more spoken words can be stored in this manner than on tape.

All audiotext is either passive replay or *interactive.* An interactive audiotext system gives you a choice of passive playback options or of inputting your voice or other information. The choices offered can be several or many. Simpler systems may provide a one-step menu, such as a choice of hearing weather reports in any of 100 cities—"press NY for New York City, LA for Los Angeles," for example. More complex systems can offer far more choices in a succession of steps, each a submenu. For example, certain travel-related audiotext systems ask you to identify different destinations to choose from, offer a wide variety of information packages, and ask you to order directly.

Interactive voice systems work with any push-button phone, or a computer-keypad modem that "talks" to another computer. Many newer systems can even work with rotary phones by recognizing the numbers you speak instead of push. This is important because, according to research by AT&T, rotary dial penetration is 38.5 percent nationally.

A Technological Revolution

Slashed hardware costs and the emergence of inexpensive PC software makes voice systems for large and small companies produce enough savings to pay for and profit from them. Most small systems can replace or assist a human voice or switch you at any time you want to talk to a real person.

More complex voice systems do what was unthinkable before. One system can process 450,000 calls in an hour. Greater storage capacity of computers allows more and lengthier answers. Some systems can instantly call up spoken paragraphs, sentences, words, even syllables. They can combine music, voices, and sound effects in any mix desired.

Voice Systems and Marketing

Voice systems help marketing in the following ways:

- They can enhance the effectiveness of any ad or medium.
- They project and increase the value of a company spokesperson.
- They link, inform, and inspire representatives, distributors, and/or dealers.
- They help measure the profitability of ad campaigns.
- They increase and personalize the contact with your customers.
- They target and attract desired prospects.
- They build a database of customers and/or prospects.
- They create instant and low-cost research.
- They launch new and unique applications no other medium can.
- They combine with nonmarketing use (phone communications) for a free-ride benefit.

The smallest marketers can benefit most from audiotext's simplest and lowest-cost forms, whereas large companies often profit most from the latest, more complex technology. Should you use audiotext? Each application must be judged on its merits for your company. This chapter shows you how others have made audiotext profitable. In addition, the Help Source Guide includes references to provide you with more timely details.

Voice Mail Transforms the Business Phone

Any phone-answering machine creates voice mail. Most executives prefer brief voice-mail messages they can answer in kind. Anyone who is away from the office a great deal appreciates voice mail as do those who do business from the home.

Depending upon their complexity, voice systems can record and send, receive and store, play back on demand, record answers and send them back. Each is a "phone post office." Each provides a "voice mailbox," space on a hard disk reserved to store all messages for each person or department.

Big companies use elaborate systems to save time, cut phone bills, reduce clerical support, and save big money. Systems costing from $20,000 to over $1 million can do a great deal more than save administrative costs. A voice system can even replace a busy signal or no answer with your own recorded greeting. The system can request and record a caller's message which can request a voice-mail reply.

Plummeting prices and new software for PCs now give many of the same advantages to small businesses. Voice mail software costing just several hundred dollars, combined with your PC, can do the work of many answering machines and much more.

Increased Sales at Little Cost

A voice letter supplements a fax and is faster, easier, and simpler than a letter. It's personal and friendly. It can be sent at night, at the lowest phone rates for the next morning's delivery, and sent to as many people as desired. The same voice mail message can give the latest news to all representatives in order to help make sales. Voice mail enables a firm with 20 representatives to personalize a mail message to each of the representatives' 50 accounts, for a total of 1000 personalized calls.

A big firm can send personalized calls for dealers, distributors, or representatives by the tens of thousands. Such calls are usually welcomed as a way to keep up to date about any new, important, specific information that will help salespeople sell more of the firm's products. With many systems, a customer can phone, enter his or her "mailbox number" and "password," and order. The customer can leave questions about delivery or a counterproposal about price. The customer can then check his or her box hours later and find the answers.

Anheuser-Busch sends the latest prices and news of promotions to 770 wholesalers by voice mail and gets orders by return voice mail. William Morrow and other publishers use voice mail to quickly tell representatives of an upcoming author interview in the area and ask for last-minute orders. Frequent-buyer trade accounts often find voice mail a cheap, fast way to ask and get answers and to order. Retailers and catalog houses use voice mail to tell customers that desired merchandise is on sale or available again after being out of stock.

Instant, Automated, Interactive Ordering

Customers call the Federal Express (FedEx) 800 number, tap in their account number, zip code, and the number of parcels to be picked up. This goes into the company's computer system, COSMOS, which schedules a pick-up. It's the simplest, fastest way to order and the easiest way for FedEx to get more business from competitors.

For United Airlines, a voice systems program allows frequent flyers to access their mileage to date and how much more they need to meet quotas and win free trips. Travelers, ticket buyers, car renters, trade show and seminar attendees make reservations this way. College students enroll in specific courses by push-button phone. Voice mail has more uses daily.

Should you use voice mail for marketing? Yes, if you can come up with a service your customers and prospects will value. Only use outbound voice mail if those called request that you do.

Start Simple

You may be able to use your firm's present voice system. Ask your phone company or your supplier for its voice mail marketing department. It may supply voice mail services or suggest a voice mail facilities service bureau.

Start any audiotext project as a test with 10 or a 100 voice letters. If the project proves profitable, try more. Expand only as you have assimilated all the information your employees, customers, and prospects have requested. As you expand in audiotext, do it with a variety of smaller uses rather than relying on one huge system.

This chapter's Help Source Guide gives phone numbers to find out about voice mail from major phone companies. The magazines and newsletter listed can keep you apprised of the newest applications.

Talking Ads

Audiotext can extend and increase the power of any ad medium and measure its sales cost. An audiotext talking ad can be the simplest recorded commercial message to supplement what you say in your ad. It can be a complex voice system that can answer any of various questions about what you say in your ad. But once produced, each time the ad is dialed, the cost to reach a prospect is a tiny fraction of that of a live operator. The ad can be dialed at any time of day or night, weekday, or weekend. The message is as controlled as if printed. A voice system computer can count each call received and report the time received.

Glastron Boats got a bonus for buying its half-page ad in *Boating* magazine. The bonus was a free 30-second message on an 800 number paid for by *Boating*, with a voice access system provided by Touch-Tone Access, Inc.

By dialing the *Boating* 800 number and pressing the number shown in Glastron's ad, readers were able to access the name and address of Glastron's nearest dealer. All that was required was pressing the buttons for the reader's zip code. By pressing other buttons, either the dealer came on the line or you could request a call back from Glastron. In the first 60 days many calls came in, and dealers reported selling boats for $10,000 and up from these audiotext leads.

A classified ad or a tiny display ad can feature a voice system number to call for more details. Think of the small ad as the headline and subhead inducing the reader to call for more details. The voice system message then becomes the advertisement's "body copy," using perhaps 10 or more times as many words. The system may ask for an order or record a request for further follow-up. The system can qualify leads and switch hot prospects directly to a live salesperson.

Small space in a catalog can communicate only a few details in print, but an added line asking that a reader, viewer, or listener call your answering machine makes any ad talk, offering much more information about a product. The service may be free with an ad, at cost, or sold at profit.

Do you advertise on TV, cable, radio, in magazines, newspapers, or Yellow Pages? Many advertising media offer voice system messages ranging from 30 seconds to 5 minutes. One simple version is an "electronic bingo card system" to phone a magazine's 800 number for return literature from its advertisers.

Talking Ads on Hold. An upscale sports car repair shop became a car dealer simply by advertising to callers on hold that new cars could be bought there. In just the first month, car sales were directly traced to the ads delivered while callers were on hold.

Telephonetics International, Inc., a production company for AT&T, offers syndicated and customized recorded phone messages for many kinds of businesses. Dozens of firms offer such software. It is often the lowest-cost way to reach customers by voice media. And you can do it all in-house with a PC and voice-system software.

A customer calling the classified advertising department of a newspaper can be presented with information on special ad placement rates while waiting to speak with an order processor. A catalog or retail customer may hear news of the latest sale. With your own tape recorder or voice system, you can create you own message and test it. It's your own telemedia.

A 10,000-Choice Voice Catalog.   Imagine a catalog where all the items for sale are spoken information in one field—investments—and are constantly updated. It's DowPhone, a subsidiary of the financial publisher, Dow Jones. From all over the world, the latest stories, reports, and statistics that concern investment and business are transmitted in digitized form, via Down Jones' own satellite. DowPhone broadcasts are like radio broadcasts: they have their own editorial staff to edit and announce from their own studios. For subscribers only, DowPhone offers 10,000 choices of financial information and advice. Each pays an annual fee plus use charges. Some heavy users spend $300 to $1000 a month.

Musical Telephone Catalog.   The San Francisco Music Box Company has its own telephone catalog, called DIAL-A-TUNE. By dialing (415) 420-TUNE, listeners can select by push-button any of 350 tunes in three lengths of musical movements—18, 36, and 72 notes. The music boxes in the catalog range in price from $9.95 to $3800.00. The customer pays to make the phone call at regular toll costs.

The first season, between 1000 and 1500 people phoned each day for the three months before Christmas. Of those, close to 600 redialed the company's toll-free number for more information. Of that group, about 30 percent placed an order. The sole advertising was the print catalog, which also produced its own orders. The second season response dropped off but was still profitable.

Should you try a phone catalog? Only if your product is ideal for spoken or sound presentation, preferably if it has late-news value.

Sponsored Telemedia

Sponsored telemedia are the phone equivalent of short commercials on radio programs, often for far less ad cost, to reach fewer but highly targeted listeners. Each feature is called a "program." A feature may involve simply listening (passive playback), or it may be *interactive* where callers participate and "converse" as they ask questions and activate answers by push-button phone. No live operator may be needed, or one may be accessible.

Telemedia programs are provided by information providers (IPs), which may be a media group, business, or individual. An IP may provide one or many programs. What credentials does an IP need? That depends upon the subject. If it's financial or investment news, obviously an organization with the resources and reputation to deliver this information in a timely manner is needed. Other subjects, from astrology to "zoo news" (if there is such a thing) might require more promotional expertise than an established reputation. IPs range from the largest corporations to individuals with some knowledge and a lot of initiative.

There are over 3000 national and thousands more local and regional telemedia programs. Calling the feature phone number is like selecting a TV channel. Sometimes a short feature is all that's offered. In other instances, one phone number offers a wide choice of features in one field, as do specialized cable channels or trade or professional magazines. The Help Source Guide includes a number of listings. Call *InfoText* and *Voice Processing* magazines and the National Association of Information Services to get the latest lists of sponsored telemedia IPs.

A telemedia feature may offer news, entertainment, information, or advice. Some features are unique to telemedia. Many are syndicated. Some newspapers have created a phone edition with up to hundreds of verbal features. In turn, some TV and radio stations have created their own telephone "newspapers" that can be updated frequently. Telemedia content includes information about a product, company, event, or personality. It may tell where to buy what. Content may be a game or sweepstakes, or it may explain how to play one.

How Sponsored Telemedia Works

Audiotext telemedia obviously encompasses many formats and options. Let's explain some of these telemedia options, starting with those that are sponsored and free to the consumer, except perhaps for the cost of the call.

Each program is paid for by advertisers in sponsored telemedia. For example, in the largest U.S. cities, Dow Jones has a financial news service by phone, featuring reports on the ten largest publicly traded companies. In many cities, this service is distributed by Reuben H. Donnelley and promoted in the yellow pages of its phone book. Donnelley and most other phone book publishers are IPs of programs in each of many cities. They create their own programs and distribute more that have been syndicated by other IPs elsewhere.

Many newspapers, radio, and TV station IPs offer dial-it services for sponsorship. Most are syndicated. Some are programs featuring local media personalities. Media often join to offer and promote programs or cross-promote programs.

Each Telemedia Factor Must Be Right.   The interactive stock report line, StockLine, supplied by Brite Voice Systems is one of an average number of 12 audiotext phone programs on Sundial, offered by *The Baltimore Sun* newspaper. StockLine receives an average of 145,000 calls a month. The *Sun* ran its own ads for the StockLine almost daily. The local office of Fidelity Corporation is one of five rotating sponsors; Fidelity's 15-second commercial reached 29,000 callers a month for $600 monthly. On a per-caller basis that's less than the cost of a freestanding newspaper insert and a fraction of the cost of a direct-mail piece.

Fidelity manager Keith Graham wrote the copy and Sundial manager Thom Pemberton used his own voice in the ad. The copy stated that Fidelity was not just in the fund business but was also a broker and offered a free financial seminar and a request to reply by phone. Fidelity launched this audiotext campaign with a three-month test. The campaign turned profitable the first month. The ad cost per lead was lower and the quality of leads higher than for any other Baltimore advertising: 40 to 50 people a month phoned Fidelity. Half of them bought stock. In 1½ years, from Sundial customers alone, Fidelity earned over $200,000 in commissions.

Offer and Program Must Match. Baltimore's 105-year-old Mid-State Savings & Loan, in the worst five months of the savings-and-loan crisis, pulled in over $1 million in deposits directly traced to its audiotext ads on StockLine. But President Kitty Gerling explains, "We had to offer high enough interest." She means that it took *The Sun*'s constant promotion of the StockLine plus Thom Pemberton's voice and copy, with frequent changes in the 15-second commercial to make it a success.

In Boston, an employment agency ran a typing contest in its ads on horoscope audiotext programs featured in a talking telephone book. These audiotext ads pulled 6667 phone entrants representing 97 percent of its signed-up clients from all media sources. Fortunately, the horoscope program had the highest call count of any audiotext service promoted in the telephone book and audience demographics matching the agency's job applicants.

Telemedia: Simple, Cheap, Sometimes Risky

You can produce your audiotext message yourself, write it, and record it. An ad can have background music. It can have your own voice or a professional's, one voice or several. You can change it as needed at no added cost. Even an amateur can add: "And today's specials are...."

Far more local firms and smaller regional firms sponsor announcements in other IPs' audiotext shows rather than produce an entire program themselves. However small and specialized your business, there may be a program to sponsor that's right for you. Although most large, sophisticated marketers have held off being partial sponsors, many in-experienced small firms have rushed in to sole sponsorships and failed, usually unnecessarily. Note carefully the following seven telemedia ad mistakes:

1. Careless copy without benefits or incentives
2. The wrong approach that continues unchanged
3. The wrong "fit" of the ad's offer to the company's service
4. Repeating the same offer to the "hard-core" repeat callers
5. Unchanged or "out-of-season" copy
6. Failure to trace and analyze response
7. Wrong length of copy for the job

A 15-second message can only succeed if the firm is known, if callers are ideal prospects, and if the offer is describable in 15 words and the re-quest for action in another 15. This is tough for obscure firms. For those selling complicated products or services with much information to get across, the task is impossible. But these same firms can often succeed with the correct-length message, just as the six other mistakes above can be avoided.

Creating Your Telemedia

Select a program that interests your customers. Select a professional writer of phone commercials, telemarketing scripts or radio commer-cials, or your most successful salesperson. Select an expert in that order. Next, choose a voice. The voice may be a trusted expert in your field, a radio personality or telemarketer, your company's spokesperson, top salesperson, or yourself.

Select the offer and copy that's currently your most successful in other media. Determine how quickly it generated enough response to be a winner. If you can't measure the results of your present advertising, create an offer with an incentive for response, whether a sale, a guaran-tee, a giveaway, or whatever. Have your writer adapt this for the phone. Tape the working copy in different lengths—15, 30, and 60 seconds. Listen and decide which length gets your offer across or if you need a still longer commercial.

Check these points:

1. Is the program you want available from IPs? Or a good alternative? Can you create your own program? (We'll discuss when that's feasible and how to do it.)

2. What length commercials are available on the desired program? What is the cost of each length?
3. What cost per thousand (CPM) can you afford for an ad in audiotext service? And how should it compare with CPMs in other media? Obviously audiotext costs vary by copy length. The right dial-it program for you may have a good deal higher CPM than the wrong one. But the CPM should be between the cost of the same-length message reaching a similar audience via radio or print media and that of direct mail.
4. How long a commitment does the media owner want versus how long a test period is right for you?
   a. For over 50,000 a month call-count, the time it took for your present media to prove success should be sufficient.
   b. For a call count of 25,000 to 50,000 a month, 30 days or even two weeks for a promotion may be enough. But also consider longer periods of three months if you think your business requires continued impact for significant sales results.
   c. Finally, lower phone counts obviously require longer runs.

If you're in a business where your expertise is vital, perhaps you even can start your own audiotext advice number. As the only sponsor, the program can become so closely associated to your business that your product or service is, by association, being sold throughout the call.

Use Your Expertise.   Owner Bob Ellenby of Safe Harbor's Travel in Baltimore is a travel guru and computer bug. By combining his own software with that of each airline, he created his own audiotext program featuring his own Best Air Fares Line selections. Few small IPs promote enough to cause a profitable number of prospects to call their programs. But, *The Baltimore Sun* newspapers introduced Best Air Fares Line with a burst of promotion. In five months, over 15,000 people called.

Callers selected from 38 bargain destinations by push-button phones and heard airfare descriptions. Ninety seconds of copy made the offer and asked for action. Each caller could be connected with the agency when open or could leave a voice mail message after hours. Over 1700 people responded. Over 400 took trips. "Best Air Fares" proved more profitable than any other advertising used by Safe Harbor's Travel. But few small firms create breakthrough programs.

Big Marketers Succeed More Often.   If your firm is big, use your clout. Phone technology makes it possible to take many calls in one hour and create unique interactive programs. Most large packaged goods advertisers run audiotext programs with the help of top ad agencies and technical specialists, promotion idea gurus, and telemedia consultants. Together, they uncover new advantages and extra benefits. Huge advertising creates unprecedented call counts.

A program can be national or localized for the smallest dealer. It can be integrated into overall marketing. For its Benadryl product, Warner-Lambert runs a PollenTrak 800 number to give daily pollen counts for each area covered. Callers are asked if they are Benadryl users and can get cents-off coupons by giving their name and address, thus building the mailing list.

Make Your Packages Talk.   Each Frito-Lay chip bag asked purchasers to call the contest number. A voice system guided each caller to play a trivia game against a computer. The contest lasted six weeks. Printed clues on selected chip bags helped entrants win. This was explained on packages and by toll-free number to callers; 600,000 calls were completed. Frito-Lay chip sales soared.

"Captain Crunch" breakfast-food packages showed a map with specially marked locations where a pirate named "La Foote" buried his treasure and a toll-free number to call for treasure locations. If the locations on the phone message and map matched, the family won a bicycle. In just four months, millions of calls were received, and Captain Crunch's market share jumped 33 percent.

Marketing Via 900 Numbers

Pay "dial-it" calls are paid for by users. Charges include the toll cost the phone company charges plus fees for specific information or entertainment service given over the phone. The amount paid varies widely and has been the subject of some controversy and legislation. Prices can be fixed or charged on the basis of so much a minute. Billing also varies—fees can be collected by the phone company, the phone company can collect and divide the income with the IP, or the service can be billed direct or via credit card. The first minute can be free. Access can be free to an 800 number or can be limited initially to the cost of accessing a regular toll call. Then the caller can be asked to have her or his credit card billed for additional minutes.

Entrepreneurs pioneered this category of audiotext as moneymaking ventures in themselves, sometimes not to market legitimate products or services. But now, *Fortune 500* companies (and far smaller marketers) have transformed pay dial-it into a medium that is successfully promoting many kinds of products and services. Often, a pay dial-it plays a versatile, key part of these marketing campaigns. I'll shortly cite some examples.

Pay dial-it can even be profitable PR. Customers or fans often willingly pay to hear programs which publicize a star, author, or event. More and more people are willing to pay to be informed about a training method, a hobby, or a how-to product. They are eager to pay for advice of many kinds, which often prequalifies them and then leads to a larger sale.

But pay dial-it must provide information or entertainment that satisfies. It must get enough calls. To produce them takes effective advertising, advertising that often "rides along" in existing promotions packages and other advertising.

Advertising

Tom Haynes's Tackle Shop.   Tom Haynes has a tackle shop in Melbourne Beach, Florida. His biggest stock in trade is his fishing expertise. He is famous in the area for the science with which he divided up nearby Sebastian Inlet into 20 zones and tracks where fish are striking by the day and hour. Customers come to him for his fish-catching system, to see his latest charts of where to catch the fish, and to buy tackle.

Tom's most popular service is Tom taped on the phone, automatically calling subscribers when fish are striking. He has not spent a penny to advertise it. It is a very simple voice system that can make up to 110 calls an hour. An optional phone service is Tom discussing fishing topics. Another service consists of the latest bulletins from the Florida Fishing Commission—both regulations and announcements.

About 25 people a day phone Tom at the shop for live advice. For still more help they come to the shop. His fish-catching phone service keeps growing without advertising. It got him interviews on three TV stations and six radio stations and a feature on one network. Then he began to write for *The Orlando Sentinel* on local fishing—all as his shop has increased its tackle sales.

Frank Covich's Brokers' Association.   For ten years Frank Covich was a successful business broker, earning good commissions for arranging purchases and sales of businesses. He saw the need for a national organization of specialists as knowledgeable as himself which could help buyers or sellers anywhere in the country to find and conclude deals with each other. He would run it, seek only those qualified to be members, further train and update them, and secure for them and supply to them prospective buyers and sellers.

With a two-line classified ad, he launched The National Association of Independent Business Brokers. Typical members are accountants, lawyers, and owners of financial services. Each pays $12,500 down and a total of $25,000 to join and be trained. With member-brokers Frank has trained, the NAIBB operates the Business Transfer Network and its information line (1-900-872-4545). Small ads in business publications produce calls. The program consists of Frank. It's designed to help callers while qualifying the leads it sells.

The 900-number phone line costs $2 for the first minute, then $1 a minute. An average caller stays on the phone 11 minutes, yielding around $3 for each $1 of operating cost. A caller selects from eight kinds of advice. Callers interested in more help phone Frank's 800 number. Some want to buy or sell businesses or earn a referral fee—these are leads for Network members. Some are prospects for membership. Frank follows up by phone, mail, and personal visits. Several new members are trained each month. The total sales are about eight times all the ad and follow-up costs.

Big Companies Dominate

ABC introduced SoapTalk, a 900 number for soap opera fans, with the taped voice of an ABC soap opera star. Each day a soap actor or actress "in character" told callers about that day's show. Fifteen-second TV spots during ABC soap operas promoted SoapTalk. This pay dial-it program, in turn, promoted ABC soap operas. SoapTalk received over 900,000 calls for 50 cents in the first week and over 3.5 million in its initial six weeks.

After three years, ABC, building on SoapTalk, launched a magazine, *Episodes,* devoted to ABC soap operas. The same kind of 30-second TV commercials asked for calls to subscribe to the magazine for $3. In 16 weeks this secured 1.6 million subscriptions, the greatest number of subscribers in history secured that quickly for the launch of a new magazine. Two years later SoapTalk still generated substantial call volume every week. When we went to press, according to James Ivers of Strategic Telemedia, over 150 magazines were using or testing 900 numbers.

Self-Liquidating Response Media

Big marketers use pay dial-it in many ways. These range from promoting a premium (a "one-shot" or self-liquidating promotion) to using it as an instant, cheap research tool. Each pay dial-it program may be a profit center, a no-cost extension of PR, an adjunct to an ad campaign, or a medium. The pay dial-it program's mission may be any of the following:

Extend image.   Pepsi-Cola and *Billboard* magazine jointly sponsored 900 HOT-ROCK; 100,000 callers a month pay for a choice of rock trivia or rock news and rock gossip.

Attract exact target audience.   Huggies diapers offered tape of lullabies personalized with the baby's name; over 100,000 parents phoned 900 number for 45 cents to hear lullabies.

Developed instant phone fan club.   Sport, TV, movie, theater, record stars give vignettes, confide, explain, advise, gossip, sell.

Create Instant Sweepstakes.   Over a million WH-1 cable channel viewers paid over $2 a call to register for a chance to win 36 vintage Corvettes.

Promote recipe offers.   Clorox charged $1 per call for recipes and sent each caller a salad dressing recipe book.

Create new profit center and cross-promote.   Callers can win prizes as they pay and play game shows such as *Jeopardy* or *Wheel of Fortune.*

Involve through fun polls.   Programs promote TV programs, radio stations, newspapers, sports events, products, and services.

Sponsored Pay Dial-it

Some 900 dial-it services carry commercials. Consider Dow Jones. It operates a dial-it service 24-hours-a-day, and its closing report stays on overnight for Far Eastern and European callers. The 1-minute report concludes with a 7-second commercial. Advertisers include American Express, Hertz Rent-A-Car, and Travellers Equity Sales.

Gannett has 900 numbers on sports, weather, Lotto, and horse racing. It too sells promotional announcements of 5 to 7 seconds on its Sports Center, offering them only as a bonus to advertisers buying a quota of ads in Gannett media. Nike Shoes, Chevrolet, and Epson are among its sponsors.

Whatever your firm's size, there's little chance that mentions this short will get measurable response. These are strictly image-building. Can your own program compete? Frank Covich knows the business brokerage business inside and out and how to advise people soundly. His brokerage business was already successful before getting into audiotext. Still, he admits that creating his audiotext program was "the hardest job I did in my life."

If you create a program that's right for your business, it may be more profitable than sponsoring part of someone else's phone program. First note these six ways that program providers most often fail:

1. A phone program people do not want
2. Quick-fade fad after big initial response
3. Failure to replace a burnt-out winner
4. Copying others' success—after saturation
5. Failure to induce callers to stay on the line
6. Failing to advertise effectively or enough in the right medium—or paying too much to do it

Local Market Tests

Some audiotext IPs start with a low-cost answering machine, record a program on it, and arrange with their local phone company for an extra phone and number. The amount of advertising to promote the line dictates how many lines are needed. A very small IP in New York City might start with 4. Cancellation can be at once. To install and supply four lines for three months can cost $300 to $400. Use of special software costing under $500 with a PC gives interactivity and handles up to 32 or even several hundred lines. Phone companies bill the consumer for the service and the call but not for products sold by it. But you may decide to credit the cost of the calls to the customer in some way.

For most types of pay dial-it services offered by marketers, the local or regional phone company assigns you a number beginning with 976, bills callers for you, collects, and pays you. It usually charges about 25 cents a minute plus another charge of 10 to 12 cents. But big volume can reduce this. You can start out with a local phone company in a small way and go into other areas gradually. If the areas are adjacent, you may use the small regional phone company. You could make local arrangements all over. But this costs more, requires much detailed work, and can be a nightmare.

The cost of failure is lowest if you make a small-scale test in one city and spend under $1000 a week in advertising for a month or so. All costs might be $10,000 to $20,000 but can be closer to $6000. Some small firms test for even less. Testing in several cities increases all costs and risk.

Big marketers want unique audiotext creative and marketing features, and usually interactive capabilities. They research more and launch on a much larger scale. They usually use a promotion house and may extend a successful 900-number test to five or ten markets and then gradually take on the entire country.

900 Numbers

Most dial-it services use one 900 number after the first test. Some IPs start in several cities with a 900 number. AT&T, MCI, and Sprint each offer 900 numbers. Many intermediaries do. Charges vary for each company. Usually, a company charges about 33 cents to transport each call from one phone company where the call originates to another phone company where the dial-it number is located. Another 10 or 12 cents is charged to record the call. Usually a minimum of 2000 calls a day is required. There are other much smaller costs.

Dial-it Service Bureaus

For legal reasons, phone companies cannot perform all services needed by IPs. A small IP can perform these functions for simple tests. This is far less practical, as success requires more and more time, equipment, and technical expertise. Most who use 900 numbers use a telephone phone service bureau to take over what the phone companies do not do.

Telephone service bureaus operate a "gateway." This is a special audiotext software and hardware system that allows many different programs and services to share the same system and telephone trunks. Your program may have a special extension of their phone number. Yours can have different extensions for various programs or for each ad you promote. Each ad can be keyed and results traced. The cost for a service bureau may only be $1000 to $3000 more for a local test and less nationally than doing it all yourself. Another advantage to hiring a telephone service bureau is that it negotiates for you with the phone company. Besides being more convenient for you, it often provides free consultant service. A service bureau already has phone lines and its own advanced software and hardware. With access to as many lines as needed, a bureau can handle a big surge of calls.

A dial-it telephone promotion house is a service bureau with creative services capabilities from idea to final production. Perhaps 20 percent of all dial-it programs are created by promotion houses, but they account for a bigger share of dial-it programs with the biggest marketing successes.

Parting Cautions

Don't use interactive telemedia in areas with few touchtone phones and no recognition equipment to recognize spoken numbers and letters. If you're small, look for narrow-niche success. Listen, view, read commercials and ads for dial-it services. Phone dial-it numbers and listen to the programs. Extend your know-how into the simplest telemedia and the most successful advertising you now do. Use do-it-yourself research. Exchange know-how. Team up with others small or large. Start with the briefest tests in the simplest ways.

If your firm is big, research more and investigate telemedia experts, facilities, and the latest technology. Join with other large marketers to share risks.

Whatever your size, ask for action from your callers. And track your response versus other forms of promotion. Compare results with cost. Stop if it's a bust. Modify the test if results are borderline. And only expand your successes with great care. Use the Help Source Guide below. Read the recommended books. Call magazines; get back issues. Look for lists of the nearest service bureaus and promotion houses.

Help Source Guide

1. *Ameritech Audiotext Services Inc.* publishes a *free* IP quarterly newsletter. Also available is a *free* kit providing a generous amount of information on starting an audiotext venture: 600 S. Federal St., Suite 122, Chicago, IL 60605. (800) 432-0080; Demo line (800) 733-7790.

2. *AT&T's* information line on national interactive and passive 900 service is (800) 243-0900. Voice mail information line is (800) 247-1212.

3. *Brite Voice Systems* makes, sells interactive voice response, audiotext systems. Available *free* is a list of 50 most-called Brite phone programs with names and addresses of providers/localities: 7309 E. 21st St. N., Wichita, KS 67206-1083. (316) 652-6500.

4. *InfoText* and *Voice Processing* are two fine audiotext magazines. Buy special issues on and listing of audiotext service bureaus, software, and equipment. Catalog and back issues available. *InfoText* sponsors the InfoText Annual Expo; *Voice Processing* sponsors the Voice Conference and Expo. Both have top audiotext experts; both also have videotapes and audiocassettes. Also, read *InfoText* publisher Rick Parkhill's *The Power of 900: A Guidebook to Caller-Paid Services.* Essential for marketers, this book is fact-loaded and reader friendly, listing services, citing costs, telling what to do. *InfoText* magazine: 34700 Coast Hwy, #309, Capistrano Beach, CA 92624. (714) 493-2434. *Voice Processing* magazine: P.O. Box 42382, Houston, TX 77242-9901. (713) 974-6637.

5. *MCI Telecommunications* provides *free* information re their 800 service if you call 800-223-0540 and their 900 service if you call 703-506-6258.

6. *National Association of Information Services* makes available an NAIS consultants' list describing type of service of each. Also provided is advice to set up and operate an IP service: 1150 Connecticut Ave. NW, Suite 1050, Washington, DC 20036. (202) 833-2545.

7. Top expert Marc Robbins has written *Voice Mail Reference Manual/Buyer's Guide (1992)*; *Speech Recognition Reference Manual/Buyer's Guide (1992)*, covering technology/approaches, cost justifications, applications, case studies, much more (225 pages); and *Voice Response Reference Manual/Buyer's Guide (1992)*, which details interactive voice response technology, vendors, systems to turn touchtone phone into computer terminal (290 pages): Robbins Press, 4901 Henry Hudson Parkway, #7M, Riverdale, NY 10471. (212) 796-5534.

8. *Teleline, Phone Entertainment Co.*, provides *free* video for marketing executives and *free* talking brochure: 5950 Wilshire Blvd., 2d fl., Los Angeles, CA 90036. (800) 343-4633.

11
Fax Marketing

The boom in telephone facsimile (fax) sales is the biggest business equipment phenomenon since the PC. In just nine years, U.S. fax ownership jumped over 18 times to more than 6.5 million units—and grew almost 100 percent the next year. Fax ownership worldwide was expected to pass 100 million the following year. Now that fax machines are universal in larger businesses, most new sales are now to small businesses. In fact, the fax sales are the fastest-growing equipment sales segment to small business and also are going fast to home owners. And some think that as costs drop, fax sales will grow faster still.

Besides in the office, a growing number of public fax machines are sprouting up—in banks, hotels, restaurants and airports, upscale railroad and bus stations, conventions, fairs, and any public place. Each unit is an electronic "post office" which people can use to send or receive written material or faxmail.

The transmission of printed material over telephone lines has been commonplace because fax machines have become ever faster, more versatile, cheaper, and easier to use. In addition, computer fax-board and scanner sales are hot. First a convenience, then a way to save money and time, the fax is now a routine medium to assist in sales and receive orders. As fax machines and transmissions proliferate, so do the marketing opportunities to master this new electronic medium. This chapter will show you how.

Should You Use Fax Marketing?

If you sell directly to average- or lower-income people in homes, be cautious about using the fax as a marketing medium. In most other instances, you should consider fax marketing now, but only in the way best suited to your business. Use it as soon as possible if you

- Are a retailer selling to executives
- Sell through sales representatives or a national sales force
- Have a network of dealers, wholesalers, or distributors
- Sell via export to hundreds or more accounts
- Are in any branch of the media or information business
- Are an agent, consultant, or sales representative
- Sell business to business, including institutions, branches of government, or professionals.

How can you best use fax marketing? First, use do-it-yourself research and commonsense analysis combined with trial-and-error testing. We'll suggest how as we describe several kinds of fax marketing. At the end of this chapter we'll tell you where to get more information as fax marketing methods evolve. The three main forms, listed below, each has a variety of applications, advantages, and disadvantages:

1. Faxmail marketing: To create more sales than mail alone

2. Fax-enhanced Ads: To increase pulling power

3. Faxcasting: Information services to create sales

Before we describe each, let's discuss some fundamentals.

How Fax Works

A fax machine scans, reproduces, and sends a copy of any printed or written material within a given size. Any fax machine can send, receive, and communicate with any other fax machine in seconds. It converts what it scans into digital pulses. These turn into audible tones and go over telephone lines to any fax number you dial. The receiving fax machine turns these tones back into digital pulses and prints a copy of whatever is sent as a series of lines much like those forming the image on a TV screen.

The quality of fax varies with the machine and the fax paper used. Some fax machines can send photographs and half-tones. Others have close to laser-printer quality. But most have a standard resolution (image sharpness) of about 200 horizontal lines per inch and 100 dots per inch vertically—only good enough for text and drawings. Some are many times faster than others in transmitting and receiving, and more and more can send color. But the highest-quality and fastest-sending fax machine is still limited to the speed and quality of the receiving fax machine and the quality of the fax paper this machine uses.

Computers Turn Fax into Medium

Computer capabilities can be added to fax machines, and fax capabilities can be added to computers. Fax machines with memory function can send the same message to any number of people. More sophisticated fax machines have chips and special software that allows them to perform faxmail functions and to respond automatically by fax to fax messages, dial the specific number desired, and receive a number of faxes at the same time and save them in memory.

These fax capabilities can be added to a computer by connecting to it a faxboard modem and a scanner. There are fax modems for PCs, for minicomputers, and for main frames. A faxboard inserted in a PC allows it to send faxes to and receive faxes from any fax machine or other PC equipped with faxboard. New PC fax software provides continually increasing capabilities.

Polling allows a fax machine to call another to request a document rather than to send one. Here's how it works. A supplier of fine china, for example, has 100 independent salespeople selling door to door. Each salesperson has a fax machine. At the end of each work day, every salesperson makes a fax report but doesn't send it. Instead the manufacturer's fax machine automatically calls each salesperson's machine, requests and receives every sales report, all without an operator.

A computerized fax machine or faxboard can transmit continuously the same message or different ones using a combination of internal memory and stored fax numbers. These transmissions can be scheduled for the lowest telephone rate, off-peak hours, saving as much as 75 percent of the transmission cost. Here's a comparison of what most lower cost fax machines and fax boards each do best.

Fax Machine	*Faxboard*
To install, just plug into outlet and connect to phone.	On screen, you can edit graphics and text together.
Can usually send as soon as switched on.	Can receive and send without paper
Easier. Little or no training needed. Many people can use one machine.	Can store transmitted pictures on disk. You save time, cost, space.
Can send photos.	Can fax drawing from computer, without printing.
Many will store and later send up to 60 documents.	Can be programmed to fax thousands of names from files.

Costs more but is self-operative.	Costs less but needs scanner and PC.
Best for office needs.	A must for fax marketing.

Faxboards do more than fax machines, including the following:

- With a scanner and the right software, you can send text and graphics from your computer to the faxboard of any other computer (even those that are noncompatible in other ways).

- Multiple copies are laser-printed, giving you better reproduction.

- Computers with faxboards insert names and addresses to personalize your fax letters.

- Fax automatically all night while you sleep.

- Some faxboards can store transmissions and transfer them to your hard disk when there is free time.

Fax and Faxmail Marketing

On a computer, a few strokes can call up videotext, audiotext, or stored fax. This gives fax some capabilities similar to videotext, many capabilities similar to an audiotext request, and some advantages over each. Dialing a fax response is as simple as an audiotext and can be done without a human operator.

Every year fax machines cost less and can do more. It's the same with faxboards. Marketing uses are proliferating, with much trial-and-error testing. Fax computer service bureaus are usually also phone service bureaus. The result is that you can start marketing in a tiny way with your own equipment or public fax. Or you can test with the most advanced technology supplied by a service bureau or a phone company or both, with no equipment investment.

Fax can be instant, two-way correspondence. Customers send questions by fax. Answers are faxed back. Fax interacts as it speeds sales: It can request financial information, clear and get an order, all in the same day; make proposals; quote prices or revise them, and get the OK by return fax (a legal commitment). A fax can verify order data, send product photographs, blueprints, schematics and sketches to customers, or issue press releases to the media.

Addressed to one executive, fax is a sales aid. But when one fax message can be customized to many prospects and customers, and used by many salespeople in a firm, it is then a marketing medium. Faxmail can announce a new product or line; the visit of a demonstrator, salesperson, or celebrity; a price drop, limited offer, or ad blitz; or that new inventory of a previously sold-out product is just in. A manufacturer can update material every Monday morning to a list of preprogrammed fax numbers of reps and customers.

The advantages of faxmail are that faxmail

- Is far easier to use than electronic mail by modem
- Transmits text and pictures which can't be done via an ordinary phone call
- Provides an aura of urgency—it gets read
- Offers speed—faxmail can be delivered immediately
- Offers savings—faxmail costs far less than a far longer phone call; late-night fax costs less than regular mail, with even greater saving versus overnight courier.

The biggest strength of fax is its ability to extend and supplement what your executives, salespeople, telemarketers, and direct mail now do. It may clarify, illustrate, or add last-minute information at the crucial moment of the buying decision. Fax often saves money as it creates extra sales and profit.

Disadvantages of faxmail marketing are that

- Special fax equipment and/or services may be needed
- Resolution on the receiving fax machine is often worse than a photocopy
- Color is only possible between two color fax machines
- The widest use of the same message often fails
- Recipients prefer lengthy, less vital material by mail
- Transmission cost varies widely according to the speed of the receiving fax unit
- Fax etiquette and a growing number of laws constrain the use of cold soliciting

Should you use faxmail? Yes, but correctly. Faxmail can be your best first step and succeed more often than other fax marketing methods. But forget color for wide use. Avoid buying equipment for your first tests and stick to simple drawings. Start with narrow-niche faxmail to small segments of your customer or prospect lists. Test with one to several pages. Check transmission speed. It often irritates and rarely succeeds to send out fax messages soliciting orders cold. Use permissible faxmail marketing. That means faxing to customers and prospects information they want you to send them. Avoid these nine faxmail mistakes:

1. Wrong product, timing, or offer

2. Wrong fax copy

3. Wrong equipment for your purpose

4. Casual or hasty use without a plan

5. Expenses not estimated before use

6. Expenses not tracked as used

7. Inquiries and sales not traced to each fax use

8. Profit or loss of each test not precisely calculated

9. Failure to roll out a successful test to a safe maximum

There's no magic in faxmail. It's a form of advertising and marketing, and your product, timing, offer, and presentation must be right. Many tests will fail, but they can be made for as little as a hundred dollars. Projecting one success can wipe out test losses and show overall profits. You can learn fast.

Learn as you experiment. If your firm is small, your first test may involve using your fax machine or a dedicated PC and faxboard or using a public fax with your own fax mailbox. If your company is larger, before you test be sure that your department has reasonable access for marketing purposes to the equipment you need to use when you need it. You may get better control from the start by using a fax service bureau. Using a bureau may cost more, but it will give you the exact costs and just the right equipment for your purpose and for future growth of faxmail.

Whatever your firm's size, when several tests succeed, investigate more possibilities before you expand your faxmail program. Call the faxmail departments of AT&T, MCI, and Sprint. Talk to several of the nearest fax service bureaus. Each can teach as you get their costs. Your trade association or leading trade magazine may tell you of a new way in your field to use fax profitably. The books, newsletters, and magazines listed at the end of this chapter can also help.

Fax Breakthroughs

Find your breakthrough. There should be a unique, profitable way for you to use fax or it's not for you. Travel agencies submit trip choices and prices and reservations by fax. Banks quote loan interest and terms, get applications by fax, and often fax back first-stage approval. Theaters fax seating layout with available ticket locations and get orders back by fax. For one restaurant, 10 percent of those to whom a faxed discount offer was sent came to lunch.

Hotels and motels offer room space, get reservations, and confirm by fax. Restaurants and delicatessens fax menus to business customers and get reservations and orders. Dayton's department store in Minneapolis keeps names of executives interested in specific kinds of suits not yet in stock. It faxes them on arrival and gets a fax order back.

One stockbroker who sent out 99 identical faxes at 8:30 a.m. reported that his share of a new issue was sold out in hours by fax. A single brokerage firm may store on disk 20 to 30 lists for fax broadcast, with addresses and fax numbers of 1000 to 2000 people on each list.

PR by FAX! Many public relations firms fax their news releases to news agencies and their clients. They believe that fax gives the information an aura of urgency and importance. The giant PR firm of Hill & Knowlton uses fax a great deal for releases. News releases that used to arrive by overnight mail now arrive by fax. Digital Publications of North Cross, Georgia, came up with a PC program to send press releases in volume by fax.

Cold faxmail often fails. Jack Miller, president of Quill Corp (a business-to-business catalog) tested out-bound fax telemarketing. In an interview with *DM News*, he said: "We found it costly to use and a very slow way to disseminate a lot of messages. The response rates were not as good as those we received when our messages go out by mail." The same cold fax is resented most when it costs you most, during daytime office hours. In some states it is illegal. A cold fax is resented least when it's cheapest to send, from 11 p.m. to 8 a.m., because it's delivered before office hours.

Fax-Aided Business Catalogs. According to *DM News*, when the Quill Corporation print catalog asked for orders by fax, it had a quite different result. When I contacted Jack Miller, he verified this and gave me further details. The 16 incoming lines on PC in the Order Processing Department received about 2300 orders daily, with an average order of $107. Other catalogs with business, institutional, educational, and government customers have had similar success.

Software Developers Company of Hingham, Massachusetts, sends out catalogs to programmers who often want more detailed information fast. SDC features a service called "FastFaxts." Anyone can call SDC's fax number, press on a push-button phone key numbers featured in its catalog, and at once get the material faxed back as part of the call. Over 100,000 SDC customer fax calls were handled this way in one year. FastFaxts is completely automated and uses no people time, and all costs of faxing are paid by the customer. Erik Sherman, director of Technical Service for SDC says: "To send this by mail would take one full-time phone operator and four people to pick and mail the material—and cost us $125,000 plus postage even when we get material free from manufacturers. We get tremendous savings and our customers get fast service."

DM News reported that Day-Timers and Edmund Scientific have received an increasing share of orders via fax for years, just by putting their fax numbers for orders in their catalog. John Ravage of the Day-Timers business-to-business catalog told *DM News*, "Some faxed-in orders run up to ten pages."

How to Write Faxmail Copy.   Write and send a typical, personalized fax letter or memo to a customer or prospect you know. Provide new information that's wanted and even has been requested. Ask for action, but give a reason that is vital to the recipient. Put one hand-written sentence on top. Write your fax as if it were a favor, perhaps something extra you promised to supplement or clarify during a visit, phone call, or letter.

Design your fax as the final closing effort or as part of a chain of follow-up. Offer to phone with still more information about to come in, or just ask if more help is desired. If this effort succeeds, fax in the exact same way to other prospects and customers. Broaden its use by different salespeople. Design a series of special niche efforts to small lists personally known by your representatives, distributors, and dealers. Then fax to bigger lists.

Fax-Aided Ads.   Fax-aided ads are ideal for anything sold to businesses or to executives for personal use. We added our fax number to a *Wall Street Journal* ad for our Sea Eagle inflatable boats and offered to fax information on any specific boats. By noon, we had four fax requests. We faxed pages of our catalog to fit those requests. By 1 p.m. we got back by fax an order with enough profit to pay for the merchandise and the ad.

A big percentage of direct mail from business firms and ads in business publications feature fax numbers. Even FTD Florists promote flowers-by-fax.

Fax boosts least-cost promotion. A classified ad or an inch ad can be transformed by featuring a fax number. When the fax inquiry comes in, a full page or more of features, testimonials, and documentation of your product benefits can be instantly sent to interested inquiries. Other low-cost fax ads abound. Any product shipment or bill sent to a business can include another product offer and the promise of more information by fax and a request for a fax order.

Handouts at trade shows ask for and get fax orders and inquiries. A salesperson's leave-behind literature can do the same. Executive business cards with a fax number can get a fax response. A big share of trade orders for our Panther-Martin fish lures come by fax, just from listing our fax number on our letterhead. For some companies, most orders are now placed via fax. *Advertising Age* magazine gets 70 percent of its orders for classified ads via fax.

Fax-Aided Inquiry and Order Handling.   Some of fax-provided advantages for inquiry and order handling include the following:

- Fax is always available. After-hours phone orders are no longer lost.
- Fax eliminates wrongly transcribed phone orders.
- Fax avoids duplication of confirmations and phone orders.
- Each fax order costs less to handle than by live phone.
- A fax call is more apt to get through via fax auto repeat functions if the fax order line is busy, whereas a jammed phone order line lose orders.

The more you promote your fax order number the more "junk fax" you will receive. It's a lesson to fax others as you wish others to fax you. Fax owners form a club. You are a member. Observe fax etiquette. Do not junk-fax others. Let others know what you do and *don't* want to be faxed and when. Find out from prospects and customers if and when they wish you to fax them. Follow their desires. Publicize your fax number discreetly, via targeted mailings, media, and handouts.

Voice-Fax Response.   Some voice 800 or 900 phone numbers feature an interactive voice system which offers you choices of phone information and then further response by regular mail, courier, or fax. If you want a fax, you give your fax number. Both parties benefit because prospects and marketers contact each other and exchange fax numbers only as desired.

Voice and fax communication can be combined into a powerful, personal, and fast-paced marketing tool. The phone is used for whatever can be orally explained. Fax is interjected as needed to send drawings, detailed price break-downs, or unfamiliar nomenclature; legal or scientific or other highly specialized information. Jut remember to add the personal touch to your otherwise businesslike faxes. If you market something complex and high-priced where a fast decision is needed, fax and voice mail are an ideal combination.

Multichoice Voice-Fax.   For any of Sprint Gateway's more than 300 services, you can get instant fax literature. An 800 phone number offers you a digitized voice menu. You select by push button. And for more than 40 of Fidelity Corporation's 200+ mutual funds, Fidelity will fax customers and prospects the requested information. The fax is the standard way to respond in many business situations. Many brokerage houses store information on virtually every public company and fax it out on request.

Fax "Bingo Cards."   Many business and professional magazines offer fax "bingo cards": A voice system 800 phone line takes an inquiry's name and address with a fax number option. These names are faxed to you or sent by mail or UPS. You get leads while they're still fresh, in contrast with the circled bingo card numbers, which take weeks to process. Be aware however that many fax bingo inquiries' level of interest and quality often are only a little higher than those of responders from printed bingo cards.

In a variation of the bingo format, fax numbers of participating advertisers are printed on a magazine page with a suggestion to fax for more information. Here too, the quality of the inquiries is often only a little better than that of printed bingo cards. Sometimes the magazine loads fax literature from each participating advertiser on its equipment to provide instant response to each inquiry. Although this eliminates junk fax to the advertiser, many of those responding only give fax numbers. This makes it harder to trace the resulting sales. One solution is for the magazine voice system to require a name, business address, and business phone as well as a fax number.

Trends to Watch

Fax Service Bureaus.   As more customers and prospects want similar sales information faxed to them, fax marketing multiplies. And as more complex technology provides far more fax services, fax service bureaus become needed for state-of-the-art equipment, larger-volume capacity, tight cost control, and investment avoidance.

Fax Newsletters and Faxpapers.   Some fax publications are flash updates of printed publications, and others sample on-line data. Some carry ads. Several morning papers have an evening fax edition. Paid-subscription fax editions of newspapers have been less successful than free fax newspapers supported by ads. A paid subscription fax is more successful in niche fields or when it's translated into another language and faxed overseas.

Fax on Line.   WeatherFax, an aviation weather service, is available to subscribers who pay $125 a year to be able to call any time for the latest weather flight conditions. And Fidelity Fund offers hourly fax updates of price-per-share quotes for 36 of its funds.

Fax Marketing to Consumers.   Growth of the home fax market is as fast as the use of fax and faxboard purchases, spurred by tumbling prices. As consumer access to fax machines increases, a growing percentage of consumer catalogs are asking for fax orders.

Faxcasting. Sponsored fax program via 800 and fax 900 services are increasing. Some of the requirements for success are similar to those of audiotext. Although much of audiotext appeals to wide audiences, faxcasting appeals mainly to narrower niches.

Faxed Catalog Pages. A firm may send out a big catalog once a year to preferred customers and a small catalog more often. The smaller catalog also lists models not in it, but covered in the big catalog—with an offer to fax any desired page.

Anywhere Fax! You can fax from virtually anywhere with a portable laptop computer and faxboard. These portable fax machines can even plug into your car cellular phone.

Fax Customer Support! Any service problem, with clarifying diagrams, can be answered by fax on demand via an 800 or 900 line. Faxing needed information wins respect, loyalty, and reorders.

Almost-Free Fax! Any electronic fax relay sends fax over dedicated data telephone lines, without interfering with its normal data traffic. To send fax on lines already paid for costs virtually nothing extra.

Summary

To start in fax marketing, follow these guidelines:

1. First study, don't spend. Get into fax gradually.
2. If you don't sell to business people, first use fax to contact your representatives, distributors, and dealers.
3. Plan fax tests but don't buy any new equipment.
4. If your office has a fax machine or faxboard, use it. If you don't, use a public fax machine or fax service bureau.
5. If you have access to a fax machine, list the number on your letterhead. If not, get a faxmail box from a nearby fax service and list that number.
6. If you sell to businesspeople, list your fax number in each ad, mailing, or catalog you produce.
7. If enough orders come in, get a fax machine or faxboard. Don't get the cheapest or the most expensive. Shop for the best value. Check each claim with other owners. And reconsider a fax service.

8. As your increasing volume requires it and profit from fax justifies it, upgrade and add equipment or use a fax service bureau.

9. Note the fax numbers of each incoming fax order and ask for fax numbers of all inquiries. Ask permission of prospects and customers to fax them future bargain offers and product news. Build a "yes"-list, your fax-number database.

10. During the appropriate season, create a tempting offer of an exciting product. Write persuasive short copy.

11. Fax the letter to 100 to 500 of your yes-list names, after 11 p.m., when phone costs the least. Track your exact costs and response.

12. Compute your profit or loss. If successful, roll out cautiously. Increase your yes list. Create additional small, niche tests.

13. Investigate any new fax success stories, especially within firms similar to yours. These include fax-aided ads, fax bingo cards, fax how-to information, and niche news via fax response 800 and 900 lines.

14. Be skeptical. Buy the smallest ads that tell your story well enough to ask for fax response. Stop as soon as the first results fail.

15. Expand each small success in fast, safe increments.

16. Keep looking for the fax marketing use that's uniquely suited to enhance your newest marketing campaign.

Two parting words: *Be cautious.* For many fax uses that seem right for you, there may be more smoke than fire. The most tempting use for you may not yet be proven. Keep watching continuing changes in fax technology in the near future that can affect you most:

- *Ever-faster-speed* fax that receives on plain paper, pays for itself in months, and cuts costs thereafter versus older, slower fax machines that use fax paper.

- *Ever more dots per inch* that improve the quality of text and graphics you send and receive via fax machine or board.

- *Improved software* that *scans* faxes received, sends to a computer, and converts to editable form.

- *Many more* fax machines, faxboards, and software, that are far faster—and send and receive better-quality color text and graphics.

Help Source Guide

1. *Brite Voice Systems* makes and sells interactive fax response systems. For a *free* list of most-called Brite fax programs, names and addresses of

providers by localities, contact: 7309 E. 21st St. N., Wichita, KS 67206-1083. (316) 652-6500.

2. *Brooktrout Technology* designs and manufactures electronic-message-integrated voice and faxboards. Allows sending and receiving fax from PCs: 144 Gould St., Needham, MA 02192. Fax (617) 449-9009. *Free* demo fax: (800) 333-5274.

3. *Fax Info Network of America* offers a *free* information kit and pamphlet: 20 Max Ave., Hicksville, NY 11801. Fax (516) 942-1000.

4. *Probe Research* is a facsimile and voice services newsletter, voice and fax conference, business strategy studies and forecast on fax: 3 Wing Dr., Suite 240, Cedar Knolls, NJ 07927-1097. (201) 285-1500.

5. The following can be counted on for special issues, stories on fax, lists of fax-on-demand service bureaus, annual conferences on phone (including fax): *Inbound/Outbound* magazine—12 W. 21st St., NY, NY 10010 (212) 206-6660; *Telemarketing* magazine—One Technology Plz., Norwalk, CT 06854 (800) 243-6002; *Infotext* magazine—34700 Coast Highway, #309, Capistrano Beach, CA 92624. 900-INFOTEXT; *Voice Processing* magazine—P.O. Box 42382, Houston, TX 77242-9901. (713) 974-6637; *Interactive World*—4141 N. Scottsdale Rd., Suite 316, Scottsdale, AZ 85251 (602) 990-1101.

6. *Teleconnect* magazine publishes an annual buyer's guide that includes facsimile machines, fax gadgetry: 12 W. 21st St., NY, NY 10010. 800-LIBRARY.

7. D. Fishman and E. King's *The Book of Fax*, 2d ed., 1990, is a guide to buying and using fax equipment: Telecom Library, 12 W. 21st St., NY, NY 10010. (800) Library.

8. *The Voice/Fax Integration and Enhanced Facsimile Services Market Report & Forecast, 1993* (268 pages) is published by the Information Publishing Corp. *Report* is an in-depth, splendid, expensive guide to the forecasted market for enhanced fax services through 1995. Special Reports Division: P.O. Box 42382, Houston, TX 77242. (800) 777-4442. (713) 974-6637.

9. *Using Fax as a Strategic Weapon,* by Fax Broadcasting, is an aid to Design Alternative Distribution Channel by TechProse Inc.: 370 Central Park West, NY, NY 10025. (212) 222-1765.

12
Video Brochures

In most big businesses, a video is a key part of any large marketing campaign. Videos are also a big reason for the success of many smaller, special-niche products and services.

A promotional videocassette can reach almost everyone capable of buying anything beyond the basics of food, shelter, and medicine. Over 70 percent of all U.S. homes have VCRs. VCR penetration surpasses 90 percent among households with disposable incomes beyond necessities, and most business executives have access to a VCR in the workplace. This chapter discusses video brochures; Chapter 13, video catalogs; Chapter 14, video production techniques and costs.

The following are some of the advantages of video:

Can deliver the closest thing to a personal sales call at a fraction of the cost

Can be any length and in whatever detail needed

Has all the advantages of TV presentation

Can be targeted to only those desired

Can be used in many ways and for many years

Often can be modified and updated

Can do some things no salesperson can

Video is the next best thing to actually touching, holding, and using a product and can work better than live demonstrations in the store, office, factory, or in a home. Video can make intangible benefits suddenly clear and desirable. Do you have documentation that what you sell does what you say? Customers who swear by your product? If so, a video can show graphic-action proof. It can let real people bring testimonials to life and make them more believable. It can be as sophisticated as a Hollywood movie or as simple as a camcorder home video.

Video's many profitable uses include

Product demonstration	Company's concept/credentials
Sales meeting	Training/inspiration/PR documentary
Store display	Product-use education
Fund raising	Free or cost-priced premium
Sales training	Presentation of ad plan to trade

Often the same video has several uses. Or part of a video for one use can be converted to another function. In this way, the cost of multiuse videos can be shared between a company's departments. But the video-cassette format has constraints that prevent it from being used profitably for some products and services. Some disadvantages of videos include the following:

Costs usually total far more to reach your desired audience than via many other media.

Production costs alone are often greater than most ads.

It can be a huge undertaking to plan, make, and get a video seen.

Each use has special needs and constraints.

Videos require much time, research, effort, control, and analysis.

To make and distribute even the cheapest, camcorder-produced video "brochure" will be costly per person who sees it. Some video brochures cost 10 times as much per person reached as a very elaborate mailing piece, over 100 times more than many full-page ads, and over 1000 times as much as many inch ads. Read Chapter 14 to get an idea of what it takes to produce a video that has a chance.

Should you consider a video? Don't use a video to do anything another medium can do as well or better for far less. Don't use a video if you sell low-price staple items to individuals who buy infrequently—whether you are a small retailer with one location or a wholesaler with few customers for a wide variety of low-cost goods and with a small margin of profit. If you manufacture or import a low-priced product with a low profit margin, don't create a video to sell consumers via mail order or to try to pull them into stores.

But if you can get big orders from jobbers or dealers, consider a video. Use it at trade shows and meetings and have your salespersons use it to help induce distributors, jobbers, and stores to stock your products; also try to use it as a store display. If your product enjoys a breakthrough, competitive advantage, consider video very seriously. A large profit margin gives you an even better chance to succeed with video marketing.

If you sell a higher-price article or service—whether it be a car, home, appliance, office equipment, financial service, or whatever—video brochures are proven marketing tools. Uses keep increasing.

How Do You Start?

The following steps will help you get a start on your video:

1. Analyze who your customers and prospects are.
2. Analyze whatever success your business now has.
3. Study the video assets of your products and business.
4. Determine the use of your planned video and how it will fit into your entire marketing campaign.
5. Plan how you will distribute your video.
6. List whom in your firm you must get cooperation from.
7. Organize a team effort.

Refer to the Help Source Guide at the end of this chapter. Ask your trade association about use of videos. Also ask your trade magazines and your suppliers. Talk to your sales representatives and your dealers. Read business, advertising, marketing, and direct marketing publications. Find ads and mailings to office and home offering videos. Send for and study them.

Phone the producers of promotional videocassettes. Try to learn how successful these videos have been for firms in your business. Also examine companies that use video to sell any product or services in your price range to your customers and prospects. Ask how the videos were used, what was the response versus the expense and how this compared per dollar with the use of other media.

How much should a video cost? In Chapter 14, we'll discuss costs in more detail. Briefly, cost ranges from a few hundred dollars for camcorder-it-yourself to hundreds of thousands of dollars for a more elaborate production with top equipment and staff. Most professional videos are made for $3000 to $5000 a minute, but some are made for $1000 to $2000 a minute using hungry freelance production people.

We'll also discuss several shortcuts in Chapter 14. But remember that however little a video costs, if no one sees it, the money is wasted. Cost to distribute must be part of your budget. This cost can vary from little to tens of thousands of dollars. First, start analyzing your business and what you want from your video.

Your Company Concept on Video

The right products are more important than any advertising. But behind every great business is a concept that is more important than any product or service it offers.

Has your company's concept been expressed in a speech or article by the founder or CEO, or in an ad or booklet or mailing piece? Is there something in your concept that's different, inviting, and suited to video presentation? Get your creative people to suggest ways to include your company's concept and build your video around it.

Does Your Firm Have a Video Star?   A company's success is often due to a strong personality, perhaps the founder or current prime mover. He or she may be the ideal spokesperson for the company concept. However, be aware that to use a video to build up your boss or star you, when inappropriate, can be a catapult to disaster. A name personality who is already your firm's spokesperson may be ideal to use in your video.

However, video can be a perfect stage to showcase a talented amateur who may perfectly express your firm's concept while showcasing each product. Do you have someone in your company who is charismatic, videogenic and a natural salesperson; great at demonstration, who projects integrity and is ideal to present your firm's concept, and whom your video can bring right into the living room or office?

Do You Have a Videogenic Product?   Does your product look great on screen? If small, does it look better magnified? If big, are there small parts that have important functions and are important to feature, magnified on screen? Can your product or service be enriched with color and romanticized with soft camera shots and mood music? Spend more to use the right director, cameras, and quality tape video.

If you sell intangible products and services, start with your proven easel presentation, supported by charts, graphs, and data. These can become even more convincing with computer graphics. If you sell hobby, sports, or special interest products or services, a videocassette can educate people to get started and get more out of the activity. Perhaps it should feature a star teacher and "missionary" in the field. If you sell in a fast-changing field where prospects and customers are bewildered by choice, use of the right teacher or advisor—with simple, believable presentation—can get customers to seek your advice.

Do You Advertise on TV?

TV is flooded with many short commercials, creating clutter. There's constant competition for the eye and ear. It's often confusing for the viewer. While advertisers still profitably use 15- and 30-second commercials to saturate a simple theme, they use a video to explain their produce/service in detail. TV can attract and deliver your "headline" benefit. It can promote your video. This two-shot approach can give the flash frequency of TV a change of pace. A video can then demonstrate your product's benefits and describe each in whatever detail required.

Do You Direct Market?

A direct-response offer is the simplest way to use and measure the power of a marketing video. One of the most effective and superb videos ever made sells SoloFlex Exercise Equipment. The only talent was a parking attendant who used the equipment and an off-screen voice. The video was first created as a gift to buyers to help them get more out of the equipment. Owners made copies for friends who often made copies for their friends, resulting in many additional orders from pass-along copies. SoloFlex then offered this video to inquiries from other ads and has had a high percentage of closures for an average sale of $795.

Next, the SoloFlex video was adapted into a far more profitable use as a half-hour commercial or "infomercial" on cable and broadcast TV. It has run longer and more profitably than almost any other direct-response video. Sales directly traced from all uses passed $100 million. The SoloFlex video was so successful because

1. The model was *credible* (without bulging muscles but virile), *attractive*, and *natural* (what almost everyone wants to be).

2. The demonstration showed in a variety of ways how use of the equipment could help you look the same (uniquely, simply, step by step, and without pain).

3. The presentation sold SoloFlex not as exercise equipment but as a cosmetic to make any adult more attractive to the opposite sex.

4. The perfectionist production—from lighting to composition—increased the appeal of the model yet made the *equipment* the gleaming, hi-tech, believable star of the show.

Video Response Success

A video can be powerfully persuasive. But as in any other medium, successful videos require the right offer of the right product at the right price at the right time. With the right presentation, you too can succeed like SoloFlex. It is admittedly rare. Here are 14 steps to video response success:

1. Feature one product or service.
2. Entertain, inform, tell your story, convince.
3. Demonstrate your advantages.
4. Make claims and supply proof.
5. Feature living testimonials.
6. State just what your product or service will do.
7. Get across the integrity of your company.
8. Cite favorable cost comparisons with other products.
9. Give an extra saving.
10. Offer a giveaway.
11. Put a time limit on your offer.
12. Make a clear, simple, persuasive guarantee.
13. Feature a toll-free number several times.
14. Present the entire story in accompanying printed material.

A nebulous video gets nebulous results. To get orders, you must ask for them. Ask in the video. Ask in printed literature sent with the video and ask again in follow-up mailings. And test to see whether it pays to ask in follow-up telephone calls. Each time you ask, do it nicely, with restraint, in a friendly way. And ask less often and with still more restraint for more upscale products.

Your chances of video success are far better when your video is used to enhance other marketing tools and to help cause bigger purchases. Properly teamed up, marketing videos succeed for most kinds of business in some way.

How high-priced a unit can a video sell? By itself, a video can sell something for up to a few hundreds dollars. The video price ceiling climbs with print follow-up, still more with telephone follow-up, and considerably more again with a personal sales follow-up. The best results for items selling in thousands or millions of dollars come from a combination of all these methods, but only if there is enough up-front promotion.

In the travel industry, every airline, ship line, and major cruise company uses video brochures on the trade or consumer level. Big real estate developers also create videos, even for promoting new office buildings. Smaller firms in these fields do, too, as does the hotel business, where budget hotels have found that videos can dramatize what you get at bargain prices. Naturally, videos also convey the thrill and look of the good life of a luxury hotel or resort.

Most of the biggest video successes I have encountered were each part of a larger integrated marketing campaign. How you team up your video with other marketing tools is crucial to its success. Today, a video component to a marketing campaign is accepted by most major companies, so much so that its contribution is taken for granted and not independently measured.

If your firm is large, you'll have more marketing tools at your disposal. If your firm is small and your marketing tools are few, you may be able to use what you have more effectively and measure better what your video contributes than larger companies can. Let's review your other marketing tools.

Telemarketing a Video. Coupling telemarketing with your own video opens up a wide array of marketing options. You can offer the video through telemarketing and then follow up with another sales phone call once it's been received and presumably viewed. Or the video can include a phone order or inquiry response device which begins with a qualifying, in-bound telemarketing sales script. Offering a video over the phone may be appropriate only for certain types of customers, for a limited period, or for periodic use. Still, your video may make a major difference in the productivity of your telemarketers. It just might become the centerpiece of your telemarketing efforts, used in every call throughout the year. Test it. Just count the orders, compute costs, analyze profit, and act accordingly.

Training and Video. Many giant dealer organizations put training material on a videotape. The salesmen use the videotape to brush up on a model. Many showrooms have a VCR on which the same videotape can be run. Prospects ask all sorts of questions and get quick, reliable answers on a wide variety of details.

Salespeople Video. A salesperson may use a video on a sales call, send it first, or leave it behind to sell. Often, he or she need not visit at all—just send the video in combination with phone selling or even computerized letters. A powerful video brochure left behind at the prospect's office can become a strong ally in helping whoever is convinced to sell other decision makers in an organization.

Videos to Attract Prospects to Meetings. Do you attract prospects to meetings? Club Med does. The principal use of its videos is to convert a higher percentage of attendees to sales of its Club Med vacation packages.

Club Med's retail sales and information boutique offers videotapes of various destination offers. Rod Frankel explains:

We like to get people to come to us; to come to a meeting at one of our centers. We like to show them the video, answer their questions and sign them up there.

We have used videotapes for a Club Med open house party with a travel agent at our place. We organize events with travel agents by the hundreds. These are big parties through the year and we often do things on a co-op basis and split the expenses, (including) the cost of setting up a video. Videos play a big part.

Videos and Sales Meetings.   Do you conduct sales meetings with representatives, distributors, jobbers, dealers? The right video can set a sales meeting on fire. Richard Capalbo, president and CEO of Van Eck Securities Corporation of New York City, says

Videos are great at meetings. The importance of a video is related to the number of salespersons, number of showings made, number of meetings, number of people who come to each, and to all meetings. As more come, more money can go into more effective videos.

If you invest in a network of sales people, it pays to invest more to maximize their productivity. To get more out of sales meetings, it pays to spend more money per person at the meeting in order to make the most effective presentation to those people.

According to Capalbo, videos can extend entire sales efforts:

I've seen videos used in the course of many deals, cross-promoted in every way and tied into the entire campaign. Videos designed as sales support, when effectively made, can create extra traced sales, more than pay for their extra costs, and create good profit.

Capalbo understands how versatile a good videocassette presentation can be:

Videos can be sent to homes. Client viewing at the office is also important. Sometimes viewing with a salesperson. Often a salesperson can go to a client's home with a videotape. Videos are very good tools to get interviews for salespersons. Portable VCRs can even be provided for account executives.

I've seen the marketing videocassette effort geared mainly to salespersons. Often videos are used for seminars and meetings. In some firms, all offices have projection screens. The video has become part of the corporate culture and develops far more productivity per salesperson.

Video as Public Relations

Your video can be powerful electronic PR, resulting in valuable free publicity for your products and company. You can often get articles or stories written about your video, and the proper publicity can get free viewers for your video. If you have a product or service involved in a famous event, a public relations-oriented video brochure can often result in TV exposure. PR videos can also be used in internally- or externally-oriented sales videos. And footage of any video often can be incorporated in another.

A big share of corporate video is created for PR purposes. The biggest public relations firms have big video departments. Several small companies have used PR entirely to launch a video and have received thousands of requests and even orders. Once you have a specialized video (or footage that can be edited into one) with content valuable to anyone seeking information in a particular field, seek free publicity in media covering that field.

Video Brochures and Other Media

Do you advertise in publications, on radio, or by direct mail? Do you find that your messages are too short to tell your story? Use of a video combined with other media often improves the chances of each to succeed.

A video can support other media to make them more effective. A big ad or mailing piece can mention a video with so little space as to add virtually nothing to the cost. With pictures, copy, and headline, the ad can get across what your video consists of.

Or you can make the video the *central* marketing vehicle by reducing ads to minimal size—an inch ad or even a classified ad can pull requests for a video. Or these tiny ads can ask for calls to 800 or 900 numbers where an audiotext system can describe your video in detail and then take live or recorded requests for it. Do you send out bills in quantity? Feature your video in a billing insert. Do you use UPS to ship to thousands of customers? Include a package insert describing your video. Throughout this book you will find other electronic media which can be mated with a video for mutually greater selling power.

Retail Videos

For retail videos, the store environment allows you to promote a video brochure in a number of ways. Let customers see your video run on demand as an electronic demo. Set up a counter where customers can request and get it. Or sell your video in a bargain package with an entertainment or special-interest video best-seller. Create a display for your video. Feature it in the store window. Do you slip goods purchased into bags for customers? Slip in an insert offering your video.

However, suppose you sell to stores but can't get your goods into enough of them, or enough of your line in, or enough display. Can a video help?

Commodore.   Commodore Business Machines, Inc., used video to create prospect excitement—so much so that it closed sales for its Amiga line of computers from a bigger percentage of prospects and at a lower selling cost than it could in other ways. It did this by showing prospects examples and applications of what fiercely loyal owners often praised—Amiga's stunning graphics, animations, and sound. The feeling at Commodore was that disk-based demos were slow for the purpose and tended to run out of memory when running Amiga's complex animations but that producing a video had these special advantages for Amiga:

1. A video was an ideal way to show what the Amiga was all about and could be seen anywhere the prospect preferred.
2. Producing a tape was cheaper than "on-air" commercial time and could run any length.
3. The pressure of a "live" in-store demonstration could be avoided.
4. Video was a high-impact way to get the message to the prospect by showing Amiga's abilities in education, art, music, entertainment, productivity, and video. Besides, the Amiga was a video-compatible computer—why not take advantage of its video capabilities?

Dealers Close Sales.   The cost of production was under $89,000 for the 15-minute videotape, "Amiga Test Flight." About 20,000 tapes were sent out, 10 each to over 1000 dealers. Dealers used the video as a sales tool to help close sales. Amiga's videocassettes functioned as a tool to help get customers into the retail store and to help close the sale. Prospective customers picked up the videotape at dealers who either charged a deposit for the tape or gave it away. Most dealers opted to give the tape away. Julie Bauer of Commodore reported: "Our survey indicated that, of those who phoned an 800 number and asked to see a tape, 93 percent saw it. Of these, an average 28 percent bought. And for some dealers, as high as 50 percent purchased an Amiga. There was a wonderful dealer reaction. The video was a smash hit."

Special Problems.   Video can be the right format for dealing with special problems:

- Do you need to persuade lots of desirable candidates to work for you? Big companies make videos to describe job opportunities and make them more enticing for desired classifications of employees.

- Would you like to lower liability claims for your customers and yourself and pay for the video's costs while increasing your sales? Videos which teach how to use certain equipment have done all this.

- Want to raise money and/or upgrade donations of regular, generous donors? If your board chair is an important person and videogenic, have her or him make a videotaped, personal appeal.

- Do you want to bring industry to your area? States, counties, cities, and even smaller locations have created video brochures to get across advantages they offer for companies which might move there. The videos sell everything about the area—from cultural and recreational advantages to business advantages, while also showing specific available locations.

Multiply Your Chances of Success. A video or versions of a videocassette that *help* your dealers, distributors, salespeople, phone marketers and/or your publications and direct mail advertising sell obviously will succeed better than a video that attempts to do *all* the selling itself. Don't promise results until you test at each step and measure the response. First prove that your video works profitably for one dealer, one distributor, one salesperson, one ad, one mailing. It won't happen at once. By steps, it will.

Only if you first win enthusiastic cooperation from all those concerned will others use the video effectively. Bring them into the process early. Decide what you want each to do. Each person's biggest contribution may be to supply accurate response information, something even car companies have trouble getting from their dealers.

Avoid Video Failure

Start with your concept of your dream video. Know what you want it to do. Spell it out, in detail. Don't give it too many jobs or a purpose in conflict with others. Don't attempt a Hollywood production with a camcorder. Cut the pattern of your objective to the cloth of your budget.

At Apple Computer, Linda Tsien is customer marketing manager and responsible for the use of videos for the home and small business market. The Apple attitude is "do it right." Cost is secondary in importance. Linda says, "We select a vertical market to go after where we believe a video is suitable. We use it for a highly targeted group. We do it right at whatever the cost.

We'll spend more on the video, on the media, and on the tracking. We want to get the highest return possible on the investment, but we want a quality job which we feel is the fastest way to our objective."

Do what Linda says. Select the right market. Go after a highly targeted group. And even if your budget is a tiny fraction of Apple's, "do it right."

If Small, Think Small.   If you can only make a video in the simplest, lowest-cost way, use your own camcorder or borrow one. New features make it surprisingly possible to produce low-cost videos for simple tasks. New videotaping systems using PCs make desktop videos more sophisticated. Even simple videos are proving to be profitable, when used correctly.

Whatever your company's size or budget, you may find video shortcuts. Each must be judged as to whether it compromises the objective of the video. Is quality paramount for the video's effectiveness? Measure each shortcut on the basis that it may make possible a profitable video which otherwise could not be produced.

Do You Have Videos Already?   Does your company use training videos about the equipment you sell for your sales force? If so, consider converting these videos to train your end-users, as a customer service. As a next step, consider selling these and advanced training videos to these customers thereby creating a new profit center.

Or you might modify a customer service or training video into a demonstration video which sells as it shows. For example, do you have a video which explains to employees what other employees do and how your company operates? Consider converting it to show your customers and prospects the company behind your products.

Develop Videos Naturally.   Do you use audiovisual programming? Many AV users have found that to make a video do the same job is a small step. Club Med used audiovisual demonstrations for years to show groups of prospects specific destination tours and sign them up. So did Royal Viking Cruises and Air France.

If your company made any corporate films, converting them to videotape is cheap and may give you valuable footage that provides a low-cost start to making your first video.

Do you have a cartoon character as a trademark or symbol which can be animated in video? Do you have videotapes of focus-group sessions too long for TV but in which users of your products are more convincing than any ad? Has your product or service ever been successfully demonstrated by your company, or its equivalent by a competitor? A video demo may be even better.

Let Audios Lead to Videos. If you use audiotapes to train, sell, or for public relations, it may be a smooth transition to make a video for the same purpose. Past sales seminars or speeches by any in your organization at industry and professional shows and conventions can also provide material for your video.

Consider using videos to promote seminars. Consider selling the video and selling seminar attendance with the video as well. Videos are usually simpler to create from seminars, are a natural adjunct to them, and often can be profitably sold to attendees as well as to those who cannot attend.

Make Your Video a Profit Center

Consider combining your video with a best-selling related video or with a book, newsletter, or catalog. Build value and offer a bargain. But, make sure you concentrate on your main purpose: using your video to market profitably what you sell.

Marketing video consultant Bill Fawcett reports that very limited numbers of videos for small enterprises (and his clients) have created surprisingly large sales and profits:

A Chrysler dealer in Monterey, California, sent out 202 videotapes and sold 43 trucks and cars.

A golf course developer sent out 154 videos and sold over $3 million of condominiums.

Another country club development made 11 sales averaging $1 million—all from sending out 252 videos to a highly targeted list.

How can you achieve results like these? Bill recommends that you follow his five-step method:

First step   Carefully identify your prospects. Remember, videomarketing is a narrowcasting science, it's not a broadcast medium. Therefore, the more time you take to identify a quality list of prospects the better results you can expect.

Second step   Design a video mailer that will cause the prospect to open the video mail and play the enclosed video. Video mailers that work best appear to be gifts.

Third step   Script the video in a direct-response manner. Highlight strong benefits to cause the prospect to commit to the offer. An on-camera spokesperson will have a 3-to-1 effectiveness ratio over a voice-over narration.

Fourth step Use a three-phase telemarketing program: (1) tell the prospect that a video is coming; (2) after the video is received, make sure the prospect plays the video to qualify the prospect to receive a call after viewing; and (3) make the final call to close.

Fifth step The accountability phase. Here you make sure that whoever is responsible for the telemarketing follow-ups has done their assignment.

Bill says that

> A video must be needed, the sales strategy must be right for the situation, and the production must be professional. There are certain "musts" regarding the use of videos.
>
> To sell, videos must be seen. Sixty-five percent of those to whom we send videos do not watch them. A major problem is to convert those people who do not watch the video into people who do. This requires effective telemarketing prior to sending the video and after sending the video, as well as sales follow-up.
>
> There must be rewards; to inquire, to buy, to recommend, to do anything we request. We get 17% of the people whom we send a video to return it for some reward. A videotape must be purchased or be a gift. It should come in a package that looks like a gift. It should have a quality feeling.

Three ways to sell more from your video are:

1. *Ration your videos.* They must sell something expensive to be justified, usually to someone more successful and busier than most, who owns a VCR. But these people are short on time to watch a video and are constantly being offered more videos to watch. Don't waste their time and your money. Only make a video about something that is badly wanted by somebody. Only send it to someone who very likely wants what it offers. Target your market.

2. *Qualify your viewers.* It's easy to get people to request videos. But you need interested prospects, people who will play the video on their VCR, and are likely to *buy* what the video describes and shows. A casual inquiry is not good enough. One qualification has been to charge for the video. Some firms then give it back as a credit on the first purchase. Air France only takes video orders by credit card and on an 800 number, for $14.95 (there is no charge if the video is returned within 14 days).

3. *Promote your video as though a book.* To get requests or orders for a video, you must sell the benefits of seeing it. If you oversell, few view-

ers will buy. Start with brief copy, the sell more. Often the advertising of a video has started out as the briefest of mentions in ads. Gradually, as the video's effectiveness is proven, the marketer devotes more advertising space to sell the reader to send for the video. Finally, it features ads built around the video from the headline down to persuade the reader to send for the video.

Keep sales records scientifically. Use of videos has become accepted as a necessary part of a campaign and often is not measured when it easily can be. Measure results precisely. Analyze results and be guided by them. It's easy for retailers to compare video requests with sales. Any competent direct marketer does.

Every video should earn its keep, whatever its objective. Its performance should be measured, and the future use of any video should be stopped or improved based on lessons learned. Here are some reminders:

1. Start simply. Build from what you already do.

2. Always look for an extra, a bonus from your video.

3. Get any free publicity you can from it.

4. Track inquiries and sales.

5. Use your video in every possible way.

6. Integrate your video with your present promotion.

Help Source Guide

1. *Fawcett's Video Marketing* is a marketing, production, communications consultant. It can provide success stories about videos for car dealers, real estate developments: 13700 Alton Parkway, Suite 167, Irvine, CA 92718. (714) 380-8677.

2. *Lightscape Productions Inc.* is a production house for commercials, industrials (corporation videos for internal use or to sell products, services). Request success stories: 158 W. 29th St., 7th fl., NY, NY 10036. (212) 695-6434.

3. *Medialink* is a video PR network that reaches networks, cable outlets, news bureaus via AP newswire. *Free* 21-page *Video News Release Handbook:* 708 3d Ave., NY, NY 10017. (212) 682-8300.

4. Articles featuring direct-response video brochures are available from *Direct magazine*, 911 Hope St., Six River Bend Center, Stamford, CT 06907. (203) 358-9900. *Direct Marketing* magazine, Hoke Communications Inc., 224 7th St., Garden City, NY 11530; (516) 746-6700. *DM News*, 19 W. 21st St., NY, NY 10010; (212) 741-2095.

5. *Karol Media* offers affordable VHS video duplication; printed sleeves/mailers, and warehousing and fulfillment, sponsored video distribution for schools, organizations, and cable TV: 350 N. Pennsylvania Ave., Wilkes-Barre, PA 18773-7600. (800) 526-4733.

13
Video Catalogs

For years, almost all attempts at converting a traditional print catalog into video form failed. The only kind of video catalogs that succeeded would not even be called catalogs by many traditional catalogers. These were really video brochures of a very special type. But each was created to be a perfect marriage partner with an enclosed print catalog. And only certain kinds of print catalogs proved to be suited to a video marriage.

I call such a video format a "cocatalog." Sometimes it's a support medium to the print catalog. Sometimes it's dominant, with the attached print catalog serving a subordinate role. More often each is of equal value. Without print support, a video catalog usually fails. And without video support, a print catalog is often less profitable and more limited.

Chapter 13 explains how some of those who have succeeded with video cocatalogs have done it in what kind of fields and for what kind of products. Through others' experience, your chances to succeed can greatly improve. Let's start with some basics in judging whether you should consider a video cocatalog.

The video catalog format offers these advantages: color, action, graphics, demonstration, personal persuasion, living testimonials. This format can introduce people to your staff and show your company's departments in operation and provides a closer experience to going to the store rather than buying by mail. Since all the advantages of video brochures are applicable to video catalogs, why have video catalogs so often failed? Primarily because of the way they have been used. Video catalog disadvantages include the fact that too many items can fight each other for attention. Video catalogs make it difficult to scan, pause, jump ahead, refer back. Production problems increase with each item included, and video catalogs require more time, expense, new specialists to produce. Their cost per thousand of those reached is far higher than for a print catalog.

Most video catalogs failed because they simply translated into video form what a print catalog does without regard for video catalog's advantages and disadvantages.

Why do print catalogs succeed? Many factors make print catalogs very effective in ways video catalogs can seldom compete against. A print catalog, in sizes most often used, can be carried anywhere, read any time, and kept indefinitely. The pages can be flicked quickly to the section desired, and a wanted item easily located. People are accustomed to and enjoy catalog shopping. On a square-inch basis, print catalogs are still a low-cost way to show, describe, and sell items.

Different kinds of new technology are developing that should allow a video catalog (VC) to portray better what print catalogs so effectively do. Later in this book, we'll cover how simplified portions of or entire VCs can be made at far lower cost. In this chapter, let's see how video catalogs now succeed, mostly in ways quite different from print catalogs.

Should you consider a video catalog now? To be safe, don't think about creating a video catalog unless

1. You have a catalog concept that uses video's advantages.

2. You have some items proven successful via video brochures.

3. Most of these items appeal to the same people.

4. The average sales expected is from $300 to more than $1000 or, if lower, a high percentage of customers is expected to buy a number of times.

5. It's a field in which a video catalog has already worked.

6. You have a profitable print catalog or can create an effective one to use with your video catalog.

Some VCs which ignore these specifications will succeed and some of those that follow all of them undoubtedly will fail. But these guidelines may help you determine if a VC is more likely to succeed than fail. After reading this chapter carefully, review Chapter 12 and Chapter 6 on how to make a TV commercial. Follow up with the Help Source Guide references at the end of this chapter and read Chapter 14 on video production.

What succeeds best? Look for a field with little competition, high margins, and a better bottom line. It should be growing fast, with intense interest by new users—a market still too limited for the economic use of TV advertising, yet with products and services that video can best demonstrate and with an average order of several hundred dollars or more.

Once you've selected a field, consider products which are related to and are best used with each other; lead to a chain of future related purchases; are suited to videos as described in Chapter 12. Look hardest for products that are brand-new, or recently successful on TV or a video brochure and are available to you exclusively. The ideal is one you invent and make or import yourself, with no royalty—with maximum value to the customer and minimum cost to you. At the same time, avoid quickly changing fad or fashion products.

To build a successful catalog, either VC or print, takes the same painful item-selection process. What succeeds in print may not succeed in video. Winners may rank differently. An item, successful in space advertising or in a catalog, may fail on TV, or the reverse may occur. But generally an item which has been successful in one medium has a better chance of succeeding in another than one untested. It's usually safer to rely on what has succeeded on TV than via print. Not just highly targeted videos succeed. VCs are also used (in special ways) in more universal fields. Let's discuss one field in which a VC is widely successful and has its greatest percentage of success—education.

Education and the Video Cocatalog

Education marketers *don't* use a video catalog *instead* of, but *with* a print catalog. They leave to the print catalog listings and specifications of courses. Print does this better: Student needs differ, and choices are carefully made with much flipping back and forth. But the VC, better than print, gets across the concept, lifestyle, and range of activities from studies to sports to hobbies to fun. It visits classrooms, labs, locker rooms, fraternities. Viewers meet faculty and students.

It's built to be seen from beginning to end. Nothing fights for attention. All content works together to build overall interest. The video cocatalog and print catalog each supplement and strengthen each other.

VCs for educational institutions evolve naturally, mostly without benefit of top professionals. Video yearbooks are often produced for and sometimes by the graduating class. Film made over the years can be converted to videotape. There are decades of photos and drawings, often on slides. Campus TV stations have studios and videos of TV broadcasts about the university, plus the editing facilities and volunteers to edit it all. Often small colleges and schools use their own camera crews, students, alumni, and friends to make videos at little cost. Over 1000 education institutions (and more every year) use video catalogs to show their facilities to prospective students. Some are very professional.

The Kansas City Art Institute made just 165 copies of its video to showcase and bring alive art, the work of its students and itself, and to increase its enrollment of 500. The Institute director of admissions said

> The video catalog is very effective and cost less than $20,000. We're very selective. We target advertising carefully in art magazines and by mail to people interested in art and education.
>
> We send video catalogs to applicants. We'll send it [a video catalog] to any group. We show it to the staffs of schools who can recommend us. We show it with a staff attendant from our college who can then answer any question.
>
> We showed one to every prospective student and gave each a print catalog. We do know that our enrollment went up very substantially and better than any previous year.

Guidelines for Success

Let's review what makes for a successful video catalog. A successful video catalog

1. Covers a field uniquely suited to video presentation
2. Performs catalog functions best suited to video
3. Avoids catalog functions perfect for print
4. Features related items ideal for video brochure
5. Emphasizes the concept of the business category over specific items featured

Marco Polo

Ramesh Manghirmalani founded Marco Polo by Milani Ltd., a Danville, California, importer of upscale silk fashions. He markets primarily by mail order. Ramesh got an MBA at Harvard Business School and gained much experience in telemarketing as an executive at Citicorp. Within a year of starting his business, he applied this telemarketing experience to promoting a Marco Polo video catalog.

Ramesh imports high-quality, expensive silk garments from an Indian factory he half-owns. First he created a high-fashion print catalog and sent it to high-income women. Next, he created and distributed 2500 copies of a 14-minute video. He sent 1400 of these copies to his print catalog customers and 1100 to upscale, exclusive retail stores, each with a print catalog.

Before sending any video, he first telephoned each individual to make sure that the person really wanted a video catalog and was interested in the price range of his merchandise. Sixty percent said they were. Each person called had to agree that the company could call back for the person's reaction. The subsequent phone call was made eight days after sending out the video catalog. Ramesh reports:

> Results have been extremely good. We made a second video catalog and then a third. Our video catalog now accounts for 51% of our overall business, our print catalog brings in 45%, and stores only 4%.
>
> Of those who got our print catalog, 12% ordered, for an average of $495. But, with one telemarketing call before, and several after, 48% of video catalog recipients ordered—spending an average of $830. Of the orders, 60% came by mail and 40% by phone.
>
> Our first video catalog was 14 minutes and featured 18 items. Our second was 21 minutes with 25 items, and our third 26 minutes with 31 items. 80% of those we sent a video to have a VCR with freeze-frame and search capability. It's as easy as flicking a page.
>
> We sell a video catalog for $14.95. We offer to buy it back for $6. So many send it back that we have rotated 3,000 cassettes to 21,000 people. It would cost us $7 to $7.50 to reproduce each copy.
>
> So far, everything has been on a test basis. Our total sales are only $1,500,000. But, next year I'll open a store. We're aiming at distribution of 100,000 video catalogs and sales of $7,000,000, all in silk.

Common Questions about Video Catalogs

The following are questions to answer before starting your VC:

1. *How long should a VC be?*   Most run from ten minutes to half an hour, although we'll soon describe one of almost two hours.

2. *What does a VC cost?*   Most cost about as much per minute as a video brochure, or often more, because they're usually longer. (See Chapters 12 and 14.)

3. *How do I produce a VC?*   Find the right mix between a print catalog and a video brochure (see Chapter 14).

4. *How frequently should I make a VC?*   Decide to make VCs one by one, as results justify. Amortize each over longer periods.

5. *Should you ask for vendor funding?*   Only if you can get the right item at the right price and keep control.

Timing and Tone

How long should each item presentation be? In a print catalog, a small picture of a product with a tight description of a few words can often be productive. In a VC, a flash demo of the item rarely gets across what it is and does. Direct-response TV commercials on broadcast and cable TV are usually 2 minutes, 1½ minutes, or 1 minute. Shopping TV network personalities chat as they sell. Often 4 or 5 minutes are devoted to a single product or service.

Each item requires from 30 seconds to 5 minutes depending on how exciting, videogenic, and demonstrable it is. Spend time preparing and tightening the presentation of each item. If an item is less suited to demonstration, present it more briefly. Always get the optimum lighting for each product to make it look great.

Be friendly but discreet.   Achieve and keep the mood you wish to get across. Don't use hard-sell techniques in your video catalog. And never jam together a series of sales pitches: Competing items will fight each other to the death of most sales. Avoid this item struggle by resisting an overemphasis on any item. It's out of character with the image of a quality firm.

Study the friendliness of TV shopping shows. A prestige catalog cannot be too familiar with its customers—a Tiffany salesperson does not slap a dowager on the back. But do put a friendly feeling into your video presentation, completely in character with your catalog.

Find a balance: You should do more than a TV commercial or print catalog to answer potential questions about a product, but don't constantly and aggressively push the viewer to inquire or order. Do feature your toll-free phone number on the screen, but do it discreetly, during a product demo. Also show a mailing address every so often.

Sell other ordering methods. Your video catalog can dramatize the convenience of ordering by means of your company's various ordering systems. Use a segment of your video catalog to demonstrate to the customer how easy teleshopping is or how to use your audiotext ordering system. Explain the advantages of staying on the line and of getting more detailed information on an item by audiotext. Offer to notify those interested about future specific sales. Explain how to request such service via audiotext.

Video Brochures Combined into a Catalog: Wood Mizer

Now let's examine a case history that proves the power of video demonstration, how videos can grow into catalogs, and the big-dollar sales that can result. Wood Mizer advertises itself as the world's largest manufacturer of portable sawmills. It also makes wood-carving machines and drying kilns. The carving machine sold from $300 to $1000 in different models. The Wood Mizer log-cutting machine sells from $6000 to $15,000 and the kiln for $800.

Wood Mizer produced a video brochure for each and then combined all three into a video catalog sent with print literature. Jeff Laskowski, now president of Lastec, Inc., says: "Each product is highly related to another. The two kilns are particularly logical because any wood which is cut has got to be dried. Once a person has bought the sawmill, he has to find some way to dry it. So when we offer a way, most people take one of the two kilns. It's a highly related add-on and perfectly suited to items already shown in the video."

Wood Mizer's video catalog runs well over 1½ hours. Twenty-five minutes are devoted to showing all their products. Then, in 15 minutes, the plant and employees are shown. Although an off-camera voice describes the manufacturing process, the camera roams, showing different activities. Next, two people saw away for 15 minutes to show the entire process of how the Wood Mizer cuts a log. There's 10 minutes on a solar drying kiln. Next, there's 12 minutes on a vacuum-drying kiln. Finally, the carving machine demo completes the video catalog.

The Spiegel VC Analysis

After 100 years as the catalog of the blue-collar worker, Spiegel transformed its catalog business to appeal to upwardly mobile career women. The change, guided by focus-group research at each step, caused the most successful turnaround in catalog history.

Spiegel viewed the creation of video catalogs as a logical progression of its development of speciality catalogs, based on the same thorough, scientific research. Rod Parker, marketing programs manager for Spiegel, summed up the advantages and obstacles of a video catalog for Spiegel:

> Video allows you to present an item in a way that brings it to life, in color, in detail, and in action. You can see it move and in operation.
>
> You can't touch or feel the products. Video can't show merchandise faster. Each video competes with other forms of communication. Most people don't use a video player to search through the tape, find the desired item and stop. Some don't even have the equipment to do that. Most people look at the video throughout.
>
> Whether it be long or short, offer people what they prefer to watch. Hold interest all the way, with enough information and entertainment to keep viewers a full half-hour or whatever. Create a mood that makes effective selling possible.
>
> Have a clear-cut purpose. From the first working script, know why the video catalog is being made; what it is attempting to do. Build it to attain its purpose.
>
> Target a certain group. Go after that group throughout. Perform a service for it, in a way that holds interest, and provide something else that print cannot.

Fashion Hope for Larger Women.   One of the fastest growing and profitable specialty Spiegel print catalogs is directed to larger women. This was the area selected for Spiegel's video catalog.

There are an estimated 24.9 million large women in the United States. Research showed that about a quarter were interested in looking attractive and dressing smartly. Most in this group already were customers or prime prospects for Spiegel's print catalog for the large. Another quarter of the female large market had given up, made no effort to dress well, and were relatively hopeless prospects. But about half, while discouraged and not now making an effort, were hopeful that somehow, and in some way, they could dress and look smarter.

The half-hour VC was not marketed to the most discouraged group. Obviously, it would solicit the most prospective group—the same best target serviced by the print catalog. But the video catalog's main function would be to persuade those among the other 12 million large-size women that fashion help was on the way, that Spiegel fashions could transform their appearance and perhaps their life. The idea was to get inquiries from the best prospects among this group, send the video, encourage them, sell them enough merchandise to be profitable, and then gradually get the video seen by others in that huge universe.

Spiegel's Video Concept.   Rod Parker described the video project: "The purpose was to show how fashions had been designed to make large-sized women attractive and that certain styles could dramatically affect their look." Phyllis Lampkin, a large-size fashion expert, interviewed fashion designers, beauty and hair experts, and representatives from fashion houses which made large-size clothes. The video catalog showed featured fashions for office, home, and leisure wear. Then, demonstrations documented "makeovers," how the right fashion and makeup could change a woman's looks.

Every element built upon the basic theme. Rod Parker described, "The video was designed to knock down all the barriers the larger woman has in shopping through the mail: lack of self-confidence, fear of poorly fitted clothes, concerns of quality and a lack of awareness that fashion is available to them." The video catalog was offered for sale in the main Spiegel catalog. Spiegel sold more than 22,000 copies. Within a year, Spiegel pronounced its video catalog a success. Follow-up analysis showed that the group who bought the Spiegel video subsequently maintained "significantly higher sales volume" of Spiegel merchandise than those who did not buy the video. Rod Parker explains why: "We set out to do with the video what the print catalog could not do well. We created it to work in concert with the print catalog. But we made it information-driven. We used tips and fashion design interviews to give encouragement, confidence, to give information on new fashions and on the new-looking appearance large-sized women could now have."

Spiegel and the Future of VCs. Spiegel continually conducts market research to help develop new video catalogs from 7 to 30 minutes long. Rod explains:

> Each of our specialty markets is a marketplace we have to create and develop. For each, a video has a different job. Video creates excitement. While the printed page is one of the easiest ways to shop, we try to make the catalog experience easier by marketing the video with it.
>
> We look at all specific marketing segments. For each we ask the questions: Is there a role for video? Would it be profitable?

What does Spiegel think about the future of VCs? Rod says: "Video could get stronger and stronger. Video is the medium of youth. Kids just getting out of college have been accustomed to the TV medium. Video catalogs are a very natural way to service them with information important to the purchase of merchandise.

Here's a parting word of caution from Rod: "The easiest way to lose money in a video catalog is to view it as a way to present your product instead of providing information and service for your customer."

How to Test-Market a VC

If you are a cataloger with likely videocassette viewers as customers, offer your new VC in your print catalog as Spiegel did, whatever your business. You might also send out a video brochure appealing to the same prospect; include a package-insert offer of your VC. Whatever your business, use package enclosures, billing enclosures, and inserts in mailings to offer your VC.

If you advertise anything in any medium reaching appropriate prospects, include several lines of copy offering your VC. Feature a toll-free number. Test a quarter-column or half-column ad. Wood Mizer first offered its video with a three-inch ad one time in *Popular Science*. Or start by offering your video with an inch ad or even a classified ad. If your video is highly specialized, offer it in publications reaching the same special group. If your firm is large, include in your first test other secondary tests I'll shortly suggest. In any case, track inquiries and orders.

Here are four ways to test your VC offer:

1. Sell your VC as a part of a bargain combination offer that appeals to your prospects, such as a $29.95 value for $14.95. Include a subscrip-

tion to a newsletter and several print catalogs or perhaps an audio-tape or a special-interest or entertainment videotape. Offer a refund against the first purchase.

2. Charge $2.95 to rent. But also charge $12 for a deposit that you'll return when the video is returned.

3. Loan out the video for free but take a credit card number, credit-clear it, and specify that if the video is not returned within 14 days, you will put through a charge for $9.95. Also consider other pricing alternatives from entirely free to $7.95 on approval for the VC only.

4. Or mail the VC free to customers as Ramesh Manghirmalani did in his first test. But also phone first to qualify recipients and to get permission to call after, as he did.

I suggest that you only test the above VC offers or any others if you get at least a thousand VCs distributed each way.

Important Packaging Reminders

VC packaging is even more important than packaging a video brochure. The outer enclosure should have a sticker with big letters stating "THIS IS THE (NAME) VIDEO CATALOG YOU ORDERED" or another message that tempts the recipient to open it. The inner package should convey value, look like a desirable gift, and project your video catalog concept.

The first selling piece seen must convince the viewer to put the video into the VCR. The VC must be able to sell even if there is no accompanying printed matter. Conversely, the print catalog enclosed with a video must be able to sell as if the VC is never viewed. Yet each should help the other. It's inexpensive to include ample ordering literature. It can be black and white but must contain detailed information on any item demonstrated by video. Besides including your print catalog, consider providing additional literature on each item shown on VC that's not in your print catalog. This need not be in color. Include more models, colors, sizes, add-ons, and accessories and related items than in the VC. The added cost is nominal compared with the cost of the VC. *Don't* use a print catalog with a different toll-free number or mailing address. Confusion kills orders. *Do* enclose a catalog with special key numbers for the offer. *Make buying simple.* Anything complicated cuts orders.

Phone Follow-Up and Multiple Use

After you ship each video catalog package UPS second-day air, phone 100 people who have ordered your VC. Explain that the VC is on its way, that it's a big investment and an experiment. Ask if you can call back after the VC is received and get a reaction. For those who agree, call back in 10 days.

Your VC in various forms can be used in many of the same ways as a video brochure (many are explained in Chapter 12). If you're a manufacturer that sells through stores, use your entire VC on VCR as an in-store video of your entire line. Most stores can only stock a limited inventory. When a clerk shows your VC, the customer can select any item from a wider range of colors and sizes and models with a bigger choice of accessories than stocked by the store. Items can then be shipped to a customer's home or to the store. This may lead to the store stocking more goods.

Consider a joint promotion with a related catalog. Your video catalog becomes theirs. You drop-ship and supply the video. Your joint venture partner reproduces and distributes it to its customers.

Rolling Out Your VC-Test Success

In order to safely roll out your video catalog test, first do some simple direct marketing math—carefully. This involves checking your mail counts and actual sales, after returns. Recalculate your profit margins based on actual product costs after manufacture. If you import an item, check your landed cost based on actual bills. Calculate each cost of processing orders in house. Get all added costs, including production costs. Include in your video catalog equation the prorated cost of the smallest video catalog mention in any ad. Have your accountant make up a profit or loss statement for the video catalog as if it were a separate business. Have the accountant calculate the profit and loss in two ways: (1) with all production and talent costs applied against the VC and (2) amortizing these costs at 10 percent of traced sales

Analyze if any parts of the VC test were more profitable per dollar spent in advertising. Make a pro-forma projection of promotion and of traced sales for the next three years based on using VC advertising that was profitable in the test. If your figures are marginally profitable based on amortizing costs, make a small confirming test. If figures show a better gross profit per dollar of promotion than your present advertising, double your confirming test size.

Follow these guidelines to make a confirming test:

1. Drop the losing parts of your original test.

2. Spend half as much on marginally profitable parts.

3. Spend five times as much on the most profitable parts.

Whatever form of promotion proved profitable, do more. If free PR worked, try for a lot more. If a mention in your catalog was profitable, increase its size. If you can split-run your catalog, test three sizes of these mentions for your VC, up to a full page. If package, billing, or mailing inserts were profitable, print and enclose three times as many. If a classified ad or an inch ad worked, buy more but in the same kind of publications.

Buy each ad selectively. If your video catalog inquiry cost and percentage conversion of buyers to VCs-sent-for were both low, test for a higher-quality inquiry. If your inquiry cost was high but with high sales in proportion to inquires, test ways to lower the inquiry cost. If phoning 100 people who ordered or requested a catalog got more orders, phone 500. If phoning 100 people before and after did better, phone 500 before and after. If it was a big success, phone every VC requester before and afterward.

Proceed with Promotions Step by Step

Follow the same precepts described for rolling out video brochures in Chapter 12. If a VC mention in your print advertising worked, give it more display value and a better position. Increase the space size in careful steps. Repeat ads equally cautiously. The tinier the ad, the more often you can safely run it. But test bigger sizes. Often, a bigger-size mention will prove profitable but not as profitable per dollar spent as a smaller size. If so, run with the smallest size most often and the biggest, still profitable size occasionally.

Test making your offer stronger. Put more excitement into your copy, as if selling a book or movie. You may get more inquiries but of worse quality. Constantly track the percentage of those mailed who order, the average order, and total dollar sales per VC sent out. Where quality suffers, "tighten up" the offer and copy or raise the quality of your inquiries. Qualify by media. Also, consider making the following tests.

Card Packs. A simple way to start in direct mail with the least money, risk, and know-how is with *card packs* and other cooperative mailings that offer a multitude of products and services. Many of these coop mail vehicles are better at pulling inquiries than making an immediate sale. Some of these card packs or coop mailings include a classified section, probably the least expensive way to start.

Often a card pack publisher is also a mail order firm. It may use some cards to sell its own wares, the firm may sell some to advertisers, and the firm may, for the last cards in the pack, take advertising on a percentage of sales or *per-inquiry* (PI) basis.

Only consider card packs reaching precisely your target prospects. Avoid a per-inquiry deal—who knows how many will convert to sales?

But be open to a percentage-of-sales deal. Try a classified display or a straight classified ad. And avoid the "bingo" listing (name of company and/or product with a number to be circled) except on a percentage of sales.

For a card pack you can't make a deal with but one that reaches exactly your prospects, first test half a card in only one card pack. A half-column ad will fit nicely. But cut your copy and make the headline and display bigger. If you succeed with one card pack, buy others cautiously, a little at a time. Negotiate. Learn what others pay for cards, what extras they get, which cards pay off for whom. Very likely you will only succeed in the right specialized packs, and volume will be small.

Phoning or Writing Customers. Some combination of writing and calling your customers to induce them to get your video catalog makes sense to test. Do this if inserts or a mention in a print catalog to your customers get video catalog orders or inquiries which result in profitable sales. Try sending 1000 first-class, personalized, computer letters (signed by your CEO) to recent buyers of above-average orders (items most related to those in your VC). The CEO can thank each customer for, and refer to, specific recent purchases, describe the VC briefly, and say that an assistant (name) will soon phone to make arrangements to send the VC.

Within a week, phone, refer to the letter, and describe the VC in more detail. Explain that it is expensive, that you want to send it, but only if customer will look at it, and ask if it's OK to phone later for a reaction. Use the offer which worked in the print catalog. Ask if it's OK to ship, and phone 10 days later for a follow-up conversation. If this procedure is profitable, phone and mail 3000 more customers of related items in the same price range. If successful, phone and mail to 10,000 similar customers and then in larger increments.

Cautiously try for the jackpot. As long as you succeed and have other, recent similar customer names, phone and mail (or mail, phone, and ship the VC and then phone) more. Meanwhile, test a phone-and-mail campaign to 500 customers who ordered related items in the same price ranges but between one and two years ago. Also phone and mail 500 recent buyers of less-related items and 500 customers of lower-priced related items. If successful, phone and mail 3000 and then 10,000 of each of these groups.

Finally phone and mail to outside lists. This is the most difficult task but can produce many more direct-response sales than most other sources. To succeed with outside lists, start learning state-of-the-art know-how in direct mail. Read books by Rose Harper, Richard Benson, Dick Hodgson, and others I recommend in the Help Source Guide. Reread Chapter 9 on out-bound telemarketing. After every test, analyze why it failed or succeeded.

Judging Success at Each Stage

For a small start-up venture with little capital, a video catalog must pull in enough sales with enough gross profit from its first test to at least beak even. This must include the cost of advertising to get each inquiry; any phone expense; all packaging, handling, and shipping expense for each copy of the video mailed; and any list expense if a mailing to outside names. The production cost of the video should be divided by the number of video copies made. The amortized production cost per copy times all copies mailed in a test should be calculated and included.

Bigger catalogers may seek new customers who can be expected to have a customer life as long or longer by VC and who buy as much or more than present print catalog customers. These catalogers are willing to spend upfront in promotion expense a percentage of anticipated future profit. *Caution!* If you can't afford it, don't do it. Realize that if you spend upfront to get customers who leave you after buying less (and less profitable) merchandise than estimated, you lose.

For a small successful print catalog, a video cocatalog must produce enough *extra* sales and gross profit from the first mailing with the print catalog to cover all its costs. Judge this by comparing to the results of mailing the print catalog alone when sent to the same number of the same kind of people, whether customers or prospects.

To be statistically valid a test must be big enough to get enough individual orders to be a representative sample. Since a higher average order is needed for a video catalog to succeed, this usually requires a larger mailing, which may be beyond the financial abilities of a new entrepreneur. A smaller test will be less scientific. If the test fails badly, I advise stopping. If successful, the strategy must be retested *scientifically*. This means getting out substantially more video catalogs, with the promotion and costs involved. Because larger production and a larger test require more detailed know-how, I urge you to read the books recommended in the Help Source Guide.

Last Suggestions on Tests and Roll-Outs

Most VC successes have been cocatalogs of higher-priced items appealing to special markets distributed as the result of ride-along promotion. This involves little out-of-pocket advertising risk. Most start-up video catalogs on their own have failed, particularly when mailed unsolicited to outside lists, usually for lower-cost items appealing to mass markets.

If your firm is bigger, you may be interested in a VC only if it can produce sales of significant volume. The more your firm spends to produce a VC, the faster you may want this sales volume. Whatever your firm's size, if you have much more success than expected in your first test, you may want to expand much faster. If you have a competitor producing a VC to reach the same prospects, you may be in a race. Small firms generally should proceed more slowly. Go at the pace suited to your situation, step-by-step, and prudently. And, be aware of the newer developments in video catalogs. Watch for success stories of video cocatalogs teamed up with one or more other visual (from print to TV) and new EM media, with video a much more dominant partner, and even for video catalog success on its own, with minimum mention in co-media.

Keep up with continuing changes such as those listed below as these changes alter what your video catalogs can do best; your catalogs' chances of success, and, if profitable, of being outmoded by competitors, and how soon; and what you should do to benefit and outcompete at each step.

- Availability of high-density VCRs and videotape with the color resolution of fiber-optic cable for most set owners

- Much improved high-compression software, multiplying VCR catalog content of items, descriptions, demos, etc.

- Far better software to search VCR catalog forward and backward and freeze any frame

- Video-frame catalogs with each frame like a print catalog page but with an off-screen voice

- More interactivity to view menus of item types, followed by item menu of type wanted, then speed-scanning to correct frame, and call-up of as much information as needed about any item

- More types of V-cats, from children's catalogs in cartoon story form, animated at low cost, to interactive seminar-business catalogs with spreadsheets and charts

Help Source Guide

1. *Alternative Media* from Leon Henry Inc., a list broker and consultant firm, provides a resource on marketing freed from high-postage costs, on reaching as many as 50 million homes more efficiently than via conventional channels. Definitive tract, complete with valuable checklist of pitfalls, *Free* to direct marketers but $25 to brokers, agencies, students, consultants: 455 Central Ave., Scarsdale, NY 10583. (914) 723-3176.

2. *Catalog Age* magazine, published by Cowles Business Media, provides articles on video catalogs: 911 Hope St., Six River Bend Center, Stamford, CT 06907. (203) 358-9900. *Catalog Age* also sponsors, with the Direct Marketing Association, the Annual Catalog Conference and Exhibition and top books such as Dick Hodgson's *Successful Catalog Marketing*, which addresses how

to create catalogs, best opportunities, selecting merchandise, and L. T. Hill's *Profit Strategies for Catalogers, 1989,* which looks at how to get all sales and profits your catalog can deliver.

3. Katie Muldoon's *Catalog Marketing, 2d. ed.,* 1988, written by a top print catalog consultant, is available from AMACOM Division of the American Management Association: P.O. Box 1026, Saranac Lake, NY 12983. (518) 891-5510.

4. The *Catalog Marketer* newsletter is available biweekly from Maxwell Sroge Publishing, Inc. For a *free* copy, contact: 228 N. Cascade Ave., #307, Colorado Springs, CO 80903. (719) 633-5556.

5. The *Direct Marketing Association* (DMA), and its DMA Catalog Council, provide an annual show with seminars, video- and audiotapes, books on catalog marketing, including seminars on fulfillment and on customer service: 11 W. 42d St., NY, NY 10036-8096. (212) 972-2410.

6. M. Sroge's *How to create Successful Catalogs,* 1985 (480 pages), written by a top expert, is available from NTC Publishing Group: 4255 W. Touhy Ave., Lincolnwood, IL 60646-1975. (800) 323-4900.

7. Rose Harper's *Mailing List Strategies,* 1986 (213 pages), from McGraw-Hill, Inc., provides all-inclusive, timeless classic tips: 13311 Monterey Ave., Blue Ridge Summit, PA 17294. (800) 722-4726.

8. The Target Conference Corporation offers the annual *National Catalog Operations Forum,* at which skilled industry leaders serve as faculty for catalog operations executives: NCOF, P.O. Box 1161, Ridgefield, CT 06877. (203) 438-6602.

9. M. Sroge's *101 Tips for More Profitable Catalogs,* 1990 (122 pages), is available from M. Sroge Publishing, Inc.: 228 N. Cascade Ave., #307, Colorado Springs, CO 80903. (719) 633-5556.

10. Richard V. Benson's *Secrets of Successful Direct Mail,* 1989 (208 pages) is a sound, superb book available from NTC Publishing Group: 4255 W. Touhy Ave., Lincolnwood, IL 60646-1975. (800) 323-4900.

11. *SRDS* bimonthly directories provide direct mail list rates, data profiles—13,000 lists for business, consumer, farm, other producers. Also available are rates, data on card decks—over 700 business, consumer decks, plus 100 inserts, coop mailing programs. Profile, circ., issue & closing dates: 2000 Clearwater Drive, Oakbrook, IL, 60521. (800) 232-0772.

14

Making a Video According to Your Needs

The difference between making a TV commercial and making a video is that, due to its extended length, a video production's budget per minute of film or tape produced is usually stretched to the extreme. For example, if a video is done in a hurry, so much more can go wrong that you can wind up with an unwatchable embarrassment. In addition, if a video is made like an expensive TV commercial, the video's costs can go out of sight.

From an organizational standpoint, it's more practical for a small moonlighter to devote the time, effort, and expense to learn how to make his or her own video rather than a TV commercial. In the same way, it makes sense for a large company which makes a lot of videos to set up its own in-house video production department. However, most companies should use a middle-priced, quality-conscious production house.

This chapter covers all these video production scenarios. Along the way, you'll read the advice given by video experts—entrepreneurs and managers of *Fortune 500* companies. First, let's finish detailing the major differences between video and TV commercial production.

In video, shooting outside of the studio occurs more often. Hiring a freelance producer is more apt to be a practical course of action, as is going to a smaller city or even abroad, for the sake of economy. Contract negotiation tends to be more important in video production, hence clearing everything with a lawyer experienced in TV and video situations is imperative. The editing process is also usually more important, especially when a video mostly or totally consists of edited material with an off-screen voice.

Naturally, there are also many similarities between video and TV commercial production. Chapter 6 explains the necessity of identifying your objective, studying the successful production executions of others, and writing a tight script before you begin TV commercial production. All this also applies to producing a great video.

The Right Spokesperson

A spokesperson can be vital. Do you have a strong personality in your company? Someone who sweeps people off their feet? Somebody who can mesmerize? Anyone who can explain, persuade, or convey integrity and trust? Teach and give confidence that others can learn? He or she can be a powerful spokesperson for your video and become a valuable marketing asset for your company.

Previous Footage

Previous footage can be a big help. Airlines and cruise companies inexpensively converted to tape big libraries of film to promote the glamour of their destinations. From this huge bank of video footage, these companies constantly put together videos to promote new bargain destination offers.

Do you have video footage from previous videos or films? For training, marketing, or a message to stockholders? To show how to use your equipment? Or perhaps you can get access to videos or film footage from customers, suppliers, your trade association, or other sources which could be effectively included in your video.

Try backtracking to a natural source. Some videotapes are based on previously made audiotapes, often recorded at seminars. Excerpts from a series of videos can be combined into one video. How-to TV shows can be converted into videos. Extra footage shot for a teaching program can be used in a longer video or may lead to another that sells a product.

Teaching in any electronic medium may lead to a training video. The promotion of or programming for any form of electronic marketing may lead to its use in a video. Part of or all a videodisk, a floppy disk, a CD-ROM disk, a video conference by phone, or a business TV show by satellite can be transferred to videotape. Read the rest of this book with this in mind.

How Others Succeed

Let's now learn from a variety of people and businesses how to produce a successful video. We'll hear from small, medium and large businesses, as well as from some top video production professionals.

International Business Exchange

International Business Exchange, a business broker in Austin, Texas, for six years has based its business on making videos of businesses for sale and showing them to buyers. I asked founder Ed Hart how good the quality of a video needed to be for purposes such as his. Ed is a realist. He wants simple, low-cost video tapes:

> Look, we do these things right. There is no flicker, no flashes. It's not bad video. But we know that you can get better-quality video from the local TV station or from any number of producers. That's not what we have for sale. We use our business brokerage ability to find desirable businesses. We then show them to buyers in a friendly way, all with camcorders.

Q: How much video experience should you have?

A: I knew nothing of videotaping, but a lot about buying and selling a business, more than most people in the country. Questions every genuinely interested prospective buyer must know—questions to ask the owner—and how to present a business to the buyer.

Q: How does a small firm start to make a video?

A: I bought a camcorder and learned how to use it.

Q: What is the least-cost way to get a producer? A director? And whatever cast you need?

A: I paid no one. At first I personally went out and worked with the seller and taped the owner. I took the owner through the various phases of his business operation, by asking him questions and demonstrating the business.

The owner explained all the ins-and-outs and told of its successes and potential. I taped him, his employees at work, and everything about the business. I was the producer and director. The owner and employees were the cast. I was the off-screen announcer.

Q: Once you tape, what is the least-cost way to edit?

A: I put my son, Roy, in charge of this problem. Roy had worked in the business for years. He knew pretty much every aspect of what buyers look for in a business. Once the raw footage was taped, it came to him in Austin, and he took over. He had no previous experience either, but he was soon quite comfortable working with video equipment.

Q: How did Roy do it? What about graphics? Titles? How did he, for the least cost, put it all together?

A: I wanted do-it-yourself computer editing and producing and inserting of titles and graphics. I knew nothing about computers. When Amiga Computer, with its wonderful color reproduction, came out, we bought one. We also bought from Electronic Arts, Deluxe Video 2, and Deluxe Paint—two programs for Amiga.

Q: How did these help?

A: With them, we developed a capacity to create very exciting titles and charts in color. It was possible to convert high points from a revised pro forma financial statement and convert them into graphs. These would jump on the screen and dramatically show the profitability potential of the business.

Q: Did you need a lot of other software?

A: No, but one other program proved very effective. It was a weather atlas which showed weather maps for every state. It was therefore possible to show the business location and to show on-screen in full-color such things as the average temperature, number of rainy days per year, and other facts.

Q: As you made more videos, did you hire a lot more people?

A: No. I then began to recruit sales reps, on commission. Each rep would, on a camcorder, learn how to videotape. I would then give each the kind of questions to ask. I'd work with the rep. We'd video-tape together. After getting the knack, the rep went out and inter-viewed and taped the owner just as I did.

Q: How did you change shows? Based on trial and error?

A: We began to include, in every show, the living conditions of the area of the business. The new owners had to move there to operate. They wanted to know where this place was and what facilities existed.

Every videotape included footage of the area showing the downtown district, country club, and sports facilities; the university nearby, the arts and cultural center, and whatever was attractive—not just for the pur-chaser but for the spouse and kids of the purchaser.

We learned how to edit demographics from the Chamber of Commerce and to put all the pertinent facts on screen. We learned how to flash out the cash flow; to calculate the bank interest, and to show what payments would be each year; and what the business had to do in order to meet pay-ments for the business.

Q: How long are your videos?

A: Our typical videotape runs 20 to 40 minutes. That includes all the finan-cial information shown in charts. Some are quite simple.

Q: Doing it your way, what does it cost to produce?

A: From $1500 to $11,000. The average is $4000.

Apple Computer

Now let's learn how a highly innovative, huge company plans and makes a video. Linda Tsien, customer marketing manager, is in charge of video marketing for Home and Small Business Products at Apple Computer. Linda reports:

For some time we've been developing a program to educate customers. We wanted a new selling environment. We investigated various media. Video seemed to us to be an opportunity. It offered sight, sound, and motion in a living room.

Q: Who had the idea?

A: A number of individuals at Apple. I was a champion of it.

Q: What was Apple trying to do?

A: We wanted to reach people who used or wanted to use a computer at home or in their business; to talk to them about their needs, wants, and complaints. And to show them without hype or push what Apple could do for them...in more depth than we could in other media. This was two years ago. We went deeply into the concept.

John Sculley favored the idea. It was very appealing. We had considered it to be informative, entertaining, and in character with Apple. This was very difficult. We knew our objective but not how to accomplish it.

Q: What was the next step?

A: It was to put alternatives into script form and consider them. We looked at a lot of scripts.

Q: Who wrote the scripts?

A: In July, a writer and director team came up with something. We didn't need to write scripts, we decided. We just should let Apple owners do the talking. This made the most sense.

A: How did you do this?

A: We contacted Apple owners, with this kind of question or request: "We would like you to communicate your own thoughts about Apple. Just tell us what, why, when, where you really got into a personal computer. What you find out about Apple. Tell us the positive and negative side. We can't pay you because we don't want to have paid commercials. We just want you to sit in front of a camera and ask questions. You answer. We won't change what you say." We didn't suggest or change a word. And it came out as if we had conceived the original idea.

Q: How much did all this cost?

A: Nothing for the people but our travel costs, a lot for everything else. We don't give out these figures. But we felt it was important to do things right.

Wood Mizer

If you have any product or service that is or can be demonstrated, here are some lessons from Jeff Laskowski of Wood Mizer, Inc.

Lesson 1—Teach by Showing. Jeff says:

We didn't plan to make our first video, or think of doing it, or pay to make it. We made it for a school which bought our wood-carving machines to teach wood carving to their students. The school asked us to use their video equipment to make a training video to train their students to use the machines. The tape just showed one person teaching another person how to use it in each of various ways, step by step, very plainly.

Lesson 2—Sell as You Teach. Jeff tells how:

Suddenly, we saw how simple it was to convert a training video into a sales video, and we did. We used the same demonstration to show the same things the machine could do, but we explained how it made money for an owner; how it saved money; and paid for itself.

Lesson 3—Sell the Features, Uniqueness, Superiorities.

We just showed whatever our machine did that you could not do manually; that it did it better than any other machine; and that it could do things no other machine could.

Lesson 4—Sell What Stands Behind the Product or Service.

We taped my father, our employees and our factory. No one was introduced by name, and no one spoke on-camera. It was merely a description of the process of manufacture off-camera while the camera roamed around showing activities of the company.

But, off-screen, we told how we felt about customers; about our engineering background and experience; our guarantee; and about our customer support. We quoted what our customers thought of us.

Lesson 5—Ask for the Order

We asked just as we did in a one-to-one sales demonstration. Our costs were going up and our prices soon would. This was a chance to save the increases by acting now. We didn't pressure, but simply explained. We featured our telephone number every so often.

Lesson 6—Fit Your Demonstration to its Audience.

To the special niche of people we go after, what our machines do is news they are hungry for. What these people badly want to know and we show them bores other people. But they are not our market. We know our customers, talk their language. We don't need to be a star but to make our machine one. We're just experts.

Lesson 7—Simple Can Be Best.   For the right demonstration made for the right product or service, a simply produced test is better than none. Again, according to Jeff,

> By then I owned a camcorder and some accessories. The business bought one. With those two pieces of equipment, we got started. We bought some editing equipment. We began to edit the tape that we shot. We wrote off-screen narration which I spoke. We did everything in house. It was cheap, simple and primitive—but productive.

Lesson 8—Test Successful Videos for Other Products.   If a video demonstration works for an product or service, test a variation of it for another demonstration product or service, preferably related. Jeff says,

> We did first one and then another. We applied what we had learned. We took every bit as much care to make each. Now we have four successful sales video demos.

Lesson 9—Done Right, Long Demos Work.   If a long demo is done right, and is news for a niche audience, don't worry too much about the length. According to Jeff,

> Most people won't watch our video all the way through. But people who work with wood, who can make money cutting and carving wood, and who own trees they want to turn into money are quite interested in each.
> We combined all our videos into one very long video catalog; 25 minutes of it shows all the products, 15 minutes of it shows the plant and the employees performing different functions—15 minutes shows how the Wood Mizer cuts a log. It just shows two people for 15 minutes sawing away, during the entire process. There's 10 minutes on a solar-drying kiln. Then there's 12 minutes on a vacuum-drying kiln. Finally, there's the carving machine video.

Lesson 10—Upsell and Cross-Sell.

In our video, we demonstrate lower-cost and highest-price Wood Mizers. People can decide from the demo which does most per dollar. Our highest-priced model is over $10,000 and is our best seller.

No one who buys a Wood Mizer can cut wood and use it later

without drying it. They want to know how. We demonstrate why our solar and our vacuum dryer are each unique. Many Wood Mizer customers buy one, and some two. Anyone who cuts wood is a prospect to carve wood. Many people may start by wood carving. Some may also want to cut wood. We get many multiple orders.

Lesson 11—Trade Up Your Demos; Make Each Better.

We succeeded, but wanted still better results. We also felt that an unprofessional video made our company look unprofessional. As we made money from our videos, I took the responsibility to make our videos more profitable by putting more money into them. All our sales videos are now made outside. Anything I send out to the customer is created out of house. But we still have our own equipment inside to duplicate videos. We keep four decks going constantly.

Doug Miles

Doug Miles is a film and video producer/writer whose work includes marketing videos for corporations such as AT&T, Prudential, and Bell Atlantic as well as broadcast television and feature film. I asked him these questions about how a nonprofessional should go about marketing a product through video:

Q: Would you make your own video with your own equipment?

A: No, unless you think a home video will create the kind of image you need to sell your product. Marshall McLuhan was right, "the medium is the message." An amateur video will say "amateur product." A professional, well-produced video will say "professional, well-produced product." Hire a professional.

Q: Would you use film or videotape?

A: Either medium can be effective; however, film still delivers the impression of elegance. It says "primetime" and video says "gameshow." It's more expensive but the client wants to make a statement about the quality of the product through the look of the show. The video we produced for AT&T's AUDIX voice mail was also shot in film for that same reason.

Q: How much does it cost to make an effective video?

A: It's a fine line. You need to spend enough to create a piece that positions your product well, but you also have to be careful not to over-spend. We've done effective but simple shows for as low as $7500. We've also produced videos as costly as $300,000. An example of the low end was a three-minute meeting-opener for American Express that was shot in one day and edited in another. No script, no talent, just pretty pictures, music, and quick cuts. An example of the high end was a series of videos for AT&T corporate education that involved shooting all over the world as well as extensive graphics and animation.

For a marketing video to promote a specific product, you generally are talking about a five- to eight-minute video. The budget will most likely fall in the range of $25,000 to $35,000.

Q: What are some tips for a reader of this book on how to get an effective, reasonably priced video?

A: First of all, think about how you are going to get the video in front of potential customers. Are you going to make copies and put them into the hands of the sales force? Are you going to set up point-of-purchase monitors? Are you going to mail out copies either free or for a fee? Second, seek out the help of someone who is experienced, not only in production, but also in your product area. A marketing background doesn't hurt. Third, focus on your message. Learn who your customer is. What do you expect potential customers to do once they screen the program? Make sure you ask them to do it. Make sure you have a way for them to do it. Fourth, keep it simple. Video is a great medium for generating excitement, interest, and enthusiasm. It's not a great device for delivering lots of detailed information. Use the strengths of video to create a desire for the product; use print or a direct person-to-person selling technique to present all the detailed selling points or instructions. Above all, make sure that you have a well-conceived plan before you start. This means schedule, script, budget, and distribution method. Plan. Plan. Anticipate. And then plan some more. This is the best insurance for a successful marketing video.

Marco Polo Ltd.

Next, let's consider how practical is it to make a video, for U.S. use, in a part of the world where costs are far lower. If you attempt this, how can you best safeguard quality? Ramesh Manghirmalani, founder of Marco Polo Limited, owns half of a silk production facility in India and lives in the United States. Here are my questions and his answers:

Q: Being an Indian gave you an advantage in making your video in the Orient. Did you worry about travel costs and quality?

A: I worried a lot. I wanted to get the best people in the world to make my video, but I wanted the best price in the world for them. To get proper help, I put a call out among all the people I ever knew, and used all my connections, in order to get recommendations.

Q: Whom did you hire and why?

A: To make the video, I chose J. Walter Thompson, a very famous, international ad agency, but J. Walter Thompson of India. I got very smart, very talented people, and of Thompson caliber. But their pay scale was closer to that of India than of the United States.

Q: How much experience in videos did any Far Eastern production firms have? Were you concerned about this?

A: Texas Instruments and Chevron have also made videos in India. So I was on safe ground. J. Walter Thompson in India helped a lot and was very professional. Not only was it able to do the work for the least cost, but it also consulted with J. Walter Thompson in America for advice on how to do my video.

Q: Where did you make your video?

A: We compared facilities and priced production all through the Orient and chose Hong Kong. J. Walter Thompson people flew there with me to supervise production. Cost was very low, but quality was protected by top technical people from Thompson who supervised it.

Q: Did you fly in your cast?

A: No, we selected, in Hong Kong, five occidental models and an American actor for the off-screen voice.

Q: How much did you get into the production?

A: I had top professionals, but felt I had to be on top of it. I was there day and night as the video was being made (and for each video I have made since).

Q: What was your verdict?

A: The J. Walter Thompson people knew how to produce it, and the Hong Kong producers were top grade. The dresses and garments were modeled, demonstrated, and shown very effectively, in a most desirable way. Color reproduction was excellent.

Q: How long was it and how much did it cost, including all travelling expenses?

A: My first video was 14 minutes and cost $3.50 a video after paying $33,000 to produce it.

Q: What do you advise readers of this book to do first once the decision to produce a video is made?

A: Send for videos of others of the type you'd like to make—well before you make your own. Study them. Determine what they do that you'd like to do. Find out what that costs. Find the production level suited for your video. Find the right people to produce it.

Q: After that, what is most important?

A: Get yourself into your video personally. Expense is not the solution. Keep watching production costs. Keep expenses down at each point. Keep everything under control. Do all you can before you get to the studio.

Q: What can you do once production starts to ensure success?

A: If you do all you should beforehand, production should go well and keep within budget. And your video may be very successful. Trust your people. But, as you make your first video, study how to make the next better for less. I now know enough so that I can cut 50 percent of the cost of my first video and maybe even get a better-quality production.

Video Consultants

Should you have a video consultant? If you have enough expertise in house for the kind of video you plan, within the budget you have, perhaps you don't need a video consultant. Just make sure that you have the right people with enough expertise to ask the right questions and to analyze and judge the credibility of the answers and that you have enough time to research all of the logical, possible production firms.

Without enough expertise, you may be on the wrong track. You ideas affect expense. Only those with production expertise can soundly advise how practical your ideas are or what *parts* of a good idea are too costly or won't work. Before we move on, note the following:

Each year do-it-yourself capabilities of camcorders get closer to those of last year's local pro-video production. Abilities of local facilities and gypsy producers get closer to most recent big-city production. But newest techniques in top studies in the biggest centers offer still more tempting breakthroughs to big-budget marketers.

Whatever your firm's size and however you make your videos, keep aware of ongoing marketing-video changes such as

- Improved smaller, lighter, in-studio or portable cameras with better image quality and more features

Help Source Guide

1. D. Matrazzo's *The Corporate Scriptwriting Book,* 1985, offers step-by-step organization to write scripts for business films, videotapes, and slide shows. Available from Communicom Publishing: 19300 N.W. Saurie Islands Rd., Portland, OR 97231. (503) 621-3962.

2. *"How to Plan, Coordinate and Produce Videos"* is a two-day seminar available from Padgett-Thompson: 11221 Roe Ave., Leawood, KS 66211. (800) 255-4141.

3. *The International Television Association* can give you the name and number of the president of the local chapter nearest you who will suggest a choice of members who are top producers of corporate film and videos

near your area: 6311 N. O'Connor Rd., LB-51, Irving, TX 75039. (214) 869-1112.

4. *Location Update* magazine covers everything about shooting outside. Available *free* is "Connections," a guide to location filming in the United States and internationally: P.O. Box 17106, North Hollywood, CA 91615-7106. (213) 461-8887.

5. *MPCS Video Industries, Inc.*, offers a *free* rental guide and all the equipment you'll need to make a video: 514 W. 57th St. NY, NY 10019. (212) 586-3690.

6. *"ShowBiz Expo"* is an annual show held on both the west and east coasts—almost 500 displays. Software, equipment, demos, seminars, also available from Live Time, Inc.: 2122 Hillhurst Ave., CA 90027. (213) 668-1811.

7. Peter Utz's *Video User's Handbook* (3d ed., Prentice-Hall, 1989) is a nontechnical guide for those with no experience; includes easy steps to use, maintain, trouble-shoot every type of video equipment; to achieve quality results; to attain needed skills; to use shortcuts. Special sections on color, editing, lighting, sound: 200 Old Tappan Rd., Old Tappan, NJ 07675. (800) 223-2336.

15
Video Media

Ads in Videocassettes and Video Premiums, Ads on Planes and in Theaters

More affluent people see a commercial that precedes a major home videocassette movie release than typically see any commercial on network TV shows. Likewise, commercials shown before or after movies on planes and in theaters reach more people than the ads in magazines serving competitive fields. The use of videos as premiums to help sell another product or service has been very successful. These video media offer a wide range of choices to marketers who search for new opportunities.

Ads in Movies on Videocassettes

Let's examine why the possibilities for ads in videocassettes are so tantalizing and yet are growing more remote, and how large marketers can sometimes still profitably promote their wares in conjunction with some of the biggest hit movies on cassette. I'll also propose several intriguing ways in which ads on cassettes of smaller-audience movies can be practical and profitable for far more advertisers.

A typical VCR household rents more than two movies a month. Although video rentals per VCR household dropped from a peak of 3.26 movies per household a month to about 2.07 per household, the number of VCR-equipped homes and total sales of videos continue to increase.

This tremendous sales growth becomes even more impressive when one considers that some videos are offered for sale only after rentals slow, and some movies are only offered for sale rather than rental. Today, rental and sales income from home videos almost double movie ticket sales.

Nielsen says that each rented tape is viewed 1.3 times before being returned, and Alexander, a New York consulting firm, estimated it at 1.1 times. Early results from Nielsen showed that during 75 percent of a purchased videocassette's playback, someone views a commercial in the video.

Adult viewers of videocassette commercials were significantly younger than the primetime TV average. In fact, video ad viewership in families which watch broadcast TV commercials most is less than in other homes. Nielsen research also revealed that almost 100 percent of video viewers zip past the leader tape and the FBI warning but stopped as the commercial comes on.

By the time you read this book, almost all movies being released for home video should be encoded—more than 300 titles a year. And research to determine the audience amount, type, and value will eventually become as accurate for videos as for TV.

Ads on videocassettes possess all the advantages of TV advertising. And the potential viewership for ads in the biggest hit movies on videocassettes is enormous. So why don't more TV network advertisers switch to ads in movies on home videos?

Bob Alexander, president of Alexander & Associates, answered me:

> Video viewers are not the barrier. They did not object to viewing commercials when handled responsibly by advertisers. Big advertisers are not the barrier. They are willing to use commercials in a manner acceptable to video viewers. Big agencies are not the barrier. They are willing to recommend the use of the cassette ads if the CPMs based on research acceptable to them show CPMs comparable to those for TV network top shows.
>
> The barrier is that the total ad income per cassette based on such CPMs is too small a percentage of the income the same cassette provides from rentals and sales to interest the studios. They want advertisers to pay far bigger CPMs and, more than that, they only want advertisers who are promotional partners and can cross-promote the video, resulting in bigger cassette sales and rentals.

Each successful ad sponsorship of a videocassette to date has involved event marketing, or pulling out all the promotional stops to a degree few marketers can. But how often is it the best buy for the money for even the biggest marketers?

New Possibilities

New opportunities for far more marketers and for smaller marketers to advertise in home videocassettes have opened up. You may be able to sponsor a video which appeals to the exact target group you are after—not the widest appeal all-star movie but perhaps the most narrow-niche how-to video. Movies on videocassette offer a wide selection of video material to choose from. Video entertainment or instruction can even be customized for a sponsor's needs. Producers of many narrow-niche, special videos have been more inclined to work with sponsors. Some of these specialized video makers will even create a video from scratch for a sponsor (often simply combining and editing existing material). As a rule, these video makers try to get the sponsor to pay for all production costs for the rights to limited use (and a commercial) while retaining the ownership rights for themselves.

What giant marketers have learned can apply to a surprising number of marketers who go into video sponsorship on a smaller scale:

1. Sponsor a winner with the maximum rental or sales.

2. Be sure the movie perfectly fits your firm and product.

3. Make your commercial part of the show.

4. Pour star-power glamour into all your ads.

5. Be a tie-in promotion "Barnum" in every way.

6. Offer your representatives, jobbers, and dealers promotion deals.

Considering Video Sponsorship

Firms considering video sponsorship must understand the disadvantages of video movie sponsorship, including the following:

- The biggest movies on cassette are unavailable to most advertisers.
- R-rated movies may reflect poorly on a sponsor.
- The "right buy" for middle-sized firms is usually hard to negotiate.
- Starting as a sponsor in a modest way is difficult.
- Customizing or creating videos from scratch by pros takes much work and time on your part or may disappoint.
- Organizing video sponsorship according to the needs of marketers has been slow.

Small advertisers want to buy locally or regionally or to share sponsorship and buy into packages of videos with similar demographics. They want studios to group together video sponsorships shown in the same area. Advertising agencies want movie studios to standardize research and rate calculation methods. One major impediment is that sufficient research information is only gradually becoming available.

Unless your firm is among the top-100 national advertisers, don't bother even thinking about sponsoring a major movie in videocassette form. Sponsorship cost is comparable to that of a super event, which might get 40 million viewers. Instead, get a video winner you can afford and use this video in ways that are simpler, safer, and far less costly. Investigate the forces that have opened up sponsored videos on a broader scale:

- The vast, worldwide bank of film and video footage available for repackaging in new program forms, such as old popular TV shows.

- The existence of special-interest films and videos on every conceivable hobby and subject.

- The startling popularity of kids and sports videos.

- The unexpected pulling power of videos as premiums.

How Do You Start?   First, study how big marketers have succeeded with "nonblockbuster" sponsored videos. Specifically, investigate how marketers have profitably sponsored special-interest videos; how they have arranged with producers to create new features (with repackaged and some new content, including product and company tie-ins in the show); which videos have been most profitable when used as premiums for companies in fields like yours; what profitable direct-marketing campaigns of videos are related to products like yours; and how a mix of these methods has best worked.

Next, familiarize yourself with the scope of videos you can sponsor. What are the fastest-moving video premiums currently? Which are the most ingeniously created new sponsored videos? Shop for a video you can test as a premium or market directly through other media advertising. Most libraries contain directories of movie reviews, special-interest videos, video media distributors, and producers. The titles and other help sources are listed at the end of this chapter. The next pages will provide an overview to the task.

Big Marketers Seek Better Buys.   Ralston-Purina, for its limited-run Dinosaurs brand cold cereal, ran a one-minute spot on the videocassette release of *Denver, The Last Dinosaur*, a "B" movie for children. General Foods sponsored a far less expensive videocassette cartoon series, each with 60-second spots or two 30-second spots for brands of its cereals. For other brand tie-ins, General Foods also tested a video of shortcut tips for cooking, repackaged from segments of various cable TV programs.

A special-interest video may create the setting for a broad interest product. For example, Sanka brand decaffeinated coffee sponsored a video on walking. Colgate's dishwasher detergent sponsored one on family gatherings.

Dodge Motor Company found a way to multiply the distribution of its sponsored video of the funniest young and unknown comics, offered for $14.95. In addition to offering single copies to individuals, Dodge placed the video with comedy clubs everywhere. The club copies secured 50 to 100 times more viewing audience per copy than videos distributed through the home.

Custom-Created, Sponsored Video.   The Westminster Kennel Club Dog Care Guide videocassettes, sponsored by CalCo pet food, cost about $800,000 including duplicating 100,000 copies. Madison Square Garden Home Video produced the videocassette, which included excerpts from the annual dog show at the Garden.

Local videos based on a sports team's season usually cost between $50,000 and $75,000. A history of a team with a life beyond one season would cost more. For this, the sponsor gets its name on the videocassette box, a coupon within the box, a commercial, plus a special announcement at the beginning of the tape. MSG Home Video will consider a multiple videocassette sponsorship but prefers two with a maximum of three sponsors, with commercials placed only before or after the video story. However, MSG will also integrate into the program products or logos.

The Self-Help Profit Center

Use of ads in how-to videos is working for marketers of all sizes and growing fast. Educating people about the activities a product is designed for has always been a key to the introduction, growth, and retention of a major share of a product's market. Eastman Kodak, from its earliest years, supplied people with "self-help" tips on photography. The firm sponsors three series of half-hour videos, including 43 tapes of basic how-to subjects. Kodak film was prominently shown and mentioned throughout. Wherever possible, videocassette shows were based on previous film programs originated by Kodak for public TV and from Kodak's film library.

The Kodak series was available to anyone who joined the Kodak Video Exchange for $29.95. Members got two free cassettes, a minitripod, and an opportunity to obtain new selections—either for $6.95 each on a rental basis or for $19.95 to keep. Membership income reduces Kodak's costs in creating the videos. The deficit was considered an ad expense.

From the vast choice of special-interest videos, your company may find one to fit your product, service, and concept. Consider cosponsoring it with others in your field. Start small, even in one city, and roll out step by step, with promotion costs shared by each cosponsor.

Videos as Premiums

Use of videos as premiums is growing fast. The biggest success stories mostly come from big advertisers, but some much smaller marketers are also using video premiums successfully. Video premiums—the practice of offering a free or deeply discounted price for the videocassette, which is usually tied to another purchase—can reap profitable results. This is true even for current or new videocassette titles. Time after time, the sponsor's promotion of video premiums sparked rental and sale income for the same videos. This occurred because

1. The large growth of video rentals created mass tape duplication economies of scale (ever lower cost per tape).
2. A tape of a movie is perceived to be an ideal premium—even better when it's highly related to the advertised product.
3. The advertiser's self-liquidating premium offer promotes the retail sale or rental of up to millions of tapes of one movie.
4. Buying so many tapes makes it possible to insert commercials in premium tapes distributed at a reasonable cost per thousand.

Most videos can't produce enough rental income per square foot to be regularly stocked in a video rental store. But when General Foods sponsors cooking tips on a home video and advertises the video as a premium in a test city, distribution quickly follows—in libraries, book stores, supermarkets, and video rental stores. Advertising beyond on-package promotions to include radio, TV, and newspapers builds demand and viewership.

Videos are less of an inventory risk than most other premiums. With "pancake duplicating," companies can record a program on large rolls of tape but only load the video onto cassettes as orders come through. If orders don't come in, the tape can be erased and reused with a fraction of the loss of overstocking cassettes.

David Grossman, a video-premium consultant, suggests the following tips:

- Know the quality of the tape.
- Know the duplicator's quality-control procedures.
- Require a written indemnification from the program's supplier.
- Look for and include all hidden costs (promotional fees).
- Compare price and production quality.
- Consider the name value of any stars featured.

Further, Grossman points out,

> A 60-minute program packaged in a four-color cardboard slip-in sleeve will cost about $3.50 to manufacture in small quantities. Each additional 30 minutes will add about 60 cents to the manufacturing costs. The more copies made at one time, the lower the price. Companies owning home video rights must pay to the program producer or "talent" royalties.
>
> These can range from zero for proprietary programming and public domain programs that have no copyright protection to 25 percent of the selling price. An exercise tape could cost $50,000 to $60,000 to produce. But star cost(s) could triple this. Football player Phil Simms was paid $100,000 for his exercise tape.
>
> Video distributors want big orders with the hope of bigger reorders and maximum promotion by you. Typically, a company offers a video (as a premium) for half its suggested retail price plus a proof of purchase.

Big Marketers

Hallmark Cards offered customers a *Creepy Classics* videocassette for $4.95 with any $5 Hallmark Halloween purchase. This video premium promotion followed a successful *Spooky Sounds* audiocassette promotion. Hallmark ordered 500,000 copies of the 30-minute videotape hosted by Vincent Price. It included footage from *The Blob, I was a Teenage Werewolf,* and other thrillers. Radio spots as well as newspapers ads ran just before Halloween.

Procter & Gamble gave away an estimated one million cassettes of *Walt Disney Cartoon Classics* with the purchase of Ivory dishwashing liquid or Tide laundry detergent. More than half of the million cassettes reached families who didn't previously own a Disney video. For Disney, it was considered valuable sampling.

MacDonald's has long dominated the children's share of the fast food market, due to Ronald MacDonald, low-priced meals for kids, toy premiums and gifts, and constant promotions. Then Burger King counterattacked with its Kids' Club. Advertising featured a gang of cartoon characters led by Kid Vid. The next month, Burger King offered free Ninja-Turtle plastic characters with every Kid's Lunch. This resulted in 14 million meals sold and turtles given away. Then Burger King offered children certain *Teen Age Mutant Ninja-Turtle* video episodes at a discount price. The promotion was wildly successful. Michael Evans of Burger King reported:

> Children under 13 represent 14% of the fast-food business. Children have incredible influence on what fast-food restaurant their parents choose. We ran TV commercials to support the Ninja-video promotion for our Kids' Club. We also promoted the offer in our Kids' Club Newsletter with a circulation of over a million.
>
> Selecting a meal is often an impulse. We used in-store point of purchase signage. Up above counters are brightly colored ceiling hangers. On each cardboard banner, 9 inches deep and 3 feet wide, was pictured a Ninja turtle and under 20 words of selling copy. We moved over 7 million self-liquidating videos in 5 weeks. Peak response was 200,000 a day. On the Ninja video, a minute commercial offered a membership in The Kids' Club.

In three months after the Ninja video promotion started, sales for Burger King jumped over twice as fast as those of MacDonald's. Profits took a bigger jump than sales. Kids' Club membership of children from ages 2 to 13 jumped past 1.7 million by the seventh month after launch.

Smaller Successes

The following are some smaller successes using video promotions:

- General Foods distributed 250,000 copies of *The Crystal Light Aerobics Video* and ran commercials for appropriate products.
- Royal Crown Cola purchased 20,000 copies of *It's a Wonderful Life,* with the right to include its own commercials.
- Penn Tennis Balls ran a 30-second commercial in *Andre Agassiz Attack,* a tennis how-to video. With two proofs of purchase from Penn tennis ball cans, buyers got a $10 discount on the tape. Penn advertised the offer in *Tennis* and *World Tennis* magazines.

Smaller marketers can often find a nonmovie video that is appropriate and has an excellent chance to be a profitable medium. Most such programs can be tested as a premium (or via a direct-response offer as described in Chapters 12 and 13).

Lessons from the Master Marketer

Sports Illustrated (SI) has developed its vast video premium expertise more through its savvy than the size of its organization. You, too can apply SI's knowledge. Chuck Davis is in charge of SI's video premiums. SI has given away millions of videos for subscriptions. Over one-third of *SI* subscriptions were produced by offers of videos over a 5-year period. Offers of other videos are used to obtain renewals. Others are sold to subscribers.

It began when SI offered the 44-minute NFL videotape, *Football Follies,* free with any new subscription (but only after receiving payment)—350,000 tapes were distributed in the first campaign. To date, SI has received more than 850,000 new subscribers by giving away *Football Follies.* Excerpts from the video became the basis of a successful direct-response TV commercial. Stills from the video were used in space and direct-mail subscription ads. SI's overall subscription selling cost dropped due to the video. Even bad credit was reduced.

SI then began testing other video ventures. It released a set of three Mets baseball videos retailing for $59.95. One cassette was the year's highlights, another was the history of the Mets, and the third, *The Lighter Side of the Mets,* had plenty of bloopers. Other SI videos included supermodels Elle MacPherson, Cheryl Tiegs, and Rachel Hunter exercise videos. Another SI video offer was *The All New Not-So-Great-Moments in Sports.*

Campaign after campaign ran offering free videos with paid subscriptions. *Michael Jordan: Come Fly with Me* offered 40 minutes of basketball great Jordan's breathtaking leaps and slam dunks. It's free, but only when a subscriber has paid $59.95 for 40 issues (in three installments).

New SI Profit Center. Then SI produced its own cassettes and got advertisers to sponsor them. SI tapes usually sell for $14.95 to $19.95. Most SI videos have sponsors to help pay for production costs, which run from $300,000 to $400,000. There are no outside ads in SI videos. Soon SI was creating more videos for use as premiums for other advertisers than it made for itself: SI released a video version of its swimsuit issue, made and distributed by HBO, which sold over 700,000 copies. For Reebok, SI created *The Magicians of Sports* videocassette. For R. J. Reynolds, SI produced *The*

Greatest Sports Follies, which was offered for sale on Winston, Salem, and Camel cigarette cartons. For Dodge, SI supplied its swimsuit video, and Dodge gave it to anyone who made a test drive. SI then sold the swimsuit videos for $14.95 through stores and direct-response ads.

Not Every SI Idea Worked.   SI experimented with one cassette called the *NFL Crunch Course.* At the end of the videotape a two-minute spot was tested in two ways. Each offer was for a continuity videocassette series. One version offered *The Epic of Flight.* The other offered *Golden Moments of Sports.* Both featured an 800 number. Neither test did well enough to continue.

Every day, the variety of videos available for sponsorship and/or premium offer marketing grows. But remember: Always test-market and roll out according to your situation, as suggested in Chapters 12 and 13.

Video Magazines

The majority of video magazine launches have failed. But most did so years ago when costs were higher and VCR ownership smaller. Today, new developments open new perspectives. Video magazines are being produced by amateurs on camcorder, as are video magazines subsidized by one or a number of advertisers and combinations of print and video magazines.

Movies on longer air trips are standard for most airlines. Short subjects, in which commercials are inserted, run before and after the main feature. Total potential viewership reaches tens of millions of travelers a year, comparable to the readership of all in-flight magazines on the same flights. It's possible to buy smaller commercial tests and roll out to all planes on an airline showing video.

Airlines offer not just movies but syndicated TV shows, news, and sports. On many airlines, there's an ABC News TV magazine show, including its "On Business" special feature hosted by Sander Vanocur. An ABC Sports program highlights sports events around the world. ABC's magazine and its sports program are each a half hour on domestic flights and one hour on overseas flights. CNN Headline News is also on many airlines. All these programs carry commercials. The audience is "mass-class." There's less distraction than at home and no "zapping."

For Seagram's Chivas Regal Scotch (a product category banned from broadcast and cable TV) Seagram's got such a good reaction from an in-flight test TV campaign that it has continued ever since. AT&T's in-flight TV campaign features its USA Direct card which avoids the excessive surcharges made on long-distance calls by hotels. American

Express is another heavy user of in-flight commercials. The airlines often run their own destination videos promoting an excursion special.

In-flight video is a poor direct-response advertising medium due to the lack of immediate access to phone and fax machines. But this may change: On certain flights of Northwest Airlines, Qantas Trans-Pacific, Alitalia and British Airways, a miniature TV set was mounted in front of each seat, on the back of the seat ahead. One variation could be mounted from the seat arm. Market tests went on for 30 months. The small TV was made and installed by Airvision, a subsidiary of Philips N.V. Surveys of Northwest Airlines showed that

1. 70 percent of the passengers said they preferred the individual TV to overhead screens.

2. 70 percent said they would be more likely to fly in airlines that had individual TVs.

3. The picture was easier to see for many passengers.

4. There was more choice: Six channels offered movies, news features, documentaries, music videos, cartoons, and programs in an alternative language.

More airlines have installed Airvision on a more permanent basis. A newer model allows passengers to electronically select from up to 12 video channels with stereo and/or multilanguage audio plus up to 30 audio channels as well as many other new features.

The screen provides brilliant color pictures. There's an on-screen program guide and on-screen flight information. From their own seats passengers can order beverages, indicate meal preferences, go "tele-shopping" with on-screen catalogs, and see on-screen product demonstrations. They can convert currency; make reservations for hotels, cars, and other flights; and purchase duty-free items. They can make direct-dial telephone calls, receive incoming fax letters, and send outgoing fax transmissions. There's built-in instant billing of any purchase. Inventory is monitored, allowing automatic updating. There's instant accounting of what each passenger watches or listens to. Research is gathered on programming usage and preferences, advertising viewership, and demographics.

Other competitors are Matsushita, Sony Transcom, and GEC Marconi. Bob Worral, one of the founders of SkyMall, which has print catalogs on over 60 percent of airlines, expects that the backseat systems are the future of airline movies and is planning electronic catalogs and cocatalogs to use on the systems to give passengers extra service at more profit.

Movie Theater Commercials

Eight thousand theaters show them. Screenvision Cinema Network alone places commercials in over 6100 theaters in 205 ADIs in 50 states. A 28-day national flight reaches an average of more than 38 million moviegoers. Screenvision advertisers include Kodak, Sprite, Reebok, SEGA Videogames, Gatorade, M & M/Mars, California Raisins, General Motors, Chrysler, Mitsubishi, and Volkswagen.

Commercials acceptable to theater audiences must be soft-sell and highly entertaining. They run at least 60 seconds, and they emphasize image more than sell benefits. These commercials should still complement the brand's regular hard-sell advertising on TV or in print. Usually no more than three are shown before any feature film, in contrast to the "commercial clutter" of TV. There can be no zapping. Screenvision guarantees product category exclusivity.

Cinema advertising's day-after recall scores 83 percent. It's even becoming possible to integrate an on-screen message with in-theater materials and a call for instant response. Those who pay $5 to $7 and more per ticket to see a movie are generally younger and more upscale than average. They buy more than older folks who stay home.

Video and movie media opportunities will change and grow as technology evolves. On airlines, the move to miniaturization will only increase video media's allure and accessibility. Marketers should stay on top of advances in this field.

Keep up with continuing developments such as:

- All-star, "infomercial" movies to introduce products. More ads in top hit cassette movies so related to the product that the film becomes a near infomercial.

- More supersponsorships of superevents. PPV and then videos of the events followed by super co-promotion and PR. More such sponsorships of super local, regional events.

- Ads on far more co-video cassettes of business, professional, hobby, and other special-interest magazines (often video co-magazines); also seminars and courses.

- More ads on specialized, videocassette networks, from college rock music to classroom to hospital.

Note. Look for far more interactivity and choice to select, request, and order electronically in all of the above, and often sooner, on planes (including TV ads in movies).

Help Source Guide

1. Ask for special issues and articles on video media. Buy issues, subscribe to periodicals, or read the following at your library: *Advertising Age*, weekly (800) 992-9970; *Adweek* (212) 529-5500; *Inside Media* (203) 358-9900; *Electronic Media* (800) 992-9970.

2. Ask for issues, articles featuring videos as premiums from *Business and Incentives* magazine, 1515 Broadway, NY, NY 10036, (212) 869-1300, and from *Potentials in Marketing* magazine, Lakewood Publications, 50 S. 9th St., Minneapolis, MN 55402. (612) 333-0471.

3. *Billboard* provides international news, home video reviews, compiles national store sales reports on top special-interest videos, top video sales and rentals, and top kid video sales. Read in library, buy special issues, or subscribe: 1515 Broadway, NY, NY 10036. (212) 764-7300.

4. R. R. Bowker's *Bowker's Complete Video Directory* (2 vols., 3000 pages) is an annual directory of 62,000 titles, more than any other reference; includes over 20,000 educational and special-interest videos; contact R. R. Bowker: P.O. Box 31, New Providence, NJ 07974. (800) 521-8110.

5. The annual *Premium Incentive Show* makes products available for premiums; sell or shop there, at Jacob Javits Convention Center: 655 W. 34th St., NY, NY 10001. (212) 216-2000; show managers: (516) 627-4000.

6. *"Synergy Video Marketing"* is a *free* speech by David Grossman, a top video premium consultant: 28 Shinnecock Trail, Medford Lakes, NJ 08055. (609) 953-1998.

7. Gale Research Inc.'s *The Video Source Book* (about 2400 pages) is an annual publication of 57,000 entries in 400 subject areas. Check a business library or order direct from Book Tower: Dept. 77748, Detroit, MI 48277. (800) 877-GALE.

8. *The World Airline Entertainment Association (WAEA)* provides *free* latest information on in-flight advertising on big screen and back-of-seat small screen and how to get media kits and from whom: 401 N. Michigan Ave., Chicago, IL 60611 (212) 644-6610.

16
Interactive Computer Disks

A new generation has grown up with computers, made possible by the personal computer boom. While a growing core of intense computer users spend more time with PCs, ever-more-useful hardware, software, and peripherals continue to pour out, broadening the accessibility of personal computers to people who were formerly intimidated by the technology.

The very success of the PC technology has spawned a new marketing medium—the disk that is inserted into the machine. A higher percentage of computer disk marketing campaigns succeed, in more ways, than in many other forms of electronic marketing.

In this chapter and in Chapter 17, we'll examine how and why the computer disk has become a powerful new interactive marketing medium. This chapter will concentrate on interactive ads on disk, and Chapter 17 will explore interactive disk catalogs.

First, let's take a look at the computer disk market.

- The overwhelming majority of all but the smallest and poorest businesses each have one or more PCs.

- Most white-collar workers and a far bigger share of senior executives use PCs at work.

- Those with the most education and most-needed and newest computer skills get better entry-level office jobs and rise faster to higher levels.

- More companies provide computers to employees for home use. More owners of small firms (including almost all home office businesses) have PCs at home.

- More U.S. homes have PCs for special interests, hobbies, and to aid in education of family members in school and college and in upgrading careers lifelong.

Most executive users at work and most frequent at-home users were at first very largely men, but female home use keeps rising. Surveys show that the majority of users are married, college graduates, home owners, have passports, own VCRs, and are younger babyboomers.

Interactive disks (IDs) can be extremely simple to use, even for computer newcomers. Because prospects and customers control the viewing sequence, they benefit by spending little time to get the instant, vital information they need to know. In this way, disks supplement and strengthen the selling power of both traditional and other electronic media. Note the following:

1. These disks are interactive: When a prospect asks, the disk answers.
2. The customer can select information via simple menus.
3. Choices can include price range, color, model, or other features to see.
4. The questions asked can be invaluable research for further marketing and product development.
5. Disks are low-cost, simple, and fast to produce.
6. A disk can be mailed at the cost of a first-class letter.
7. A disk can include graphs, charts, drawings, or photos.
8. A disk can be produced in full color.
9. Animation, music, and sound effects can be used.
10. A disk can be instantly updated, often at little cost.

An ID is a very versatile medium. ID formats have included a game or a test; an ID can teach, sell or demonstrate. For example, an ID can calculate the monthly payments for various product combinations paid for over different lengths of time. It can provide documentation at the press of a key, from authorities to backup info on a questioned claim to price comparisons.

Some of IDs' marketing uses are enumerated in this list:

1. As publicity releases, getting inquiries at no ad cost.
2. To give out at trade shows and special events.
3. To mail to prospects at a fraction of the cost of a sales call.
4. For in-store placement as an interactive PC display.

5. To prequalify leads, use in presentations, or use as a "leave-behind."

6. To educate customers or a sales force.

7. After phoning first, send an ID as demonstration. Then follow up by phone.

8. After advertising to solicit inquiries for disks, using the ID to close.

9. Follow up inquiries with disks, then close the sale via mail order.

10. Distribute the ID program by computer modem.

New uses keep growing fast. MCI offers its "Portfolio Demo Disk" for companies to analyze the exact features and costs per minute of MCI phone and fax services by call volume. The Chase Education Finance Center offers "SNAP," the Student Need Advisor Program, a disk that determines any student's eligibility for college financial aid.

But also consider these ID constraints:

1. No programmed computer disk will work on all PCs.

2. Color, pictures, and animation, and sound devour memory.

3. Not all PCs have enough memory or color capability to run IDs.

4. Many older, nonfinancial executives fear computers.

5. Most older people have never used a PC.

6. Most younger women lack the time for frequent use of home PCs.

7. For most marketers, ID technology is a limited, niche medium.

For each ID marketer, success requires an ingenious application that delivers a needed service, saves time, and gives instant answers. It's not easy to figure out what role an ID should play in marketing a product, much less to develop the creativity and innovation needed for an effective presentation. You need a programmer with ID experience. Furthermore, disk compatibility is a major complication. Although IBM PCs and IBM compatibles naturally use the same software, Apple, Commodore, Amiga, and other computer makers run on a variety of incompatible software. Besides this, you'll get requests for various disk sizes and densities. The PC mix varies from offices to home PC environments and differs again for laptops.

Considering Disk Marketing

Should you consider disk marketing? Forget IDs if

1. Your customers and prospects are not generally PC-literate.

2. Your product is a one-time sale for under $20.

3. Your product or service has no benefits which can be presented interactively.

Most ID successes have been for higher-priced products and services sold to businesses, which offer potentially sizable repeat business.

The first use of interactive computer disks for marketing came out of an ID's use as a tutorial device given away with the purchase of a computer or computer software. IDs showed buyers how to use what they bought. The next step was to send the ID free in advance—a portion of the tutorial to show how it worked—and to tempt the PC owner to buy a new kind of software, peripheral, or even a new computer function.

When IBM went into the PC business, it created a tutorial disk for each IBM PC. Dealers used tutorials as a demonstration to allow a person to try out the PC in the store. Converting this ID into a marketing tool was not a big step.

After IBM mailed computer disk ads to prospects and customers, other marketers followed, first computer makers and then general advertisers. AT&T and Tandy created demonstration disks. Disks soon worked in the training field and were created for trade shows. Entrepreneurs began to see what these disks could do.

Siemens Medical Systems Inc. sent an ID to financial officers and radiologists to secure qualified leads for its sales force. The disk was also used by the salespeople at trade shows.

Welbilt Stoves created an ID to give its specifications to building engineers as well as to purchasing agents. It incorporated computer-aided design (CAD), the system the engineers used. It came in time to have Welbilt equipment specified in construction plans.

Researching Disk Marketing

Wherever you see an ID offered by any advertiser, send for it. Phone ID marketers and ask questions. Ask ID production houses for case histories of businesses most like yours which use IDs. Check your library for the most recent books on IDs. The Help Source Guide lists these sources, including how to get a free ID that demonstrates how to create and use IDs.

Study the demographics and psychographics of different classes of computer owners. Compare these traits with those of your customers. Note the following:

- Computer users are mostly younger men..

- Many younger affluents own Macintoshes.
- Special groups such as artists and ad people own Amigas.
- Traveling executives own laptops.
- Many younger, less-well-off users own other makes.
- Frequent PC users spend less time watching TV, reading books, newspapers, magazines, or even trade publications.

Each year, more people use and become comfortable with computers, including those previously resistant (such as older people and women). And each year, more ID tests succeed, and more ID campaigns roll out.

Getting Started

In short, your ID must fit into your overall marketing efforts. Analyze your business, your present marketing, and other companies' new ID campaigns, using these guides:

1. Study each ID success and failure.
2. Look for patterns, trends both to avoid and to follow.
3. Adapt these trends to your product selection and presentation.
4. Determine to whom you're trying to sell.
5. Decide what you want to communicate.
6. Determine the desired action.
7. Present your sales message in interactive fashion.

Now, organize creative and production teams, using any of the free-lance staff options described in developing other electronic media commercials. Your team must be able to develop the interactive concept for the disk, write the copy and design the graphics, develop or buy the appropriate software, create the disk "master," get the disk duplicated, and package and mail the disk.

The makeup of an ideal team varies with the intended use. But consider selecting from these types of people for your team: an innovative entrepreneur; a master of interactive presentation; a teacher, showperson, or salesperson; a perfectionist; a shrewd buyer and negotiator; and a cost-control watch dog. Creative members must think interactively. They must be flexible and develop a "feel" for what comes across interactively and for what does not and adapt the ID presentation accordingly.

Selecting and working effectively with the right ID production house is similar to choosing and using the right video production firm. Reread Chapter 14. Do-it-yourself ID production requries programming knowledge. Although Chapter 17 will detail how some small, self-taught ID entrepreneurs have made simple ID catalogs, most ID successes have involved bringing in outside expertise.

The more ID expertise you have in house, and the simpler the ID format, the lower the cost will be to create an ID. At this one extreme, with all talent inside, creating an ID can cost under $2000. A freelance creative team, working with you as the producer, can cost $5000 to $10,000. An experienced (but not top-rated) producer alone can cost $5000 or more.

Some ID production companies provide a complete, one-stop service—with disk design, duplication, and distribution capabilities in a single package. A middle production firm may charge $25,000 to $50,000 for all costs. Costs for revisions can be modest if done on a PC.

Disk duplication costs start at more than 1 dollar a disk, come down to 70 cents or so in runs of a few thousand, and can drop to 40 to 50 cents for "maximum" runs.

Raw disk prices have dropped sharply and continue to drop. Although a computer disk is usually distributed through first-class mail, at third-class bulk rates your ID could be in the mail for not much more than the cost of a quality catalog. This cost, including amortizing all your production expenses, is a small fraction of a video catalog or brochure. However, an ID still costs more than a printed direct-mail piece.

Disk packaging must identify the disk as what was requested, sell what is inside, and persuade the recipient to insert into the computer and view. If the ID is being marketed as a giveaway, it must be packaged to look like a gift.

Most offices currently have IBM or IBM-compatible PCs, including most home offices. Therefore, most business-to-business ID marketers start out in IBM PC format only. If successful, many then redo the ID in Apple Macintosh format. Most ID campaigns to date never get to other formats. Most offices with IBM-type systems now request 3½" disks. Over 75 percent of these requests are for high-density disks. Over 70 percent of requests for 5¼" disks are for the high-density version.

ID Promotion Costs

Most ID failures have been attempts to sell products to home computer owners who do not have home businesses. And, as we have noted about other electronic media, more IDs succeed when used in conjunction with other media in an integrated campaign.

Promotion costs vary widely, depending upon available media and how extensively you test. But plan to promote your ID by spending one-third of what it costs to produce and duplicate your first 3000 to 5000 copies. This usually provides for an adequate promotion test. Viable ID promotion testing may include free PR, several extra lines in existing media advertising, or extra sentences in a telemarketing script. The most cost-effective ID promotion is the use of enclosure slips in other advertising mailings, bills, or packages or simply displaying the ID with a PC at a trade show or in a store.

Remember that the greater the lifetime value of your customer, the more vital it is to *combine* promotional methods and to spend more to promote. But stop quickly if tests prove an ID to be less effective per dollar than your present selling methods.

Sales Applications

Sales for One-Twentieth of Former Cost!

By combining three kinds of electronic marketing (including an ID), Citibank slashed the selling cost of its on-line information service, *Global Report,* by 95 percent. How Citibank did this is a great lesson:

1. *Startup marketing expertise.* Robert Haddock, marketing director of Citibank's Global Report, acquired much of his expertise at Prentice-Halls' Business and Professional Books Division, where he headed mail-order operations. He also developed several new electronic publishing ventures at Ziff-Davis.

2. *The right product. Global Report* integrates information from 14 sources for its subscribers. It receives 10,000 pages of data a day and analyzes and organizes this information into some 4000 subject categories that business people understand and use often. Haddock spent two years designing and developing *Global Report.*

3. *Test the most logical market.* Haddock targeted his promotion to financial executives.

4. *If project bombs, analyze why.* At first, identifying a qualified lead cost *Global Report* $800. The fully loaded cost to get a new customer was $12,000—including salespeoples' time and expense. At that rate it would have taken Citibank several years before *Global Report* paid back on its investment. Research showed that the targeted people liked the service once they actually saw it, plus the renewals from

early subscribers looked strong. But the high cost (the bomb) had to be reduced.

5. *Consider new, even unorthodox media.*   A simple demo disk was developed to show *Global Report* to prospects. A direct-mail letter with a coupon offering a free preview disk was then sent to prospects. The demo-disk, direct-mail offer helped cut the sale lead cost from $800 to $80. The company then developed a greatly improved demo disk. Haddock found consultant Tom Lowenhaupt, who specializes in demo disks. Lowenhaupt had the know-how to make the disk highly interactive and visually exciting. The script was rewritten, and Lowenhaupt implemented several excellent alterations. For instance, the new demo disk asked for the user's job function and interest, and, based on this, gave a 10-minute, "personalized" guided tour.

6. *If the product is part of the problem, improve it.*   *Global Report* was a good product, but the potential users had to see it before they would subscribe. Haddock learned that most users needed a professional to set up the software on their PC. To solve this access problem, the company designed new software that radically simplified the setup. A first-time user could then be on-line in five minutes without help.

7. *When innovation hits the jackpot, test more innovation.*   To obtain subscriptions, other on-line services sell a "starter kit" including software, instructions, and a password for $29 to $49. *Global Report* mailed 17,000 packages using this standard approach, which included an offer for the start-up kit with one hour of time on-line for $39.

Testing against this, *Global Report* mailed 20,000 packages containing a new brochure, "One Hour with Global Report," and demo and access disks. The mailing included a letter offering a free hour of on-line usage. The package that included the disks outdrew the standard approach by more than 300 percent.

Overall, more than 4.4 percent of those who received the package with disks logged on and tried the service. Each trial session was followed up with a telemarketing call. More than one out of four of these trial users have been sold *Global Report* for a $90 minimum monthly service. Many of these later upgraded to other plans at higher minimums, some at a $500 monthly minimum. And the latest selling cost is a mere fraction of the first approach's cost. The total cost per sale including the telemarketing follow-up call came to $600—a 95 percent reduction from the original $12,000 cost.

After Citibank developed its improved demo disk for $500 plus in-house time, each later step took only a modest amount of risk. ID marketing resulted in a 60 percent growth of *Global Report's* U.S. customer base in less than three months. With the proliferation of PCs, even faster growth in sales and profits is expected. These little disks often have big successes.

Chase Manhattan's ID

A mailing that offered a financial spreadsheet ID to help business executives determine how the bank's "electronic funds transfer" system could best fit their cash-management needs got 10 percent to respond. The ID let Chase Manhattan's prospects tell their computer exactly what they wanted from Chase and also answered their questions.

The ID then instructed the PC to print out a letter that these prospects mail back to Chase specifying the kind of services their company would be most interested in. Inquiries were followed up by phone. Many other banks also use IDs for a variety of marketing purposes.

Other ID Applications

Standard & Poor (S&P) put all three of its basic commercial credit-rating services on CD-ROM. At that time, few business prospects had CD-ROM readers in their PCs. Undaunted, S&P produced an ID which interactively demonstrated and advertised the CD-ROM disc, with a special offer of a CD-ROM reader at a special price. The ID demo of CD-ROM technology also served as an introduction to Standard & Poor's data, complete with three simulated searches that showed a librarian finding the desired information.

Bill Rosenthal is president of the Warbler Group, which specializes in the creation of interactive demo disks. Not surprisingly, Warbler uses an ID to demonstrate its services and to explain how Warbler-produced demo IDs have generated an 8 to 10 percent response rate from compiled lists. Warbler's clients include Telerate, NYNEX, Reuters, and NewsNet.

Consumer-Oriented IDs. Besides the personal computer field, one consumer product category has already had considerable success with IDs: the automobile industry. A young corporate executive, Paula George, became largely responsible for initiating car companies' interest in IDs. She started by analyzing the considerable amount of research various computer magazines had conducted on the demographics and psychographics of computer users and owners versus those of customers of various kinds of products including cars.

This research indicated that people retained 20 percent of what they hear, 30 percent of what they see and hear, and 60 percent of what they interact with. Magazines, radio, and TV were passive media, but computers were interactive. Surveys indicated to Paula that promotion via

IDs could be, for certain car models and makes, more profitable for automobile companies than traditional media. Moreover, IDs could reach an otherwise hard-to-reach market.

Her other research revealed that PC penetration is highest in New York, Los Angeles, Chicago, and San Francisco. Most PCs are IBM and IBM-compatible. The average user spent over $2200 on a PC system and about $700 a year to add to the system. And when the computer home income is over $40,000, research indicates as much as an 80 percent decrease in television viewing.

When Paula launched The SoftAd Group, an ID marketing production company, she recommended that IDs be used for:

- A complex selling message
- To educate the prospect
- When the purchase is costly
- When competition is tough
- For a high-tech image
- For PC products and services

Her analysis helped convince car companies to make ad tests with disks. Buick first agreed to conduct a focus group research study before its ID campaign. Paula then got Ford to test an ID and other car companies began dabbling in ID marketing. Other ID production houses and ad agencies began to specialize in IDs and to make proposals to car companies. And large ad agencies with automobile clients began to supervise ID production. Because most of these IDs have been "catalogs" selling several models on one disk, we'll discuss them in more detail in the next chapter.

How Buick Creates an ID. One exception to the ID catalog approach has been Buick's Park Avenue, a prestige model so important that for the first time Buick made an ID all on one car and sent out 20,000 copies. Eighty percent of the ID's content was on the car, and 20 percent focused on a golf game. During the Buick Open golf tournament, shown on network TV, a Buick commercial featured Park Avenue and offered the disk and golf game to viewers. The ID golf game is played on the same course as the actual tournament—the Warwick Country Club.

How Lincoln-Mercury Used IDs. The famous racing driver, Jackie Stewart, offered a "test drive" on-disk for one Lincoln-Mercury sport sedan model. The ID answers viewers' questions on model features, options, prices, and competitive price comparisons. Red "air" streamed over a profile of a car demonstrating its aerodynamics. A picture of the instrument panel's "graphic alert module" showed what happens when doors are open or ice is on the ground. A three-dimensional rendering of the rear seats showed how they could be folded flat to increase cargo area. Color graphics compare the sports model to the Saab 900 Turbo, BMW 325, and Toyota Supra as well as other competitors.

Mike Leischner supervised Lincoln-Mercury's use of interactive disks. He told me: "The first year about 50,000 diskettes were sent out by Lincoln-Mercury. Then 130,000 were distributed the next year with color graphics. Cost per lead was good. We also traced promotional cost per sale. Disks were profitable as part of our overall direct marketing campaign." Lincoln-Mercury has used IDs for other cars and in other ways to increase sales, including for its leasing program. The Fleet and Lease Division tested use of IDs sent to businesses.

Can ID Marketing Expand?

So far the ID has been predominantly used as a profitable "niche" medium, often a "sliver niche," that is a medium with narrow market applications. But change may come. Consider Mead Data Central, which operates "Nexis News Plus," an on-line news service customized for any executive. It costs $50 a month plus search charges. Mead had 210,000 IDs bound into its ad that ran in selected subscriber issues of *Forbes* magazine. Mead ran the ad without the ID in the rest of *Forbes'* national circulation, offering the ID.

Both versions succeeded. Mead then bound in 20,000 more disks into copies of *Institutional Investor* magazine. This also succeeded. A year after the first test, Mead said conversions were excellent and that more disk-insert ads were planned.

Some ID enthusiasts feel that intelligently executed ID campaigns in business magazines will result in future sales volume that will dwarf those created by any ID to date. A number of consultants have had surprisingly consistent success for clients when sufficient research determined feasibility with follow-through on creative concept, presentation, targeting, and promotion.

Robert Stoeber, founder of The Creative Media Group, a pioneer disk production house, says, "Of all the disks we've made for clients, we have never had a failure. Everything works to some degree of success. Better input succeeds better. But no client has had a bomb." But Robert Stoeber only accepts clients he thinks have a real chance. So be careful. But don't be surprised as ID uses proliferate. More items and services for families, women, and children may soon be sold via IDs.

Ogilvy & Mather's Electronic Marketing Division—launched and headed by Martin Nisenholtz, senior vice president and director, was the first group to create a fully interactive marketing disk (as opposed to the passive demos available since the introduction of the PC). This interactive disk was created for The Equitable in 1985.

Martin Nisenholtz has kindly read this and the following ten chapters and answered questions I have asked him for you in each chapter.

Q: Martin, is the resistance by older people to using PCs now decreasing?

MARTIN NISENHOLTZ: As the baby boom generation moves into retirement age, PC usage demographics will start to skew older. But currently, PC usage drops off after age 50.

Q: Are "time-poor" women now finding that PCs at home save them time? And are they therefore more receptive to ads on disk than formerly?

MN: The notion of a PC in every kitchen has not happened. For the most part, PCs at home are extensions of office or education activities. AT&Ts new SmartPhone is a far likelier hardware platform for home banking, electronic yellow pages, and other such applications than the personal computer.

Q: What do you consider to be the most recent and exciting success stories in the use of computer disks to reach people at the office? And to reach people at home?

MN: Our disk for Hewlett-Packard's New Wave software is an exciting example of an office disk. Similarly, our disk for AT&T's Definity PBX line provides personalized "advice" for telecom managers. On the consumer front, I've always felt that the Buick disk is an exciting home entry. Prodigy's interactive demo is a terrific selling tool.

Q: Do you see IDs as basic equipment for the computer notebook-equipped salesperson? Any recent success stories?

MN: I see this as a major opportunity in categories where the sales force is acclimated to PC use.

Help Source Guide

1. *The Byte Information Exchange* [BIX], is a computer network provided by General Videotex Corporation for computer bugs. Any *BYTE* magazine reader with a modem can instantly dial and download any demo of demonstration software listed each month in a full page in BYTE (see story in Chapter 19): 1030 Massachussets Ave., Cambridge, MA 02138. (617) 491-3393.

2. *CompuDoc, Inc.,* specializes in interactive electronic media. A team of pros specializes in IDs as media from concept to production and promotion. *Free*

demo disk and *free* information kit and case studies available from: 51 Mt. Bethel Rd., Warren, NJ 07059. (908) 757-2888.

3. The Creative Media Group (Robert Stoeber, CEO) is an ID production house, consultant, and firm with ID marketing success stories in many fields: 103 Headquarters Plaza, Morristown, NJ 07960-3959. (201) 538-5619.

4. *Non-Store Marketing Report* is a newsletter with occasional ID success stories. *Free* copy available from Maxwell Sroge: 228 N. Cascade Ave., #307, Colorado Springs, CO 80903. (719) 633-5556.

5. *T.J. Lowenhaupt, Inc.* offers a *free* information kit about success in IDs, customized to your business: Box 1027, Jackson Heights, NY, NY 11372. (718) 639-4222.

6. *The SoftAd Group* offers a *free* information kit with many ID success stories: 311 North St., Sausalito, CA 94965. (415) 322-4704.

7. *The Warbler Group Inc.* produces interactive brochures and demos on floppy disks. More info, reprints of articles by Warbler CEO W. Rosenthal on IDs, and Warbler's own demo disk are available *without cost:* 63 Midvale Rd., Hartsdale, NY 10530. (914) 472-1155.

17

Interactive Catalogs on Computer Disk

An interactive computer disk catalog (IDcat) offers a menu of products that are featured in an interactive way (programmed to answer questions of a catalog user). The disk can be inserted into a personal computer. The concept is simple and deceptively closer to that of a print catalog than a video catalog. Whereas most of the efforts to electronically convert print catalogs for most products have failed, the IDcat has found its own successful niches.

I have found that success in an IDcat is usually limited to selections of those kinds of products which have been successfully marketed via IDs. I have not yet seen, for instance, any success for selections of low-cost consumer products appealing mainly to women. IDcats are quickly becoming accepted and appreciated ways for companies to sell to other businesses, and new technological developments may soon make IDcats an even more powerful marketing medium to far more businesses. The IDcat as a co-catalog sent along with a print catalog has a greater chance of success. Efforts to create IDcats without using special IDcat advantages fail more often.

Present IDcat advantages are the following:

- An IDcat's visual interactivity is a unique quality that a video catalog is only beginning to possess.

- IDcats are also more interactive than print catalogs.

- Anyone can copy an IDcat for other people, potentially reducing your distribution costs.

- An IDcat's original production cost is usually no more than a comparable print catalog.
- IDcat revisions are faster and cheaper than print.
- All the other advantages of IDs also apply to IDcats.

An IDcat allows your customer to view a wide range of product models and see any variation asked for, such as colors or styles. Beyond selecting product variations, an IDcat can calculate exactly what the items will cost, even with a monthly payment option.

IDcat users can also provide you with important research data at little or no extra cost. By inducing your customers to fill out an interactivity questionnaire on the IDcat, you can find out how best to change your IDcat concept, approach, and product selection.

The present disadvantages of IDcats are the following:

- High-quality color is impractical.
- IDcat production is too expensive to sell lowest-priced items.
- In some cases, your sales volume potential may be too small for the effort.
- There's a big difference between what an IDcat can do in theory and what is practical for an IDcat right now given today's technological standards.
- All the disadvantages of IDs apply also to IDcats.

Color from a disk can be magnificent on a computer screen, but a stunning IDcat with rich, full-color throughout is not practical. Some PCs still have too little memory to run high-density disks. And present high-density disks have too little memory for as much color as, for example, a garden catalog requires. Far more bytes on a disk are required. New breakthroughs are multiplying the quantity of bytes on a disk, but the PCs to run them will probably proliferate far more slowly.

New kinds of disks coming in the near future may be far superior for IDcat purposes. Experimenting with and testing an IDcat now may be the least expensive way to prepare for whatever computer-based form wins out—especially because a similar presentation mode may be used in whole or in part.

Considering IDcats

IDcat failures usually result from catalogers trying to translate too literally what has worked for them in print, with little regard for computer interactivity. These problems, plus the mistakes of business beginners (who are often poor entrepreneurs), litter the marketing landscape with failures.

Should you consider an IDcat? Don't proceed without a unique concept that's ideal for an IDcat. And don't expect large IDcat volume in any field, except perhaps for the high-end, technical business market. Each item should benefit from ID presentation and should sell for a relatively high price and/or have the potential for numerous repeat sales.

An IDcat makes sense if it's simpler, faster, and easier to select and order from than a print catalog. Preferably, it should also be fun. Don't produce an IDcat in an area where you have not already succeeded with an ID. And only consider an IDcat for business products which don't require much color. An IDcat requiring a great deal of high-resolution graphic illustrations will usually prove unprofitable unless you

- Distribute it widely and aggressively to many large dealers, distributors, and/or mass marketers.

- Send it with your sales force (after being trained) to sell with on their calls.

- Display your entire line on IDcat at trade shows and sales meetings.

- Use as a salesroom or dealer display of your entire line.

In these instances, you must buy or rent high-quality, high-power PCs. This requires enough showings to your best prospects and customers to justify the considerable expense. Eventually, the top-quality color IDcat will also become an ideal medium for a great variety of upscale products to consumers.

IDcat sources of proven expertise are the same as for IDs, but for IDcats you have to ask more people more questions. One ID production house may have made only a few IDcats—and none successful enough for a new version. Learn about the IDcat failures.

Other IDcat production companies have a number of successes. Ask what kind of products have worked better than others. Some production houses produce only IDcats. Ask if you can talk to their IDcat clients, and then ask these companies for their results and opinions. Study each IDcat you can get your hands on to see how it is interactive. Also analyze the service it performs—Is it fun to use? How is the quality of the presentation? How helpful is the routine for ordering? Does it suggest that you copy it and send it to a friend?

Car IDcats

Car IDcats succeed, primarily because an IDcat can let a car shopper compare by computer a number of cars. In addition to making a short-term purchase decision, these computer shoppers can also dream-shop into the future. By becoming familiar with their ultimate car of choice, IDcats spur long-term purchase desires and sales. The IDcats can be updated yearly until the customer's dream car is affordable.

Both Buick and Ford are successful IDcat users, each with its own approach. By example, they can teach you to adapt IDcats to your own firm's needs. Let's take a look at their approaches.

1. Buick gives away IDcats. Ford sells them.

2. Buick offers fun games with no advertising. Ford makes a fun game out of "test-driving" Fords.

3. Buick distributes one-half of its IDcats to those who requested it the year before and want another. Ford largely sells disks each year to new prospects.

4. Buick uses no ad agency for IDcats. Ford uses the direct marketing arm of its agency, J. Walter Thompson.

5. Buick IDcats reach almost twice as many prospects and they enhance all its promotion. Ford uses its IDcats as highly targeted, niche direct marketing but in 1990 sold over 100,000 disks.

Both companies did considerable research before deciding to create and test-market IDcats. They both also researched the demographics and attitudes of their IDcat users and traced the subsequent sales results carefully. Buick relied more on qualitative research, and Ford put more value on quantitative research. Both spot-checked IDcat users versus car buyers to determine the buy rates of those asking for or ordering an IDcat. Buick uses no direct mail to outside lists. Ford had success with one or two outside lists only, but internal lists were successful. Both advertise IDcats with big-space ads in computer magazines.

Research Reduces Risk.   In each of five model years, Buick sent out a new disk catalog for its entire line of cars to a total of 737,000 people. Before creating the first IDcat, the focus group method was used to find out how Buick customers who used computers felt about the idea. Among the focus group's findings were what computer-user consumers liked: people liked the idea of animation to demonstrate features; of the disk calculating various costs; and of a fun game to be included with the disk. Focus group participants said they preferred not to pay for it. While they did not want to be mailed unasked-for IDcats, they wanted to be offered the chance to send for them, via ads in computer magazines. The focus group discussions were taped, and their recommendations used in a market test.

IDcat Content.   Close to 25 percent of Buick's IDcat content featured one model, and another 25% was devoted to an interactive game. The rest of the carmaker's line was featured in the remaining half. The featured car model, game, and the IDcat theme differed each year. Ford's research led its IDcat producers to make a game out of road-testing different Ford models rather than Buick's primarily amusement-oriented game approach. The first Ford IDcat included three test-track driving simulation games.

Research led both carmakers to include all models of each line in their IDcats, a demonstration of every accessory, the ability to calculate costs for custom-selected combinations (and to compute the monthly payments for each combination), and *excitement* in the viewing of their IDcats.

Yet the end products are quite different. The first Buick IDcat was full of motion, color, action, and sound—animated cars, chugging engines, moving pistons and crankshafts, and bouncing shock absorbers. Meanwhile, in one Ford IDcat you could drive any of 16 Ford models in four simulated driving events—touring, drag-strip, slalom, or Grand Prix. There was also a Ford Info Center which included graphic demos on antilocking brakes, air bags, intraclean windshields, super-charging, and more features.

Post-IDcat Research and Usage Stimulation.   Both car firms' IDcat marketing strategies presumed that mailing out IDcats is not enough to ensure success. Their follow-up marketing and research efforts have included

1. Personalized letters with questionnaires to IDcat users

2. Phone surveys

3. Interactive questions within the IDcat

4. Questions in ads in computer magazines offering IDcats

5. Focus group discussions

The demographic research of IDcat users confirmed other studies of computer users but were somewhat more upscale. Their results overall showed that the big majority of IDcat users were male, married, and college graduates. Each company found that IDcats attracted a large percentage of nonowners of their cars and people with more income than the average owners of their cars. Research for Buick showed that the average disk-user spent two hours with the IDcat.

Buick printed this suggestion on its disk: "Feel free to copy and pass along this disk to a friend." Eighty-four percent of those interviewed who watched the Buick IDcat said that they gave a copy to a friend; 97

percent said they spoke to others about the disk; 69 percent gave a copy of the disk to an average of four people, and some to six or more. Ford assumed a much smaller pass-along rate but a higher retention rate due to the driving games.

IDcat Marketing Cost versus Sales. Subsequent car sales amongst these IDcat-promoted consumers were traced by

1. Inquiries about the shopping actions taken after seeing the IDcat
2. Dealer reports of showroom walk-ins and purchases
3. Spotchecks of IDcat-user names versus actual car-buyers.
4. Traces of responses by direct-marketing methods

Of those queried by Buick, 10 percent said that after seeing the IDcat they intended to buy a Buick. Some said they went right to the showroom and bought one. Dealers were enthusiastic but vaguer. Buick also tracked the sales from special offers such as certificates mailed with the disk and submitted to a dealer when purchasing.

A viewer of one Buick IDcat could instruct the computer to print out a certificate for a deluxe picnic basket giveaway for each Park Avenue car buyer. By taking the certificate to the dealer after selecting the car, Buick then sent the $250-value basket to the car buyer's home.

Although research indicated that consumers were willing to pay for the disk, Ford chose to test ways to offer the disk in computer publications. When offered for free, over 22 percent requested the IDcat. At $2.95, 8 percent responded, and at $9.95, 5 percent purchased the IDcat. Ford decided upon a price of $6.95 and subsequently measured the cost per response to specific media and ad copy.

Periodic focus groups influenced Buick to make IDcats more functional, friendlier, and simpler. One-to-one phone interviews with randomly picked customers and users also affected IDcat content.

With all this effort, it must be said that these car companies still do not consider IDcats as substantially contributing to their overall sales. But Nancy Newell, who heads disk marketing at Buick says, "People get in the habit of sending for and using our disks each year. And we get a large number of 'conquest sales' from converts owning other makes. It offers Buick a different medium to reach opportune prospects."

Larry Dale, who pioneered the use of IDcats at Ford, says, "Our disk catalogs have been a small niche, but they've been profitable in gaining us new customers of a superior kind. I consider it support for our media mix."

Other Consumer IDcat Markets

Only IDcats devoted to special areas will succeed among consumers at first. The transaction values should be large and preferably frequent. For example, IDcats are not generally used to sell private education, yet might soon routinely supplement both print and video catalogs. And, as home-computer penetration grows and more women use computers at home, IDcats may be used successfully to market appliances, real estate firms, prefab housing, boats, home heating, air conditioning, financial services, and other innovative, unusual niches.

Just remember that each consumer IDcat should be uniquely interactive and not require much in the way of detailed color. In fact, use little of the highest-resolution color (the kind needed by luxury advertisers in fashion and upscale shelter magazines). Better color capacity may soon come, but by then other upcoming technology that we'll cover in later chapters may be even better.

Business-to-Business IDcats

I asked Martin Nisenholtz (senior vice president and director of Ogilvy & Mather's Electronic Marketing Division), "What is the most recent, highly successful, business catalog on a disk that you are familiar with?" His answer was "The AT&T 800 Directory." It serves a simple, specific, universal purpose.

Business-to-business IDcats are proliferating for all kinds of products and services. Compaq Computers, for example, has an IDcat for its product line, whereas Digital Learning, Inc., publishes quickly needed books on-disk and offers a sampler disk catalog. Also consider *Business Marketing* magazine, which has a 25-page disk catalog of its line of business books.

Some business-to-business IDcats are conceived and designed as advanced software management tools. Such IDcats perform unique services for customers who buy big-ticket products and services. The most suitable ones pay for themselves, require great precision in devising custom choices, and involve much time and study by the user to compare options.

Still, the right IDcat shows business customers how to expedite the decision-making process. This includes the ability to quickly make copies of anything within the IDcat. Users can then distribute copies within their company or institution.

Business IDcats should also interactively do much of the calculation work and aid in leading the user to the correct choice with the biggest possible savings given his or her company's objective. After selecting the product, customers should be able to see the total costs, including any area sales tax, and shipping costs. Then the IDcat should allow customers to print out order forms or purchase directly by modem.

Parker Poole III is an engineer who became interested in software applications that help people understand the energy performance of machines. He is CEO of Cornerstones-Wright, which creates interactive disk catalogs and selection programs for manufacturers of a wide range of products. The catalogs consist of one to ten disks. One major client is ITT Bell & Gossett (B&G), a manufacturer of pumps and related systems.

B&G's IDcat is called ESP-PLUS (Equipment Selection Program). ESP-PLUS has hundreds of products, some with dozens of configurations of accessory products. B&G engineers and Cornerstones-Wright worked together to develop ESP-PLUS as the primary and preferred methods for engineers and customers to access product information.

For example, a B&G customer can select from a variety of complex pumping systems and determine the appropriate system for the specific application and the life cycle cost of that system. A few keystrokes display single or multiple centrifugal pump performance curves showing the efficiency and performance ratings under different conditions. ESP-PLUS saves 50 to 70 percent of the calculating and specifying time required by using print catalogs and can automatically configure and select the correct accessories for the pump system that is chosen.

ESP-PLUS comes with a detailed instruction manual, and users receive a newsletter on features and tips on how to use the program. In utilizing the program, the customer or engineer has the ability to create an order following the selection of a specific system. This feature greatly reduces incorrect orders and saves B&G significant order-processing costs.

As we go to press, over 2000 customers and engineers use ESP-PLUS. In a recent survey of several hundred engineers, B&G found that 85 percent of the surveyed customers utilized ESP-PLUS. Many of them use the program on a daily basis as part of their ongoing evaluation and consideration of B&G products. B&G estimates that orders from ESP-PLUS users are larger and more predictable than with previous methods of customer communications. They are also more accurate.

Here are some questions I asked Parker and his answers:

Q: What business-to-business marketers can benefit most from the use of IDcats?

A: Cornerstones-Wright worked first with manufacturers in the HVAC industry, the electrical products field and electronics area. But for any business-to-business (BTB) marketer the use of disk media will soon be as fundamental in selling as print catalogs and product sheets are today.

Q: What percentage of those who market-test the use of BTB IDcats fail and give up?

A: Any bad product, line, or inept marketer can fail. We only deal with quality products and competent marketers. No cataloger who has started with us to use IDcats has given up, although some went slowly. Most are more aggressive—70 percent of these IDcat users are extremely bullish because their customers like to use IDcats.

Q: Why do technical and business customers like IDcats?

A: Because using them replaces the drudgery of ordering from print catalogs.

Q: How does this sell more goods?

A: The IDcat can present more vital information and more up-to-date information on more products (particularly accessories—it's the ideal add-on medium) in the same time spent. A technical specifier could spend an hour or so on one or two products in print or by disk examine dozens of products and hundreds of accessories.

Q: Will disks replace business catalogs in print?

A: No, but print catalogs will shrink. The technical information which now takes 50 to 60 percent of print space (and is most dated) will be eliminated from print and supplied on disk. Business, technical, and industrial catalogs will be half the size and have a far longer life. Frequent revisions will be less needed.

Q: Have you found any other advantages of IDcats?

A: Their use is a whole new way to do business and the simplest, fastest, cheapest way to prepare for other electronic media. A many-disk catalog naturally extends into a CD-ROM catalog, with minimum extra cost. An on-disk catalog can evolve into a computer bulletin board or into use on an online network. It can be combined in many ways with other media ranging from literature faxing at a moment's notice to a bind-in in a business publication to use as a trade show display, a salesman's leave-behind, or sent in advance of a call. It can be promoted in any medium and integrated into your entire campaign.

IDs versus IDcats

IDcats have greater content, are more complex, take longer to produce, and cost more than IDs. But if the IDcat is well conceived, there may not be a great deal of difference in price with other marketing options. Nancy Newell of Buick says that an IDcat takes about four months from storyboard to completion. This involved about 80 hours of in-house time and over 80 hours at a production house. Moreover, the production cost of the Buick IDcat was no greater than Buick's print catalog. The business-to-business IDcats described above required at least $20,000 worth or more of in-house time plus more than that of a production house. The time required to produce an involved business-to-business IDcat can range from six to nine months or more.

Do-It-Yourself IDcats

Many consider HyperCard one of the biggest breakthroughs in software for Apple since it introduced the Macintosh. It makes programming easy for nonprogrammers. HyperCard (HC) is probably the easiest way to make a do-it-yourself IDcat. The vast majority of Macs have HyperCard. HyperCard allows the Apple and Macintosh user to arrange data in accessible forms called "stacks." Apple also offers "Stackware," which creates what looks like an index card, but on that index card anyone can put text, graphics, sounds, and voices.

One software program, "Convert-It," converts HyperCard stacks to use on IBM or IBM-compatible PCs. Another software program, "Toolbox," creates stacks similar to those of HyperCard on any IBM or IBM-compatible.

I know of an ex-Marine and ex-truckdriver who turned out an excellent HyperCard IDcat with no experience. But he says he could not have done it without a book (listed at end of this chapter). The minimum equipment needed is one Macintosh II or later model (or an older retrofitted model) and HyperCard, or an IBM or compatible PC and its equivalent. The minimum computer experience needed is the know-how to use a Macintosh or an IBM or IBM-compatible PC.

On a do-it-yourself basis, list your products, prices, descriptions, alternative models, colors, sizes, and any other classifications. Use mostly text. You can use some line drawings, charts, graphs, logos, but avoid photographs. It took one beginner about four months to do the programming. He says he spent the majority of the time writing the advertising copy. It looked like a print catalog, with each stack resembling a double-page spread in a catalog.

Customers turn "pages" by selecting the right or left arrows. The table of contents, order form, and index tabs can stick out from pages on either side of the open catalog and can be selected and quickly accessed. A listing of items is sometimes on the left side and a detailed description on the right side for one item. There can be a few hundred items and the equivalent of a 200-page (or more) print catalog. It's easy and simple for customers, on any page, to select "specifications," in which case they will then access another page and learn more details.

Production costs can be low. Costs can be only the time of one or more people. In an IDcat's simplest form, there need be no out-of-pocket expense. If the IDcat is modest in scope, it's usually offered free. Some HyperCard ID catalogers update daily. Some offer to send a revised IDcat (sometimes for a charge) if the original is returned. A small firm can start to promote its IDcat with an inch of space, a classified ad in a computer publication, or in their own print catalog. Others send their IDcats to a sampling of customers. An HC or IBM-equivalent IDcat has the same success requirements as other IDcats.

International Dataware, Inc., a mail-order catalog house in San Jose, California, uses as its main advertising vehicle the *Diskette Gazette* newsletter, a 28-page tabloid newspaper with a circulation of over 75,000. But it also distributes HyperCard catalogs (over 10,000 in the first two years). Customers with HyperCard can get notices of new products and the latest software updates available. These are updated daily instead of sending out notifications of new prices, discontinued items, new models, and so forth. Updating is free and is done via a computer bulletin board, accessible by modem.

International Dataware's HyperCard catalog replaced a second, smaller printed catalog on its proprietary products at no extra cost. The electronic catalog has created a closer relationship with its customer. Because it's perceived as a service, any customer who wants it can have it. The only promotion it gets is in the tabloid, yet it has made money for International Dataware from the start.

HC IDcat Sold to the
Fortune 1000

Sixty-Eight Thousand Incorporated of Carmel, California, offered computer software, peripherals, and machines mainly to *Fortune 1000* accounts. In addition, it sold its consulting services and supplied a three-ring binder catalog to purchasing agents of *Fortune 1000* companies. When the company created an HC IDcat, it wasn't cheap. To send out 5000 disks cost about $90,000. Another $100,000 was spent in full-page ads with insert cards in Macintosh-oriented publications.

Although Sixty-Eight Thousand already had a small house list of customers, its success secret was in "pass-along." The IDcat suggested: "Make a copy for a friend." As many as 80 people in one company saw the disk. Disks sent to 10 people at three large companies (Sandia Lab, Lawrence Livermore Lab, and Martin Marietta) multiplied to over 1000

IDcats. People wrote back to the company to say that they saw it. The IDcat cost per person dropped to about 10 cents and created a house list of 28,000 customers.

Summary

Do what the smartest marketers do. Rule out use of an IDcat unless the products you sell, including your prices and your customers, fit within the parameters of other companies successful with IDcats. Decide whether to work with an ad agency, an IDcat production house, or both (or attempt the simplest do-it-yourself approach). Then follow these steps:

- Find the "perfect marriage" interactive concept for your company or stop.
- Research before and after you test.
- Be a perfectionist but keep your IDcat simple.
- Make your IDcat perform unusually well and make it do what can't be done by print catalogs.
- Measure sales results precisely.
- If a failure, stop.
- If a success, research how to improve. And keep testing.
- Roll out your IDcat success in cautious increments.

Here are Martin Nisenholtz's (of Ogilvy & Mather Direct's Electronic Marketing Group) three do's and three don'ts for anyone considering marketing via an interactive disk catalog:

Do

1. Understand the real economics of the opportunity
2. Add value
3. Delight the consumer

Don't

1. Be seduced by the technology
2. Assume that the target audience will read any documentation
3. Assume that you will have a big business in the short term

Help Source Guide

1. For *"Buick Dimensions: Road Test a Buick in your Home,"* a *free* demo disk, write Nancy Newell, Buick Motor Division, 902 E. Hamilton, Flint, MI 48550. Indicate Mac or IBM; disk size; high-density or low-density. (313) 236-5786.

2. Send $6.95 for the *Ford Simulator Disk*. Specify IBM or IBM-compatible, 5¼ or 3½ disk size, EGA or VGA screen. 14310 Hamilton Ave., Highland Park, MI 48203. (800) 634-2767.

3. *The Inmar Group* is an ID and IDcat production house—graphics, animation, sound, interactive spreadsheets, questionnaires. *Free* information kit, including demo disk, available: 4242 Piedras Dr. E., Suite 120, San Antonio, TX 78228. (512) 733-8999.

4. *Cornerstones-Wright, Inc.,* is an ID catalog creator, consultant with engineering background, can provide case histories in IDcats for money-saving, energy-saving products: P.O. Box 4904, Portland, ME 04112. (207) 772-3900. (800) 888-8811.

18
Modem Marketing

E-Mail, EDI, Bulletin Boards

Thousands of computer networks connect millions of individual computer users. Thousands of networks alone link big manufacturers, wholesalers, and retailers. Last to develop have been the national, entertainment, and information computer networks.

What has allowed all these networks to flourish is the proliferation of computer modems. The first modem was a simple device which "interpreted" between a computer and a telephone. Modems connected to the computers make possible a "phone conversation" between two computers. The two become a computer network to send to each other various kinds of data.

A *local area network* (LAN) is a small- to moderate-size network, usually within a building or cluster of buildings. A *wide-area network* (WAN) is usually larger and further apart, often nationwide and sometimes worldwide.

Participants in wide-area networks include members of leading professional and trade associations and employees of large companies. Special carrier networks interlink each network and allow computers to communicate at local phone rates. A *gateway* connects one network to another.

Basic Modem Applications

Let's start our review of modem marketing opportunities by examining how one of the simplest applications evolved. A *bulletin board system*

(BBS) is a computer (usually a PC) and modem set up to receive calls and act as a host system. The first was an online computer version of the community bulletin board at the local grocery store. Users left and/or picked up messages. Then they "talked" online and exchanged information. This soon developed into desktop broadcasting. BBS's became little videotex newspapers or magazines, club meeting places by computer and little "mutual aid" societies.

Computer bulletin boards worldwide pour out new kinds of information on several hundred thousand varied, narrow-niche interests. These bulletin board systems have proliferated far and wide because

1. The cost of modems has plummeted while their capabilities and transmission speed have multiplied.

2. Faster modems send more information each minute for less cost.

3. Long-distance phone costs per minute dropped 50 percent in 10 years. In addition, the capacity and quality of telephone transmission lines have improved greatly with the widespread use of integrated services digital network (ISDN) and fiber-optic technologies.

4. Modems are now an integral part of most office computers and many home computers. In fact, the number of modems is an ever bigger percentage of the total number of computers worldwide.

5. Information stored on computers became accessible through new retrieval-and-analysis software.

There are often thousands of databases available which are of some potential usefulness to a single field of interest. For an ever-growing number of fields, there is a vast database network which comprises a universe of information from libraries, universities, business schools, and other primary databases available directly online from newspapers; magazines; newsletters; and research organizations covering science, medicine, the law, business, and the government.

Later in this and subsequent chapters, we'll explore computer bulletin boards and online networks in greater depth. But first, let's examine two other forms of modem marketing: *E-mail* and *EDI*. Electronic mail (E-mail) is the exchange of messages via a network or bulletin board system. One user leaves the message "addressed" to another user, who can read it and later reply. Users by the millions send billions of messages a year. Eighty percent of them are internal or within an organization. E-mail has been growing at the rate of 20 percent a year. Although big companies have their own E-mail networks, many smaller organizations use public E-mail networks such as AT&T Mail, MCI Mail, and SprintMail.

The fastest-growing kind of messaging network is electronic data interaction (EDI), the computer-to-computer exchange of standard business data in a standard machine-readable data format. Presently, about 20 EDI public networks exist in the United States alone, plus several thousand intercompany EDI networks. This number is increasing at a rate of about 40 percent a year.

Communications Tool to Marketing Media

Modem marketing (MM) is the use of any such media to create sales that would otherwise not occur. The easiest way to start is via E-mail. John C. Dvorak and Nick Anis, whose book on PC telecommunications I recommend,[1] suggest these E- mail uses:

- Distribute hot leads to your sales force in an instant.
- Receive ordering information quickly and efficiently.
- Send price changes and product announcements to customers.
- Send proposals or follow-up letters from anywhere.
- Distribute instant newsletters on products and services.
- Speed communications with dealers and distributors.
- Set up an E-mail network with your customers or suppliers.

E-mail provides for instant interactivity (which mail and overnight courier can't) while reducing the potential for errors of phone conversations. E-mail is far cheaper than communicating by courier, often cheaper than mail, and sometimes cheaper than fax. E-mail is generally perceived as urgent as a fax or a courier message and more urgent than mail. And E-mail can be combined with fax or broadcast fax via any PC and faxboard or public network.

However, people prefer to read only short letters on screen and sometimes not even that. An E-mail printout is an extra step. In addition, using a modem with a PC is not as familiar to most as using a fax. To date, modem phone numbers are known far less than fax numbers and scarcely at all compared with phone numbers. Unsolicited E-mail is rarely permissible and often is resented as "junk E-mail."

Moreover, all E-mail networks still do not have a single standard, although faxes do. E-mail network interconnection can have complica-

---

[1]*Guide to PC Telecommunications*, McGraw-Hill, 2d ed., New York, 1992.

tions and extra cost. Sometimes, interconnection proves to be impossible. Plus, E-mail has no envelope, so it can be read by anyone accessing the computers at either end (without security steps, which for new users take time and trouble).

Considering E-mail marketing? Yes! As postage, printing, and paper costs increase, E-mail becomes more useful. You can use its strengths and, with simple steps, overcome most of its weaknesses. Always use E-mail only as a service, *only* where prearranged with the customer or prospect, and *only* with short messages for most promotion. If you word-process yourself, it's easy to communicate by modem yourself, including your identification for security. If an assistant word-processes for you, he or she can E-mail for you.

If you want to use E-mail marketing, how do you start? A single letter via a public E-mail network such as AT&T Mail, MCI Mail, and SprintMail can start you on your way.

At the end of this chapter are phone numbers to get the latest rates plus suggestions for helpful books, magazines, and newsletters. Get the permission of your biggest customers and their modem numbers first. Establish with each a computer-mailbox number and a personal identification number (PIN) for each executive. Set up a computer address file.

Begin E-mail slowly. E-mail's copy format is typically unstructured. It's freeform and meant to be easily read. E-mail connotes urgency. Send E-mail to a customer only about what is important to that customer, such as a back-order has just been shipped, or a price reduction or price protection is available before an imminent price raise. To interested parties, appropriate E-mail messages may concern a looming shortage, a new sweeping guarantee, or a break-through product. Form an E-mail relationship, customer by customer. Then do the same with prospects.

As in every form of modem marketing, E-mail can create inquiries and orders by modem. These naturally supply you with names, modem phone numbers, and E-mail box numbers. Develop an E-mailing list. When this list is within one network, sending an E-mailing to everyone often costs nothing more, even to thousands (we'll later cover this in more detail).

EDI Networks

EDI (electronic data interchange) allows for instant, computer-to-computer communication of business data. One computer calls another and transmits the data. They "converse" with each other via transmission of standard business transactions sent and received. For example, one company's computer may ask for the latest inventory figures by sending an inventory inquiry transaction, and the other may answer the inquiry by returning an inventory response transaction.

Phyllis Sokol is a leading authority on EDI, and her book (*EDI: The Competitive Edge*, McGraw-Hill Intertext, 1989) has been highly praised.

Because EDI is transmitted in a prearranged, structured data format, EDI is machine-readable and can be fed directly into a computer application. EDI data are exchanged virtually instantly over high-speed telephone lines. Both EDI communication sessions and EDI processing can be completely automated, eliminating the need for and costs associated with people. EDI is particularly useful for high-volume transactions used frequently in day-to-day business such as purchase orders, invoices, and shipping documents.

General Motors orders via EDI about 90 percent of the production materials it uses in the manufacture of its automobiles. Likewise, Ford's computer network links over 4800 of its dealers and over 3000 of its production material suppliers to its corporate data center. IBM is connecting 2000 of its largest suppliers worldwide via its EDI network. Sears Roebuck's EDI network has 135,000 terminals in 7000 locations (now doubling) and at over 800 Sears suppliers. The network also reaches Allstate Insurance, Dean Witter Reynolds, the Discover card, and other Sears subsidiaries. Walmart connects close to 2000 trading partners via EDI.

A big-company approach to EDI will usually start with connections with the firm's largest suppliers, then big customers, and finally smaller customers and supplier trading partners. The plan is usually to continue bringing in trading partners until most of the important trading partners are actively sending and receiving EDI transactions.

In spite of the high up-front costs, EDI eventually saves big money and increases productivity. The use of EDI technology is growing fast in virtually every industry around the world. EDI has been particularly successful in the chemical, banking, pharmaceutical, and grocery industries—90 percent of purchases of pharmaceuticals by wholesalers from manufacturers are made via EDI. EDI use is emerging in the insurance, communications, and health care industries.

To set up an EDI network, most companies purchase an EDI translator for somewhere between $2000 for a PC and $30,000 for a mainframe. (The cost of each continues to decrease.) Then the companies spend some money on application programming, training, and other expenses. Then they usually use a public network, as do 80 percent of EDI network users. Prices for third-party services are minimal, mostly based on volume of data being transmitted. Those companies that use their own communication networks already had networks that were being underutilized, including Sears and Walmart.

EDI, once set up correctly, virtually eliminates the clerical costs associated with the keying in and processing of incoming orders, shipping documents, and invoices. EDI eliminates the costs of paper materials such as envelopes, paper forms, and stamps, and cuts out the errors resulting from misunderstanding or incorrect key entry. A sales manager can distribute increases in product prices to 3000 people in minutes. A company can reduce the cost of issuing a purchase order by up to 90 percent. Even small-to medium-size companies can save from tens to hundreds of thousands of dollars by reducing their inventory and safety stock requirements. Large companies can save over $100 million.

With EDI, manufacturers and distributors can use incoming orders to monitor customer demand; EDI's fast and accurate information allows these companies to forecast for their own manufacture or purchases more accurately and be better prepared to respond more quickly to unexpected surges in product demand. EDI makes just-in-time manufacturing schedules possible. Customers send more frequent, smaller orders based on their actual forecasts; their suppliers receive the orders, process them, and deliver product faster. All in all, EDI improves the relationship between trading partners while also streamlining the way they do business together.

However, data transmitted by EDI must conform to highly structured standard data format. Although there is room in the standard for all the information a company will need to send or receive, EDI is much more effective when the data are codified rather than sent in a narrative form. This may be a challenge to do. Sometimes, accompanying data either are sent outside of the EDI transmission, as, for example, a contract or CadCam drawings, or are augmented with telephone calls. You can send the purchase order but not always more detailed information about the order. However, some flexibility can be built into EDI beforehand. EDI combined with some phone or fax contact allows more flexibility.

EDI Preparation

Successful EDI largely depends on the standard data format. Various standards are being used, but no one is universally accepted. However, the American National Standards Institute (ANSI) X12 standard is very widely accepted in North American EDI transmissions currently. By supporting this standard, both large and small companies can conduct electronic trade with one another, regardless of the size of the computer they use to implement EDI.

EDI is not for daily wheeling and dealing. Price negotiation takes place beforehand. Participation requires cooperation, a joint-venture attitude, a partnership relationship. With EDI, business cannot be adversarial. Customers can't effectively use EDI to make sudden demands for instant delivery of a product never discussed, and EDI is not a way for vendors to avoid adhering to rigid delivery dates. It requires much mutual confidence and working together.

Prior to setting up an EDI relationship, the business customer and supplier must meet. A good, working, business relationship should be established first. A detailed agreement is made. Ongoing customer needs of certain models, sizes, or colors in whatever quantities are determined. A probable stocking program is agreed upon. Further sales expectations are discussed. There's a lot of up-front work, preparation, and debugging needed.

How EDI Works

An interesting EDI application being used by some companies today is for the supplier to generate its own orders by using either inventory or point-of-sale information from the customer. Algorithms that control the replenishment of stock are agreed to by both customer and supplier and usually cover basic stock items. Fad and seasonal items are rarely handled this way because their demand is more volatile.

After merchandise is shipped, the bill can be transmitted via EDI. Payment can be transmitted by check or EFT (electronic funds transfer). Either may be accompanied by EDI payment remittance information.

Even though EDI transmissions can be conducted totally unaided by people, EDI is not a passive system. Business users constantly monitor transmission and receipt of important business transactions. Some large companies set up an internal post office to pick up from and route EDI data to various company locations.

In a five-month test at four J. C. Penney stores, sales of Penney brand suits went up 59 percent after the stores linked via EDI with the apparel supplier. EDI made it possible to replenish supplies quickly enough to meet the season's demand.

SuperValu stores handle 200 vendor-promotion announcements per week on EDI to take advantage of vendor promotions. The vendor or broker puts promotional screens into SuperValu EDI files with the buyer's approval. The computer program recognizes a promotion opportunity, places the order, and then calculates and passes on allowances to the individual stores. This creates new sales and profits for both SuperValu and the vendor.

The retail fashion business is seeing a trend to introducing a new style each month rather than one per season. Liz Claiborne, Inc., Milliken & Co., Hagar, Dillard's Department Stores, and Levi Strauss & Co. lead in EDI. Wrangler in Greensboro, N.C., calls its EDI program the Wrangler Wire. Wrangler's retail partners scan bar-coded inventory weekly with a handheld scanner. Upon receipt of the data, Wrangler's EDI system automatically generates orders, taking into account what is in transit, unshipped, or already received.

The use of EDI by small companies to increase export sales is an important trend. EDI greatly reduces the crushing volume of required paperwork for export. This is happening because EDI networks are being connected worldwide between and with members of the European Economic community, in the Far East, and in Eastern Europe. Jerome Dreyer, past president of the EDI association, says

> The enormous paperwork of export has shut out most small businesses. But EDI is the great equalizer, allowing even small businesses the opportunity to find niches in world markets. It may be the only means a small firm can get in on export for a big share of its sales.

Considering EDI

EDI is fast becoming a must for any firm to sell to many giant buyers and to be a dealer for many giant sellers.

Should you initiate EDI? If your company is big and you don't establish EDI, you are liable to be at a disadvantage competitively. An EDI feasibility study can show you the dollar savings and investment payback probability. Companies with a large number of transactions to a small number of trading partners may choose to build EDI networks specific to these companies. But note the following:

- If you get only small orders very infrequently, don't use EDI now. And if you sell infrequently to the same customers, forget EDI.

- 85 percent of EDI is now via public networks. These third-party or *value-added networks* (VANS) offer a more practical way for most companies to initiate EDI and the only way for small ones to do so.

Small suppliers make up 90 percent of all companies doing EDI to big companies, from national retail chains to automobile manufacturers. Small suppliers, asked to join an EDI network, can do so after the purchase of a PC translator for an investment of only $1000 to $3000.

An EDI caution is warranted here: Expect some problems to start. The network must handle unpredictable peaks and lulls of EDI traffic. It must not delay customer orders, remittances, or acceptance notices coming or going. Vendors may send a large batch of orders, once a day, once a week, or, occasionally, once a season. Even with EDI, working with your trading partners will continue to require much effort. EDI transactions need to be handled with extra care. Thorough preparation is a must.

Marketing Information Online

Computer-based bulletin boards and online networks are fast becoming significant media—even dominant for the distribution of certain kinds of software. According to Dvorak and Anis,

> Anyone can inexpensively set up shop and publish information electronically for profit. You can become an on-line service and charge others to access your information. For giant companies it's difficult to acquire, organize and maintain specialized information. Generally, they just buy it from people who create it.
>
> For a few thousand dollars and a few years of effort, you can become the authority for a field of study. As you become known as a central point for that information, others with similar interest will bring more information to you. Collect and organize the information into accessible and presentable form. You can do it all with two PC's, two phone lines, and two modems.[2]

Online PR

Public relations is mining the rich new online "vein" in a variety of ways. Online news networks, specialized news networks, and databases are all sources of necessary background information for TV and radio stations, newspapers, trade media, professional journals, local business publications, newsletters, and other forms of communication.

No giant PR campaign is complete without putting its story online, and no big PR firm is without an online department. Many have BBSs (bulletin board systems) with all possible back-up material for a launch of a huge new project or product introduction. Even the smallest moonlighter can send releases to the appropriate online media. A one-person start-up firm in any of many fields may begin with a BBS. The Help Source Guide suggestions at the end of the chapter include help in do-it-yourself research and start-it-yourself BBS.

---

[2]*Guide to PC Telecommunications.*

Shareware

A BBS's biggest product is self-published "shareware"—software offered free or sold for very little. People are asked to pay more if they like it. Here's how this unusual marketing concept works: Name-brand software is expensive and forbids copying. Shareware invites people to copy it. This public domain software is royalty-free, can be copied by anyone, and often is available free. But top-quality software is hard to find. The best shareware is considered by computer user groups and by experts to be as good and sometimes better than name brands.

Scott Watson is a programmer who operates The FreeSoft Company of Beaver Falls, Pennsylvania. He created White Knight (first called Red Ryder), a communications program for the Macintosh computer. Spending no money on advertising, but simply offering Red Ryder on BBSs allowed Watson to market what became the number-one communications program in the country for the Mac. He did not sell it in any store. All he asked of those who downloaded the program into their computer was that if they like it, they might send him $40. (To download is to receive data on a computer from another computer, network or BBS.) He later said: "I took advantage of a problem: piracy. Many program-users copied them free. I assumed that, if I offered something free and asked people who liked it to pay, that some people would; that maybe I'd get a bigger percentage than people who sell software."

This new kind of "on approval" selling worked beautifully. There was never a follow-up. The cost was a fraction of what competitive software sold for. Often people who gloried in copying sent in checks.

Each BBS sent the program online free to anyone who asked for it. Anyone happy with Red Ryder copied it for friends and passed the word to others, who then got Red Ryder from their bulletin boards.

Macintosh magazines rated Red Ryder higher and higher for excellence. People asked computer stores for Red Ryder. Scott rejected orders from both computer stores and distributors and just concentrated on making Red Ryder better. More new bulletin boards ran his offer.

Then Scott made a command decision. He doubled the price to $80 simply because he wanted to keep getting the $40 he always had plus a little more for his improvements. He sold to stores but still refused to sell to distributors, because they wanted 60 percent. He concentrated on making his product still better and on servicing anyone who wanted help.

Next, Scott Watson came up with a program for anyone to create a BBS. It's called Second Sight (previously called Red Ryder Host). Scott introduced the new program in the same way he started, on bulletin boards everywhere. By then, Scott Watson operated his own bulletin board. Anyone could order directly from him. He had proved the power of the simplest bulletin boards as media.

Scott explained to me how his marketing evolved:

Bulletin boards help distribution. Our store sales tripled in three years since going into stores. There has been a switch-over. As volume increased (with no overhead increase), our cost per disk dropped.

At the end of our third year selling to the trade, we began to sell through a distributor, Ingram-Micro D. At the same time we started to advertise. We began to run for six months a full-page ad in three Mac magazines. As soon as the ads started, we had a big burst of sales.

Caution! Scott's two products were perfectly suited to sell via a BBS. White Knight universalized the Mac, enabling it to communicate with most other PC and mainframe makes. Second Sight enabled anyone to set up a BBS with a Mac and modem. Both were superb and are constantly improved. Scott had introduced Version 11.12 as we went to press. Many others have also succeeded in marketing software through BBSs, and the quality of the product is paramount to its success.

Dvorak and Anis point out that putting a program into shareware distribution can cost only a few hundred dollars. Shareware authors typically offer competitive programs to many famous name brands. Every major shareware company has its own BBS and accepts payments via charge cards as well as making use of as many BBSs as possible to let anyone download. BBSs want shareware programs to upload (put into their systems) for users to download directly. Thousands of BBSs post (announce on screen) shareware programs for downloading and libraries of shareware programs. A BBS often gets 40 percent of its income in the "connect time" charges to users downloading shareware. (Connect time is the time you spend online with a database.) Some BBSs charge $60 a year or so for unlimited access.

A BBS must have a dedicated phone connection. But local accessing is too limited for profitable marketing, because most people won't pay long-distance charges to connect with your BBS from far away. National access can be offered via packet-switching networks which take calls at local rates from almost anywhere. The BBS pays a differential as well as set-up charges and minimum guarantees. If a BBS can promote enough national accessing, this approach is practical.

To call a single-user BBS is like a normal phone call. To call a multiuser BBS is like a conference call. This makes chat lines and forums possible. A multiuser BBS offers real-time (immediate) online interaction with other people, without the delays of a single-user BBS. An eight-line multiuser system costs $160 a month at a residential rate or $400 a month if the BBS charges for access, which then involves a business rate from the phone company. (Dvorak and Anis can tell you far more about BBSs.)

Product-Support BBSs

Most leading computer hardware and software companies now provide some online access to technicians as well as technical information and software updates via BBSs. Many now take their most frequently asked technical support questions and answers and post them on the BBS. Anyone using the board can see the answer.

Some have two BBSs, one for the public and one for advanced professionals. Large companies often use a support BBS as an after-hours backup. Even the smallest companies can buy the simplest PC system, connect a modem, set up a BBS, and offer 24-hour technical support. Minor questions are answered by the software developer personally or by a part-time tech person. When the BBS is open to all users, many of the questions are solved by other users of the product.

Marketing Advantages

XyWrite of Billerica, Massachusetts, started a bulletin board for product support and charged $50 a year for access. The top 130 questions most often asked about applications and use problems, and complete answers to each, were put into the database and on printing drivers. Those inquiring could communicate via the BBS with each other and exchange experiences. There was more user satisfaction with the support. The cost of handling each inquiry was dramatically reduced. The BBS became a profit center.

XyWrite was also getting marketing advantages. It could conduct surveys, get product improvement suggestions, offer new products, get testimonials or recommendations, give commissions on sales. More new users of the support service increase marketing benefits. XyWrite then cut the price in half. The BBS still made money, and, even more important, the marketing advantages were significant. XyWrite then gave the service free because of the marketing benefits.

Service and Cross-Selling

Ashton-Tate (A-T) software has a free BBS on TymNet for customer support. The caller pays for the modem call, but the BBS is free. Ashton-Tate's BBS is also a PR medium, and in-house ads appear on the screen for various A-T software items. Customer support BBSs serve as PR tools, order-takers, and software update distributors. These BBSs may also give database access, such as back-order status or part number cross-reference.

By using BBS's software, developers can poll customers, hold round-table discussions, and expand the usability of their products while increasing sales. Companion products or utilities can be cross-marketed if users can see the benefits of using the two together. Epson America, Sierra Online, and many software and hardware firms benefit from BBSs in some of these ways.

BBS Take-Off under Way

New technology is transforming the BBS into a far more desirable service. Service bureaus, including those operated by the phone companies, enable users to also set up a bulletin board as an extra service. Some can also print incoming orders or inquiries on a printer or printer station dedicated for this purpose.

Baud speed (the measure of computer data transmission) is leaping far faster. PC ability to handle high-speed modems will soon grow. Modems are on the verge of becoming standard equipment in average-price PCs, after which online use will skyrocket.

From the early days of videotext, through the growth of bulletin boards and electronic mail, Ogilvy & Mather Direct has been busy in these fields. I asked Martin Nisenholtz these questions about the future of online applications:

Q: What newspapers anywhere are succeeding with online services? Any with classified ads such as for real estate or help wanted?

MN: Gannett is now supplying Prodigy with classified ads. I think it's going well. America Online has recently formed a venture with Tribune Company in Chicago to supply online services.

Q: Will banking online revive?

MN: Home banking has not died. It has just gone underground. [Within days after Martin's answer, *The New York Times* ran a lead story in its business section headlined "A Renewed Bank Push for Pay-by-Phone."]

Q: Are far more people afraid to log-in online versus slipping in a disk? If so, will new easier-to-use software overcome this?

MN: This depends on the procedure used. AT&T SmartPhone is totally transparent. So are interactive TV systems. You shouldn't assume that the PC is going to be the only, or even the dominant, interactive device in home.

Virtually every field of business and special interest will support BBSs soon. Many will be start-ups. At the other end of the spectrum are the "super-BBSs" which have become information and entertainment networks. We'll discuss them next in Chapter 19. In Chapter 20 we cover catalogs online and via BBSs. And in Chapter 21, we describe marketplaces online and via BBSs. Should you consider your own BBS? Read all three chapters first.

Help Source Guide

1. *Boardwatch* magazine covers BBSs and online information services. To subscribe contact: 5970 S. Vivian St., Littleton, CO 80127. (303) 973-6038. Also available is *Boardwatch* On-Line BBS: (303) 973-4222.

2. *AT&T Easy-Link Services* offer AT&T Mail and AT&T EDI. AT&T offers *free* information kits re EDI network design, software, integration, standards, and AT&T features 400 Interplace Parkway, Parsippany, NJ 07054; (800) 367-7225.

3. A *free* information kit is also available from *MCI* Mail: 1133 19th St. NW, Washington, DC 20036. (800) 444-6245. *Sprint* has a *free* information kit also with E-mail rates in detail and features of *SprintMail*: (800) 736-1130.

4. John C. Dvorak and Nick Anis's *Dvorak's Guide to PC Telecommunications* (1128 pages), 2d ed., 1992, Osborne/McGraw-Hill, has a BBS section that is a must for marketers: 2600 10th St., Berkeley, CA 94710. (415) 548-2805.

5. *EDI Reporter* is a newsletter from Input Advisory Services. *Free* sample issue available: 1280 Villa St., Mountain View, CA 94041. (415) 961-3300.

6. *EDI Yellow Pages, Spread the Word! USA* (400+ pages) (the international edition is the *Business Partner Directory*) is an annual listing of EDI users, vendors, consultants; seminars, workshops, publications; EDI Bookstore's videotapes: P.O. Box 811366, Dallas, TX 75381. (214) 243-3456.

7. *The Electronic Data Interchange Association* (EDIA) sponsors EDI research, background, software, annual conference; cassettes, speeches, articles, success stories, and education programs. *Free* information kit and *free* issues of EDIA newsletter available: Suite 550, 225 Reinecker's Ln., Alexandria, VA 22314. (703) 838-8042.

8. *The Electronic Mail Association* provides a *free* information kit, report on E-mail, list of E-mail service bureaus: Suite 300, 1555 Wilson Blvd., Arlington, VA 22209. (703) 875-8620.

9. *Infonet Services Corporation* provides a *free* information kit on single-source network 24-hr. nodes and direct support across the United States, worldwide. Toll-free 24-hr support numbers: Commercial Services Division, 530 5th Ave., NY, NY 10036. (212) 398-2828.

10. *PSL News* is a low-cost magazine on latest, best public domain and shareware, multiple software. *Free* sample issue available from P.O. Box 35705, Houston, TX 77235-5705. (800) 242-4775.

19
Information and Entertainment Networks

Videotex and
the Super Bulletin
Boards

Compuserve originated the information and entertainment (I&E) or videotex format for computer networks by accident. Originally, CompuServe was in the business of managing the sharing of computer time among large business users, almost all during business hours. Then, CompuServe began to share after-hours time with members of a computer-user club who each had a PC and Modem. Members asked each other technical advice and answered online. A more experienced member guided the process. User clubs started for each major make of computers, then for peripherals, and most of all for software.

These were the first online special interest groups (SIGS), now called forums. Computer companies found that helping such groups was a great form of customer support. It was great PR and increased sales.

Next, forums went online via CompuServe for hobbies or other interests shared by CompuServe members. CompuServe became an online "super club" by offering access to a staggering array of forums, to database networks and databases, to automated bulletin board systems (BBSs), and finally to virtually every kind of news, ingenious service, and entertainment.

This chapter will explore several videotex or I&E computer networks for their marketing potential. Although CompuServe has pioneered this burgeoning electronic medium and thus earns the largest amount of discussion in this chapter, several newer potentially formidable competitors are also noted.

CompuServe

CompuServe is the mother of BBSs and the first super BBS. For many years CompuServe successfully attracted computer users, information providers, and marketers without relying on fancy graphics or splashy colors. While it now features both, as its basic business premise CompuServe offers

1. An endless stream and wide choice of many kinds of much-desired, highly specialized information (by the minute) that people badly want—often before it's available anywhere else.
2. The opportunity for any modem owner to participate, meet and form friendships with others who share similar interests as he or she participates in small intimate discussion groups by computer for each of a great variety of niche subjects.

Each kind of information and each discussion group tempts some people, and each is a small profit center for CompuServe. Well-off "addicts" can spend more and more, often for information that makes money for them.

A local phone call in most U.S. cities and in 100 foreign countries can access CompuServe—90 percent of the U.S. population can access CompuServe at local phone rates. Owners of the cheapest to most expensive computers and modems can subscribe. As IBM, Apple, and Microsoft are standards for the creators of PC software and peripherals, CompuServe is a magnet for innovative information providers. It attracts diverse, unique, and innovative programming— perhaps yours next.

CompuServe offers access to general news, financial news, and business news networks, plus a veritable smorgasbord of other services which collect the latest news on many specialized subjects from all over the world. CompuServe gives new online services a way to get in touch with more than 30 percent of computer media network users. As it has grown, CompuServe has learned, through trial and error, more lessons in new computer network activities and format than any other organization.

CompuServe appeals to experienced computer and modem users. More than 80 percent of CompuServe members are male, and they have higher incomes and more education than average computer owners. More of them are in industry, the professions, and high-tech businesses. These subscribers use more E-mail, are younger, and are harder than average computer owners to reach through other media.

CompuServe's successful business premise was to always sell enough services to users to pay for its overhead. So as CompuServe helped develop new services, it avoided risk. It went into many joint ventures in which its "partners" or information providers take the creative, production, and service-operating risks. CompuServe's partners sold information by the minute to make money, and CompuServe shares in one way or another. For a small percentage of services, it also added a "connect-time" surcharge.

Marketing Via CompuServe

There are two ways to use CompuServe for your company's marketing program. First, if you market information, you may be able to become a CompuServe "information provider." The electronic information you provide is usually related to or a by-product of your core business. Becoming a CompuServe info provider allows you to publicize your product or service, plus many other benefits discussed in this chapter.

Most companies use CompuServe as a marketing tool by becoming a "merchant" on The Electronic Mall, an online shopping bazaar. The Mall is a fast-growing major income producer for CompuServe, and it has made money for many of the "merchants." Each year, the number of subscriber accesses to the Mall go up. More important, product orders via the Mall are climbing faster as the Mall habit takes hold. The average sale for all stores on the Mall (and also repeat orders) keeps climbing too.

Electronic Mall Promotions

"Merchants" and CompuServe each promote the Mall. Some stores offer free merchandise and/or services, some a catalog, and some simply a credit card application to fill out online, while others run contests or auctions.

Sometimes CompuServe Mall visitors are asked one online question. Those who complete an online entry form and answer the question correctly are entered into the week's Mall drawing for 40 prizes.

CompuServe Magazine (monthly), with one of the largest circulations of a magazine reaching computer users, is a powerful promotional medium for the Mall. News articles about store offers go in the magazine and are then sent out as PR. An electronic companion magazine is

On-Line Today, which is online every day; it offers far more material than the print edition, with more promotion for mall stores.

Success Stories in Many Fields. CompuServe has grown consistently and made high rates of profits. I have found an unusual percentage of success among marketers using CompuServe, including more small ventures than in most new electronic media.

For years, executives of some big company sponsors of CompuServe's Electronic Mall told me that it was profitable but that the volume of business was too small to be interesting. But small marketers I spoke to were very happy with the amount of business as well as the profit they reported. Big companies as an experiment for the future, and smaller ones for present sales, in high percentages renewed their contracts with CompuServe.

CompuServe's Disadvantages

As a merchant, a year's commitment was required to try out The Electronic Mall (although the minimum cost was modest). And succeeding takes a lot of work. For beginning computer users, CompuServe could be confusing and was and is expensive. For years, searching for what you wanted was often difficult. Later, CompuServe was still a plain text medium, and a black-and-white medium to most users. It was not very advertising-oriented.

Besides a PC you needed a modem, communication software, an extra phone (or you tied one up), and some software for your presentation. Typically, the initial volume of sales and profits was small versus the same effort to create success in a highly projectable medium. But a growing core of subscribers were fiercely loyal, a growing number of providers found CompuServe profitable, and CompuServe always made money.

CompuServe Improvements

Special CompuServe software (the CompuServe Information Manager) speeds access and makes it easier to get where you want to go on the system. It is now free for new subscribers. How about color? The CompuServe Graphics Interchange Format (GIF) can be viewed with nearly any computer system. GIF creates a four-color picture with high resolution. Each month more color-capable new PCs are bought.

Before considering marketing through CompuServe, read the rest of this chapter to compare CompuServe with other I&E networks. Chapters 20 and 21 provide more CompuServe case histories.

Prodigy

Prodigy, owned by IBM and Sears, has invested the most research and the biggest concentration of marketing brains of any U.S. information and entertainment network. As we go to press, the number of Prodigy subscribers has soared up to almost half of all subscribers to all computer media I & E networks.

Prodigy was the first to offer subscribers graphics in bright, splashy color plus many other features that were superior to those of any competitor—or not even available elsewhere. Subscribers got all this for a low monthly charge per unit. Advertisers get a medium created for marketers by marketers designed to produce sales for advertisers to lower selling cost, with far more volume than possible before.

Prodigy is as easy to use as a TV set, even for computer beginners. An easy-to-read menu guides the user through easy-to-read text and graphics. One tap on the computer key starts a dialogue. It guides, asking only for one keystroke at a time, as it brings up whatever service or product information is needed.

Whatever editorial or noncommercial service is onscreen, the bottom fifth of every screen is a teaser ad with an onscreen button marked *Look*. There are only eight command words displayed along the bottom.

An Electronic Magazine

Prodigy subscribers are 75 percent male, and most are married, but Prodigy is geared toward families, women, children. The information services are the editorial matter. There is news from *USA Today* and the Associated Press. Prodigy offers almost a thousand features. There are departments for communication, entertainment, and information; travel services, education, and brokerage; consumer information, banking online, and shopping; games and bulletin boards; stock quotes and news; consumer information. Prodigy has over a hundred public discussion forums.

Prodigy features well-known experts on subjects of broad interest. Subscribers can make and check airline, car rental, and hotel reservations; check animated weather maps in full color; read a movie review; or order running shoes for home delivery.

Within Prodigy are mini mail-order catalogs, offers of single items or for print catalogs, and the names of stores nearest the member which stock his or her desired items.

When a member is shopping, Prodigy calculates cumulatively the total for each order. It records each inquiry as well as each purchase. It builds a reminder list and helps you to find best buys.

Prodigy also helps to find the best prospects for its advertisers. It gets to know each subscriber as no publication or broadcaster can know each reader, viewer, or listener. Marketers can reach a greater variety of specialized groups through Prodigy than by geographic, demographic or psychographic editions of any publication. Prodigy subscribers can be targeted by age, occupation, interest, income, and combinations thereof.

Prodigy instantly counts orders or inquiries for the clients' use. Failed copy can be dropped. Copy, as soon as successful, can be run in remaining circulation. New copy can be tested. Advertisers can update and quickly change many parts of their ad on-line virtually as fast as wanted.

Advertisers can telescope direct marketing from two or several separate steps to a continuous series of steps, all on Prodigy. Brightly colored graphics illustrate each electronic page on screen. There are three-or-four line "awareness" ads almost constantly on the bottom fifth of the screen.

Each "awareness" ad attracts viewers while qualifying. Instead of writing for more information, a viewer can call up more information. With a single keystroke, one item featured may lead to several, even a mini-electronic catalog. Only interested viewers ask to see more. Those most interested can ask to see more pages describing more.

Prodigy is a research treasure house, gathering various information about how its members use the service. When they enroll, members provide information about their name, address, gender, and birth date. Much of this is voluntary. Prodigy services both members and advertisers by delivering specialized advertising that matches a member's particular interests and matches the parts of the service they like to use.

However, this information is not available directly to Prodigy's commercial clients. Prodigy offers any company the opportunity to target advertising or electronic mail on the basis of demographics and interest groups. Commercial clients receive the names and addresses of members only when a member chooses to act on an offer and requests information or orders a product.

Direct marketers can easily test offers online and can track usage screen by screen to find which of several offers have the greatest appeal.

Prodigy Providers and Advertisers Succeed

Rosenbluth Travel. Rosenbluth Travel, Philadelphia, has over 450 locations in the United States and sells over $1.8 billion of travel services a year. Chief Operating Officer Lee Rosenbluth told me:

We've been with Prodigy since the inception and have had documented success. Fulfilling requests for air travel reservations is our largest revenue area on the service. Currently, Prodigy has a choice of three travel companies that are authorized to fulfill ticket requests. Our share continues to grow as we enhance our overall services. The average ticket price is approximately $300. This reflects the orientation of the service to the vacationing consumer who is able to utilize heavily discounted airfares.

Prodigy members are very loyal yet determined to receive the best value. Our experience with the membership has led to members utilizing us for airline tickets and then calling upon us for their vacations or cruises.

PC Flowers. Bill Tobin and Peter MacMurray are the founders of PC Flowers via Prodigy. Bill is an "idea entrepreneur" who has founded 12 companies each aimed at a new niche without competition in a new high-tech field. Peter had owned and sold a chain of florists.

Bill and Peter became interested in Prodigy and studied the demographics and psychographics of its members to the degree made available to them. Meanwhile Bill had discussed with Peter the characteristics of flower shop customers who wired flowers and found a strong correlation with Prodigy members. He and Peter saw a unique opportunity.

FTD had the only electronic network between florists and a central distribution location. Prodigy had the most members and had made the biggest investment to simplify and speed communications between members of any U.S. I&E network. What was needed was unique "bridge" software and a technological infrastructure to take inquiries about and orders for flowers ordered by computer. To process each order required transmitting the order to FTD for retransmission to the nearest flower shop of the person receiving the FTD order. The shop could then deliver the order. All this would have to be done in a small fraction of the time FTD members take using the traditional manual input methods and with a small fraction of the errors normally expected. The bridge software when combined with Prodigy software and the FTD electronic network had to transmit orders with the least possible human involvement.

It took a big investment and a year and a half to put it all together. Bill and Peter bought three flowers shops, joined FTD, and formed PC Flowers. Its software displays the FTD selections in color. To take an order and process a credit card took 52 seconds. Errors were less than 0.25 percent, and all ordering was accomplished with minimum involvement of people. By the fifth month of operation, PC Flowers became the number-10 retailer in monthly electronic sales among the 25,000 FTD members. By September of that year it became number 2.

In the first year, 24,000 PC Flowers orders were taken through Prodigy. Sales jumped to 80,000 the second year. Of people who logged on to Prodigy and then used the menu to shop on PC Flowers, more than 30 percent became customers. Each new customer of PC Flowers, on average, purchased again through Prodigy three to five times in the next 12 months. By November of that year, sales were $100,000 a week.

PC Flowers sends a monthly basic newsletter on one 8½-by 11-inch page by electronic mail, through Prodigy, to each PC Flowers Prodigy customer—at a fraction of the cost of direct mail. The newsletter features the care and maintenance of various flowers and plants appropriate for a timely floral holiday.

At the end of the first half of the second year, Bill and Peter started a new business, PC Balloons, for people who wanted to send balloons instead of, or in addition to, flowers. Five months later, weekly sales of PC Balloons were running 30 percent of PC Flowers.

Meanwhile, PC Flowers was expanding into other I&E networks and additional gateways beyond Prodigy. A phone kiosk test in Giant Supermarkets was a large enough success to prompt a national rollout of kiosks in select supermarket chains. Avenues for new gateway opportunities were opening up as fast as Bill was able to come up with new ideas.

In the first year, the investment was 90 percent in technology and only 10 percent in people. When the business doubled, people expense did not quite double. Program updating was required, but at a small fraction of the first year's dollar investment in technology. Two PC Flowers managers, stationed at FTD, oversee a core of seven PC Flowers employees. The core swells to 30 or 40 people at holiday time, drawing from trained FTD part-time workers. The same employees handle the operations of PC Flowers through Prodigy and other gateways and of PC Balloons as well. The more business increases, the more profitable it becomes per dollar of sales.

The average PC Flowers online order is $32 before tax and a service charge of approximately $5.95. At least 50 percent or so of total sales through Prodigy are from repeat orders. PC Flowers already get many overseas orders through Prodigy. Bill and Peter are now developing the software to use foreign networks and are working with U.S. phone companies to use similar software on their gateways. They will very likely be on Minitel in France and other gateways in various countries by the time you read this book.

I asked Bill to tell how others can have similar online success:

Q: How important to your success was your research before going online?

A: Of the utmost. You must study the advantages of the I&E network you select and take full advantage of them. You must also study the disadvantages and adjust to their limitations.

Q: How important is promotion? Does Prodigy promote PC Flowers? If so, how?

A: Very important. The best promotion we get from Prodigy is their daily Highlights Screen (the first screen seen by every member who signs on), which features news headlines and events of providers and advertisers. [The screen] features PC Flowers along with each floral holiday. And every time the Prodigy Highlights Screen features us, for days after the reminder of our business, it triples or quadruples.

Q: How much and how close must be the cooperation of the marketer and the network?

A: It is all important. The color and graphics capability of Prodigy can be a big advantage. Prodigy's graphic department is very talented and can do a wonderful job. Cooperation is crucial. We make the best FTD selection. They come up with the best possible color reproduction. They create graphics to get across our offer in the clearest manner in the fastest time. Online, time is money. The fastest conversion to a sale from inquiries and biggest percentage of conversions maximize profit. We have the shortest time periods for shopping decisions on Prodigy because graphics and text get across our message so well and so fast.

Prodigy helps us in many ways, including our online newsletter. One example is that, with their help, within eight hours of receipt of an online order, we put a confirmation of shipment in the member's Prodigy mailbox online. In return, we wrote extensive software built into our database to give Prodigy (and us) instant feedback on results.

Q: Why do some succeed so dramatically marketing through I&E networks and so many others fail or get only a fraction of potential sales and profits?

A: If you have a traditional retail marketing mentality, you're at a disadvantage. You must create from scratch a business with a technological infrastructure that parallels the technical infrastructure of the service provider network. You must produce marketing programs that take advantage of the computer language and graphics capability of the computer language of the I&E network [such as "NAPLIS" that Prodigy uses].

Q: What is most important?

A: You must react quickly to change, modify your game plan, and accommodate to change—and perhaps try a different product mix. You must communicate your needs. You must foresee problems and prepare for them. We initially received bigger bursts of orders than Prodigy could handle, but they accommodated by updating their software. We updated our order-handling methods. Consequently, we have had bursts of up to 5000 orders per day and up to 11,000 orders in two days, handled in such a manner that we had only 34 complaints.

Prodigy Costs, Requirements, Benefits

Prodigy has established separate rate cards for different marketing objectives: media advertising, lead generation, and merchandise selling. It offers CPMs competitive to other media. Sponsors pay for ads, and Prodigy gets a commission on sales. Ads are on part of the screen for almost every page of information. There are no time-based charges by Prodigy, which results in far more shopping time per member.

Prodigy has no limit to the number of screens for an ad. In some cases animation is used to make the point. There can be up to 64 characters to a line and nine lines of text to a screen, assuming solid copy with no illustration and no display graphics. Prodigy clients send an online acknowledgment of an inquiry or order within 24 hours of receipt. In this way, marketers build an E-mailing list and even E-mail thousands of prospects for a cost lower than direct mail.

Some Disadvantages.   First, Prodigy was slow. Its system is improving, but it's still irritatingly slow on some PCs.

Second, some computers are still incompatible with Prodigy. Most IBM PC models and IBM-compatible PCs can get Prodigy. Most of the Apple Macintosh line can get Prodigy. Basically, much older and underpowered models of IBM-type and Apple/Mac have varying difficulty. All users need a 1200 or 2400 bps Hayes or compatible modem, but Prodigy has gone to the extent of giving such Modems free to new member household subscribers.

Further, each IBM PC and compatible must have VGA/MCGA/CGA Hercules or compatible graphics capability and one disk drive (5¼" or 3½"). Each must have a VGA or EGA graphics card. Not all Apple computers can view Prodigy in color. They must have one megabyte or more of memory, system software 4.1 or higher, and at least an 800K disk drive—the same modem requirements as for IBM PCs.

Finally, Prodigy users can't download from Prodigy to their computers. But this, too, may be possible by the time you read this page.

Considering Prodigy?   Study the field first. If you are a niche advertiser, one of the other I&E networks may do better. If you sell upscale items or services with broader appeal, Prodigy may be more suited to you. If you have a truly mass product at a low price, very likely you should forget I&E networks.

Don't worry too much about the shortcomings of Prodigy. It keeps improving! Prodigy's technology is constantly evolving. New breakthroughs are expected. Users love it. More advertisers are succeeding, and subscriptions are rising far faster than for most new media.

Other I&E Networks

Phone each I&E network mentioned in this chapter for its information kit (phone numbers are at the end of each chapter). Log in to each, particularly to the electronic shopping malls. If you have decided to market through an I&E network, select the one best suited to you.

GEnie

GEnie, the second fastest growing national I&E computer network, is owned by a subsidiary of General Electric. It makes money for itself, for its providers, and for "stores" in its shopping mall; GEnie is directed to the same users as CompuServe. GEnie is text-based and therefore harder to use than Prodigy but easier to use than CompuServe. Members download for free its navigator software system, Aladdin. This speeds and eases access to any GEnie online service.

GEnie sells user services just as a cable TV system does. It offers over 100 basic services, including mall shopping with unlimited use, for a monthly basic fee which is less than half the charge of Prodigy. GEnie's basic package, which offers less than Prodigy, includes E-mail use, news, weather, sports, closing stock quotes; columns, an encyclopedia; leisure, professional, and GEnie-support BBS; all its software libraries; and unlimited shopping. GEnie offers other services (including some of its most desirable services) for an extra charge per minute of use. Still, it is far cheaper than CompuServe. It has its own magazine, *Livewire*.

Byte Created BIX

McGraw-Hill publishes *Byte* magazine, which for years operated the Byte Information Exchange (BIX). BIX started out as *Byte Online*, a service to get anything that ever appeared in *Byte*. Next, BIX added a daily news service online called *Microbyte* and expanded to more than 250 interactive forums. BIX then started *DemoLink*, which offers three downloads of demonstration software listed each month in a full-page ad in *Byte*. Any *Byte* reader with a modem could instantly dial and download any demo offered in the ad. Six months later BIX surveyed callers. Six percent who downloaded a demo had already bought the software, and 10 percent more stated that they would.

Anyone can log in to BIX after paying an annual subscription fee; tens of thousands of subscribers already have. BIX subscribers are mostly programmers, consultants, and computer enthusiasts. BIX is growing as it evolves. It includes more info about computers than any print publication can. It may become an important trade medium plus a showcase for a broad spectrum of wider databases and forums. Its demo marketplace concept, if promoted intensively by a marketer in all important computer magazines (and then widely by direct mail) may be a demo marketing revolution. BIX is now owned by Delphi, another I&E computer network organized like CompuServe.

Delphi is often most highly praised for simplicity and ease of use and for its easily understood manual. It offers a light-user plan for less than Prodigy's membership charge. But this includes only one hour per month at no extra charge. For heavier users, Delphi offers 20 hours each month for more than Prodigy but for a small fraction of what CompuServe charges. Delphi has far less variety and amount of content than either CompuServe or Prodigy. It does have a shopping mall, Merchant's Row. And it's growing. Check it out.

Two Other I&E Networks to Watch

America Online. America Online offers an online service for Macintosh and Apple owners. It also has a PC-compatible version of its service plus an online service for Commodore computer owners and another service for owners of Tandy computers. More marketers offering products and services have experimented with the online service, but it has concentrated on adding more and better programming. America Online is highly praised for being easy to use and is growing fast. It may burst out because of heavy joint promotions with computer manufacturers and media owners who are often also partners and investors. Watch its progress. It may already be a bargain marketing medium as you read this.

Main Street. Main Street is the I&E network of General Telephone and Electric (GTE). Its operation has been experimental and more technology-minded than entrepreneurial.

The French Connection

The French government phone company, French Telecom, has given away computers to a big share of households and offices in France. These serve the purpose of a phone book. The computers are connected to the Minitel Network. Each Minitel (when desired) gives phone numbers instantly for a tiny charge each and will ultimately eliminate phone books.

Check and Compare Networks

Memberships in and overall use of I&E networks are growing rapidly and promise to become a major new marketing mechanism during this decade. Usage of shopping services is growing faster now that subscriber connect-time charges for shopping have largely been eliminated.

As we go to press, the "baby Bells," regional telephone companies, hitherto prevented legally from owning and operating their own I&E networks, may enter the field (although appeals from competitive media, if granted, could upset the decision).

One trend is certain. More networks will carry ads. And according to a report by Arlen Communications, by 1995 45 percent of all PCs in U.S. households will have modems either built in or as peripherals.

Ogilvy & Mather Direct's Electronic Marketing Division has been increasingly active in the marketing use of I&E networks since the launch of most of them. I asked Martin Nisenholtz these questions for you:

Q: Will there be a service equivalent to Minitel in penetration in the United States? If so, will this be via telephone companies, newspapers online, or both, and how soon?

MN: The US West/France Telecom joint venture is the best hope in this area.

Q: What are your views on future projects of regional bell operating companies (RBOCs) in networks to compete with Prodigy and CompuServe?

MN: This is a big question. RBOCs are much likelier to compete with cable MOSS long-term than CompuServe. In my view, CompuServe will either be bought by an RBOC or will continue to succeed on its own.

Martin Nisenholtz also notes: A very important new online network called SeniorNet has been set up to acquaint older people with PCs.

My interviews indicate that two consistently profitable uses of I&E networks have been for catalogs online and for marketplaces online. These applications are covered in Chapters 20 and 21, respectively, as well as both applications via BBSs.

Help Source Guide

1. *America Online* offers a *free* starter kit with software; contact: 8619 Westwood Center Dr., Vienna, VA 22181-2285. (703) 448-8700. (800) 827-6364.

2. B. Schepp and D. Schepp have written *Complete Guide to CompuServe*, 1990 (650 pages), Dvorak-Osborne/McGraw-Hill: 2600 10th St., Berkeley, CA 94710. (800) 227-0900.

3. C. Bowen and D. Payton offer *CompuServe Information Manager* (416 pages), Bantam Books: 666 5th Avenue, NY, NY 10103. (212) 765-6500.

4. *CompuServe Information Services Inc.* offers *free* electronic mail information kit and copy of *CompuServe* magazine: 5000 Arlington Centre Blvd., Columbus, OH, 43220. (614) 457-8600.

5. *GEnie, GE Information Services,* offers a *free* information kit and *free* issues of GEnie *Livewire* magazine: 401 N. Washington St., Rockville, MD 20850, (800) 638-9636.

6. *Alfred Glossbrenner's Master Guide to GEnie,* 1991 (600 pages), Dvorak-Osborne/McGraw-Hill, includes Aladdin on 5¼" disk, makes use of GEnie easy, fast: 2600 10th St., Berkeley, CA 94710. (800) 227- 0900.

7. *Main Street* from *GTE* (General Telephone and Electric Corp.), offers a *free* information kit: One Stamford Forum, Stamford, CT 06904. (203) 965-4302.

8. *Prodigy Interactive Personal Service* offers a *free* media kit. Get more information from 800-PRODIGY or contact 445 Hamilton Ave., White Plains, NY 10601. (800) 822-6922 ext. 726; (914) 993-8843.

9. Pam Kane's *Prodigy Made Easy,* 2d ed., 1992, Osborne/McGraw-Hill, can be a great help when you subscribe: 2600 10th St., Berkeley, CA 94710. (800) 227-0900.

20

Online Catalogs

Consumer, Trade, and Special-Purpose Markets

More online catalogs are succeeding every month. Although the tiny among them account for only a few thousand dollars a year in sales, some of the big online catalogs generate hundreds of millions to more than a billion dollars in annual sales.

An online catalog sells a number of items through any variety of computer networks. Some sell consumer items directly, whereas others promote items sold in stores. Many sell industrial, office, or professional items to the appropriate field. The rising costs of postage, paper, and printing make online catalogs increasingly competitive with the standard print alternative. Advantages of online catalogs are the following:

- Items and prices can be updated continually, quickly, and at a nominal cost.

- Backorder expenses and complaints are greatly reduced.

- The printing, postage, and handling costs of a print catalog are avoided.

- Customers give their name and address in the process of generating an order.

- The interactivity of an online catalog eases the ordering process and speeds customer service.

- Online catalogs collapse the long interval between catalog inquiry and receipt by providing instant catalog delivery.

- Used properly, customer relationships can be built to increase the lifetime value of the customer to the catalog.

An effective online catalog performs services people want and can't otherwise easily get. An online catalog overcomes the frustrations and hassle of store shopping while arranging information simply and quickly for easy use, clarity, and fast reference. The catalog is also fun to use, not a chore.

An online catalog can often expand to whatever amount of information is needed for a buying decision on any item. It can be downloaded on a floppy disk and given to a friend with no modem.

Some disadvantages of online catalogs are the following:

- Ordering online is a slowly acquired habit.

- Achieving big volume online often requires a big investment.

- The products and services offered must fit online's capabilities.

- Creating a good online catalog takes know-how and work.

- Most online catalogs have small volumes versus the effort involved.

- Even the best online catalogs fail without effective promotion.

An online catalog doesn't seem user-friendly to many older people or women. It's not convenient to carry and read an online catalog from time to time, as many people peruse print catalogs. In addition, an online catalog can't show most PC owners a large number of high-resolution color pictures like a glossy print catalog or provide the color action of a video catalog.

An online catalog can be accessed from

1. An I&E computer network
2. Its own BBS
3. A private network organized for it

Most consumer online catalogs, particularly smaller ones, run on an I&E network. Each network encourages subscribers to log on to the catalog. The cost is modest to try one out. Some I&E networks can help create the online catalog best suited to you. But others have limited capabilities. And the marketing constraints of each vary (see Chapter 19).

Smaller industrial and business-to-business marketers sometimes start their online catalogs via their own BBSs. I&E networks typically do not attract enough of the specialized customers these marketers require. At a small software cost, more capabilities can be built into BBSs.

Some firms sell mainly to business customers who communicate often, make special requests, and buy in large amounts cumulatively. For these customers, an online catalog may need more advanced equipment and software and a private network with PCs often given away to bigger customers.

Considering an Online Catalog

Weigh carefully whether you should launch an online catalog. First read the rest of this chapter and reread Chapter 19. Get from each I&E network a list of all online catalogs it carries. Next, get the latest list of BBSs from Boardwatch magazine listed at the end of Chapter 18. Look through the list for catalog BBSs. Don't seriously consider an online catalog until you own and use a PC, modem, and communication software. Join at least CompuServe and Prodigy. Log on to their cataolgs and to BBS catalogs.

An online catalog using a private network can cost well under $50,000 up to far more, considering all associated expenses. If this option makes sense, read your trade publications and ask your trade association for the names of online catalogs organized through private networks. Phone the online catalog operators of these private networks; ask for the marketing manager in charge of catalogs; explain your interest in an online catalog. You don't want to compete with them, but you would appreciate some advice. Then ask what has worked and what has failed. Listen and learn. Ask to log on. Do it.

I&E Networks for Online Catalogs

Which I&E network is best for you? Each has somewhat different advantages and drawbacks. Most online catalogs launch on CompuServe or Prodigy because the subscriber volume on either is enough to provide for an adequate test. In addition, both of these I&E or videotex networks have ample experience with catalogs and can give valuable advice and help you promote your catalog.

Here are several online catalog reports from the field: Jeanine Sek of Hammacher-Schlemmer (H-S) notes that success took over a year on CompuServe but came faster and bigger for the same catalog on Prodigy. H-S is making money on both CompuServe and Prodigy.

The Heath company catalog finds CompuServe ideal for its purpose and has not used any other I&E network. For Heath, CompuServe attracts high-income customers oriented to its kind of consumer electronic products. Heath makes money on CompuServe while it helps build its image.

Most of the online catalog operators on CompuServe I have interviewed say they make money. To date, Prodigy has been more successful in marketing family items, lower-priced ones, and more general items. CompuServe is better at reaching men of higher income, especially those with high-tech interests.

Leveraging Your Online Experience

An increasing number of online catalog operators use several networks. For example, J. C. Penney has online catalogs on Prodigy, CompuServe, GEnie, and U.S. Videotel. Sears uses Prodigy, CompuServe, and GEnie Direct for its online catalog. Micro has a catalog of computer supplies and accessories at discount prices on GEnie, CompuServe, and U.S. Videotel. Godiva Chocolatier has online catalogs on GEnie, CompuServe, Delphi's Merchant Row, and GTE's Main Street.

What's the value of marketing on competing I&E videotext networks? Many feel doing so makes the volume worth the effort. Gerald M. O'Connell is the founder and CEO of Modem Media, a South Norwalk, Connecticut, consultant and advertising agency specializing in online media. Gerald says,

> Separately, [online catalog] volume is small. Together, volume becomes worth the creative and production effort. Success depends on leveraging your online catalog to all the major networks, promoting it heavily, keeping it dynamic, and assuming the costs of shopping activity.
>
> Our experience is that if it works for one network, it will work for them all. After the first success, the rest become straight media buys rather than creative and people drains.

Formerly, converting the software for an online catalog to another I&E network took a programmer several months and was an expensive process. Now it's fast but still not cheap. It's subject to negotiation for Modem Media customers, which has developed such conversion software.

Low-Cost Phone and Promotions

Some networks offer inbound phone numbers for online shopping at costs of 8 to 12 cents a minute, about half what it costs to operate a standard WATS line. This can cause a dramatic increase in shopping volume. Greg Stone of Heath explains:

> We purchase weekend access time at a good rate from CompuServe and give it free to our shoppers. We time the offer of a free weekend during big shopping weekends, like Labor Day. We feature several key items then. Our sales soar on free weekends. This is helped because we send out E-mail to announce it.

Each videotex service has a magazine or newsletter to supplement its online promotional activity. Get the maximum promotion to drive people to log in. Gerald O'Connell cites some of the online promotions to consider:

> For some networks, anyone using the service can type in the name of another catalog and instantly access it. Often a catalog is listed on and can be accessed from several main menus, giving more exposure. Within a catalog the same item can be listed under different classifications.

Sponsoring an event is usually possible using the service's online conferencing software. This might be a product demonstration, a seminar, discussion with experts, or a public forum. Also look into other log-on promotions, including combining with other mall merchants for joint efforts.

Greg Stone says, "We get a lot of promotion in the Go-Mall section of *CompuServe* magazine. This always jumps sales." And Glenn Ochsenreiter of Walden Books says, "We take advantage of all promotion we can get from CompuServe. Each is a golden opportunity to get new customers."

Other Promotion Ideas

There is no shortage of promotion ideas. Be creative and aggressive in applying promotional features to your online catalog. For example, an online catalog can consist of a BBS announcing coming promotions, sales, free connect-time, shopping days, or any incentive. Gerald O'Connell points out,

Special online ads can be run in various parts of an online catalog. These might feature a hot item outside of its classification or any kind of promotion or savings.

When a product is ordered, a complementary product can be instantly displayed for cross-selling. Often it is possible to have several customer forms in an online catalog, one to order products, another to qualify leads, another to request more information.

In the Direct Micro catalog, products are cross-referenced under several categories.

A large part of J. C. Penney online orders are placed by consumers reading the Penney print catalog. By encouraging this type of online ordering, Penney and many other catalogs reduce the costs of providing and staffing an 800 service line. Sears has an online order-blank capability which allows an online shopper to order any item listed in any current Sears print catalog. Greg Stone of Heath notes, "There is a small mention in our print catalog that customers can order online, and some people prefer to. But many order online who never would have from print."

Hammacher-Schlemmer has pulled over 10,000 requests for catalogs from Prodigy. Some of these people order from the print catalog, whereas others get the catalog and then order online. CompuServe's Electronic Mall has a "Catalog of Catalogs" that lists catalogs that can be ordered online.

Get all the free PR possible. Send a simple release announcing your online catalog to your trade publications and to online news services. Mention your online catalog in all your ads, mailings, package enclosures, and billing enclosures. Direct Micro runs print coupons in computer magazines. The coupons are redeemable online.

Online Catalog Items

What Items Pull Best Online?   Jeanine Sek of Hammacher-Schlemmer remarks that sometimes a product that's a loser in the print catalog is a winner online. But many items sold online continue to do well: electronic items, personal care items, and auto accessories. The best items use the online advantages of a particular I&E network, such as color and graphics, or appeal particularly to computer and (even more so) to modem owners, such as computer software and peripherals.

How Many Items in Your Online Catalog?   As few as 15 to more than 1000 items featured in an online catalog have worked for various marketers.

Online gift catalogs often feature few items, whereas specialty catalogs feature a greater variety. The Penney catalog on CompuServe contains over 100 items. The Sears online catalog on GEnie offers over 1500 products. Hammacher-Schlemmer's online catalog on CompuServe has about half the 192 items featured in a typical H-S print catalog. The OnLine Store has 1500 computer-related items.

The trend is to cut the number of items and describe them in more depth. Greg Stone runs the Heath catalog on CompuServe. He says, "We used to offer over 1000 items online. Then we cut that number to 100 to 125 items, taking our most successful print catalog items. We call the online catalog the 'Heath Electronic Shopping Center.'"

How Much Copy per Item? Hammacher-Schlemmer's online copy for each item is identical to its print catalog copy—about 50 words. Greg Stone of Heath says, "We use ample copy but short copy blocks. Per item, we average 3 paragraphs of about 7 lines each with 7 or 8 words a line, or about 55 words a paragraph and 165 words an item."

One Specialty or Many? Most online catalogs have one specialty. The Chef's Catalog has mostly kitchen gadgets. The TSR Games Shoppe online catalog just offers games—older classics like Star Trek, Dungeons & Dragons, and Buck Rogers, to more recent ones like ElfQuest and Hunt for Red October. Publishers Clearing House has a catalog of magazines by classification from travel to computer. Direct Micro and Computer Express each has an online catalog of computer supplies and accessories.

The trend is to specialize more. Penney has eight categories to choose from that span athletic footwear to toys. Sears features online products in home electronics, home office, videotapes, video games, and special value promotions. Each month, Sears features online about 50 items emphasizing home electronics and office equipment with special offers from its print catalogs. H-S has nine categories in its online catalog, about 12 items in each.

Online Catalog Cost? A catalog of 50 items on GEnie might cost well under $10,000 plus several thousand dollars of equipment. A year's contract is required. Usually even a simple catalog of 50 items or so requires substantial time from at least one person to change, update, check results, and manage.

The Online Store gave CompuServe $10,000 to start with 1500 items. However, with all the additional software that had to be created, its online entry cost jumped to at least $35,000 not including management's time.

The I&E networks are growing so fast that these costs can only increase by the time you read this. On the bright side, the sales per dollar of expense are rising faster for those who create on-line catalogs. All those I've interviewed say that the cost of entry for the cataloger is nominal compared with the investment of the network in time and promotion to make the catalog a success.

Tips for Success

Use Your Strengths.   Do what your firm is good at. McGraw-Hill has had an online catalog on CompuServe for more than five years. The company started by offering many kinds of books but then decided to concentrate on offering its line of computer and business books. Likewise, Software Discounters of America offers online just the software in which its great volume allows for big profit margins and where it has expertise. But Glenn Ochsenreiter of Waldenbooks says selling software online doesn't make sense for his company. He explains,

> Software is a direct-response business which requires very aggressive pricing. I wanted higher margins. I decided to target customers I could give our best service to, so I converted the online services to offering all our computer books.
>
> I've marketed computers, managed book stores, run Walden Software, and been a computer book buyer. I believed in the online catalog and knew what it required: (1) new products, (2) organization, (3) customer service.
>
> I asked for and was given a chance to turn it around. By 18 months after I took over, we had over 1000 computer books online. I think of it as a store. We wanted to be the place to rely on for computer books.
>
> We offer for sale and perusal a list both by titles and by authors. We give each book a page of description, about 50 to 75 words. That's more than in our print catalog. It's a very well organized, new structure. The first menu offers 10 choices by computer program. It's a very simple breakdown.
>
> We offer free access every weekend. We feature various giveaways. We doubled our business. We quadrupled our annual rate of sales in four months.

New Online Look Improves Success.   Greg Stone, of the Heath online catalog, says,

> When I took over, we listed all products by name, weight, price. We had been running for three and a half years on CompuServe and

making money. Most people used the online catalog first and then went to the print catalog to get more information and to order.

We redesigned the online catalog to help customers. We divided it into sections. One was a "What's New" section. Another was the "Blockbuster Specials" section, designed to sell excess inventory without affecting normal sales.

In the first two years of the new format, sales jumped about 65 percent. Our costs were lower because the second year we cut down to a smaller plan.

One reason more people don't buy a product they're interested in is that they still have questions. Provide these online shoppers with more information as they ask for it. Prodigy can highlight product features with options for more detail than any catalog. There can be as much copy for each feature as in an entire mailing piece. It's there if they ask for it.

Increase Your Average Order. Here's how Waldenbooks On-Line increased their average orders. Glenn Ochsenreiter says,

Eight hundred and fifty of our online computer books are basic and widely available. But 150 of our books online are more specialized and not widely available.

The real excitement is toward these higher-end books. Often they are advanced books available only in textbook stores, such as a book on connectivity or chip architecture. These books run $60 to $80 and on average have better margins. Obviously I want to sell a lot more advanced books.

Although the average Hammacher-Schlemmer sale online is about $85 versus $110 in print, H-S has sold slot machines online profitably at $375. Meanwhile, the Heath average sale online is about $190, close to that of its print catalog. Overall, the average sale and annual sales per customer varies with the type of goods sold and the medium used. They are lowest for consumer catalogs on I&E networks.

Encourage Buying by Modem. When people order on a bulletin board, they themselves are filling out the data by ordering. All the information that is going into your computer is what they're typing out. For this reason, Sears, J. C. Penney, and many national catalogs are equipped to take orders on modem and promote that ability. CEO Stan Snyder of The On-Line Store says, "Our repeat orders come more and more on a modem. This is our higher-profit business; I handle more business with less people. We now clear the credit cards entirely electronically. We're entirely automated."

Update Catalog and Promotion.   Gerald O'Connell says, "Nothing's worse than a stale, stagnant, out-of-date information center or catalog. Keep your online catalog lively, dynamic and up-to-date. Modem Media clients that have been most successful use monthly specials, newsletters, giveaways, and message boards."

Greg Stone of Heath says, "We have a list of over 10,000 CompuServe members who have bought from us online, with their E-mail box numbers. It costs us nothing to send an E-mail message to them. We keep an E-mail letter to 50 words or so—a little memo, short enough to be read on one screen. The memo highlights upcoming Heath promotions. People appreciate it."

Direct Micro uses E-mail to promote quantity discounts. And Sears acknowledges online orders by sending E-mail to the subscriber's online mailbox.

Some Catalog Reminders

Feature Your Guarantee.   The OnLine Store has a 90-day lowest-price guarantee to meet or beat any regularly advertised price.

Tie-In with Your Retail Store or Chain.   Any online Sears order can be shipped UPS or picked up at a local Sears store.

Feature Credit Card Payment.

Consider Co-op Money.   Glenn Ochsenreiter of Waldenbooks says, "Co-op money is important. All our books are promoted cooperatively, with publishers contributing."

BBS Catalogs

BBS catalogs are used mostly by businesses to sell to other businesses. Although online catalogs have succeeded on I&E networks because all the promotional support was supplied by the network, with a BBS, you're on your own.

The business and computer store of Willow Grove, Pennsylvania, has The Book BBS, which offers information on computers and features an online catalog of 2000 computer books. JDR Microdevices of San Jose, California, has a BBS which offers information and an online computer hardware catalog. One Point, a California company, also has a BBS catalog of computer items. Computerland has connected its largest business customers to its own online catalog so that they can get instant price quotes and place orders for their computer, peripheral, and software needs from their own offices—a considerable advantage for Computerland over some of its biggest competitors.

There are many other online catalogs in other fields such as Multimedia Software, Mount Airy, Michigan, which offers the MusicNet BBS with a CD catalog, music news, music files, and Top 40 listings.

Buying Online Catalog Software

The major BBS, Galacticomm, sells the hardware to start a BBS for several thousand dollars and the software for under $100. Look in the Help Source Guide at the end of this chapter for more information.

The Shopping Mall edition software of the Major BBS automates on-line entry, catalog sales, and credit card-based purchases of products. It can be modified to your product line, pricing policy, discount schedule, and shipping methods. Users can search by product category, browse catalogs, place and cancel orders at will. The Shopping Mall Edition can calculate the exact shipping costs. There's even a built-in credit card number validation routine.

You don't even need "host" BBS equipment to start if you use a public network such as SprintMail. You will still need a program for your catalog, demo, or interactive service, but you can simply start by sending your catalogs on disk to your customers.

Some online catalogs are huge. The biggest sales volume online catalogs use private EDI networks with the most advanced programs and equipment. The Ingraham Book Company and Baker & Taylor (both book jobbers) have very big book catalogs online with sophisticated software that allows them to process orders and deliver books anywhere in the United States within 48 hours. Among other large online catalogs are a seller of used computers and two coin companies who have online catalogs via satellite.

The Genuine Parts Company sells over $2 billion worth of auto parts to over 6000 dealers and distributors. Most are connected by computer to one of the company's 64 NAPA distribution warehouses. Every time a jobber sells an item, the sale is logged on a computer at the warehouse. The computer updates a list of parts to be delivered the next day to replenish the jobber's stock. Mechanics often use laptop computers to order parts electronically without leaving their service bays.

Some catalogs have many capabilities. Camfour, of Westfield, Massachusetts, is a national distributor of firearms and related products. The first year Camfour offered its online catalog, one-fifth of Camfour's customers used it. Now, virtually all its business is transacted via online catalog. More than 6000 items, including all existing inventory, are listed and updated daily. Using PCs, dealers can access up-to-date pricing, product availability, sales promotions, and serial numbers at the time of placing the order.

With its online catalog order system in place, Camfour's 1200 customers dropped to 300 but sales volume increased. More important, Camfour needs only one-third the people to handle its online sales compared to its competitors. Vice President Russell Kanzinger explains:

> We spent a fortune for software, created internally by three programmers. It is very efficient and easy to use. The big savings is in time. There is more flexibility and more accuracy. We did have five full-time sales persons. We replaced three of them with one telemarketer and the online catalog.
>
> We give every customer an IBM-compatible PC if they order a minimum volume. We look for customers who pay their bills and give us few problems. We stick with just these people. We first achieved the same volume with one-quarter of the accounts and far more accountability. Then we doubled the volume with no more personnel than before and greater profitability.
>
> We deal in serialized inventory. By law, a bound book must be kept by each dealer, recording all gun sales. We show onscreen a form the dealer's computer can print out requesting a government variance to allow the use of computerized records. The government grants this upon proper application. The dealer's use of our online catalog for all purchases and control of its inventory automatically keeps the required government records.
>
> Our catalog has many capabilities. For any serialized product, punching the letter A will bring up all accessories on screen. In addition, it presents our entire marketing sales program. It is more effective than a trade magazine. The ads are right there as customers are online and interested.
>
> All serialized sales by the dealer are maintained on computer. We can provide a summary of this information to manufacturers to guide them in production schedules. We have hundreds of screens of specials and promotions. We show graphic pictures and specifications of products in color. The online catalog offers all kinds of promotional opportunities.
>
> A dealer can order via modem from exclusive onscreen offers; 60 percent of dealers respond to special offers. A customer who wants a better deal than the prices and terms onscreen can phone the account's telemarketer, who listens and relays to management competitive information. This adds a personal touch.
>
> As a service to customers, we supply free ads to buy and sell excess inventory from each other. A Utah customer can create an ad on his PC and modem it to our mainframe computer, which puts it in the system, on screen and in color. It's very high-tech.
>
> We send our open account monthly statements via computer. We don't mail. They have our statement on screen. We put a reminder

on screen the first three days of the month. If they don't pay by the 5th of the month we stop shipping. Our credit losses are minimal. The online catalog leads to smaller orders more often. There's no need to maintain large inventories. It's a just-in-time capability. A customer always knows if an item is not in inventory but can backorder.

Here's another question for Ogilvy & Mather Direct's Martin Nisenholtz:

> Q: What is the most successful online catalog operation you know where equipment was sold, rented, or given to customers?
>
> MN: Probably Baxter Healthcare, but it depends on how you measure success.

Online catalogs have led to a new phenomenon we'll take up in Chapter 21, online marketplaces.

Help Source Guide

1. All *I&E networks* listed in Chapter 19's Help Source Guide are good sources. Look in their magazines and newsletters for catalogs online. then access.

2. C. Bowen and D. Payton's *Complete Electronic Bulletin Board Starter Kit* (436 pages), Bantam Books, 1988, is very helpful. A proprietor of one bulletin board told me he could not have launched it without this book: 666 5th Ave., NY, NY 10103. (212) 765-6500.

3. *CompuServe's Catalog* of Catalogs lists catalogs that can be ordered online. Many can be accessed on CompuServe: 5000 Arlington Centre Blvd., Columbus, OH 43220. (800) 848-8199.

4. *Galacticomm Inc.* (Timothy Stryker, CEO) provides a *free* info kit and a *free* online demo of the Major BBS and online catalog system. Stryker has invaluable experience and provides great access: 4101 S.W. 47th Ave., Suite 101, Ft. Lauderdale, FL 33314. (305) 583-5990.

5. *Modem Media* (Gerald M. O'Connell, CEO) provides agency services to develop campaigns. Represents online networks and serves as production house, consultant, specialist in online catalogs: 12 S. Main St., Suite 401, South Norwalk, CT 06854. (201) 853-2600.

6. *Teleconnect Marketing*, TeleComm USA (TeleConnect), is owned by MCI. *Free* info kit available re access from anywhere at local rates to your catalog online. 12 W. 21st St., NY, NY 10010. (800) 728-7000.

21
Online Marketplaces

An online marketplace can be a sophisticated extension of electronic data interchange or the simplest kind of computer bulletin board (see Chapter 18), I&E networks (see Chapter 19), and online catalogs (see Chapter 20). Online marketplaces (versus online catalogs) typically encourage competition within the same product or service category. An online marketplace is a service for buyers and sellers that usually charges both.

Millions of items are listed, and billions of dollars of sales are made through online marketplaces every year. There may be an online marketplace reaching prospects and buyers for your products and services. It may be possible to list and price some of what you sell for very little money, perhaps a tiny percentage of sales.

Anything for sale can become part of a databank of things for sale. The host computer assembles and classifies such data according to categories. It lists item numbers and information such as quantity available and price—with the firm's name, address, and phone, fax and/or modem number. The computer arranges this in small or huge files. It can update, as often as desired, facts such as the latest inventory availability and price. For anyone shopping for anything, the computer can search in a flash and call up onscreen a choice of sources and price quotes for an article or service.

This is an online marketplace. Of the many different such marketplaces, each has been born because a need was seen and filled, and each came about in its own way. Some grew out of an information service online while others developed out of an online catalog. Often a trade association organizes one for its members. Often the online marketplace is a joint endeavor.

Online marketplace advantages include the following:

- The buyer seeks you. An inquiry is qualified.
- It can be the fastest, easiest way to locate hard-to-find items.
- The online marketplace is the most discreet way to sell distress inventory.
- The buyer chooses the seller. It's direct, one to one.
- The cost to locate or to sell can be very low.

An online marketplace's equipment needs vary from the simplest to the most sophisticated. The marketplace can be created with a BBS or on an I&E network, or on more than one. The biggest online marketplace may involve an investment of hundreds of millions of dollars yet list products and services for modest cost. There are always more marketplaces to choose from.

Some online marketplace disadvantages include

- Large volume and wide use in some fields may come slowly.
- In niche fields, even after long use, volume can be small.
- To list anything for sale may require a year-long contract.
- Online marketplaces suffer from the limitations of computer modem ownership.
- It's hard to project success from one instance to others.

Shopping on an online marketplace is a habit that often is acquired slowly. Far fewer consumers shop online marketplaces than in business-to-business situations.

Should you market your wares on an online marketplace? Yes, but only where the marketplace fits your field, where someone is profitably selling a product or service comparable to yours, or where the risk to you is nil.

Finding Online
Marketplaces That Fit

Associations sometimes start online marketplaces. Trade publications often report on related ones, particularly new ones. Phone the associations, trade papers, and newsletters in your field. Read the Help Source Guides at the ends of chapters 18, 19, 20, and 21. Newsletters reporting on BBSs can update you on the newest BBS-based online marketplaces. Each I&E network can give you a list of the marketplaces on their network. Gerald O'Connell of Modem Media (see last chapter) can update you. He ran one. Ask your business library to help you find stories on online marketplaces. An online "clipping service" can come up with more at very little cost.

Make a list of those marketplaces that fit your field and send for an information kit from each. Now let's look at how varied the online marketplace is in cost structure and customer appeal.

Online Marketplace Examples

I asked Ogilvy & Mather Direct's Electronic Marketing Division Director Martin Nisenholtz: "What is the biggest success story of a computer marketplace on line that you know of?" Martin answered: "CompuCard [the Corporate name is CUC], by far." CUC offers 10 to 50 percent savings off manufacturers' list prices on a huge range of consumer goods via its online marketplace. The CUC computer calculates the lowest price delivered to your door. It also offers automatic, two-year warranty protection coverage up to a full year on items bought, and online service 24 hours a day, 7 days a week.

To be listed with any of the more than 250,000 products on *CUC International*'s online marketplace of brand name consumer items costs the seller nothing. CUC typically makes a commission of 6 to 8 percent of sales.

The subscription shopping service is a product of CUC International. Its 3.3 million shopping members pay a $39 to $49.95 fee each year. The online members, for years, paid online time to shop on some online networks. The online members are not idle shoppers but are looking to buy. CUC's online marketplaces are on virtually every I&E network and on many online data banks and services. In magazines or newsletters for each, publicity and ads promote CUC online shopping. CUC produces nine to ten catalogs each year. Its average sale is $182.

The Salvage Marketplace Network

AutoInfo of Maywood, New Jersey, has brought the technology of satellites and computers to the auto salvage industry. The company offers several services including: (1) Orion Trading Network, (2) Checkmate Workstation, (3) Insurance Parts Locating Database. AutoInfo's Orion Network is a satellite-based trading system used by over 1300 dealers in the United States and Canada to buy and sell auto parts. Over 4 million messages are sent yearly over the network. The company's Checkmate workstation is used by more than 500 auto salvage dealers to profitably analyze potential trades. The insurance parts database contains information on over 10 million used auto parts. AutoInfo also operates a motorcycle parts network and a cattle feeder network.

The Orion Network allows auto salvage dealers to send parts requests to other dealers. The monthly subscription price of $375 includes software, hardware (satellite dish, PC and terminal, maintenance and communications). The salvage dealer just supplies paper, ribbons, and a telephone line. Martin Rubin, president, says:

> The Orion Network has changed the way auto dismantlers conduct business. Instead of dealing with only local dealers, the salvage dealers can deal with fellow dealers hundreds or thousands of miles away. Our system is less expensive and more productive than telephone or fax.
>
> Our first year online, we had 50 customers and did about $198,000 in revenues. We lost money. Five years later, our sales and after-tax profits were $9.6 million and $2.4 million respectively.

Sometimes, the marketplace existed previously in another form and just needed a new delivery system.

The Online Yacht Marketplace

BUC Marine Sales Network (BUCNET) is a worldwide marketplace for yacht brokers and sellers of boats. It's a multiple-listing service paid for by the membership of over 500 dealers and brokers. The minimum membership charge is $780 a year. Dealer/broker subscribers are charged 35 to 65 cents per minute to use the Network.

The BUC Marine Sales Network is without charge to buyers and sellers until a boat is sold, at which time a commission (traditionally 10 percent) is paid to a broker member. BUC also offers a *New and Used Boat Price Guide* and BUC's Personalized Boat Evaluation Service.

BUC offers a database of the selling prices of new boats and another one of used boats. BUCNET also has a Marine Lender Listing Service which lists boats taken back by lenders and available for sale via its members.

BUC President Walter Sullivan says: "Listings on BUCNET are much more detailed than the typical real estate listing. The result is comprehensive information describing each vessel listed on the network, rather than summarized reports."

Bargain Ad Marketplace

If you make any of the 200,000 kinds of fasteners in the world, you can list your entire line of inventory on the FASTFINDER online marketplace for only $35 a month. It's used primarily to list inventory available below the market price.

On FASTFINDER, just enter a description of the part you are seeking. FASTFINDER locates the item, quantity available, and any possible substitute parts. An average search takes about 45 seconds. Access is possible around the clock. FASTFINDER is continually and easily updated. Williams & Watts President William Van Etten reports on FASTFINDER: "We list our inventory online. Our phone number is on-screen. People call us. There's no effort. To update, we just run and mail in a computer tape."

PUBNET

PUBNET offers publishers' books to bookstores. It was launched in college bookstores, backed by the 20 publishers who sold 85 percent of all college textbooks. The PUBNET system was advanced technology EDI and required a very big collective commitment. But PUBNET has saved bookstores a great deal of money in processing orders. PUBNET offers a package for small publishers with a PC and modem. About $1250 buys the software and use of a mailbox. The publisher must take direct orders and must have its own warehousing and shipping capabilities.

A publisher pays 25 cents each time it loads into the database plus 25 cents each time it writes in a new price or a change in availability. It also pays 4 cents per month to store each title on the database plus a charge of between 65 cents to $1.10 for each order it receives. The charge varies by the system-wide volume of orders and time of transmission.

PUBNET states in its promotions to retail bookstores that ordering by phone costs the average bookstore $100 a week in people time and phone cost but can be done via PUBNET for $5 to $10—without the people mistakes by phone. PUBNET's marketplaces increase book shopping by increasing the range of choice and availability to both bookstores and their customers alike.

PUBNET was offered free to book sellers for the first six months. A bookstore can join the network for $250 and receive a mailbox and software. The software can be used to access the database, to create and send purchase orders, and to receive purchase order acknowledgments.

Each purchase order can be created on-line or off-line. Publisher inventory can be kept on the database. Purchase orders sent by the bookstores are processed daily by publishers. When publishers process orders via PUBNET, customers get orders faster. The faster process enables bookstores to have fewer out-of-stock situations. Bookstores get more sales as a result.

PUBNET's E-mail system can be customized so that publishers can notify any store by E-mail when an author will be in the area, what author interviews will be on TV and radio and newspaper, plus other PR are listed along with the availability of the author for a store appearance.

Jim McLaughlin, director of marketing of PUBNET explains: "PUBNET is an advanced EDI network. Publishers can save a good deal of money. Stores write their order directly into the publisher's computer. There are fewer mistakes and fewer workers required. 800 numbers are no longer needed, which also saves personnel time."

Participating publishers on PUBNET report that although they get smaller orders than traditional distribution channels, the greater frequency of those PUBNET orders adds up to more total sales.

Other Online Marketplaces

A division of the Plenum Publishing Corporation is Career Placement Registry (CPR) in Alexandria, Virginia. CPR is available online via Dialog. The CPR database ranges from 4000 to 9000 job applicants. About 60 percent are students and 40 percent are experienced. Adults pay $15 to $40 to be listed, while a student pays only $8.

Every month, between 400 to 500 firms pay $95 an hour plus one dollar a résumé to search through CPR. They extract between 1900 to 2600 résumés at an average cost of $25 to $40 (including both search charge and the $1 a résumé). CPR estimates that it costs $4000 to $6000 to qualify a typical job applicant for interview, versus only $250 using CPR.

How big is a marketplace? Edvent II lists more than 125,000 seminars, workshops, training programs and meetings in North America, run by over 5800 organizations. Inventory Locator Service, Inc. (ILS), of Memphis, Tennessee, offers online 16 million items. ILS processes over 45,000 part number inquiries per day from its 2000 customers worldwide. CBD (Commerce Business Daily) OnLine reports on over 200,000 upcoming government procurement offerings worth more than $400 billion.

The many wide-appeal marketplaces include US GasNet of Denver, Colorado, which identifies natural gas buyers and sellers in the gas market on any given day. MEMA has a bulletin board of after-market auto parts. Pronet tracks wholesale prices and commercial availability for the produce and floral industries 24 hours a day. Fish Exchange Inc. of San Francisco, California, runs an online marketplace to link buyers and sellers of fresh fish nationwide. Dun & Bradstreet's BBS, BidNet, lists the latest requests for bids from the thousands of state, local, and U.S. government purchasers nationwide. J. P. Morgan sells bonds by computer auctions via Capitalink. *Globex*, developed by Chicago Mercantile Exchange and Reuter's Ltd., enables markets to operate online after hours. Conway Data, Inc. of Norcross, Georgia, offers *SiteNet*, an online directory of commercial real estate with 20 research files. Worldwide Exchange is an electronic bulletin board for people who want to swap houses and apartments. *Travel Scan* has a service called "The Last-Minute Club" that reports on discounts being offered by tour operators to sell seats in the final days before departures. American Gem Market Systems of Moraga, California, provides an online marketplace and laboratory for the gem industry.

Results

BUC President Walter Sullivan says, "The average price of a boat sold via BUC is close to $300,000, although vessels ranging in price from $5000 to $36,000 are available. And over 90,000 vessels have passed through BUCNET in its six-year history." For most business-to-business marketplaces, the average size of purchases range in the hundreds to thousands of dollars. For job bank marketplaces, it can represent a number of years of executive income. And for an online bond issue marketplace, it can run from hundreds of thousands to millions of dollars.

When Williams & Watts purchased the Jacques Group, a business supplying fastener parts, and decided to sell off below-market about 3800 of its 6000 items, it used FastFinder. President William Van Etten told me:

We have been on FastFinder for three years. We list all our inventory and sell discontinued inventory at slightly below market. For FastFinder's charge of $35 a month, we have sold $600 to $700 of inventory each month. In the last nine months, we sold about $5500 worth for $280.

Ruklic Screw Company has done even better. Vice president Jay Ruklic says:

We've been online for two years with about 300 items. We sell excess inventory to other fastener firms...under the market price but at profitable discounts. In two years we have sold over $200,000 for a

total listing cost of $2400, a 1.2 percent selling cost, with no produc-
tion cost, and no special software.

Marketplace Tour de Force

American Airlines Chairman and President Robert L. Crandall, in a series of brilliant moves, transformed American into a winner by the following:

1. Helping create SABRE (Semi-Automatic Business Reservation
   Environment), the first PC airline reservation network
2. Installing custom PCs in 13,000 travel agent offices, in 24 countries
3. Instituting a frequent flyer program tracked by SABRE
4. Creating SABRE for individuals and Commercial SABRE for companies to make reservations by modem directly.
5. Matching passenger names signed on tickets with the biggest computer databases to get address and phone.
6. Following up frequently by mail and phone to frequent fliers, offering extra incentives and special deals.

SABRE is an excellent system with fine software. Conceptually,
SABRE started as a constantly updated online catalog of every
American flight. It became an online marketplace when SABRE added
one-stop airline shopping, including flights booked on other airlines.
Travel agents could communicate with all major airlines through it.
American Airlines travel agent business went way up. AA air freight
zoomed up. SABRE profits came, then leaped.

Other airlines set up their own online airline reservation systems.
Today, travel agents account for 75 percent of all tickets sold. In the
United States, 95 percent of the travel agencies have a computer reservation system, and 88 percent of all airline tickets are issued through
these systems.

Before SABRE, booking a round trip from New York City to Buffalo
required a dozen employees performing a dozen separate steps in a
three-hour job. Now SABRE connects over 160,000 computer terminals,
with ticket and boarding pass printers in airports and travel agencies
around the world. The SABRE is used by over 17,000 travel suppliers
worldwide. It has information for over 650 airlines. Besides airfares,
SABRE accesses over 22,000 hotel properties, over 35 tour companies,
and 57 car rental agencies. All told, SABRE has information on more
than 45 million fares.

SABRE's Bonanza of Bonuses. When a SABRE-originated ticket is generated for another airline, American Airlines benefits from the "float" of money. That's because the money is held by the airline that collects it until the flight coupon is used. The flight coupon is then turned in and the money paid.

Moreover, to book through SABRE to, for example, New York to Paris then to Rome, there is a charge for each segment of the trip. SABRE charges other airlines (and its parent company) $2.25 for each segment. The round trip brings it to $13.50. SABRE charges for billions of segments. The profit from SABRE alone for American Airlines over the years has been well over $1 billion, with other benefits:

- Commissions have multiplied on hotel reservations, car rentals, and other services.

- Its telemarketing facility became so successful that American set up a telemarketing subsidiary to offer these services to others.

- SABRE created a $30 million mail-order business by mailing and telemarketing offers to frequent flyer members.

Do-It-Yourself Travel Marketplace. AA became a true online marketplace when it introduced Commercial SABRE and EAASY SABRE Systems to corporations and individuals with PCs and terminals. Modem users can log on and make their own flight, hotel, and car reservations and arrange to pick up tickets at a travel agency or ticket office or even receive them by mail.

Other airlines offer their marketplaces for do-it-yourself travel, from the WorldPerks Program of Northwest Airlines to TWA's Frequent Flight Bonus Program.

How does a small business get involved in these large electronic marketplaces? If you are in the hotel industry, VIP Reservations Inc. of Menlo Park, California, will list your hotel in all the major airline reservation systems. Bookings are received online and printed out in hard copy at your reservation desk.

Travel agencies book adventure travel online for clients via Ultran of Colorado Springs, Colorado. Qualified tour operators, from the United States and 60 foreign countries, provide information in a database of over 6000 trip departures.

Independent Travel Marketplace

The Official Airline Guide Electronic Edition Travel Service (EETS) is an online travel service that offers millions of direct and connecting flights for over 600 airlines worldwide. Fares are displayed from the lowest to the highest price. The service can be subscribed to directly or through many online services by anyone with a modem.

What makes it a marketplace? Besides being able to purchase tickets through Thomas Cook Travel, you can also make hotel reservations and car rentals. Plus, there's information on actual flight arrival/departure times; over 35,000 hotels and motels; tours and cruise discount packages; over 85,000 vacation and leisure choices; frequent flyer programs; flights that arrive on time more often; the weather in cities all over the world; the quality of lodgings nearest any destination; other travel news; and last-minute travel bargains with savings up to 63 percent.

Starting a Marketplace

It is more profitable to create and own an online marketplace you also use to distribute your own products or services. It is also much more dangerous. Success requires a combination of the right idea plus talent and experience. For example, the concept behind the Inventory Location Service (ILS) market started when the founder wanted to create an online catalog listing with all his airplane parts. But then he thought, "Why not pull together everyone who has aviation parts—all the different aviation parts in the world—and put them on one listing, and become the service between buyers and sellers." This idea blossomed because John Williams, ILC's founder, knew the aircraft parts industry intimately; because he was a born entrepreneur; because he combined his talents with those of his sister, Minnie, who was a skilled computer programmer; and because there was a need and the time was right.

Official Airlines Guide online started as an information service, a variation of its print edition. When people kept requesting the ability to make travel purchases, it became a marketplace.

Caution! Any risk can be a loss. Play safe. Listen to CUC CEO Walter Forbes, who says:

> From inception, we've gotten 17 million members by direct marketing through third parties, including more than 6000 banks, with no risk. The shopping catalog is no risk; it's part of what a member pays for with the membership fee.

99 percent of our U.S. business is not by computer. But members from online buy totally online, with the highest renewal rate and the highest average order. In France due to the Minitel system, 60 percent of our business is via computer. That's why we're on every major computer media network but we don't invest heavily in marketing technology. Everything to date is basically the same, and interim. Only real pictures can change this. The technology just is not here yet.

Meanwhile, we will participate with any real service but take no technology risk. The result is that, while there have been huge losses for others, we're here 17 years later. Our sales are in the hundreds of millions, up as much as 50 percent in a single year.

CEO Walter Forbes has held to a visionary concept with iron risk control. His example is particularly applicable if you sell consumer goods where color illustration is important. For business marketplaces, often computer matching ability is vital and color is far less so. The higher the cumulative transactions the more this is so. But Walter Forbes's attitude can help keep you safe, however promising any area of electronic marketing is.

Help Source Guide

1. *BIX BBS,* General Videotex Corp, 1030 Massachusetts Ave., Cambridge, MA 02138. (800) 227-2983. Ask for *free* info kit on DemoNet, the online demo marketplace; read it and access: (800) 444-4444. *Free* demo: (918) 586-4536.

2. *EDI Exec Monthly* is a newsletter on latest case studies of EDI marketplaces. *Free* for subscribers is a 96-page handbook *International Guide to EDI Products and Services* published twice yearly. Available to buy is a 20-minute nontechnical video: 1639 Desford Court, Marietta, GA 00064. (800) 633-4931.

3. *Electronic Data Interchange Association* (EDIA) can provide marketplace EDI case histories and information in "EDI: Steps for Success": Suite 550, 225 Reineckers Ln., Alexandria, VA 22314. (703) 838-8042.

4. *How to Use EDI Seminar* is sponsored by the American Management Association: P.O. Box 1026, Saranac Lake, NY 12983. (518) 891-0065.

5. *Information Industry Association* is a source for information businesses. Members get information on latest technology applications/development, new markets, business opportunities, competitive intelligence; can locate buyers, sellers of information companies, form partnerships, alliances. Other topics include new ways having to do with customers, capital, niche markets, business problems and solutions. An annual conference is also held: P.O. Box 1653, Washington, D.C. 20013-1653. (202) 639-8262.

6. S. Schlar has written *Inside X.25: A Manager's Guide.* X.25 is open systems interconnection (OSI) standard that allows data communications hardware

of various manufacturers to communicate freely. This work addresses how X.25 works, what products support it, how they function together. Includes detailed case studies and covers integrating IBM, Apple PCs, and ISDN, discusses the billions of dollars spent in the United States in the 1980s on packet-switching equipment. The book guides communications engineers to maximizing equipment. Telecom Library: 12 W. 21st St., NY, NY 10010. 800-Library.

7. *Modem Media's* CEO Gerald M. O'Connell ran one of the biggest marketplaces online. Ask him for the newest marketplace success stories on I&E networks: 12 S. Main Street, Suite 401, South Norwalk, CT 06854. (203) 853-2600.

8. To find out about *Sears Communications Company's* EDI Information and Services, ask re EDI marketplace case histories: 231 N. Martingale Rd., Schaumburg, IL 60173. EDI projects: Sales (800) 366-2722. Implementation: Customer Services (800) 877-4210.

9. *SprintMail* provides a free 174-page computer-based service directory and free information on how to use Sprint EDI international access. (800) 736-1130.

10. *X.500 and the Electronic Directory* (244 pages) addresses commercial trends in the early marketing of X.500 products and services. Includes 22 detailed case studies: 10 corporate electronic directories users, market leaders; 6 public service providers, 6 essential directory and applications software firms. FIND/SVP: 625 Ave. of Americas, NY, NY 10011. (800) 346-3787.

11. *The Business Side of EDI Implementation Seminar* is provided through EDI Center/ORDERNET Services—a course and video catalog. For information call: (800) 677-3342.

22
CD-ROM

Catalogs and Marketplaces

Catalogs and marketplaces on CD-ROM are still in their infancy. Their rapid growth has been scarcely appreciated because the use of CD-ROM in publishing, libraries, and education has been growing much faster. But CD-ROM developments now being perfected may catapult this exciting new medium into a powerful electronic marketing tool as CD-ROM becomes more universal. Chapter 22 explores how CD-ROMs are being used profitably today to market a growing list of products and services.

First, let's describe what CD-ROMs are. CD-Rom stands for Compact *Disc Read Only Memory*. A CD-ROM disc is the same size as an audio CD, but it stores text and graphics as well as sound—from drawings to full-color pictures of good quality, animation, and motion video. These images can be taken off a main frame, minicomputer, or PC, and changed by computer. A CD-ROM drive can show CD-ROMs on a computer screen. All CD-ROM discs conform to a world standard. A CD-ROM disc contains up to 680 megabytes (MB) of information, about 100 million words, which, in print, is about 275,000 pages of text or 200 pounds of paper. A variation of an audio CD player transfers text to computer. To do this, a laser moves back and forth reading the data selected by the user.

Any CD manufacturing plant can be adapted by software to make CD-ROM discs. The same plants can also manufacture video discs, usually with the same masters and techniques.

In 1991, Freeman Associates (Santa Barbara, California) reported that 798,000 CD-ROM drives were shipped worldwide, increasing the total number to 1.62 million. In 1992, this market research consulting company projected 1.15 million additional shipments.

CD-ROM's advantages include the following:

- It can deliver text, data, graphics, drawings, talk, stereo quality sound, full-color photos, and video.

- It produces the equivalent or better image quality as broadcast TV.

- It's more interactive in more ways than any other medium.

- It's faster to use than a big, complex print catalog.

- Disc cost per megabyte is under $0.001 versus $4 on paper, $1.70 on floppy disk and $10 on a hard disk.

- CD-ROM drives are low-cost, work with any DOS PC, and are as easy to install as a modem.

Provided that your customers possess a CD-ROM retrieval system, a CD-ROM for marketing purposes is easy for customers to use and lessens the likelihood of errors. It is more durable, can't be wiped out by magnetic field like a floppy disk and has no mechanical parts to damage.

Some CD-ROM disadvantages include the following:

1. Data on disc cannot be changed.
2. Data on CD-ROM are basically far slower to access than hard disk.
3. Searching through a multisensory document can be daunting.
4. Creating original graphics for a CD-ROM is costly.
5. A CD-ROM drive or player costs $400 to $800.
6. Full-video images eat up storage.

CD-ROM uses CLV, or *constant linear velocity*, as its rotation technique. This slows access time. Like a floppy disk, a CD-ROM disc must be used with a computer, but it also requires a CD-ROM drive (player). CD-ROM does not replace other media. Special software is needed to build, set up, and select whatever goes on a CD-ROM disc.

Should You Market Via CD-ROM?

Most firms marketing consumer products shouldn't rush in to produce a CD-ROM. However, promising technical advances may soon change this proviso. For business-to-business marketing, a growing variety of CD-ROM catalogs display extensive product lines. CD-ROM is ideal for these:

1. Huge catalogs of products sold to businesses
2. Wide choices of complex products and services
3. Combinations of big manuals and parts catalogs
4. Aiding engineers to specify products
5. Combinations of many demos with tutorials for each
6. Combinations with online catalogs and marketplaces.

The best CD-ROM search software can overcome some of its slowness. As CD-ROM prices drop and PCs come with built-in CD-ROM drives, new marketing uses will proliferate. We'll describe some of these new uses, including how to share CD-ROM marketing costs and how small firms can participate.

Marketing Uses

CD-ROM integrates easily into online ordering systems. An online system provides up-to-the-minute price and inventory information but is far more expensive than a CD-ROM to use. Therefore, Ford and other car companies use both CD-ROM and online parts catalogs. CD-ROM is preferable for frequent reference and online for the latest updates. Travel agent reservation systems also combine online catalogs with CD-ROM for pictures and related information (CD-ROM drives are shared on local area networks in agent offices).

Baker and Taylor, the world's largest book distributor, uses a CD-ROM catalog to list its inventory of some 10 million books from over 14,000 publishers. For sophisticated cataloging, ordering, and delivery, it uses its CD-ROM and online catalogs in tandem.

CD-ROM can satisfy your customers fast. 3M produces a CD-ROM catalog with information on over 50,000 products, for internal distribution to more than 50 countries. The catalog contains product codes, descriptions, pricing, and import/export information to aid distribution personnel.

Nearly every company that publishes its own huge catalog to sell to organizations can cut costs, increase efficiency, and make more sales and profits via CD-ROM. One CD-ROM can contain a huge catalog or even a group of catalogs. Some companies update their CD-ROM catalogs quarterly, monthly, and, even occasionally, weekly. If only a small portion of the content needs revision, a good alternative is to send floppy disk as auxiliary updates.

Auto Parts Catalogs on CD-ROM

Bell & Howell's electronic parts catalog system on CD-ROM includes the Chrysler parts catalog, the Jeep-Eagle catalog, the General Motors parts catalog, the Honda parts catalog, the Acura catalog, the Nissan catalog, and Volvo catalog. In addition to the Mercedes-Benz of North America catalog, the system is now including Mercedes-Benz of Europe starting in English and going to four more languages. The system stores a number of years of parts, diagrams, and text. The system can retrieve any catalog information or illustration in clear detail.

Ford Motor Company has its own system; not only does it have a CD-ROM parts catalog, it also installed CD-ROM drives in over 500 of its dealerships. And Barry Quinllin, director of sales and marketing for GM Service & Parts Operation, comments "Our computerized system will eventually eliminate our printed parts catalog."

For the more than 500,000 customized Mack Trucks produced over the past 20 years, each requires a customized parts catalog. These print catalogs amount to 875,000 pages of paper and 330 feet of shelf space to store. This is too expensive and slow to transmit on-line. On CD-ROM it takes 7 discs including 23,000 pieces of art. These are updated three times a year. Now with the MACSPEC search system and a touch screen, a dealer can quickly find (usually in 1½ to 3 seconds) and order what is needed. Waiting time for people in line is cut, service improved, and cost of handling customer inquiries reduced.

Most Mack distributors paid for the system and CD-ROM drive on a lease basis of $333.33 monthly. It was soon in over 300 dealer locations. Enhancements let dealers fax or modem retrieved information to customers. A dealer can download from the CD-ROM just the pages needed to "desktop publish" a print catalog for the parts for a single truck.

Jet Parts Catalog

A shop manual for a jet engine contains up to 50,000 pages of text and line art. The engine's illustrated parts catalog has from 10,000 to 20,000 pages. Because each jet engine is built to custom specifications, each plane has a unique manual and catalog. Even for the same model, make, and year, some changes are made during construction, and changes are made as the plane is updated.

Regulations require that every page of each manual be maintained and updated for more than the previous ten years and that the unique manual and illustrative parts catalog be present at each takeoff and landing site used by the plane. Multiple copies of a 70,000-page set may be needed in different shops in each location.

British Airways responded by putting an entire maintenance manual for a Boeing 757 on CD-ROM. Its repair people can find an illustration of a missing part by tapping a few keys. If it's not in stock, they can order the part by computer for delivery in hours.

CAD/CAM Catalogs

An engineer who purchases has to specify exactly what is required. To do this, he or she must make an engineering drawing that is geometrical for each part ordered. Now, computer-assisted design (CAD) and catalogs are being integrated into a CD-ROM. The new process requires finding the appropriate catalog pages and then working with a CAD/CAM (computer-assisted manufacturing) program to design each. If you sell anything to engineers which must be specified—and you supply CD-ROM catalogs—you can offer engineers huge time savings and get a big sales advantage.

NoreLem, a French tool company, made a variety of mechanical vices. For it, Informatique (a subsidiary) put its CAD/CAM drawings and product catalogs in a CD-ROM. About $250,000 was spent on software development. For the 1000 CD-ROM catalogs distributed, the average order amounted to 250 vices, about $212,000. Total sales were over $1 million. And the cost to produce more was only $2 each in the same volume.

Both companies were acquired by Applied Power, a tool manufacturer in Milwaukee, Wisconsin. When Applied Power (AP) brought Informatique to the United States, it changed the name to Norminfo. The first U.S. client was Vlier Enerpac, a manufacturer of similar devices and an AP subsidiary. The software produced for Vlier Enerpac is very interactive and can perform complicated geometric calculations. It even adds to the bill of materials the specifications suited to it.

New CD-ROM Sales Method

How would you like to sell once and then get repeat sales with no further product costs—no packaging, shipping, and handling costs, and with customers delighted with the value received? Greg Kalodziejzyk, a commercial artist from Calgary, Canada, founded Image Club Graphics Inc. with a mail order ad in *MacUser* magazine. He sells other artists' "clip art" and type fonts on floppy disks. He became so success-ful that his full catalog uses 75 hi-density disks.

Greg then had a simple, big idea. He offered a huge bargain on CD-ROM—with a CD-ROM drive included. On the same disc, he included other bargains accessible only via a separate secret password. Each ex-tra batch of clip art could be purchased later by phoning in a credit card number and order and getting the password to unlock it. The idea worked. Greg started the Image Club CD-ROM business by a PR release and mentions in his ads in *MacWorld, MacUser,* and *Personal User* maga-zines for floppy discs.

Two years after Greg started the "unlock" method of selling as an op-tion, the Image club had six CD-ROM products all with additional of-fers locked in. Image Club no longer sells CD-ROM drives. Both art and type Image Club discs are bundled with CD-ROM drives, peripherals, and software sold via computer stores. One out of four buyers unlock for more sales.

NEC Technologies Inc. developed and marketed its own CD-ROM LOCK unlocking technology for both the Macintosh and IBM PC envi-ronments. NEC first tested the unlocking CD-LOCK, CD-ROM sales method for type fonts and then for clip art. Within a year NEC had a to-tal of six products with the unlocking option. Sales results were good enough for NEC to plan a considerable unlock expansion into more areas.

CompuGraphics has a CD-ROM disc of type fonts and sells using the unlock method. So do Multi Ad in Canada and MonoType in Europe. Mike Wegman, product manager for NEC CD-ROM software, calls un-lock CD-ROM a trend that can only multiply as CD-ROM gets built into more laptops and PCs. CD-ROM can be used for public domain or clip music, clip sound effects, clip excerpts and quotes from stories, drama and public domain clip video. Public domain material grows as fast as the royalties run out.

Martin Nisenholtz, director of the Electronic Marketing Division of Ogilvy & Mather Direct, began to explore CD-ROM the year it started in 1985. I asked Martin:

> Q: What is your opinion of the marketing future of the unlock CD-ROM method? Will this be used by Publishers Clearing House for unlock sub-scriptions? Will a CD-ROM unlock college education be offered? Will there be an unlock book club of books to be read on-screen or digitized, recorded books to listen to?
>
> MN: It's too early to say definitively. The answers will be mostly technol-ogy-driven.

Creating a CD-ROM Catalog

Creating a CD-ROM catalog is complex and can be expensive; sometimes, however, creating a CD-ROM catalog can be simpler than you might fear. Reread the previous chapters on electronic catalogs. Read the fine books recommended in the Help Source Guide at the end of this chapter as well as issues of the excellent newsletters listed. Also, ask the Optical Publishing Association for guidance. Plus, ask *PC Week, PC World,* and *Byte* magazines for the latest lead articles on CD-ROM.

Linda Helgerson has helped the most newcomers start in CD-ROM. Immerse yourself in her magazine, *CD-ROM End User,* for the latest applications and developments in technology, software, and peripherals. Another Helgerson must is the "CD-ROM Shoppers Guide," a quarterly compilation of all CD-disc titles published.

As soon as you get a CD-ROM drive for your Mac, IBM, or clone, access the *CD-ROM Sourcedisc* published by Helgerson Associates, Inc. (president is Linda Helgerson). It's a catalog for previewing and ordering CD-ROM titles that contains a phone directory of CD-ROM publishers and suppliers plus other facts and figures. If you can't afford the catalog, find it in a business library.

Business catalogs that succeed on floppy disks have a good chance of success in an expanded CD-ROM format. So do those that greatly supplement an online catalog. Huge, untried endeavors can turn into big disasters. Small tests at little expense for untried areas often fail, but some tests work after modest risk.

The following are some CD-ROM start-up questions:

- How much promotional material do you have on computer?

- How many of your customers have CD-ROM systems that can run your discs? How many are willing to buy systems, even at your cost? How many buy enough from your print catalog to make selling them a system at a loss or giving them a system worthwhile?

- Are you willing to risk that your CD-ROM catalog will take away business from your print catalog? If you restrict your disc catalog it may fail.

The initial money should be spent researching these questions. If you have a strong marketing department, most of or all your research can be done in house.

Next, make sure you have the latest PC with the necessary extras. These include a big memory hard disk, a CD-ROM drive, and the peripherals and software needed to run CD-ROM discs.

Then shop service bureaus. Compare discs of their work. Send for catalogs on disc and carefully analyze those that can be models for your CD-ROM catalog.

Ask CD-ROM experts for their latest case histories, and the names and addresses of other people to talk to with experience in CD-ROM catalogs, marketplaces, and "unlock marketing." Look for reports in your own trade papers and check your own trade association. Get more names and numbers. Phone around and ask if they've been successful, and always ask advice and for the names of other catalog firms on CD-ROM. Keep talking to all of them—ask which created a CD-ROM catalog in house and which used a service bureau and which method each recommends.

Should You Use a Service Bureau?

CD-ROM service bureaus typically charge more, but you get the use of far more experienced sophisticated equipment and software. Besides being able to do it all for you, the expert advice from service bureaus can be crucial. Using any of a growing number of excellent service bureaus can be far safer than attempting to produce a CD-ROM catalog in house.

Another option is to contract with a hybrid software development bureau. These shops completely produce your first catalog on disc. They will then license their CD-ROM software to allow you to make subsequent CD-ROM catalogs in house.

A third approach is to use a service bureau for your first (or several) CD-ROM catalog. Once you learn enough you can move to your own in-house CD-ROM catalog production without the service bureau's software. This requires buying special software, the necessary peripherals, and the in-house expertise to keep up with technological and creative developments. Only do this when you know you will make many more new CD-ROM catalogs regularly.

I suggest starting with the simplest CD-ROM catalog that suits your products and using a service bureau. If you make money with it, proceed cautiously.

In-House CD-ROM Production

Software written in house is usually created for simple or small applications. Even shorter programs that dare to venture beyond text can take a huge chunk of a senior programmer's writing time. Fortunately, off-the-shelf software exists to guide you to organize the text of your catalog on the CD-ROM. Also available is software for easier, faster, and simpler retrieval from a CD-ROM. With the right software, the hugest CD-ROM catalog, if it's in all-text form and is already on computer, may be practical for in-house production.

Ford New Holland has a huge CD-ROM parts catalog for its agricultural and industrial equipment. Carmen J. Martin of Ford New Holland knew computers but not CD-ROM. With software programs purchased from Dataware and after only one day of training, Carmen built a dealer catalog of 300,000 Ford New Holland parts and components. Every part, price, and specification for all agricultural and industrial equipment Ford New Holland manufactures and sells worldwide was included. The catalog is easy to use and has had only minor problems—no more than those produced by most service bureaus. Ford NH now plans to produce a new CD-ROM version with diagrams, color, and interactivity.

What Should CD-ROM Catalogs Cost?

Each year, the range of possible price widens. While it gets more practical for do-it-yourselfers to produce the simplest CD-ROM, service bureaus keep getting newer equipment to produce CD-ROMs faster and cheaper with features impossible before. The dilemma is that the easiest-to-produce CD-ROM may not tap the potential of what a CD-ROM catalog can do for you or distinguish you from the competition. You pay for what you get. Producing a CD-ROM can cost as little as $3000 to as much as $250,000 or more. But the lowest cost can mean more risk in quality control. And this doesn't include the initial investment in equipment of at least $30,000 and often far more for a low-cost, good quality in-house production. This investment may take a number of catalogs and several years to amortize.

Ken Wegman of NEC Technologies states that the cost to make a disc like its Type Gallery PS is as little as $1500 and then $2 a disc to reproduce. Producing the average disc can vary from $10,000 to $40,000 in a service bureau. Costs can be far less if you have the CD-ROM catalog material on computer disk or tape.

If you produce in house, an authoring program can cost from $795 to $30,000. Retrieval programs usually charge according to the number of CDs you intend to press, starting with several thousand dollars. Leading premastering systems cost $25,000 to $30,000. These costs can be amortized over many discs.

Whether you produce your CD-ROM in house or use a service bureau, the most price-sensitive issues are: How much of your catalog is already on computer? How much material exists in completed, reproducible form? Does a new catalog have to be created from scratch? If so, how much is text and how simple or high-tech are the requirements for the balance? Using existing video and animation can add greatly to expense. In fact, producing them may be prohibitively expensive. Supporting customized software created for your catalog can be like signing a blank check.

How long does it take to produce a CD-ROM disc? Premastering one disc takes about two hours. Mastering and pressing 100 discs can take three days. Each step has its own time requirements. Creating material rather than transferring it can take weeks to years depending on what you attempt. *The McGraw-Hill CD-ROM Handbook,* which I strongly recommend, suggests that when selecting a manufacturer, you ask these questions:

How much experience has the manufacturer had in making CD-ROM discs?

Is premastering available? Is there an extra cost for this?

What is the cost of mastering? What is the turn-around time? Is there a check disc available? Does it cost extra?

What is the minimum quantity run acceptable? Cost per disc? Quantity breaks? Turn-around time?

Is packaging, back cover, front cover booklet, and label printing included in the price?

What are the lead times necessary for scheduling?

What are the CD-ROM master tape requirements and label/booklet printing requirements?

CD-ROM Marketplaces: Sharing Costs

Now let's examine another way to create a marketing CD-ROM that is much lower-cost, simpler, and faster. For those fields that feature them, putting your catalog on an existing CD-ROM marketplace may be safer and a more profitable marketing option than either the in-house or service bureau route.

Eclat Inc., of Pleasanton, California, distributes quarterly a CD-ROM library used by architectural and engineering product specifiers on electrical, mechanical, and additional/engineering products. The quarterly contains comprehensive text, full color, CAD details, animation and performance calculation programs on 250,000 products from 30 plus manufacturers, currently. Eclat runs in the Microsoft Windows environment. CadCom systems animate exploded drawings with extended parts, performing calculations to aid in specifications and product selection.

Each electronic binder is maintained and updated by Eclat, adding and deleting products through the year.

The Mannequin Marketplace

Display Net is a CD-ROM catalog and computer- and fax-ordering system. It's a marketplace of products from more than 60 manufacturers of mannequins, displays, and other retailing fixtures. A typical Display Net disc contains 4000 to 5000 color images with full text descriptions. Studies showed that buyers at major department and specialty stores spent an average of 120 hours a month shopping and ordering from traditional catalogs of display materials but that Display Net could reduce this time to less than 20 hours.

Display Net users can zoom in to inspect a photographed item and compare up to three items at a time on-screen. To make a selection, the buyer points to it using a "mouse." The computer adds the selection to a shopping list as the user keeps shopping. Once shopping is done, the user may compare items chosen or delete items not wanted. Each order is automatically sent to a main computer, separated into individual vendor purchases, and sent via fax to each manufacturer.

Display Net is produced by Electronic Catalog Corp. (ECAT), which services subscribers and resources 24 hours per day.

Catalogs are issued quarterly with new products and updated prices. Display Net can include store-planning CAD files, shipping tables, inventory records, and other special functions. Advertisers pay a membership fee of $300 a year to use the system, including the fax response system; $50 for each picture shown and $10 for each item shown in the picture for descriptive text; and a 5-percent sales commission for any sales made. The average vendor-advertiser spends about $5000 plus commissions.

Display Net has reduced the system cost down to the price of a good-quality PC in order to appeal to a larger number of smaller organizations buying display material. To date, Display Net has reduced the equipment cost to less than $4000 or for $150 a month for a lease.

General Display Corp. (GDC) was one of the first vendor-advertisers. For months, General Display had little sales effect attributed to Display

Net. Then GDC got an order for $220,000 through Display Net from an account it had been unable to sell for years. Another sponsor, Foam Boards, Inc., also got big orders. Display Net's other advertisers also reported getting profitable amounts of orders in relation to the money spent.

Furniture Marketplace

John Neering pioneered catalog marketplaces on CD-ROM. He is an alumnus of Herman Miller, a leading fine furniture company, and a consultant to them. Neering became an expert in building, furniture manufacturing, and planning and founded Computer-Aided Planning, Inc. (CAPI) in Grand Rapids, Michigan. CAPI first created mainframe, then PC-based, computer programs to help managers make commercial interior design choices based on the level of traffic expected. He next created a CD-ROM marketplace called "CAD Libraries" for 20 furniture manufacturers. Soon the marketplace had 800 subscribers and 1300 users. It was highly profitable.

When John sold his company to McGraw-Hill, it became CAP Electronic Sweets, a marketplace that includes CAD Libraries and 35,000 graphic designs of virtually every commercial furniture manufacturer and their order forms. The CD-ROM system can accommodate a myriad of specifications needed to create an order. Each dealer may have a CD-ROM drive and floppy disk system for every salesperson.

CAP Electronic Sweets downloads new design data directly from the mainframe computers of the furniture manufacturer. To tap into this electronic system, each subscriber buys a microcomputer work station that includes a CD-ROM drive. These very complex CD-ROM catalogs are updated monthly, generate a very high average order, and save substantial processing costs.

Subscriptions to CAP Electronic Sweets cost an average $2000 a year; purchasing costs about $8000. But orders created by Cap Electronic Sweets run from $1000 up to $500,000 and $1 million. Out of $9 billion of furniture and equipment purchased in a recent year from the contract furniture industry, $2 billion were specified using electronic catalogs, primarily CD-ROM.

The Spread of CD-ROM Marketplaces

John Neering believes that CD-ROM catalogs are more efficient, easier to use, and less costly for buyer and seller than other print or electronic media. Moreover, he predicts that most business-to-business catalogs (other than the smallest) will be distributed on CD-ROM—not individually, but as part of huge, cooperative marketplaces for each field. The most complex marketplaces, especially those with high average orders and detailed specifications, are leading the way.

I asked Martin Nisenholtz the following: "What are the most innovative CD-ROM catalogs and the most successful CD-ROM marketplaces that you know of?" Martin answered: "Probably those serving the government market."

Discovery Systems sells a CD-ROM sampler marketplace. Owned by Jeffrey Wilkins, also the founder of CompuServe, Discovery Systems excerpts from many of the best new CD-ROMS. The sampler includes many demonstrations in full color and with multimedia capabilities. Discovery Systems' sampler is either sold for $26 or included with another purchase as a premium. Being included in a sampler is obviously ideal for anyone starting a CD-ROM.

MacWorld Nautilus, published by Discovery Systems, is a CD-ROM magazine. It's another Jeffrey Wilkins project. Every 28 days for $10 each, a new Nautilus CD-ROM disc arrives, packed with a lot of features with color, pictures, sound, and some video via DVI. Each issue has multimedia presentations, name brand software demonstrations, and programming resources. The disc reviews public domain software and shareware and delivers instant software.

Jeffrey is full of plans for "The Nautilus Mall." He pictures a consumer product CD-ROM marketplace bigger than any online, one with no access charges and far lower sales costs to promote any product. He describes a future Nautilus where small ads can unlock big catalogs at no cost or offer literature or sell any kind of information for instant delivery. Nautilus may be the forerunner of a galaxy of CD-ROM magazines.

CD-ROM Offshoots

SONY's Data Discman is handheld CD-ROM in which everything from an encyclopedia to a language course is stored. It may be the perfect medium for CD-ROM catalog discs.

Rick Stauffer, CD marketing director at Intel, says, "Our view is that by the mid 1990s, every PC sold will have a CD-ROM drive in it and have DVI." DVI has been called the first true multimedia CD-ROM. DVI provides full-screen, full-motion 30-frame-per-second video directly off a CD-ROM disc. DVI enables a PC to display more than an hour of full-motion video, text, 3-D graphics, still images, special effects, and multi-track audio voice and music played from a highly compressed digital data stored on a single, standard CD-ROM disc.

Larry Dale, who pioneered the use of IDcats at Ford, says:

> Our computer disk catalogs have been a very small niche but profitable and gaining us new customers and of a superior kind. I consider it support for our print catalog. I see another advantage.
>
> By 1995, CD-I...with superb color...should be available to a very wide public. It should do in the mass what our disk catalogs now do on a niche basis. The same presentation should work on a vaster scale and we will have mastered it.

We'll describe compact-disc interactive technology (CD-I) in more detail in Chapter 23.

Help Source Guide

1. The *CD-ROM Expo* is sponsored by World Expo Corp., division IDG, providing a perfect regular update. Big companies should attend; small should buy audiotapes of any sessions on catalogs, marketplaces: P.O. Box 9107, 111 Speen St., Framingham, MA 01701-9171. (508) 872-2700.

2. C. Sherman's *CD-ROM Handbook* (512 pages), 2d ed., 1992, McGraw-Hill, Inc., allows high tech experts to detail capabilities, complexities, constraints of hardware, peripherals, software.

3. *DataWare Technologies, Inc.* provides a *free* information kit re its fine authoring and search software systems. Also free is "Corporate Guide to Optical Publishing," excellent for newcomers to CD-ROM: 222 Third St., Suite 3300, Cambridge, MA 02142. (800) 344-5849. PR dept.

4. *Discovery Systems* offers a CD-ROM sampler disc and a *free* information kit and free introductory disc for newer *Nautilus* magazine on CD-ROM or *free* phone information: (800) 637-3472. *Free* information is also available re disc production. 7001 Discovery Blvd., Dublin, OH 43017. (614) 761-2000.

5. *Helgerson Associates, Inc.*, 6609 Rosecroft Place, Falls Church, VA 22043-1828, (703) 237-0682, publishes: *CD-ROM End User* magazine. Easy-to-read, understandable high-tech information, information on all aspects of latest application; *CD-ROM Shopper's Guide* quarterly, lists CD-ROM titles, publishers, distributors, CD-ROM drives, specs.; *Disc Magazine*, a highly technical periodical, covering all aspects of CD-ROM production and dissemination (each issue includes a CD-ROM disc [for DOS or Macintosh] with about 100 megabytes of more information, demos, ads, speeches with audio, text, and graphics); *CD-ROM Sourcedisc* is a CD-ROM for both DOS and Macintosh computers—describes over 800 CD-ROMs, demonstrations of many.

6. Meckler Corp. offers an optical information systems quarterly, a multimedia review quarterly, "CD-ROMS in Print," annual conferences, micropublications, newsletters, software, videos. Good but expensive publications; check your business, college, or science library, or contact 11 Ferry Ln. W., Westport CT 06880. (203) 226-6967.

7. *Optical Publishing Association* (Richard A. Bowers, executive director) provides latest list of service bureaus, software houses, and peripheral manufacturers and a *free* information kit on CD-ROM: P.O. Box 21268, Columbus, OH 43221. (614) 793-9660.

8. *Verbum Interactive* is Verbum Inc.'s new multimedia CD-ROM magazine for multimedia PC platform. Features reviews, demonstrations of multimedia programs; showcases animation, interactive multimedia works. 670 7th Ave., 2nd Fl., San Diego, CA 92101. (619) 233-9977.

9. *The International Conference & Expo on Multimedia and CD-ROM* is sponsored by Microsoft Corp. & Cahners Expo Group, San Francisco, California. For information, call (203) 352-8224.

10. Send to these firms for catalogs about CD-ROM sources (some in print, some on computer disk, and some on CD-ROM disc): *Bureau of Electronic Publishing*, 141 New Road, Parsippany, NJ 07054. (201) 857-4300. *CD ROM Inc*, 1667 Cole Blvd., Suite 400, Golden, CO 80401. (303) 231-9373. *Compact Disc Products*, 272 Route 34, Aberdeen, NJ 07747. (800) 634-2298. *DAK Ind.*, 8200 Remmet Ave., Canoga Park, CA 91304. (818) 888-2695. *EBSCO Electronic Info.*, P.O. Box 325, Topsfield, MA 01983. (800) 221-1826. *Faxon Co.*, 15 Southwest Park, Westwood, MA 02090. (617) 329-3350. *Gale Research Inc.*, 835 Penobscot Bldg., Detroit, MI 48226. (800) 877-4253. *Updata Pubs.*, 1736 Westwood Blvd., Los Angeles, CA 90024. (800) 882-2844.

23

Electronic Marketing Machines

Atms, High-Tech Multimedia, and Simpler Kiosks

Atms

The automatic teller machine (ATM) is the most mass-produced, generic, electronic-marketing machine in the world. Atms are used in banks, outside them, and elsewhere, are interactive, and allow you to conduct various kinds of banking transactions without any banking personnel. John Kristoff of InterBold, the largest manufacturer of Atms in the world, describes the full-size ATM as "a mechanism that makes a cash withdrawal and makes a transfer of money between accounts." The smaller model John describes as a "cash dispenser" that "can do everything but take deposits."

The over 80,000 Atms in the United States handle almost 6 billion transactions yearly. There are over 271,000 Atms worldwide. Older Atms are simpler and newer ones more complex. They vary somewhat as customized for different banks. They're made by different manufacturers but usually with similar basic parts, often from the same parts makers.

Citibank designs its own Atms, buys components, assembles them, and considers them better engineered for the bank's needs. Citibank created its own software for the functions it requires and has its own quality control and maintenance to service its ATMs and to make its units stand up better under the uses required. Citibank calls its ATMs "Citicard Banking Centers" and feels that they have dramatically advanced banking technology. They let you do 55 different banking transactions by machine and, in the United States, operate in English and Spanish. As the use of "Citicard Banking Centers" expands to the 40 other countries in which Citibank conducts a consumer financial services business, its ATMs will function in 11 languages.

James Walker, vice president of Electronic Banking at the Provident National Bank, says that "roughly 50 percent of teller transactions can be done at the ATM and it's not farfetched to think that ATMs will handle 75 percent of teller transactions, particularly if banks use the new ATM features available." Eighty percent of Citibank transactions at its New York City branches are via its ATMs. Interbold's John Kristoff says its latest models are capable of performing 90 to 95 percent of banking transactions now performed by tellers.

Multimedia Kiosks

The word *kiosk* was originally defined as a Turkish garden house, then a booth in a Turkish bazaar, then a newsstand or glass-enclosed free-standing ad display on a Paris Boulevard, then a staffed booth in a shopping mall. Today the word *kiosk* increasingly describes an electronic marketing (EM) kiosk, but these kiosks still inform, help sell or complete a sale—or give service and support to a customer—interactively.

Ideally, in an EM kiosk, multimedia combines hardware and software elements and interactively for far more effective persuasion. William J. Comcowich, chairman of the Interactive Multimedia Association, says:

> Video possesses enormous power to sell, to tell a visual story, to get people emotionally involved with an idea or product. Computers offer instant access to enormous quantities of stored information and rapid analytic capabilities. Interactive multimedia combines the visual and emotional impact of video with the depth of computer databases, and the intellectual impact that comes from the active participation and involvement of the viewer.
>
> Multimedia is the convergence of TV and computers. It offers the impact of television with the power of computers. It integrates text, graphics, sounds, still photographs, and motion.

Some of the EM kiosks that we are concerned with became possible with the development of Microsoft InfoWindows software and then

Windows software created by Microsoft working with IBM. Many other kiosks have used the Apple system rather than MS-DOS and Windows. Some use still other variations and systems.

What a Hi-Tech Electronic Kiosk Contains

INTECO Corp., a top research firm, defines a multimedia kiosk as one which "allows the user to interact at his or her own pace and that in addition to text and/or computer graphics, contains at least one of the following: sound, still images, animation or full-motion video." James E. Strothman, editor of *Computer Pictures* magazine, states:

> Information kiosks provide information only, guided by the user's commands. A typical version consists of a cabinet containing a personal computer, touch screen, and video disc player. Some contain printers, and have CD-ROM drives and hard disks for easy updating. When the information is relatively simple and required in multiple locations, kiosks can consist of a cabinet containing a CD console, such as CD-I or CDTV player, and a touch screen.
>   Sales kiosks are usually used for selling complex and expensive goods and services. Typical locations are home furnishing stores, car dealers, and retail bank branches. Onsite kiosks often consist of a cabinet containing a personal computer, touch screen, video disc player, printer, modem, speakers, and credit card reader.

Much Promise, Many Failures

Despite the promise, there have been many kiosk marketing experiments and relatively few traced-sale successes. Of all forms of electronic marketing described in this book, electronic kiosks have probably had the greatest percentage of marketing failure.

Michael Liebold, manager of Media Architecture Research for Apple Computer in Cupertino, California, says:

> Kiosks had problems. Newspapers and other general media had a far lower CPM. Kiosks had smaller exposure and high CPM. The cost of production was a far higher percentage of media cost. There was more complex production of a software ad message at a higher price than the production of a TV commercial. Production was very complex. It required a variety of fairly expensive production titling tools for media or production and delivery.

Joe Serino of Alexander Associates, leading consultants in the field, says:

Kiosks were often not integrated into the overall marketing plan. The kiosks were hidden away. There often was not adequate promotional support for the retailer. Customers often didn't understand the nature of the kiosks so that they failed to use them enough to justify the cost of producing the devices.

Jack Noon, president of Midi, a top kiosk developer, adds, "Often kiosks did not have enough speed. Many were poorly designed and not properly maintained. Users were frustrated."

Some authorities have blamed kiosk failure on the overemphasis on technology by the kiosk creator. Many of them ignored what shoppers wanted in the use of kiosks; placed kiosks in the wrong locations; didn't realize that, even in high-traffic locations, those passing by had to be attracted to the kiosk and that those people who stopped had to be tempted to interact with the kiosk and persuaded to go on at each step. People had to have a reason to use a kiosk, a simple way to use it. And the response from the kiosk had to be clear and easy to understand.

Kiosks often complicated shopping and required extra time shoppers did not have. Instead of helping a salesperson sell, the kiosk often made more work or even was designed to compete with and lessen the income of the salesperson. Often the kiosk sold little more than an ordinary display which cost a fraction of that of a kiosk.

INTECO Corp. tracks use of kiosks and states that by the end of 1991 total kiosks in the United States totaled substantially less than ATMs alone.

High Production Costs. Production costs to go first class with a high-tech kiosk are still higher than most marketers realize, unlike the average multimedia kiosk hardware cost per unit, including peripherals and enclosure, which has dropped in recent years. The total project development cost is still substantial, including content material. Yet these costs did not bar success in the right marketing situations.

William Comcowich, who is also vice president and creative director of Effective Communication Arts, Inc. of New York, says the cost of developing programs has come down. The entire production cost runs $150,000 to $300,000, with a greatly increased level of interactive sophistication in the current programs. This budget range represents a much improved value compared with a few years ago.

Some Consistently Succeeded. Despite every problem, smart marketers who best understood how to effectively use kiosks have succeeded. The success stories described in the next three chapters are examples that prove what could be done while others failed. Top creators of kiosk programs have consistently made money for a goodly number of clients despite high costs.

The Comcowich Approach to Kiosks. In the ten most difficult years for electronic kiosks, Bill Comcowich came up with successful kiosk applications for big company clients. He did it by selecting an industry and a use most suited to kiosk promotion. By skill and meticulous care, he overcame common obstacles to kiosk success, judiciously achieving quality production. He made the kiosk's considerable cost a good investment.

First Bill Comcowich carefully analyzed the strengths of kiosks. Then he selected the pharmaceutical industry as one for whom the use of kiosks was ideal. He saw a way for kiosks to aid in product introductions by reaching a variety of professionals and executives at different levels who are rarely seen by salespeople. These highly desirable businesspeople are often in allied but different areas of distribution. They could influence or make buying decisions at all levels—including brand prescribers (e.g., physicians). The extra sales to be attained were very big. The long-term repeat sales were far greater. The margin for promotion was large and the potential extra profit enough to more than compensate for the expense of first-class kiosk presentation.

Comcowich chose trade shows and big professional meetings as ideal kiosk locations for the purpose because, he says:

Multimedia offers these major advantages and benefits in exhibits and meetings:

Impact: Video is the most powerful media of persuasion. We live in a video world. Consumer products use video very effectively in their marketing programs. We need to apply the emotional and psychological appeals of video more effectively in more kinds of marketing.

Depth of information: The combination of text, graphics, photography, and video provide an unmatched repository for information—instantly accessible.

Involvement: Multimedia replicates the traditional time-honored case study approach that executives and professionals prefer.

Individual: Multimedia delivers information individualized to the specific needs of professional and business viewers. By making simple choices the viewer is able to obtain the information he or she wants.

Extraordinary presentation efficiency: In multimedia courses for professionals, learning time decreases by about 30 to 50 percent.

Fun: A well-designed multimedia program is an enjoyable information-absorbing experience. We all find out more and feel better about it when we enjoy the process.

These major benefits provide ample payback for the relatively steep financial investment required for multimedia equipment and program development.

Today, says Bill Comcowich, "The major pharmaceutical companies use kiosks in exhibits on the convention floor. The audience and prospects are recommenders and prescribers. The most important factor of success is to determine what it is that the audience wants and then the delivery method."

How Pharmaceutical Companies Use Kiosks. Bill Comcowich continues:

The interactive videodisc is the system that has been used most frequently in medical marketing applications by companies such as Burroughs Wellcome, SmithKline Beecham, Miles, Sandoz, Winthrop and others.

The interactive videodisc player is connected to a computer—providing an entire range of capabilities: up to 60 minutes of video, 54,000 photographs or drawings, hundreds of computer graphics, thousands of pages of text—all accessible within one or two seconds.

Some interactive video programs are extremely successful, with physicians, nurses, and pharmacists literally waiting in line to view programs. Others are costly failures. Interactive videodisc criteria for success are:

1. Finely honed objectives which should be short, simple, specific, and should ideally specify some changes in behavior.
2. Substantive [programs]. The sizzle of interactive technology can initially attract, but few programs succeed without a substantive content. Multimedia programs must provide knowledge or assistance that the convention or show attender judges to be crucial to his or her work. Purely promotional programs almost always fail.
3. Practical and useful [information]. Professional and business attenders want information that can be applied to their job and career. They want to improve their skills.
4. Interactively challenging [programs]. Dull interactivity is a common cause of failure of interactive programs. Some current programs use very simplistic interactivity—basically multiple-choice questions about information presented. That kind of interactivity was passable five or seven years ago. Today, forget it.
5. Quality production. In video, quality is elusive. The notion persists that low-budget is acceptable. The viewers, however, are accustomed to the high-quality production of network broadcasting and television advertising. Their level of expectations has risen. Simply put, quality video production is more persuasive. It is cost-effective because it sells more.

The emergence of multimedia development firms such as Effective Communication Arts, Inc. of New York and extraordinary creative talent like Bill Comcowich has made the marketing use of kiosks far safer. Often, a big contribution is simply to stop failure before it occurs by questioning whether a would-be client has a real chance in using a kiosk for the intended purpose.

Effective Uses of Multimedia Kiosks

Bill Comcowich asks:

So how do you judge if your solution is appropriate for multimedia? Just what are the indications for multimedia?

An audience must be big enough to justify the cost. As little as 1000 potential viewers may do if a very high-priced purchase or series of purchases is possible. But many times more viewers are required if your prices and margins are much less.

Interactive multimedia is especially useful if the audience is composed of individuals with different skill levels. A perfect example is SmithKline Beecham Pharmaceuticals' program on depression, produced by ECA. It was designed to be viewed by psychiatrists, primary care physicians, pharmacists, nurse practitioners, and social workers. There was different content for each subset of audience.

Ideally, a multimedia program requires video. Not just talking heads. But photography. Or imagery. Or "how-to" procedural demonstrations. Visual content. Multimedia is best utilized where the subject is stable. It is usually unwise to produce a videodisc if the subject matter is likely to change substantially in a short time. Question the wisdom of using multimedia if the project doesn't meet at least most of these criteria.

If the would-be client passes this Comcowich test, the next question is what kiosk approach is right for the purpose. Bill describes one method he has found successful in helping customers select the right product out of a wide choice:

An expert system is a computer-based multimedia program which offers the knowledge and analytic ability of an expert. The user provides the system some information about a problem by answering some questions. The system then provides its recommendations based on a set of expert rules that are contained in the software.

One easy-to-understand expert system, for example, is "Racquet Selector" for use in retail sporting goods stores. A tennis player answers ten profile questions about physical ability, type of tennis game, level of tennis ability, and racquet preferences. Based on the information provided, the system recommends five racquets from a database of 120 racquets made by different companies.

Expert systems can be applied to almost any field of expertise on different varieties of products and services. The possibilities are virtually endless. With deep knowledge bases and well-designed logic, expert systems represent a potent technology that can become a powerful consultive service that is as indispensable in the future as phone and fax consultations are today—but instantly available and based on the knowledge of the nation's preeminent authorities in each specialty.

Comcowich is a strategist in designing a kiosk to get maximum value out of a booth's passing traffic. He describes his method:

> An exhibit will be more successful if it offers multiple layers of information appealing to the many different depths of information which executives and professionals desire.
>
> An island booth, for example, could have a conceptual design that involves three rings. In the outermost area of the exhibits—the area next to the aisle—there is relatively superficial information, just the bare bones of the product or service information. In media terms, the outer ring is the roadside billboard of the marketing plan. It contains one powerful image and one finely honed message. The outer ring is the carnival barker. It is the movie marquee. The outer ring announces what's playing inside. The outer ring promotes questions and inquiries—to stimulate interest in the offerings in the exhibit.
>
> In the middle ring, there is available information and media in substantial depth and substance. At this level, the customer can get answers to basic inquiries. The exhibit sponsor also delivers the short version of the product pitch. These encounters usually require from one to three minutes.
>
> Finally, at the core of the booth is information in substantial depth—a database of extraordinary detail. Everything anyone in the field in a variety of capacities ever wanted to know about the field and the product. And the comprehensive database of information is accessible at many different depths, accommodating a variety of different information-acquiring styles.
>
> The amount of contact time can range from five minutes to over an hour—depending on each individual's needs.
>
> This notion of depth of information is extremely important to the entire marketing plan. The reason is simple. The exhibit is often the only place where companies may gain lengthy access to hard-to-reach top executives and high-rank professionals. These are precisely the people who want great depth of information.

Most of what Bill Comcowich has just told us is excerpted or modified from an article by him in the July 1990 issue of *The Pharmaceutical*

Executive magazine. Thanks also to Bill for the time he devoted to interviews with me. There is expertise available for a wide variety of kiosk applications. Top kiosk program developers make a real effort to explain to a marketer the limitations and chances of success and failure for each type of kiosk concept considered.

Big Changes Expected

An entire series of developments in hardware and software, and efforts by a variety of manufacturers in different fields, continue to improve kiosks. Software firms, teams of creative people and consultants, and innovative marketers all have developed new ways to create unique multimedia combinations and breakthrough services offered in kiosks.

The introduction of multimedia PCs for the home brought more standardization, the beginnings of mass production, along with simplification and lower costs of components. Joe Serino of Alexander Associates says:

> Kiosk marketing is a changing situation today for several reasons. First, people are just more and more used to interfacing with technology. They've seen more of these devices and are less shy about touching them. Design and operation has surely improved. Although I haven't seen it yet, shrinking disk drives and increasing success with compression technologies could really reduce a unit's required "footprint," making table-top units a possibility.

INTECO Corp. predicts 1.5 million kiosks in 1995, a twenty-three-fold growth in four years. James Strothman, editor of *Computer Pictures* magazine, told me, "That's because of new, lower-cost technology, the new mass production of hardware, easier-to-use software, the expected volume production of units also designed for home use, and the expected sharp drop in hardware costs."

In 1991, Vicki Vance, multimedia manager of Apple, told me that a Mac kiosk with all hardware, peripherals, and software needed for programs of top professional caliber could be produced for under $100,000. But by 1992, Apple came up with several breakthroughs. Michael Liebold, manager of Media Architecture Research, told me the following:

> For the last two years Apple has been working to develop Macintosh hardware and software and peripherals for kiosks and other applications. These developments now help keep the cost of kiosk devel-

opment and program production down. Less hardware is needed. Desktop production can be possible with $10,000 to $15,000 invested in hardware. Apple QuickTime System software has enabled the creation of a rich collection of video animation software tools from third-party developers. It extends video, animation, and sound. A kiosk is enhanced as new technology develops. Time and cost are both dramatically reduced because there are so many interoperational design programs. It takes much less investment.

Bill Gates, founder of Microsoft, has pushed CD-ROM and multimedia ahead. Microsoft has been influential in setting up multimedia standards by an entire group of top computer companies (outside of Apple and IBM). Microsoft's Windows 3.1 and Windows Multimedia Extensions (which now includes software-based video) have resulted in big advances and lower costs for kiosks.

As this book went into production, IBM announced plans to

become a leader in the multimedia merchandising and public-access kiosk marketplace by offering a set of standard integrated kiosks and tools, custom kiosks and applications and related kiosk support services.

IBM's initial entry, designed to be delivered as a totally integrated solution, is expected to save time and make installations less complex for the customer. State-of-the-art technology, including an advanced touch display, can make it easier for customers to design multimedia applications that will attract users to the kiosk. Simply touching the screen activates the unit, allowing users to navigate through visual programs and interact with various scenarios. Visual programs can use analog or digital technology to deliver sound and motion; a credit card reader and a printer can enable users to purchase goods or services and receive a printed receipt of the transaction.

IBM offered

a comprehensive set of kiosk support services including:

- Integration and/or installation of hardware and software

- Distribution of kiosks to customer's location

- Product warranty and ongoing maintenance

- Site services

IBM offered standard kiosks with the advantage of a bigger run, but each model could be customized "by utilizing IBM selected business partners."

All hardware, peripherals, and software can be bought off the shelf, but together there are more features of an advanced kiosk with more memory than in the IBM basic multimedia combinations offered for home entertainment. IBM priced its kiosks substantially lower than kiosk hardware and software systems had cost in the past. And the IBM units had new advantages.

Meanwhile, in computer magazines, IBM's Ultimedia have gotten high marks for the sound quality from IBM's internal speaker and audio card, for the speed and color reproduction of IBM's XGA graphics and the search program of its CD-ROM/XA.

Much simpler and lower-cost authoring systems are now available and make kiosk presentation easier. Most let you specify in certain ways where users can make choices to proceed and use the interactivity available. Kiosk servicing is available nationwide by General Electric Computer Service and other top organizations, although GE must first approve the equipment. Even by the time you read this book, your chances of marketing success using kiosks will have increased due to the new computer hardware and software and kiosk development whose impact few marketers fully realize. Two exciting developments, DVI and CD-I, are competing to achieve multimedia capabilities—ultimately with the least equipment and cost—and in time to slash kiosk system costs.

Digital Video Interactive (DVI) Technology

According to Mark J. Bunzel and Sandra K. Morris, of Intel,*

> At the most fundamental level, DVI technology is a set of video processors and software that give manufacturers the ability to create a digital, personal computer or platform. These video processors, the i750 PB/DB (pixel processor and display processor) are high-speed, special-purpose computer chips that are dedicated to the task of compressing, decompressing and displaying video in the personal computer.
>
> DVI allows all media—the video, stills and audio—to be stored digitally, and to be treated the same way as other digital files. Motion video, stills, and audio can be captured by the computer and stored on hard disk as files. This information can be edited: video can be cropped so that unnecessary parts of the images are eliminated; digital video files can be transformed so that they are brighter and darker; alternative audio tracks can be added to video; special effects can be written in software—zooms, wipes, fades, starbursts can all appear without expensive postproduction; graphics or text can be added to video or to still images.

*Multimedia Applications Development Using DVI Technology, McGraw-Hill, New York, 1991.

Compact Disk Interactive Technology (CD-I)

Bob Harris, vice president of Professional Media Systems, Philips Consumer Electronics Company, calls CD-I

a multimedia technology which allows a designer to utilize graphics, moving video, high-quality sound and text on a single screen. It is packaged in one box and installed with a monitor and input device. Its principal components are a compact disk drive and multimedia controller/processor. It can run all CD-I discs produced in accordance with the worldwide CD-I standard. It operates via a mouse, touchscreen, or keypad. A CD-I player is extendable for CD-ROM. It processes digital video and audio.

For CD-ROM discs, additional software can be incorporated. The CD-I then acts in the same way as a CD-ROM drive, peripheral to a computer system. Some models include Full-Motion Video (FMV). This uses an MPEG algorithm to compress natural pictures at a compression rate of 140:1. Similarly, the audio algorithm can compress a stereo CD disc at a ratio of 7:1. For playback, a demultiplexer in the player distributes the data from the CD-I to the appropriate processors and decoders and to the system decoder which handles the whole interactive presentation.

Creating a CD program starts with program design. After multimedia production/collection of audio, video, graphics, and text analog [are] converted to digital. There is control software coding, then disk-building, next emulation; after this mastering, and finally CD-I copies.

DVI versus CD-I

Almost as soon as DVI was first available on a test basis, Ogilvy & Mather began to apply it for clients. The firm has evaluated every major vendor's approach to kiosks from the IBM InfoWindow to the NCR 5682. Here are four more questions I asked Electronic Marketing Director Martin Nisenholtz:

Q: What are your views on the future of DVI versus CD-I?

MN: They serve different markets short-term. DVI probably has better prospects long-term, but it's too early to tell.

Q: What is your opinion of the new developments in hardware, peripherals, and software to make kiosks lower-cost and more effective for use?

MN: Kiosks require industrial engineering specs, per NVR 5682. I haven't seen an industrial grade spec using most makes of PCs in high-traffic locations.

Q: What manufacturers have the biggest possibilities of breakthroughs in kiosks?

MN: Hardware is secondary to application. My view is that applications must drive hardware development activity, as it did say with VideoCart.

Q: What breakthrough peripherals are contributing most to the next generation of kiosks? What new software?

MN: Flat panel displays. Reliable, miniature printing technologies, compression.

Creating Kiosk Programs

Steve Floyd is president of Floyd Design, a leading multimedia development firm whose clients include Coca-Cola, IBM, Delta Airlines, and Sears, and author of *The IBM Multimedia Handbook*. Steve's book is not just for big marketers. It is based on the IBM PC, with constant references to inexpensive peripherals and software that many businesses can afford and work with. He describes first-class kiosk projects but also points out how to go budget-class. Steve also predicts how the future may soon make kiosk programming easier, faster, and cheaper.

He is a superb organizer of the program creation task and a master teacher of his art. Steve Floyd guides both clients and his 40-person organization step by step with the least friction and expense to achieve a desired result. He believes in thorough research, in first focusing on the intended purpose and then on preparation and planning. He also believes in questioning, at each phase, the fundamental assumptions of all concerned. Steve preaches that *groups*, often a number of groups, create kiosks and programs, and how important the right mix of the group is for the purpose (including the members' ability to work together) to increase chances of success. He believes strongly in selecting, orienting, and getting the most out of a multimedia creative and marketing team.

It is impossible to cover in depth in this chapter how to create a kiosk presentation. For that, I strongly urge that you read Steve Floyd's book. To help you, I asked him these questions:

Q: How best can retailers or small marketer-entrepreneurs with low budgets profitably use kiosks?

SF: Graphics only.

Q: Is a standard kiosk in a retail or mall location—to be rented one week at a time with different software programs used for different advertisers—feasible for simplest applications?

SF: Not really, unless fees cover a lot of administrative overhead.

Q: Is desktop kiosk software production by an amateur possible now for simple applications that have a real chance for the right small marketer?

SF: Yes, using AVC, a storyboard and other simple tools.

Q: Does DVI or CDI now make substantially lower-cost kiosk program production possible with less equipment and people?

SF: No—costs will be higher, *not* lower, initially for CD-I or DVI *software.*

Q: Can you "guesstimate" minimum cost to make the simplest kiosk application by 1995?

SF: It depends on the size and complexity of your project and on existing resources, but probably will range from $20,000 to $30,000.

Help Source Guide

1. *Ask* which recent issues of the following magazines have stories on latest kiosk technology or multimedia. Read at the library, and buy specific issues on kiosks, multimedia, or both: *Computer World* (508) 879-0700. *MacUser* (415) 378-5600. *MacWeek* (415) 243-3500. *MacWorld* (415) 243-0505. (212) 503-3801. *PC World* (415) 243-0500.

2. E. Miller and W. Miller's *Discovering CD-I, 1991,* is a guide to CD-I multimedia systems applications for business and consumers, covering design, development, costs, authoring requirements: Knowledge Industries, 701 Westchester Ave., White Plains, NY 10604. (800) 800-5474.

3. *Hypermedia* publishes a newsletter and catalog and offers *free* issues of each. Available are items on new kiosk applications, equipment, software, producers: 3501 Ryder St., Santa Clara, CA 95051. (408) 737-6113.

4. Steve Floyd's *IBM Multimedia Handbook: Complete Guide to Hardware and Software Applications, 1991,* is available from Brady Publishing, Simon & Schuster, NY. In libraries, computer and book stores.

5. *IBM* offers a *free* video about its IBM Personal System/2 Multimedia and new multimedia applications: (800) 255-0426, ext. 58. (914) 288-2094. *IBM Advanced Education Systems,* P.O. Box 2150, Atlanta, GA 30066. (404) 286-4646.

6. M. Bunzel and S. Morris's *Multimedia Applications Development Using DVI Technology* (McGraw-Hill, 1991) is a thorough, well-written coverage of DVI as it teaches basics of multimedia. At libraries, computer and book stores.

7. Multimedia Computing Corp. (MCC) is an information source on industry, investors, end users, offering: *Multimedia Computing & Presentations,* a twice-monthly report for industry professionals on market and product strategies; *International Directory of Interactive Multimedia Producers,* a guide to companies and persons producing computer-based multimedia; and

Multimedia Producers Legal Survival Guide. Multimedia: Achieving Competitive Advantage in the 1990s and Beyond, 2 volumes of market analysis: MCC, 3501 Ryder St., Santa Clara, CA 95051. (408) 737-7575.

8. *The Interactive Multimedia Association* (IMA) is at 800 K St., Suite 204, Washington, DC 20001. (202) 408-1000.

9. The *Multimedia & Videodisc Monitor* makes available a *free* sample issue and *free* catalog. Includes ample coverage kiosks, multimedia. Future Systems, Inc.: P.O. Box 26, Falls Church, VA 22040. In VA: (703) 241-1799. Out: (800) 323-DISC.

10. Tom Sheldon's *Windows 3.1: The Complete Reference* (950 pages), Osborne/McGraw-Hill. Read in business library or contact 2600 10th St., Berkeley, CA 94710. (800) 227-0900.

11. *Media Expo* is a 2-day annual multimedia show, sponsored by *MacWorld* and *Publish!* For information, contact Mitch Hall Associates: 260 Milton St., Dedham, MA 02026. (617) 361-8000.

24
Retail Marketing Machines

There is a big reason for the growing conviction that in-store kiosks can increasingly become profitable for quite a variety of products and purposes. The biggest cost in retailing is labor. There is now less employee time available to answer any question. Kiosks that are simple to use and provide desired answers fast are often welcomed.

As the cost of computerizing drops ever faster, automation of more retail sales functions will increase. Retailers will compete electronically in new ways to substitute for or to help employees increase their sales per square foot. John M. Kawula, president of the Point-Of-Purchase Institute (POPAI), says, "More and more retailers will use the advantages of interactive kiosks to overcome a worsening labor shortage, cope with consumer demands, and satisfy the demand for greater return on their in-store investments."

If you are in the retail business or if your firm manufactures, imports, or wholesales anything for resale through retailers, these trends of the 1990s directly affect your business:

- There are several million fewer retail employees.
- The remaining salespeople possess less knowledge of products.
- Real disposable income of most store customers is either flat or dropping.
- The cost per sale by in-store company demonstrators continues to rise.
- Average shopping time per customer has dropped 42 percent.

- The cost per square foot of floor space has soared.
- More retail competitors are willing to lose more money longer to gain market share.

Multiuse kiosks can help sell, save labor, do research, and get inquiries at the same time. This cost-sharing among functions requires less sales per kind of use. Chapter 25 will cover successful marketing in mass-market stores via low-cost shelf computers and a wide variety of other electronic media. In this chapter, we'll discuss retail success via more high-tech kiosks.

The following are retail kiosk advantages:

- Saves customer time.
- Can answer instantly the most-asked customer questions.
- Can demonstrate the uses of many products and services.
- Can show many models and colors not stocked.
- Can offer unique services otherwise unavailable.

A kiosk can often sell certain products and services better than a salesperson. A kiosk can teach new salespeople as it informs customers, help a salesperson sell more, and cut a retailer's selling cost. If the kiosk is linked to a central warehouse, it can inform customers and store personnel of the status of any order.

Smaller retailers often have the most innovative ideas for new applications of kiosks. Larger firms have the means, see the objectives more clearly, and generally analyze their business better.

Some in-store kiosk disadvantages include the following:

- Customers acquire the kiosk habit gradually.
- Constant incentives and promotion may be needed.
- To amortize large start-up costs may require many kiosks.
- Store personnel may resist working with kiosks.
- Breakdown of kiosks can be costly and annoying.

Stores want kiosks which save labor, are paid for by vendors, and create more sales overall per person and per square foot. Salespeople who receive sales incentives want them on kiosk sales or are allergic to kiosks. Store personnel who get no incentives want kiosks which reduce employee strain. Vendor marketers want kiosks which increase sales at less selling cost. Conflicting interests can prevent success. Avoid these additional causes of failure:

1. As in any marketing test, the product, its price, the timing of the test, the offer, or the presentation may be wrong.
2. The kiosk service seems unique to the vendor-marketer or retailer but has little interest to customers.
3. The kiosk service is desired and used by some but annoys other customers, most store personnel, or both.
4. Each kiosk sells or helps to sell, but not enough to justify the costs involved.
5. The kiosk service intrigues, attracts use, sells, or helps sell for a while. Then use of kiosk shrinks.
6. The presentation slows people up instead of speeding them through the shopping process.

Considering In-Store Kiosk Marketing

If your firm is a retailer with one store in a niche field with little traffic, you probably should not try in-store kiosks. If you have heavy traffic you should, if vendor-suppliers pay for it. Few retailers can afford to pay for kiosk costs and operating and amortization cost out of profits from increased sales. Usually it takes a combination of vendor money, labor cost savings, and profits from extra sales to justify the use of in-store kiosk marketing.

If your firm sells through large traffic retailers, you should probably consider kiosk marketing. But your product or service must respond to promotion, be appropriate for kiosk presentation, and have enough profit margin for the extra cost of kiosk marketing. Locations with less traffic need a higher average sale. Products which need explanation, demonstration, or advice in selection are more suited to kiosk presentation. No firm should test kiosks before careful research.

Researching In-Store Kiosks

Refer to sources on kiosks in the Help Source Guide for each chapter. Ask your trade association for case histories of in-store kiosk success in your field. Look through your trade magazines for mentions of in-store kiosks.

Go into other stores to look for kiosks which sell products you sell or to customers like yours. Each time you go to a store, supermarket, or mass market outlet, look at any kiosk. Look for those customers flock to, those which offer customers a unique service, even if it's in a field completely different from yours. It may provide you with an approach you can adapt to what you sell. Retailers have learned the following:

1. Marketing machines which help sell succeed best.

2. Kiosks require less sales versus expense if they also save labor, do research, get inquiries, or perform other functions for which cost can be shared.

3. With increased automation, more computers, interactive video, and other electronic tools can perform kiosk functions as well at little added cost.

The ATM Model

The automatic teller machine first served to save labor costs and to reduce bank customer annoyance at waiting on long lines for tellers. ATMs made fast banking possible 24 hours a day, 7 days a week. Once learned, ATM use was addictive. At first, mostly younger people, those better educated and more venturesome, used ATMs.

The first ATMs were stand-alone. But, soon, they were connected. The next step was for customers of one bank to use ATMs of another. Customers of both could get cash at more ATM locations and then make ATM deposits and use other ATM services. Later it became possible to change programming from a central point. Soon flexibility was added: Changes could be made here but not there. Then announcements could be programmed in, for several machines for a branch; or for all the machines of a bank in one area; or for all the machines of all the branches of all banks owned by a bank holding company.

ATMs Go Network

The ATM networks came first in a metropolitan area, then in a region, then in several. Banks joined local, regional, and national networks. Then networks began to exchange ATM use privileges. The ChemPlus ATM card works on NYCE, MAC, CIRRUS, or PULSE cash machines. The MOST system interconnects most Washington, D.C., banks. The New York Cash Exchange network of ATMs, NYCE, operates in the

New York City area and in the Northeast. NYCE became a member of CIRRUS, a national network. MasterCard owns CIRRUS; VISA-USA and 52 financial institutions own The Plus System.

Cirrus and The Plus System have over 70 million cardholders. About 75 percent of the teller machines in the United States belong to either network. Overseas, the two networks have thousands of ATMs and connect to ATM national and regional networks. Some worldwide banks have their own ATM networks. John F. Love, president of Faulkner & Gray, which publishes banking magazines, says: "We are rapidly approaching the day in electronic banking when all banks in the U.S., and all banks in the world, will be offering the same availability of ATMs."

ATM Habit Took 20 Years

To create the ATM habit took about two decades of the biggest expenditures in bank advertising history and a lot of incentives. This worked predominantly on an entirely new generation growing up, and cost far more than banks anticipated.

Most bankers say they cannot precisely quantify people savings or profits from ATMs but believe that they are now indispensable. A Citibank executive told me:

> The ATMs have made all the difference in the world to the branches. The percentage of those who use them is now substantially 70 percent of our depositors. Our newest models just out increase transaction capability per machine 15 to 20 percent. Installing more ATMs is increasing ATM use per branch another 5 to 20 percent.
>
> The ATM is one of the most important sources of customer satisfaction that we have. Each user of an ATM saves a very sizable amount of time. It's overwhelmingly the most popular service the bank has.

Joseph Boutin, president and CEO of the Howard Bank in Burlington, Vermont, told me: "We have 17 full-size ATMs and two cash-dispensers. We take five years to amortize a $30,000 ATM. Most of ours are over five years old and therefore quite profitable versus the same transactions in the bank. We've organized, with other banks, a statewide network of 55 ATMs."

ATMs Keep Improving

The Maryland National Bank earns nearly $1 million a year by charging a $2 fee for the use of an ATM that prints statements. Latest ATMs also print receipts and can interface with videodiscs. In pilot tests in Pittsburgh, Interbold-manufactured ATMs accepted, processed, and displayed an image of a check to convince the customer that the bank has recorded the deposit. Check deposits via ATMs increased substantially. Upgraded equipment can add newer features to older ATMs. Some ATMs dispense cash *and* coins.

How Kiosks Can Succeed

Vincent A. Wasik, the CEO, and John D. Livingston, the chief information officer (CIO), of National Car Rental, Minneapolis, are a unique team. Jack Livingston tells this story:

> We bought the company because we saw ways to make it more automated and make more money per dollar of sales than previous management. We wanted a better way to rent. We had the conception, even before takeover, of creating what we later called The Electronic Advantage and which so far has consisted of three different type services. We developed them one at a time and then kept refining and improving them.
>
> We first launched The Emerald Club, a frequent renter program. Each customer profile of information given when applying is online. For instance, the grade of car is usually specified. Also if a renter gets into an accident, the renter is responsible for the accident liability to the car unless the corporate member gets a waiver from National in return for paying an extra fee for each rental. The corporate member can also for an extra charge have personal accident insurance for each employee who has an Emerald Club card. All this goes into the electronic application, is barcoded right into the membership card and then printed out in a complete contract simply by inserting the card in a special card-reader at the National location.
>
> National provides additional member benefits. We have travel partners. If we are in a Northwest terminal we ask each member: "Did you fly Northwest?" If so the member gets credit for extra Northwest bonus points simply for renting from National. Our computer automatically accredits mileage for each of our marketing partnerships for car mileage of each of our members who belongs to our partner's frequent user program. To join we first charged $50 a year.
>
> To get members, we let our customers know. We mailed millions of car rental customers. We went into files for those who rented four or five cars or more a year. We promoted with mailings and telemarketing. Our ads primarily were to rent cars but they explained the benefits and availability of the club and how to join. We determined our breakeven point, the number of members we had to re-

cruit, and the ad cost we could afford to gain a member. Response was more than anticipated. We secured a sufficient number of members at a low enough ad cost to be within our budget.

Th next year, we developed The Emerald Aisle, which offered The Emerald Club members the capability to go to a location and select a car off-lot from a separate aisle of premium cars. The choice of cars was manual. The member could then put his or her membership card through a reader, have the contract printed out, sign it, present a driving license, be given the key, and drive away. All this could be done in less time than going to the counter.

The next step was to automate more by use of an electronic kiosk. Our first kiosk tested took over some functions formerly done manually. It was a standing unit with a customer representative and a booth and a terminal. The program was profitable, but we felt that our kiosk could do more. From the start, we wanted to create a better kiosk than our competitors.

We drew pictures of what we thought the machine should be. We wrote down what we needed and outlined our requirements. We identified the components. We went to Hewlett Packard in San Jose and told them what we wanted to build. They did. The result was Smart Key, our improved kiosk, which is speedier and less costly. We included a touch screen, a PC, a dot matrix printer, a modem, graphics, and an interface to do the key-dropping mechanism. Customers can choose cars immediately available from a touch screen. When a car is selected it goes into the contract printed out by Smart Key, which then drops the key for it. All we now need a representative to do is to make sure a person has a license and is sober. We can use a part-time representative to make sure the machine is not out of keys.

We started Smart Key in three locations. Customers were delighted. Before Smart Key, a car rental took three minutes. This was cut to 30 seconds. We asked customers "Do you like Smart Key?"One hundred percent said yes. We asked "How should we change it?" The answer overwhelmingly was, "Put it everywhere." We then rolled out Smart Key in a little over 18 months.

We used highly focused advertising such as *The Wall Street Journal, The New York Times,* and *USA Today.* Our agency, Chiat/Day, arranged for National to be the first advertiser to run island ads in the middle of the stock-listing pages to launch SmartKey as part of promoting The Emerald Club and The Emerald Aisle. Rather than using inflight magazines, we ran in travel magazines for business which reached corporate travel planners. The promotion included enclosures in the club newsletter to members near airports where Smart Key was installed, signs in airports and at the counters, and free publicity in the paper of the airport city, as well as ads in the same city paper.

Customers of The Emerald Club using Smart Key rent with 100 percent more frequency versus nonmembers. Four-times-a-year renters rent eight times a year. There have been other valuable, identifiable benefits to National. When someone uses Smart Key, it can ask: "Do you need your hotel reservations?" It can send your needs to affiliated hotels, get your reservation. It can do the same for airline reservations and tell you where to collect your tickets. And as we have increased member benefits we now charge $75 for membership in The Emerald Club.

We have two versions. The big Smart Key kiosk costs us close to $30,000. The smaller one costs us a lot less, more like half. The big version drops the key. The smaller kiosk doesn't drop. We now have 250 Smart Key kiosks with 50 more scheduled in 1992. We put in two machines or even four in locations where there is waiting on one. To avoid running out of keys, use of the machines is monitored.

On average, renting at National using Smart Key takes 60 percent less time versus competitors. We have already created—with The Emerald Club, The Emerald Aisle, and Smart Key—multiple millions of dollars of income we would not have had without them.

Why fail when you can succeed? Jerry Kelly is president of LTV Video Services, which operates the Laser Travel Network of Irvine. Jerry, who has created kiosks which have been successful for travel agents for the past six years, says:

The new untried was rushed into too fast. The most high-tech often cost too much. Custom manufacture was sometimes done when not necessary. Kiosks failed often because they were too expensive. There was not enough education of marketers in the selection of kiosk components and selection and creation of software.

I was a resort property manager. We created videos to market our resorts to travel agencies and used this method. The travel agencies liked what we did and I got the idea of creating a business to supply them with discs of cruises from various sources.

I have 400. Each unit has a Pioneer model IVD 3000 videodisc player. I supply videos of trips on laser disc and supply an intelligent key pad with which the travel agent can call up any video of any trip a prospective customer wants to consider. He or she can show a cruise promotion; show the ship; show a still, motion video, or an actual action video. The key pad is a controller. It is simple and very necessary, cost-effective, and user-friendly. The combination is fairly fast and adequate and only costs about $1500 a unit with no real development cost.

We lease the system to the agent for three years for $79 a month (about breakeven). We get over 70 percent renewals, at which point the income is our profit. We also from the beginning give the option to preview more videos on disc. About 80 percent of the 400, or 320, are actively renting more discs. We are a publisher. We have produced 40 videodiscs in three years. The average active customer takes 70 percent of discs offered at $24 each. This is excellent-profit

business.
The system doesn't sell. It helps sell and is very productive to the travel agent. One agency sold 64 people on a cruise at $2000 *per person* after a one-hour presentation to the group.
Probably a hundred people have called me to ask how to apply in another field what we have done in travel. My advice is to have knowledge of your industry, obtain full knowledge of the equipment and software choices, and know what you want to accomplish with your presentation. Most don't.

Salesperson Upgrade

Ron Palmich, IBM's director of Advanced Education Systems, says, "It's important that a kiosk assists the master salesperson; not replaces, but *upgrades* the salesperson; takes away the mundane, the less important; and releases him or her for the really important part of selling." Cosmetic companies have led the way in learning how to use kiosks to assist their in-store salespeople. In one application, the cosmetologist paints on-screen the consumer's face with a new makeup combination. The customer then selects one effect after seeing several. The cosmetologist would then put it directly on the customer's face. The process worked equally well for all age groups, skin types, and color, but took time—about 30 minutes, including the time to apply cosmetics.

Variations and additions included printouts of what the customer should do to make up, pictures of the customer with different makeup combinations the customer could take home and think about later, pictures of the customer at different stages and hues to see whether the use of moisture cream and so forth improved the skin. Microscopic photographs compared one month to the next.

Kiosk "Successes" Can Fail.   Elizabeth Arden spent a reported $1 million to create "Elizabeth," its makeover machine. Elizabeth stayed two or three weeks at a location. A single Elizabeth had terrific sales increases for Dayton-Hudson Corp. in Minneapolis and in Detroit. In two-and-a-half weeks in the White Plains, New York, Bloomingdale's, Arden sales jumped from number 5 to number 2. Three Elizabeths stationed in Bloomingdale's Short Hills, New Jersey, store averaged $5000 per day and more. Soon, 10 Elizabeths traveled the United States, apparently very profitably.

But Elizabeth had bugs and was a logistical nightmare. The kiosk was big and cumbersome, expensive and prone to break down, personnel-intensive, and expensive to move from store to store. Arden dropped Elizabeth, even though it was a sales success. But Elizabeth proved that a makeup-simulator kiosk could greatly increase the productivity of a skilled human demonstrator. A number of other cosmetic companies subsequently developed their own unusually imaginative kiosks.

Shiseido's Success from Arden's Failure. When the Japanese cosmetic company Shiseido developed its own makeup simulator, it made sure the Shiseido machine was smaller, lighter, and cost far less. That made it easier to move around, less personnel-intensive, and more breakdown-free. Shiseido scheduled its team of simulator demonstrators for fewer days per store. The average sale following a makeover on the Shiseido machine was three to five times normal, and repeat business ran about 50 percent. Shiseido used the makeup simulator for two years in every country it sold to in the world. Two simulators were deployed in each country, traveling only to the most important stores just twice a year.

Study Kiosk Methods

The way a kiosk proves profitable for one firm may not fit your business. Few kinds of products require calculating monthly payments or complex diagrams. If your product categories are common, they won't need long explanations. If you mainly offer quality and style, lots of interactive questions and answers about products may drive away customers. Customers want to find out what they want fast.

A really big advantage of a kiosk can be to multiply your store inventory with no extra space or personnel. Your kiosk can be the world's smallest store of your kind with the world's largest selection in the field. A small store location cannot stock the variety it can offer via a kiosk. Without a kiosk, if you don't have a particular style, size, or color in stock, you may lose a sale.

Retest in Different Ways. Be sure to test market a kiosk in each of the kinds of outlets your products are distributed in which are most vital to you—a leased department in a bigger store, next an independent dealer, and a company-owned store—in different kinds of trades, in bigger and in smaller stores, and finally in a saturation test.

The biggest failures have come from rushing full-blast after the first test. Expand from one to a few stores. You may then go to 50, 100, or over 1000, depending on your kiosks' success, your size, capital, and needs. Kiosk success doesn't come easily. But when it comes, success can usually be increased, with constant effort.

Kiosk Presentation. Ask kiosk marketers for the precise sales and profit figures from their use of kiosks. Some won't tell, but many will. Ask those who succeed with kiosks how much their development cost was, how much the prototype kiosk cost, how many kiosks were then made and at what cost. Ask how different the final approach was and how much extra it cost to test that approach. The cost of making the final change that makes the kiosk venture profitable can be a small fraction of the total cost.

Ask how much of the kiosk presentation's content was derived from successful advertising in any other form. Levi Strauss & Company tested kiosks shortly after spending $30 million, largely on TV, to promote its new "501" line of jeans.

Some TV commercials for Levi jeans had been very successful in Europe but had not yet run in the United States. These TV commercials used a music video format: fun, entertainment, dancing, and rock music. Snatches from them were intertwined with kiosk interaction to create the "JeansScreen."

Levi's target audience was male, age 15 to 24. The JeansScreen was an interactive catalog that seemed like a video jukebox; it entertained as it sold. Music videos helped locate styles and sizes. Band members wore the styles. They could be touched on the screen for more information on that model. Customers were guided interactively to all styles. The JeansScreen introduced other Levi jeans, jackets, and shirts for young men. Customers began to order more jeans featured via the kiosk. Much of the inventory shown on the kiosk was not in stock in most stores.

Gradually, more customers began to buy from the stores jeans that were not stocked in the stores. They could order whatever clothes they wanted to be delivered to their home or sent to the store and picked up later. Jeff Harlowe, who directed the kiosk campaign for Levi Strauss & Co., reports: "Our customers generally buy jeans in the same style and size all the time. So they normally don't try them on. We get many cash customers. They order on the machine, get a receipt, bring it to the cashier and pay. This has influenced the stores to then stock other jeans, additional sizes, color, and styles—once stores saw the proof of demand from the use of our kiosks."

Expand Cautiously, Measure Results.   Jeff Harlowe of Levi Strauss continues:

> After testing six JeansScreen kiosks, I then bought 50, redid the disk, and placed them in 50 locations for 12 months. Then I bought another 50. Results were excellent, even great. We were very pleased.
> We measured the effectiveness very scientifically. We matched test stores versus control stores. We put machines in one location and no machines in another. Sales went up much faster, about 20

percent faster on average than in the stores which did not stock the machines. We then increased to a total of 250 units. The kiosks have been a fine assist to retailers.

Orders via the kiosks which are paid to the cashier in cash are measured very accurately by simply counting the receipts. We don't use credit card readers. Many of our retailers sell Levi's exclusively.

From JeansScreen users, a database has been formed. Terminals are the front end of the order processing. They collect the data enabling the company to track all sales. They can also keep track of those who are just browsing through the system and leave their names for literature.

Ingenious In-Store Kiosk Services

Benjamin Moore & Company was the first paint manufacturer to supply a computer color matching system to its dealers. It consists of a spectrophotometer mated to a custom PC. This allows a customer to bring a color sample of any material into the store where it can be analyzed and instantly converted into a custom paint formula while the customer waits. The machine scans the sample and then prints out a formula, specifying a base paint and tints. It's a free service. Moore supplies it at cost to dealers. Over three-quarters of Moore's 3600 dealers have it. Now computer color matching is almost standard in the industry among top dealers, but Benjamin Moore is on its seventh generation of improved model.

Later, Moore launched Moore's Video Color Planner. It's a kiosk that looks something like an arcade game. In it are stored color photographs of several dozen home exteriors and interiors and all of Moore's 2000+ standard and custom paint colors. Customers can select the picture color scheme of their choice. They can then compare different color schemes to see what they like best. A color photograph of the customer's home can be scanned into the unit if desired. Often, customers use it with no assistance from store staff. Usually, it takes a skilled employee working with the unit to do all this and often a half hour time of the employee as advisor and the customer. The Moore sales representative is thoroughly trained to orient sufficiently the store personnel.

Do-It-Yourself Design Kiosk

Innovis Interactive Technologies, then a Weyerhauser subsidiary, developed the Design Center kiosk put into 400 home centers and lumberyards throughout the United States. A customer can design a deck, shelving system, or garage and see a color perspective drawing of the design, a construction plan, a complete materials list, and total estimated price. A print-out is produced in minutes, under the control of the salesperson.

A customer, answering questions from the salesperson, can "think aloud" about a desired project, not yet planned. The salesperson, via a trackball and a button, inputs the information learned from the customer. On the screen both see the deck being created in three dimensions and full color. The kiosk will show exactly how the project appears in final form, and look at it from any angle, including underneath the structure.

Retailers can input their own prices in the system, which can determine for each customer project the amount and cost of the material needed. If the price is beyond the customer's budget, the salesperson can suggest ways to simplify and save, feed in revised information, and show the revised project on-screen and then the revised quote.

In the first year, over $250 million of decks alone were designed on the system, and a very high percentage of decks that were designed were sold. Then garage and shelving capabilities were added. The Design Center can be purchased from Innovis. Some stores charge a $10 to $20 fee to buy the printout from the design center, applicable toward purchases.

I asked O&M Direct's Electronic Marketing Director Martin Nisenholtz, "What are the most innovative new retail kiosks with the most exciting success stories?" He answered: "The remodeled Delta Shuttle ticketing kiosks are very good. I like the Amtrak kiosks. In general, I like retail machines that serve a defined consumer need."

Kiosk Market Research

Many types of kiosks prove to be great research projects. Each unit gathers information created by each person who uses the kiosk. It generates reports and indicates preferences, such as which colors and at what price Levi's jeans sell best for various styles, materials, models, sizes, and accessories. All data are put into the computer as fast as the kiosk is used and are instantly available. The following is a summary of some key points about high-tech kiosks:

1. The easiest way to make money is in a store.
2. Upscale outlets need high average sale.
3. Success in upscale outlets often depends on a kiosk teamed with a great demonstrator.

4. Far wider product selection on kiosks than the store stocks often succeeds.

5. The cooperation of sales people is essential. Give them incentives.

6. Unique-service kiosks for a field often succeed.

7. Adding new features and adapting presentations may salvage failure or improve success.

8. Asking, observing, and learning from other marketers first can avoid much grief and greatly improve your chances of success.

Help Source Guide

1. Check with the editorial department of the following magazines for stories on kiosk case histories, read them in the library and buy special issues featuring kiosks: *American Druggist*, 60 E. 42d St., NY, NY 10017 (212) 297-9680; *Retail Week*, 370 Lexington Ave., NY, NY 10016 (212) 532-9290. See also *Women's Wear Daily:* 7 E. 12th St., NY, NY 10003 (212) 741-4361.

2. *ATMs & POS in Retailing & Finance,* by The Freedonia Group, assesses U.S. big-growth markets for electronic transactions via ATMs, point-of-sale (POS) terminals, related online EFT systems, more. Projects demand through 1995 to 2000. Profiles IBM, AT&T, Sears Roebuck, American Express, Diebold, others: Find/SVP, 625 Ave. of Americas, NY, NY 10011. (212) 645-4500.

3. *Barnard's Retail Marketing Report* is a newsletter: 25 Sutton Pl. S., NY, NY 10022 (212) 752-9810. *Product Marketing* is a magazine (women's cosmetics and men's grooming products): 343-361 Park Ave. S., NY, NY 10010 (212) 686-7744.

4. *Innovis Interactive Technologies* offers a *free* video, *free* information kit from a top production house for kiosk presentation: Park Center II-21, Tacoma, WA 98477. (206) 924-2900.

5. *By-Video, Inc.,* is a CD-ROM production house that offers a *free* information kit from this pioneer producer of kiosk hardware and software: 225 Humboldt Ct., Sunnyvale, CA 94089. (801) 645-8290.

6. Instruction Delivery Systems provides bimonthly publication, *The Magazine of Interactive Multimedia Computing.* Issues focused on include design technologies, digital audio, video & DVI, CD-I, CD-ROM. *Free* to qualified professionals. Also available is the *Special Issue Buyer's Guide*, dealing with interactive multimedia products, services. Communicative Technology Corp., subscriptions, 50 Culpeper St., Warrenton, CA 22186. (703) 347-0055.

7. R. Amend and M. Schrader's *Media for Business, 1991*, (246 pages) discusses effective media whatever budget, type of information. Gamut of business

and industry media uses includes: overheads and slides; slide and cassette programs; multi-image; film; videotapes; interactive video, print; also covered are advantages, disadvantages of media, production design, graphics, written by two professionals: Knowledge Industries Publications, 701 Westchester Ave., White Plains, NY 10604. (800) 800-5474.

8. Contact the *National Retail Federation* (NRF) re reports, audiotapes and videotapes of seminars on retail kiosks. NRF Business Services: 100 W. 31st St., NY, NY 10001. (212) 244-8780.

9. N. Iuppa and M. Wade's *The Multimedia Adventure, 1992,* combines audio, graphics, text, animation, live video, interactivity. Covers capabilities, use, production of interactive videodiscs, computer-based training, CD-I. Knowledge Industries Publications: 701 Westchester Ave., White Plains, NY 10604. (800) 800-5474.

10. *Truevision, Inc.* a pioneer in video image-altering to show customers future changes, offers a *free* info kit: 7340 Shadeland Station, Indianapolis, IN 46256. (317) 841-0332.

25

Mass Outlet In-Store Electronic Media

Kiosks, Couponing Machines, and Narrow Casting

Point-of-purchase (POP) advertising expenditures now exceed spending on magazines, radio and cable TV combined. Electronic POP consists of new kinds of mass promotion media in mass-market stores. Although there has been much failure to date in this type of electronic marketing, I anticipate more success in the future, but only for those who know what it takes.

Few large supermarket chains have not tried some forms of in-store electronic media. Besides supermarkets, many hypermarkets, superdrug stores, specialty stores, and discount stores have experimented with electronic media. Even pharmacies may have a health-info kiosk with a blood pressure testing machine with on-screen ads and a VCR with health info and ads. The in-store electronic media we'll discuss are:

Shelf computer kiosks

High-tech single-media kiosks

Simple single-media kiosks

In-store TV broadcasting

In-store radio broadcasting

Couponing machines

Electronic marketing in high-traffic stores ultimately may generate big rewards for marketers of mass appeal products. Most of these in-store media have a variety of applications, and some offer a great many. Some forms and applications evolve quite differently than planned. Many successes are unexpected, and some major hopefuls become surprise failures. Some failures have resulted from barriers which many feel will soon be overcome. In-store media's *coming* advantages include

- Many choices and very low entry costs for some
- More standard equipment with less development cost
- Hoped-for lower customizing costs and lower software cost
- Possibilities for testing your own display for short periods of time
- Availability of purchase of in-store ads just as other media are purchased

Simple, in-store electronic sales aids may become basic components of marketing for larger firms and low-entry marketing vehicles for smaller companies. Market testing may be done for far less, and a roll-out may tie up less money and be achieved more safely, tied to increasing store sales.

In-store media's present disadvantages include

- The increasingly bewildering multiplicity of choices
- Confusion of media claims versus results
- Big turnover of suppliers and consultants
- Rapid obsolescence of some forms
- After-purchase plummet in value of the medium
- Resistance of store personnel to some forms

It's tempting to include exciting new electronic displays or media in the marketing plan. Some advertisers have made major commitments to in-store electronic media without first testing them or even making a thorough investigation and comparison. Success can be prematurely assumed because sales results were not precisely measured. Any of the newest electronic displays and media could have unexpected drawbacks or bugs. The supplier may suddenly go out of business.

Your store salespeople may not like some features. Store personnel may unplug your displays or media, thus eliminating the in-store audience. Or your competitor may develop or find a dramatically improved version at a cost far lower than yours.

Considering In-Store Electronic Media

If your firm is a big-traffic retailer or sells promotable items through these stores, consider in-store electronic sales tools—but only very cautiously. Only the very best for your needs have a chance. Much of the cost of a high-tech kiosk (described in Chapter 24) may be for abilities you will never use. Or the kiosk may cost more than you can afford.

If you want the electronic abilities that cost the least and sell the most per dollar spent in-store, find out which kinds work and which fail in your field for your kind of product. Check stores for the latest entrants in the electronic sales and ad race. Observe which successes in other fields seem applicable to yours. Look to adapt those successes for your firm in ways that none of the present marketing methods can.

Analyze your present customers, their demographics and psychographics, your latest marketing methods and ad campaign, and those of your competitors. What media is now most profitable for you? And how do you use your spokesperson, product packaging, and point of sale display material? Study how competitors use in-store electronic displays and media in your field. Observe the kiosks and in-store electronic media each uses. Learn the detailed, hard facts of success and failure of each form.

Read in your trade magazines reports on the features, successes, failures, and even the bugs of the newest in-store electronic promotion. Look in the Help Source Guide of chapters 23 through 26 for the magazines, newsletters, and books that cover multimedia and kiosks. In them find the names of kiosk manufacturers and kiosk developers. Ask the marketing departments of the manufacturers for a recommended list of developers. Phone some until you find several familiar with your marketing field. Ask about their knowledge of failures and successes that might indicate your chances. See several and find one you trust.

If you fail in your first in-store electronic media attempt, analyze why. Investigate all electronic media failures and successes with different price ranges of equipment in mind, including the cost versus sales. Let's now examine what's in store for electronic marketers.

On-Shelf Computer Kiosks

Intermark Corp. is a display company that sells small, on-shelf kiosks using simple, interactive computers. A team of marketing, computer and electronics specialists, including computer professor Dr. Terry Countermine, invented a simple $400 kiosk for Intermark. The kiosk was computer-based, battery-powered, and used a liquid crystal display (LCD) screen. It was small, light, and interactive. The kiosk showed a series of questions which the customer was asked to answer using a key pad. The computer analyzed responses and displayed recommendations of appropriate products.

Intermark made its microkiosk the centerpiece of a shelf display system of surrounding items immediately available for purchase. This system was constructed in various shapes and customized for each manufacturer. The system had the excitement of an interactive kiosk. Its design could be integrated into packaging and display material, and its program did not need a salesperson's time. It was designed to profitably sell goods priced from $2 to $100—for the right marketer.

Noxell Corp., which owns Noxema and Cover Girl Cosmetics, was bringing out a new line of cosmetics called "Clarion." Clarion was higher priced than mass-market brands but lower-priced than most department store brands. As a new line, Clarion Cosmetics needed to win shelf space in chain drug stores and other outlets in order to build acceptance. Clarion could not afford the computer merchandising which had been successful in department stores. Intermark's price per shelf computer display came down close to $300 in Clarion's rollout quantities. This was after customization. It seemed ideal for placement in self-service drug stores and supermarkets where women couldn't get cosmetic advice. Clarion decided to go ahead.

The first step was a 250-store test *purely* to determine whether the marketing concept of the computer display for Clarion was on target. Once Clarion rolled out, both the print and the TV campaign focused on the computer display. It then built a saturation TV campaign around the display, made another 250-store test, and got prime in-store placement. The TV commercials showed how easy it was for a woman to ask questions on the computer and get precise answers on which cosmetics were best for her. The customer typed in the color of her eyes and the type of her skin. The machine immediately showed the base, blushers, eye shadows and lipsticks she should use. Customers felt that they were selecting colors right for their individual looks. The computer made her feel safe. She could reach for the right products immediately and put them in her shopping cart.

Clarion's interactive presentation capitalized on the color analysis which became well known from the book *Color Me Beautiful*. The shelf-computer display did, without a demonstrator, what some of the high-tech kiosks did for luxury cosmetics in department stores. It reached a brand-new public and they went for it. Retailers loved it. The tests were successful.

National Rollout

For Clarion, Noxell combined a $30 million TV campaign with satura-
tion national distribution. Noxell bought 20,000 more microkiosks.
These did so well it bought 2500 more for Canada. In the first few
months Clarion did over $25 million in sales. The next year, it did over
$70 million in sales, all built around the shelf computer. A year later,
Noxell sales were close to half-a-billion dollars a year. A significant portion came from Clarion. Debby Alfred, manager of corporate affairs at
Noxell Corp., reports:

> We keep a very close check of customers' reactions. We get tremen-
> dous sales benefits from our computer displays. They don't bring
> new people into the store. They bring more people in the store to our
> counter.
>   The same people buy more often, and more make multiple pur-
> chases. The store stocks more items. The original Clarion line had 85
> different items which we got a store to handle. The line now has 135
> units.
>   We constantly reprogram the computer displays with new mate-
> rial. Customers keep using the computer display, eager to see the
> newest shades and colors that we have and which of these are rec-
> ommended for their own situation.
>   Women see new recommendations, reach for the cosmetic and buy
> it. This induces the stores to widen the line. We increase product
> sales and get more retailers to put in more products.
>   When we introduce a new Clarion Skin Care line, we use the same
> computer to ask what you like in a color analysis and skin analysis.
> The display makes us more bilingual. We have a Spanish program.
> We have a French program in Canada. Each works as well.

By Noxell's fifth year using LCD kiosk displays, it had placed 57,000
of them—37,000 for Clarion and 20,000 for Cover Girl. Intermark's total
installations for all its customers were close to 100,000. Prices per LCD
unit had dropped to $150, then to $100, and finally to just $55 for the
simplest models, like the Cover Girl displays. Intermark achieved these
prices by simplifying the shelf computer combined with dropping component prices. Lower component prices were mainly due to simpler circuit board designs and better housing designs, which lowered labor and
assembly costs.

Variations of Shelf Kiosks

Maxell, for its line of audiotapes and videotapes, placed an in-store
shelf computer featuring questions and answers to help consumers se-

lect the proper blank tape. Likewise, L'Eggs Pantyhose Advisor shelf kiosk helped women select sizes and colors. In sales tests, it created panty hose sales increases of up to 40 percent, and was then put into 2000 outlets.

The Old World Automotive company used a shelf kiosk display for its SpitFire Spark Plug. The customer pressed a button to see a spark simulation of the SpitFire in action on the screen. By pushing any of four other buttons, an explanation came up on-screen, each for a different feature. Interactive audio messages explained more. The displays cost about $150 each.

Don't waste shoppers' time. Mass outlet shoppers are in a hurry. Half of all supermarket shopping trips are 22 minutes or less. The average superdrug store visit is 16 minutes. A shelf kiosk fails if it only attracts attention or gives an unwanted service, unneeded information, takes too long, or is frustrating to use.

Self-service store shoppers look for packages they recognize and brand names they trust. Although 78 percent of shoppers see some store displays, a shelf computer must be an integral part of regular packaging and display. The combination must give only explanations the shopper wants and can't otherwise get.

Fun Kiosks

A shelf kiosk that is fun to use has a better chance of success. Let's take a look at a few examples.

Microkiosk Games

LCD screens with interactive computer games are typically placed in mass merchandise outlets for four- to six-week promotions and in supermarkets for two weeks. Game cards are on-pack or take-ones and can be matched with what pops up on screen to see if the consumer holds a winning number. K-Mart in Canada has run "Scan & Win." By simply scanning in your PC code, a voice chip told you if you were the winner. You just went to the cashier to redeem your prize.

Also in Canada, Sunoco used an LCD screen microkiosk which features an interactive game. It functioned like a slot machine at gas stations. The promotion ran for eight weeks in an area and is reported to have attained a 25% sales increase. Sunoco rotates the promotion from province to province.

LCD screens are becoming flexible. By changing the artwork, software, and text, the same unit can be used for different promotions for one product and even for different products.

Single-Media Electronic Sales Help

Simple and low-cost single-media kiosks can be tested fast, and their use is often a good first step before jumping into a multi-media kiosk marketing program. Retailers often own the simple kiosk hardware and rent the use to vendors for very little cost or commitment. These retailers require only the marketers' proprietary software, which the marketer may already own for another purpose.

The most widely used in-store electronic sales help device is motion videotape on "perpetual" or activated commercial VCR. Next most popular are audio chips and sensors that are activated as you pass displays. Then come videodiscs on commercial players. Floppy disks on color PCs and now CD-ROM discs in PCs with CD-ROM drives are also spreading fast as display formats.

VCR Demonstrations

Some VCR demonstrations are rented for $50 a month each. L'Oreal perfume has created dramatic sales increases through VCR demos in supermarkets. And in its Junior's or Young Men's Department, Dayton-Hudson, the Minneapolis, Minnesota, department store chain has permanent monitors which play the latest music videos interspersed with customized messages.

Roger Hong Foods has also profitably sold Chinese seasoning with VCR demos, starting first in Seattle and then successfully expanding nationwide. Roger began his video career as a Chinese TV cook who demonstrated as he offered recipes. Roger warns of these VCR demo pitfalls to avoid: "We use it [the VCR demo] for an introductory period in some markets for a maximum of two weeks. After that, store employees turn it off. The repetition annoys them. We rest it and use it again later. This way, it's one of our tools (not the only one) which has gotten us national distribution."

In-Store VCR Networks

At least one and often a number of portable VCRs are in each of more than 100 Dayton-Hudson-owned department and discount stores. Each runs videotape on-screen at the point-of-purchase. Most of the video spots are provided by advertisers. The cost is only $15 to run your video for one week in one store, with no commitment.

On a larger scale, AdVision Video Merchandising Systems of Portland, Oregon, owns and operates a network of 4500 of its own model VCRs in stores throughout the United States, including some of the biggest mass retailers. AdVision produces commercial demonstrations and has furnished VCRs to over 117 clients, including a few *Fortune 500* companies and many small entrepreneurs. Clients have started video advertising in one or several stores. A video may cost under $2000 to produce, only several hundred dollars if it's an animated motion demonstration, or nothing at all if you already have your own TV or video demonstration.

Talking Displays and Products

Digital audio chips let products "talk" about what they can do. A display can invite you to push a button and hear a message about product features, a coupon offer, or a premium. Or a tiny, digital voice-chip may be hidden anywhere with a brief message to get you to look at a package and display. As you walk by a display, it may be activated to offer you a special. Or on the floor may be a pressure-sensitive mat, so that when you stand on it, the selling starts. Or if you open the freezer case door to reach in for an item, you may activate a special audio offer. Although high-cost kiosks often have trouble selling low-cost products, low-cost audio displays can often sell high-priced products.

Computer Disk Displays

In New York's Penn Station railroad terminal, the Montgomery Grant computer store has a bank of 15 color computers mounted on its wall, each running a computer marketer's demonstration disk featuring its advantages with constantly changing graphics but without sound. People watch carefully, compare, and ask store personnel for more information on a make and model desired. It is far more effective than a cardboard display, yet the cost of a floppy disk is far less and is the manufacturer's only expense. The PC is already there. The entire demonstration was created on the PC at the maker's office.

When the Staples chain of business supply and stationery super-discount stores introduced the Leading Technology PC, it placed a "header card" in a reverse L-shape on top and to the right of the Leading Technology PC screen. On-screen ran a floppy disk memo reinforcing the same advantages stated in the header card but in more detail. The screen was at eye level and flashed from one frame to the next. This electronic display (although not interactive) amounted to a powerful shelf demonstrator. And at the time, it was the only computer brand sold in Staples.

In-Store Electronic Ad Media

The marketing quandary with in-store electronic media is that although new kinds keep getting introduced and there's great overall growth, there's also a good deal of mortality among these media ventures. Each new in-store medium is usually 100 percent vendor-paid. Although some retailers own or lease equipment and software (and sell co-op ads to vendors much as they do for other forms of advertising), more often the equipment and software is owned by, and all ads sold by, a media company. Sometimes the two methods are combined. Types range from sophisticated multimedia kiosks to the simplest single medium.

These in-store media may present ads only or be combined with one service or several. Media may be placed at a cash register, a key point of sale, or throughout the store. Ads may feature incentives, such as sales, premiums, or sweepstakes, or product advantages, or both. Your commitment as a marketer can range from a number of months down to one or two weeks and may involve only one store at a time or a minimum number of stores in a specific area. The total cost can be hundreds of thousands of dollars and more, down to just $15 to $30 to run your own videos or audio in one week in one location for one store.

In-Store TV and Radio Broadcasting

An increasing number of supermarkets show 30-second commercial videos to customers who are waiting in the check-out line. Video monitors above aisles slanted down toward moving shoppers run video ads with specials. Some supermarkets have one monitor every 2000 square feet with a computer action, graphics presentation. There's no sound and only 15-second commercials. In each of many warehouse stores, one 8-foot-by-10-foot screen shows 50 percent advertising plus educational, entertainment, and public service messages.

The Check-Out Channel, the in-store TV network from Turner

Broadcasting, offers 2.5 minutes of commercials run in an 8-minute loop. It is a computer-animated ad network. CPMs are $4 to $5. Another in-store network, The Shoppers Video network, offers a $3.50 CPM and reports that sales went up over four times as much compared with shoppers buying the same products in stores not carrying the network. Research showed that 75 percent saw the Shoppers Video monitors and that on-shelf electronic ads had the highest recall.

The POP radio network is being piped into supermarkets and super-drug stores nationwide and reports a growing number of success stories for marketers.

Health Information and Ad Network

Stand-alone, computer-based kiosks called "Pharmacy Information Centers" (PICs) are being installed in pharmacies nationwide for consumer use. Each PIC unit has a collection of authoritative health databases compiled by leading medical sources, including a comprehensive medication file with descriptions and possible side effects of nearly 5000 over-the-counter and prescription drugs, by both brand and generic name. Consumers use the touch screen to call up the information on medical conditions, such as heart disease, cancer, arthritis, and diabetes, along with recent news from selected consumer magazines.

Pharmacists can design their own in-house ads, notices, coupons, or take-home messages. Two hardware configurations are available, for $3495 and $6995. National advertising opportunities are available on the system, and over three dozen major companies have successfully participated on PIC units. Advertising can be national or retail in scope.

Ron Kline, marketing manager of Bausch & Lomb, says, "If a specific group of stores has an older demographic, for example, we can focus more on general eye care and discuss an issue such as 'dry eye.'"

PIC printouts (in regular or large type) allow consumers to take a copy home of whatever they wish from the system. In its first four years, there have been over 10 million look-ups and over 6.8 million kiosk printouts. Wal-Mart found that sales for products advertised on PIC went up an average of over 20 percent versus the same products in control stores without PIC. At the time, there were over 30 PIC advertisers and more than 600 kiosks in place.

Look for specialized national kiosk media networks in other fields in stores. Perhaps any field that can support a big circulation magazine has national in-store kiosk potential.

Video Preview Kiosks

Since movies began, the biggest promotional tool has been the movie trailer of the next scheduled film. Various efforts have been made to provide a movie trailer, catalog counter kiosk for video stores via videodisc. Usually the kiosk is high enough for good visibility of a color screen. Below are miniature video jackets for each selection. Each is backlit. A touch on any jacket brings the sample video on screen.

Home video movie companies also sponsor the showing of videos, but only make available B movies and movies over 90 days old. Despite this, a 10-month test of MusicLand and Sam Goody audio/video stores indicate that sales increased 29 percent.

Various video-selling kiosks have failed. More are being tried. Survival and success will require supplying more and better movies and possibly a number of videodiscs in order to become a true super-catalog of cassettes. Choices available on special order can also be included.

In-Store Animated Sign Networks and Direction Kiosks

In-Store Advertising, Inc. has several thousand stores carrying its electronic signs. These signs are 5-foot long LED electronic billboards hung above aisles. Each runs an animated company message. It's not interactive and there's no sound, but scanner data analysis showed an increase in product movement of up to 195 percent on products ranging from motor oil to iced tea mix. *Fortune 500* marketers have jumped in as advertisers.

Rick Smith created exciting kiosks for Giant Supermarkets in Pittsburgh and then formed InfoSmith to do the same for supermarkets nationally. One InfoSmith kiosk module for supermarkets creates a store directory. Customers touch a computer screen to be directed to the location of the product they're looking for. The kiosk lists over 750 products and categories, which can be customized for each store. The kiosk becomes a bulletin board, saves time for the customer, and enables advertising to be inserted.

The Advertising Video Wall

The advertising video wall is a full-color, spectacular, ever-changing billboard, with or without an audio channel. It consists of row upon row of video screens. Each is part of a giant screen yet with the intensity of a small one. There may be fewer than five screens to a row, with five rows, or many more screens. Usually video walls feature 15-second or 30-second commercials and editorial features.

The New York City Abraham & Strauss department store has featured three video walls. Bloomingdale's has featured a wall of video for Vive La France. A 48-foot screen played clips of the lush region of Poitou-Charentes and featured footage of the Tour de France, French sporting life, and the native foods and wines of Provence. The video wall of Dayton-Hudson (D-H) Department Store in Minneapolis features a constantly changing cycle of advertising and customer-service programming. Vendors pay D-H $1500 for a 30-day run of a 60-second spot, for an average of 3,000 repeats of a program.

Caution! A video wall can be a spectacular conversation piece. But the measurement of in-store, passerby audience and those who stop and watch is just beginning. Proven CPMs of viewers and case histories of sales versus cost are still lacking. This may soon come.

The Couponing Kiosk

It may become as universal as the ATM and a bigger marketing success. The couponing kiosk should soon have its biggest success in supermarkets. Here's why. Coupons given and redeemed at point of sale can create extra sales with little persuasion. Sixty-six percent of all purchase decisions are made in the store, 53 percent of all grocery purchases are unplanned, and 89 percent of shoppers shop without a shopping list. But despite huge sums invested and many kinds of coupon kiosks tried in retail stores, the big breakthrough is still being promised rather than delivered.

The cheapest shelf computer kiosk with a rudimentary printer can create coupons. Some kiosks show on-screen product coupons or lists of items and coupon values offered. When the consumer touches, the kiosk prints out each coupon. The buyer purchases the item and presents the coupon to the cashier.

Some supermarkets have reported kiosk coupon redemption of 15 percent to as high as 35 to 50 percent. But thus far volume has been too small, with too few outlets in one area for any one type of coupon kiosk to dramatically succeed.

Combining Media and Couponing

A high-tech couponing kiosk can be both a media kiosk and a couponing kiosk. It can offer a sweepstakes game, give coupons for answering research questions, and perform other unique and appealing services. Supermarkets keep trying different types of couponing kiosks, including those at the checkout counter, staffed or not, where a voice offers instant refunds, premiums, sweepstakes, and other discount programs.

With frequent shopper programs, regular customers are offered a card with an identification number. This ID number, along with the customer's name and address, is stored in the store's computer. Each shopping visit, the customer hands the card to the checkout cashier, who inserts it into a computer. This adds the total of the day's purchases to a cumulative total of all past purchases by that shopper. As this total hits certain levels, the shopper gets rebated or receives more coupons or other specific incentives. A chain store may quickly get hundreds of thousands of frequent shopper program members—and large gains in market share.

Coupon Targeting and Tracking

With some kiosks, as soon as a shopper touches the screen to get a coupon for a desired product, the kiosk also issues an extra coupon for a tie-in product. If a peanut butter coupon is selected, an extra pops out for jelly. An advertiser who sells diapers can have a special offer printed out every time a shopper buys baby food. Or a manufacturer can arrange to automatically print out and issue a discount coupon to those who bought a competitor's brand.

Eighty percent of coupons have barcodes which indicate the discount level and the issuing source, whether it's an ad in a specific issue of a magazine, a mailing to a specific list or a kiosk, or whatever. These codes can be read by a scanner. The other 20 percent are keyed to be read by humans. Kiosks with scanners which read coupons can redeem encoded coupons.

Some computer-based kiosk systems can scan, verify, redeem, and void bar-coded coupons at the checkout register. Some also produce reports of coupons issued versus redeemed. More elaborate kiosks can track coupons issued versus redemption in a number of stores locally, regionally, or nationally.

Some kiosk systems can merge household purchase history and demographics of frequent shoppers to build purchaser profiles. A kiosk can segment more specialized lists, such as people who buy hot cereal, have two children with both parents working, separately eat out but often rent video movies. Soon a packaged goods marketer can be more scientific than a direct marketer.

This type of in-store kiosk can become a personalized marketing mailbox, popping out coupons for the products most wanted by each person. Big purchasers of any type of item can be offered a special incentive to buy still more in that category. Sometimes promotions can be integrated with electronic funds transfer, check approval, and electronic cash register tapes. The kiosk will tell management exactly how many coupons have been redeemed and how many recipes printed out and report on other interactive activities. These kiosks are sometimes sold to the stores, but the kiosk maker usually coordinates for the stores the sale of the advertising over the system to vendors of each store.

Three-in-One Kiosk

It issues coupons, performs a service, is an ad medium, and can provide a store directory. Shoppers can also access information about check-cashing policies, film developing, and video rental.

The Rolling Microkiosk

"VideoCart" is a 6-by-8-inch LCD videoscreen, mounted on the handles of shopping carts and programmed to run commercials when the cart passes shelf space of advertised products. Electronic "triggers" call up, from the unit's memory storage, the suitable message. A 10-second commercial flashes on just before the customer walks past a product advertised. VideoCart claims a 33-percent average increase in sales for products it advertises. This is based on a sample of scanner sales data. A touch of a button creates paperless coupons at the store shelf containing the product. The coupon value is given to each shopper when the item's barcode is scanned.

VideoCart displays continuous news, information, and even games. It emphasizes shopping information instead of entertainment. Advertising is sold on a category-exclusive basis, for a CPM of $3 versus a CPM of 3 to 37 cents for normal displays in the store over the course of a year. Research has shown that 22 percent of shoppers see shopping cart ads.

Some marketers say coupon kiosks are too complex, cumbersome, and expensive. Others feel that efforts to strip them, simplify them, and cut costs have made coupon kiosks less satisfactory to use. Many feel that the success of couponing kiosks is inevitable but that to succeed some type of couponing kiosk must be very widely distributed and very heavily promoted, perhaps for a long time.

Martin Nisonholz, head of the New Media department of Ogilvy & Mather Direct never stops studying kiosk change. I asked him the following questions for you and here are his answers:

Keeping Up with Change

Q: Is in-store supermarket electronic ad media growing?

MN: It's growing fast.

Q: What are biggest new success stories traced and proven of users of various forms of in-store electronic media?

MN: ActMedia's coupon machine and that of Catalina Marketing.

Q: What is your opinion of the future of frequent shopper clubs in supermarkets—and how will new technology affect it?

MN: Loyalty programs will continue to grow. My view is that "Instant Off" promotions work best. The mega-scale Citicorp-type ventures have fallen off for the time being. I think the industry is more focused now on retailer-driven approaches to consumer loyalty.

Q: How successful has the new Nintendo kiosk been in the 1800 locations placed? Are its competitors into kiosks?

MN: All major videogame companies have demo machines on-site. It's difficult to say how important the demo machine is in the total scheme but I'd say that trial at the point-of-sale is fairly critical in this market.

Q: Do you see a future trend in the toy industry to design products and kiosks together?

MN: The dominant trend in the toy business today is building toys on successful TV or movie characters. So integration with a number of new media technologies will happen as these media proliferate.

Electronic kiosks, displays, and media in mass stores are in transition. Don't be left out or left behind. Serious efforts to study what is being done and continually "supergrade" your know-how may put you and your company ahead of most of your competitors. Keep spot-checking stores from your first market test through rollout. Talk to customers and store personnel. Measure point-of-sale results precisely versus cost. And act accordingly to drop or change your programs and hardware.

Help Source Guide

1. *ActMedia* pioneered and now leads the in-store marketing field. The company's many products include POP radio, aislevision, shelf-talkers, coupon machines. Ask for information kits desired. 301 Merritt 7, Norwalk, CT 06856. (203) 845-6000.

2. *Advanced Interactive Video, Inc.* (AIV) offers a *free* video and a *free* information kit. The firm produces video kiosks, organizes in-store networks. Ask about latest research, projects, case histories: 909 West 5th Ave., Columbus, OH 43212. (614) 464-2777.

3. *AdVision Video Merchandising Systems* provides in-store TVCR networks, offers a *free* video demonstration and a *free* media kit and rates: 2420 S.E. 11th Ave., Portland, OR 97214. (503) 234-1234, (800) 678-8770.

4. Ask re latest articles on in-store EM, kiosks in the following magazines and read them in the library or buy latest special issue on them: *Advertising Age* and *Electronic Media* are both at Crain Publishing (Chicago, NYC) 220 E. 42d St., NY, NY 10017 (212) 210-0100, (800) 992-9970; *Premium/Incentive Business* from Gralla Publications (latest articles on in-store premiums, couponing via EM, kiosks), 1515 Broadway, NY, NY 10036 (212) 869-1300.

5. *Intermark Corp.,* which makes shelf computer kiosks offers a *free* information kit, case histories, various types of electronic displays: 475 10th Ave., NY, NY 10011. (212) 629-5777.

6. *Pearlson Development Corp.'s Interactive Systems Division* established 1992's first low-cost interactive multimedia kiosk for standard video and computer design components. To request information kit: 8960 S.W. 87th Ct., Miami, FL 33176. (305) 598-3018.

7. *Point-of-Purchase Advertising Institute, Inc.* (POPAI) sponsors an annual trade show with many EM exhibits, reports, audiotapes, videotapes on in-store EM. Ask for POPAI's magazine articles on in-store EM and kiosks, read them in library and buy the latest special issue on them: 66 N. Van Brunt St., Englewood, NJ 07631. (201) 894-8899.

8. *POP Radio Corp.* is a subsidiary of ActMedia Corp., providing in-store ad network and *free* media kit and rates. Ask about latest research, case histories: 301 Merritt 7, Norwalk, CT 06856. (203) 845-6000.

9. *Site-based Media Inc.,* of the Shoppers Video Network offers free media kit, rates. Ask for latest research and case histories: 369 Lexington Ave., Suite 1500, NY, NY 10017. (800) 252-5646.

10. *VideoCart, Inc.* offers a *free* media kit, rates, research, success stories on shopping cart TV: 300 S. Wacker St., 3d fl., Chicago, IL 60606. (312) 987-5000.

11. *Kiosk Infoware Development, Technology Applications Group, Inc.* offers information on SAM authoring systems, multimedia courseware development, knowledge center CBT courseware, MECC education courseware: 1700 W. Big Beaver Rd., Suite 265, Troy, MI 48084. (313) 649-5200.

26

Electronic Marketing Machines in Public Places and Trade Shows

Wherever people gather in big numbers, public access kiosks will follow. Despite many failed experiments over two decades, the numbers and kinds of electronic kiosks successful in public places have grown in:

Airports	Fairs	Public shows
Bus stations	Hospitals	Sports Events
College campuses	Hotels	Theme parks
Convention centers	Malls	Trade shows

A public kiosk can function entirely on its own, or it can be staffed. It can offer a single service, several combined services, or many. Some public kiosks originally designed for in-store use are later adapted to public access.

Advantages of public kiosks include

- Larger audience potential than in most stores
- Wide variety of locations and demographic selections
- The kiosk can be adapted to different jobs and audiences

You can market to only wealthier people via kiosks located in luxury hotels, to younger men at sports events, to mostly women in the main halls of malls, or to families at theme parks. You can reach blue-collar people at bus stations, suburbanites at commuter stations, and business executives at convention centers. You can also reach those with special interests and hobbies at public shows catering to them. Your software, hardware, and peripherals can be designed for or modified to a specific audience type, including even the probable time available to the user of your kiosk.

Some kiosk disadvantages include

- The attraction of fewer customers than strangers
- All the difficulties of outside selling
- Busy, tired, impatient, or indifferent passersby who may be poor prospects
- Difficulty in completing a sale
- Extra management skills required for determining kiosk location and presentations

Although your customers often visit kiosks to buy (and may be disappointed if there's nothing new to entice them), strangers must be attracted strongly to use a kiosk offering a product or service they don't know. They are less likely to be convinced to buy. They may stop at a kiosk and even interact with it but not really understand the offer or have a real need for it. Every type of public kiosk has its shortcomings as well as its advantages.

Yes, public kiosk marketing makes sense, but only if you do your homework and plan to crawl before you walk. Before you invest in any form of public electronic kiosk, carefully read the previous kiosk chapters and all the chapters referring to videos, floppy disks, and CD-ROM. Certain kinds of public kiosks can be among the first types of kiosk you should consider, whereas others should be among the last. Some should not use kiosks at all. Let's analyze them one by one.

Direct-Marketing Public Kiosks

Kiosks that solicit inquiries, complete transactions (or both), or are sales assistants to salespeople are direct-marketing kiosks. Why? Simply because they all capture a name and address, thus allowing your company to market directly to that individual. The transactional kiosks can sell single items or several, or contain entire electronic catalogs.

Of all the types of public kiosks, the transactional kiosk has had the greatest failure rate. But some unique, innovative transactional marketing machines do succeed, sometimes after enjoying success in retail stores.

In-Bank ATMs Go Public

Consider the ATM, which has enjoyed a broad, long, and successful history as a public transactional kiosk. Now ATMs can be found on train platforms, in hospitals and airports, and even on college campuses. Joseph Boutin, CEO and president of the Howard Bank in Burlington, Vermont, told me:

> We had a branch on the campus of the University of Vermont with five employees and one ATM which cost over $200,000 the year before we gave it up. We replaced it with four ATMs but no bank building. We had an inexpensive promotional campaign of some ads in the college paper and incentives offered to ATM users—red stars which could win gift certificates. The first year we made over $20,000. Deposits hardly dropped and then grew.
>
> I believe we can expand this. We give students a credit card. A student could apply by ATM via a computer terminal with software I want to try. We can now add a laser printer and a phone and combine printouts of requested information with the availability of a human voice at the main office to answer any question. I believe in a combination of ATM, POS unit, modem for computer, and phone-in action center. I'd like to set up self-service bank branches like self-service gas stations, with an office for one personal banker. I hope to also test a set of unmanned ATMs with phone access to a human voice at a full-service branch. The same use of ATMs can grow area by area.

Citibank has opened The Financial Center, near Grand Central Station in New York City, staffed from 7 a.m. to 7 p.m. with investment consultants and tellers and 20 Citicard 24-hour banking machines which also accept cards of the Cirrus ATM network connecting with 55,000 ATMs in 20 countries.

Public ATM banking may have no future limit. Meanwhile, probably 90 percent of ATMs are still within a bank or are "through-the-wall" for use after hours. ATMs have also become important teaching and habit-creating machines that ease and speed the use of electronic kiosks in any field, particularly public, transactional kiosks.

Fax Kiosks

The first public kiosk success to rival the combined public and in-bank sales for ATMs may be the fax kiosk. Hotelecopy Fax-Mail Inc. offers 24-hour fax service at 80 percent of the hotels with 400 rooms or more. It pioneered fax kiosks and other related kiosk services. In most hotels, Hotelecopy operates business centers and offers fax-mail boxes. In close to 500 locations, the centers are unattended, which requires more sophisticated (and more expensive) equipment.

Hotelecopy offers 24-hour secretarial service via kiosk. Just touch the "help" button, then word-process on the keyboard or dictate by phone. Within two hours, your document comes back in fax form or a letter-quality printout. Hotelecopy also features a frequent fax club with discounts. The same kiosk also sells airline tickets. Just fax the cities you want to fly to, when, and from where. A dial-it system faxes back your options. You then select your flight by fax and get confirmation and where to pick up your tickets by return fax. Hotelecopy is in 2300 locations, including airport clubrooms and lobbies and even 263 post offices.

Public fax is growing as fast as public ATMs in their early years. Fax kiosks may become a comparable success. Success may be even more clear-cut because each fax kiosk is judged on its own to a greater degree. The success of each ATM is intertwined with the operations of the bank which supplies it. If the U.S. Postal Service expands its use of HoteleCopy fax kiosks to 30,000 locations (as expected), and the same pattern follows in other public places, fax kiosks may rival ATMs in numbers of locations.

Other Unstaffed Transactional Kiosks

Other unique unstaffed transactional kiosks include

Kiosk-delivered airline tickets.   They save traveler time, airline labor cost, have a higher than average order, attract repeat customers, and are successful.

Phone connection.   The Bell of Pennsylvania Customer Convenience Center is a transactional kiosk that allows college students to apply for new phone service at the beginning of the semester. They get their new phone number on the spot from the kiosks; at the end of the semester, the kiosks can disconnect at their request.

Help for home movers. Ryder Truck Rentals created kiosks to help supply its customers with maps of the area they're traveling to, packing instructions, and even local mortgage information.

Change of address notice. The U.S. Postal Service's "Postal Buddy" computerized address-change kiosks are being placed in 10,000 post offices, and in grocery stores, shopping malls, military bases, and a university. A catalog customer or magazine subscriber who is moving can type in his or her new address just once instead of filling out numerous written notices. Customers can also order new subscriptions or catalogs. Companies pay $500 to participate and 30 cents for each name.

Phone service demonstration. Indiana Bell, N.Y. Telephone, and other phone companies use interactive kiosks in malls. Each has a videodisc-based Direct Order Answering System. The kiosks promote and demonstrate any custom-calling service feature or plan requested by a touch. Upon selection of the desired new services, your charges are computed and a date of installation is provided.

Transactional kiosks often fail for these reasons:

- They offer staple items that are widely available elsewhere at lower prices.
- Too-small profit margins don't pay for the kiosk's cost.
- The interactive demonstration takes more time than the passerby has.
- Average sale is too low to create the needed volume.
- Customers resist putting credit card or bills in kiosk.
- Lack of ad promotion or poor presentation defeats sales.
- Poor targeting or poor planning produce too costly a kiosk or one with bugs.

Other hurdles to negotiate include the fact that buying via transactional kiosk is usually the last kiosk habit to be created and that to succeed with unique kiosks can take a cumulative investment far beyond small entrepreneurs. Moreover, kiosk catalogs take more time than a passerby has unless he or she is waiting for a later departure in an airport, bus, or railroad station. Because of the higher demographics of air travelers, airport catalog kiosks continue to be tested. One day they should work. Keep checking.

Unstaffed Inquiry Kiosks

It is easier to get a lead via a kiosk than to complete a sale. But even just getting quality leads or enough of them can be hard.

Unstaffed, public kiosks as lead-getting machines for different kinds of financial services often have had the same problems. Kiosk development cost was too great. Lead volume was too small, and lead quality was often poor. Most such projects failed. Now that kiosks cost less, targeting is more easily done, and there are more success patterns to follow, so projecting successful tests is easier. But doing so still takes thorough research and planning.

Staffing Public Kiosks

The public kiosk which assists a human to make a sale has a far better chance of success. A growing trend is to integrate a kiosk within a public display booth as part of other attractions. These range from celebrity appearances to how-to seminars, live demonstrations, and sampling.

The kiosk may involve complex multimedia presentations or the simplest single medium. At some booths, you can make a purchase. At more, you can request more information. At many, you can be referred to the dealer nearest to the booth or to your home. Within a mall, this can create business immediately.

For Clairol, a kiosk showed on-screen how a woman looks with different hair colorings. The Clairol coloring specialist worked with the machine. She became the star. The kiosk was her helper. She photographed the customer with a broadcast-quality video camera. She moved the image electronically on a color monitor with a light pen, creating up to four looks. They could be shown on-screen at once in quarter sections. A range of different colors could be displayed. A customer didn't have to dye her hair to see how she would look. She could make her selection immediately or take the pictures home, show others, and come back later to buy the hair coloring. She also got a printout by mail by leaving her name and address.

Lily Mahlab, then vice president of sales and marketing for Intermark, reports:

> Clairol's interactive display was called "Colorvision" and was elaborate, sophisticated, and very compelling in a category where fear (the fear of making hair coloring mistakes) can make or break the sale. There was one setup with three or four terminals which were all housed in a custom design exhibition done specifically for mall tours. It had quite an effect and became a very major promotion that ran for nearly six years.

The software and hardware investment was substantial. However, it was always quite a spectacle and tapped thronging traffic in each super mall. Women made appointments for makeovers. People crowded around the display whenever shown. The kiosk and demonstration was a magnet to this vast traffic and attracted a far bigger audience than any demonstration within any store.

But it was salespeople who convinced individuals to purchase. The kiosk was a sales assist, not an effort to take the place of the salesperson. It was a micro store in the mall, always with salespeople. Cumulatively, it was like an ongoing world's fair exhibit.

It went, as a traveling show, to a hundred malls. Clairol got an incredible amount of PR from it. It drove customers into the stores in the mall and created sales at a profit. It was a continuing ad campaign for Clairol, more targeted to key prospects than any single medium including TV.

Malls have proven to be the best public locations for both big electronic kiosks (when teamed up with master demonstrators) and for small, simpler models (as sales assistants in almost any kind of product display booth).

For years, automobile companies exhibited their new models on a circuit of airports, railroad stations, sports events, fairs, and malls. It was not a big step to include an electronic kiosk in these traveling exhibits. Buick, Pontiac, and Ryder Truck have used kiosks in malls. The kiosks travel around from mall to mall, always with a highly trained person or persons. The kiosks satisfy, by providing lots of information, the inquiries of huge numbers of people. Kiosks assist and save a lot of time for the master salesperson.

To interact with Buick's traveling information kiosk, you only needed to push a few buttons to get answers. This aroused interest and desire to talk to a Buick representative, who was right there. Each wore a Buick blazer, and was polite and friendly. The Buick representatives gave more information to everyone who approached them and carried the preselling process further, even to help them contact their closest Buick dealer.

Big Mall Traffic

The International Council of Shopping Centers reports that, in a typical month, 174.4 million adults shop at malls. In fact 70 percent of the adult population shops for an average of 34 minutes at the big regional malls an average of 3.9 times per month. They learn about, interact with, and look for products and services. At malls, kiosks are great lead-getters.

People prefer getting information from kiosks as well as talking to sales-people *before* making a buying decision. Their names can be forwarded to dealers and follow-up checks can be made regarding eventual sales. *Good Housekeeping* magazine licenses the use of its name to big exhibits which travel from mall to mall. The NBA and CBS Sports also have had similar arrangements. Each exhibit stays two to three days at a mall, usually taking over the entire main hall.

Scott Lange, who as a consultant and marketing executive has pioneered many electronic mall kiosks for clients, says:

> Almost every big sponsor exhibit features video monitors. Many use sound chips. Quite a few have interactive kiosks. One idea for CBS Sports was an interview with a local sportscaster. Prompted by video, the consumer asked sport questions while on camera. Then he or she see themselves on screen asking the question combined with the answers of the local sportscaster.
>
> Another mall kiosk idea was "Teeth-Tac-Toe," a kiosk game for Listerine tooth paste. Another was "Harvey Hardwood," the talking tree for the American Hardwood Association, using a digital recorder. "Test Your Charisma" for Chevrolet was a kiosk game. The Diamond information Center used a Scan N' Win game.
>
> Scan N' Win games typically involve interactive product demos, video presentations, interspersed with live exhibits. The Scan N' Win merchandising video and display kiosk features graphic panels, video, "take-one's," and other literature. Shoppers entering the mall are given game cards and take their cards to the Scan N' Win display of the participating sponsor, listen to a 30-second commercial, and learn if they have won a prize.

Mattel's Hot Wheels brand cars used a kiosk in 25 malls in connection with the Indianapolis 500. It featured race video clips alongside a track where children could race Hot Wheels cars. The NFL Super Bowl's 25th anniversary tour included historical video footage in its mall presentation. And CBS Sports has toured with a "mallwall" of sports events.

Kiosk Lead-Getting

A kiosk must produce leads at a cost comparable to other media. (This cost per lead should include promotion, kiosk operation, and amortizing the investment.) Leads also must be qualified enough to be closed at a similar rate to those of other media. If the kiosk's lead cost is low but closures are poor, drop the kiosk project or alter the sales approach.

The kiosk's authoring system should be flexible enough to permit changes to the offer and presentation simply, fast, and at little expense.

The software presentation must be experimental at first. Now you should find the right mix of attracting people to use the kiosk while qualifying these people to screen out worthless prospects. Decide on your goals: the number of inquiries each kiosk should produce; the percentage of conversion to sales by the method or methods used; the average sale; and the number of follow-up sales.

Test-Market First

Follow the rules of direct marketing. Create software to attract passersby to access. Tempt those who do to find out more. Convince them step by step, qualify their interest, and persuade them to respond. To select a location for your kiosk, study passerby traffic counts and research the demographics of the traffic. Naturally you want those people with the demographics and psychographics most like your customers. Test your kiosk in one location for enough days or weeks to get 500 to 1000 leads.

Give these leads only to your own people or to one dealer or sales group who believe in your program and who will follow up the leads effectively. If your lead cost is low but conversions to sales are poor, qualify more in your presentation. If your lead costs are high and conversions to sales good, attract prospects more aggressively and qualify less stringently. If results are poor, abandon the project. If successful, make secondary tests to secure several thousand leads and forward them to the appropriate salespeople.

Expand with Caution and Trace Results

Even the biggest companies with the largest dealer or sales networks can fail in rollout campaigns with kiosks that have been successful in tests. The leads may be followed up improperly or not at all. In one case, only 10 percent of dealers followed up on the kiosk leads forwarded to them. The second year the company itself sent out literature to the leads. This produced walk-ins and phone-ins to dealers, requesting a demo. Gradually the dealers and the dealers' salespeople began to follow up on the kiosk leads as well.

Small firms, with fewer dealers or salespeople, may find kiosk lead-following easier. Both big and small companies must orient all concerned before each step.

The same inquiry-getting kiosk can be profitable in one location and a waste of money in another, or its success may swing from one presentation versus another. A public kiosk may be profitable for a period but drop off in results thereafter. The length of time a kiosk is productive may vary by type of location. Testing and measuring the results of each test amounts to a small part of your overall kiosk investment of money, time, and effort. Yet this evaluation can determine the best of several kiosk methods, or even the kiosk's very survival.

Use all the measurement tools available to you. Persuade your dealers and salespeople to do the same. Computers can match names of everyone who inquires via a kiosk with those of every buyer or at least with those who send in warranty cards. A percentage of conversion from inquiry to sale can be determined. Ad cost per lead and per sale traced to kiosks can be calculated. Each lead-producing kiosk is one part of your overall promotion. But the results of each kiosk can be measured scientifically.

Kiosks in Trade Shows

Many booths in trade shows include some form of electronic display. A practical and profitable kiosk form exists for most trade show situations for even small budgets and firms. It can often be rotated to a number of trade shows. A videowall can be spectacular. A unique high-tech kiosk can be the centerpiece of a multibooth space and launch an exciting new product or line. Constantly changing computer graphics, motion photos, or action video can attract many new customers.

Consider first the simplest, easiest, and cheapest marketing machines. Sound chips that activate when a passerby pauses can draw him or her up to the booth. Interactive PCs can answer questions and animate charts to help salespeople convince prime prospects. Video demonstrations help close sales. If you have created the simplest winning kiosk to sell your product through retailers, there's no better way to demonstrate the kiosk to dealers. If you have already market-tested the kiosk and have sales figures to prove its power, build a presentation and perhaps a video to show how profitable it has been.

Ogilvy & Mather first explored public access kiosks for clients as diverse as General Foods, Ryder, and AT&T in the mid-1980s. I asked O&M's Director of Electronic Marketing, Martin Nisenholtz, "Can you cite some kiosks you have created primarily for use at trade shows, and what success required, with some results?" Martin replied,

This is an area of kiosk development that has had real success. Last year, we created a kiosk for American Express designed into an exhibit booth aimed at minority recruitment. The kiosk provides a range of good information about Amex, its corporate culture, employee benefits and career opportunities. Kiosks like these tend to succeed because they can be fielded without massive investment and serve specific, clearly identified needs.

Some company-involvement PR kiosks include the following:

- Brooklyn Union Gas public kiosks can be used by anyone or any firm moving into Brooklyn that wants to apply for customer service.

- In their headquarters building in Chicago, Quaker Oats placed a cylinder-shaped kiosk with the graphic design of a Quaker Oats cereal canister.

- Ogilvy & Mather created Ogilvy-on-Line, a touch screen which featured agency and client news, new TV spots, and video interviews with various executives.

Kiosk Market Research

American Airlines uses a videotape-yourself kiosk booth to get feedback from passengers who have just stepped off a flight. Comments range from complaints to suggestions to thanks and praise. The reactions are used to help the airline's advertising copywriters and could even lead to a candid TV testimonial.

Many companies use interactive kiosks as a form of interview. A big share of kiosks produce much more marketing research data as a byproduct. Often this helps justify the cost of developing the kiosk.

Other Kiosk Uses

Direction Kiosks. In huge arenas— whether they're used for shopping, entertainment, sports fairs, theme parks, or airports—people need to know where to go, what's where, how to get there, and even where they are. The direction kiosk has touch maps to show where you are, where you want to go, and how to get there.

Travel direction public kiosks tell you how to go from one theme park to another, from one city to another, and from one part of a city to another. The same kiosk often becomes an ad medium for restaurants, hotels, airlines, car rental firms, department stores, and gift shops. Local networks of such kiosks may soon be part of larger local and regional kiosk networks. More editorial features will probably be added to these public kiosks.

Travel Kiosks. Local networks have emerged with kiosks in multiple locations joined together. Networks have begun to expand to more cities. The user demographics of individual kiosks are determined by where each is located: Convention centers get executive travel prospects. First-class hotels get business and first-class travelers who want local buying information.

The newest travel kiosks put information on screen in 1½ seconds. If you're interested in a restaurant, punch in the kind of food you want and the part of town you are interested in. Press more buttons to receive information on each restaurant's menu, whether it serves alcohol and has entertainment, and what you should wear. Push another button and pick up the kiosk's phone. Then call the restaurant toll-free and make a reservation.

Mall direction kiosks are expanding into community bulletin boards of present and coming events. A simple, effective use is a combination bulletin board and community "paper" for the stores within the mall. For a small cost, a mall store can advertise. A vendor, sending its representative to demonstrate, can advertise the event on these mall community kiosks. The kiosks can presell the audience for higher conversion to sales.

It's a service to let patrons get more out of the mall and not miss anything going on. Ask the kiosk what is on—from what is on sale at which stores, to if a famous author is autographing books, or if there is a demonstration of cookware. The kiosks will let you know.

Expo Guide. One very effective use of electronic kiosks has been as a guide to a huge fair. IBM has installed as many as 80 units throughout the grounds of a world's fair. Each interactive kiosk is a guide for the entire fair. Each has touch-screen technology and is able to communicate in different languages. Installations become a combination of a newspaper and a magazine about the fair.

Super Sports Event Kiosk What makes this interactive kiosk program solely devoted to a "super" event truly super is its *huge* electronic file background material. These kiosks usually tell what you want to find out about each event before you watch it. You can call up by touch screen the world record for any competition, get the information about the stars of today and yesterday; plus find out history and nostalgia. Such kiosks are beginning to run advertising from car manufacturers and computer companies.

College Info. College USA kiosks are in high schools with a combined enrollment of over 1.5 million. These kiosks offer students interactive videodisk information on 600 universities and 4000 colleges, including messages about career opportunity and financial aid. Students complete response cards with the names of colleges from which they want catalogs and return them to College USA. Every two weeks these names are forwarded to college admission offices.

Blood Pressures. The Health Monitor Center Kiosk gives anyone a 45-second blood pressure reading free while seeing ads. Three advertisers share sponsorship of one kiosk. Bausch & Lomb lens cleaner and Actifed cold pills also have sponsored kiosks.

Mall Kiosk Networks. Via their interactive, multimedia platforms, mall kiosk networks may include a directory of mall retailers, their locations, and a summary of mall events. But they may also offer a selection of coupons to encourage users to answer consumer research questions. Usually the kiosks can be programmed with video, animation, still photos, and audio. Up to a 35-inch screen projects 30- and 60-second TV commercials four to six times an hour during store hours. Some static versions just flash out messages. Behind it may be up to a 40-inch × 50-inch back-lit advertising display transparency.

Media kiosks have several or many sponsors. Ads may refer users to nearby stores or to outlets everywhere. Some ask for direct response.

Videowalls (see Chapter 25) are increasingly becoming mall ad media. Combination ads are being offered in videowalls and on kiosk screens. Variations of these networks are in airports and other public access locations with the biggest traffic.

Turnover of these media companies is high. Check *Electronic Media* magazine for the latest entrants, talk to them, and check with their advertisers. Only negotiate when you find success from someone who is selling to customers similar to yours.

Help Source Guide

1. *American Automatic Merchandiser* magazine offers to qualified marketers *free* copies of latest stories on new, future kiosk trends, vending: Johnson Hill Press, Fort Atkinson, WI 53532. (414) 563-1732.
2. *A. V. Workshop* is a pioneer renter of videowalls, mainly for trade shows.

Free information available re uses, specs, costs of videowall equipment: 333 West 52d St., NY, NY 10019. (212) 397-5020.

3. Ask about latest stories on profitable use of kiosks, EM media in the following magazines. (Read issues in library and buy special issues.) *AdWeek:* 49 East 21st St., NY, NY 10010 (212) 529-5500; *Inside Media:* 911 Hope St., Six River Bend Center, Stamford, CT 06997. (203) 358-9900.

4. Herb Jamic, of *Jamic Industries,* is a design consultant, vending expert offering advice on constraints, latest status, and future of kiosk vending: 7 Oak Knoll Dr., Wallingford, PA 19086. (215) 565-2772.

5. *International Council of Shopping Centers,* of the ICSC Marketing Institute, will provide information re reports, audiotapes, videotapes on mall direction kiosks, and other mall EM kiosks and media: 665 5th Ave., NY, NY 10022. (212) 421-8181.

6. The *"International Market for Hand-Held Terminals"* (297 pages) is an MIRC report that forecasts, 1987 to 1997, applications specifics and identifies key technical trends, fast-growth market segments: FIND/SVP, 625 Ave. of Americas, NY, NY 10011. (800) 346-3787.

7. *Shopping Center World* magazine has articles on success stories of mall kiosks and other mall EM media: 6255 Barfield Rd., Atlanta, GA 30328. (404) 256-9800.

8. *Telxon* offers a *free* information kit on handheld computers for sales research and tabulation: P.O. Box 5582, Akron, OH 44334-0582. (800) 321-2424.

27

Direct Broadcast Satellite Business Television Marketing

Direct Broadcast Satellite (DBS) business TV is a unique way to market to TV audiences that never existed before. DBS TV can reach across the United States or the globe—through events, programs, and networks that deliver audiences comparable to many business and professional magazines. In short, DBS business TV provides new opportunities for marketers who never before used TV. This chapter will explain how to tap into this new electronic medium.

Priceless help for much of this chapter has come from Elliott Gold (publisher of Telespan's *Business TV Guide*), who then kindly edited what you will now read. In five years, business TV grew from about 200 hours of programming a year to over 30,000, with over 100 networks and over 10,000 programs available and has kept growing. Some of the biggest U.S. businesses are setting up their own satellite communications networks. There are over 100,000 sites with dishes to receive DBS business TV, including thousands of motels and hotels nationwide.

At home, the viewer accepts free broadcast TV programming in return for interruptions by ads. Business TV started with and is dominated by paid business and professional education. Programming is not viewed for entertainment but for the help it gives. It is seen during work hours by busy, successful, top leaders and upwardly mobile employees.

It shows how to do jobs better and faster to help advance careers, enable firms to save more money, sell more goods, and make more profit. Programs that don't help deliver more savings or productivity per dollar spent fail.

A standard DBS business format is a seminar which, in one session, packs in more participants than a traveling seminar reaches in a year (without the travel cost). Two hours of real help will be intently watched and win product and company loyalty from exactly those you may need most to sell. Sales can be faster, bigger, and more easily traced than with your present marketing methods.

How Business TV Works

When Ted Turner created The Super Station he bounced his TV signal from a studio via an uplink (transmitting antenna) to a transponder (channel) on a satellite 22,300 miles above the earth. The signal was sent back to earth by the transponder, picked up by a downlink (receiving antenna or dish) of cable systems, and sent by cable to cable system subscribers. Business TV works the same, but the signal goes not to cable systems but from DBS to business TV downlinks and then to sites owned by or available to businesses.

Two kinds of satellites, C-Band and Ku-Band, use different frequencies. Most satellite TV is C-band (requiring an 8- to 14-feet-diameter dish), but most business TV is transmitted via Ku-Band, which is received by 6- to 9-feet-diameter dishes and is far less expensive and much easier to install. On the ground, the TV signal moves via cables from the downlink to a standard TV set for viewing.

Business TV usually offers one-way video. But in many cases its broadcasts are live, which allows viewers to call in and ask questions of the people speaking. This usually is done by placing a phone call to the number flashed on the screen or by writing the question down and giving it to a "site facilitator" who phones the question in. Some questions are immediately chosen from those called in and answered live during the broadcast.

Some of the many DBS business TV advantages include

- Immediacy! DBS business TV offers instant impact and has interaction.
- It goes anywhere—satellites cover the globe.
- DBS business TV reaches select groups committed to being receptive.

- Business TV is cost-efficient to reach big, niche audiences.
- It provides an information-hungry environment.
- Business TV offers the power of personal persuasion without the travel cost.
- Business TV subscribers pay for you to "sell" them.

Business TV's unique impact comes from combining audience participation with audio and visual communication. Studies show that people who see, hear, and discuss a message retain 75 percent more than people who only read it.

Most *Fortune 500* companies understand, use, and value accepted training methods for their top professionals. Business TV marketing is an extension of business TV training. Executives and owners as well as middle and lower management and salespeople don't have to leave their territories for business TV marketing or training.

Some of business TV's disadvantages include

- Entertainment-dominated programming rarely succeeds.
- Commercials unrelated to programming seldom work.
- Hard-sell commercials are resented and usually fail.
- Just as on a radio talk show, few callers can be answered.
- Business TV is poorly suited for most products advertised on standard TV.
- Used improperly, business TV can be counterproductive for anything.

Business TV is not meant for personal pleasure, relaxation, or escape. Nor is it for those who respond to a general shopping commercial or any impulse item—even one that the same viewer might consider after business hours. Most efforts to sell or persuade or even entertain the viewer that do not contribute career help are not only ineffective but deeply disliked.

Business TV Costs

An uplink to transmit a message can cost hundreds of thousands of dollars if to a C-band satellite or about two-thirds as much to a Ku-Band satellite. Satellite time can be $700 an hour. Each downlink that connects a C- or Ku-Band satellite to individual receiving sites over the United

States can cost under $10,000 to install. Each individual receiving site may cost under $3000 to install. If a firm has franchises, dealers, or distributors, each branch may pay for its own dish, or costs may be shared. You should be able to quickly earn back all DBS costs in extra savings or sales. Check all costs—they keep dropping.

An uplink to a Ku-Band satellite to transmit data only, not video, can cost under $10,000 to install. More sophisticated technology raises the cost of downlinks but makes satellite transmission cheaper and capable of sending color, voice, and more kinds of graphics and broadcast video as well.

Companies can produce and originate their own specials from their own TV studios or from rented public, private, or commercial TV facilities. Business TV programs are either broadcast live or taped and rebroadcast. Organizations can see the programs if they have the proper receiving equipment and subscribe to business TV channels.

Financing arrangements for business TV ranges from small cash expenditures to multimillion-dollar extravaganzas. For example, a retail chain may organize a network and contribute the location and on-the-spot staff but offer little cash. Instead, co-op advertising paid for by vendors contributes the difference. This may be as little as several thousand dollars a year for each vendor. To produce a one-time event with in-house talent can cost from $3000 to $10,000. An event or program can be put on an independent network at an hourly charge without setting up a network. A 30-second message on an existing program can be bought for as little as $150. A star-studded spectacular can cost over a million dollars.

Considering Business TV

If it's suited to you and your company's background, abilities, and resources, you should consider business TV marketing. Here are ways it may be good for you:

1. If you're a retailer, wholesaler, or distributor, you may be able to participate in DBS networks that are paid for primarily by vendors. Or, for a small initial expense that's quickly retrieved in savings or sales, you may be able to organize and create a network largely at vendor expense.

2. If you're a manufacturer or importer of consumer products, you may be able to participate in DBS networks of a big retail chain and profitably sell far more to the chain. If your company is big enough, you

may be able to set up your own DBS network with the help of many dealers.

3. Whatever your firm size, if you make or import products or services which advance professional or business effectiveness (and you demonstrate how best to use it), you can sponsor an event, program, or message on an *independent* network.

A good first step is the Help Source Guide at the end of this chapter. Among the sources listed, it's important to read *Telespan's Business TV Guide*, a program guide and newsletter. Although education use gets heavy coverage, there is plenty of news on the latest DBS marketing successes. The *Guide* lists producers, production firms, DBS conference room companies, and the latest new networks. It's vital to view business TV programs and sample-view business TV networks.

Investigate subscribing to a network in your field or advertising on its network. Consider sponsorship of a simple one-time event. Talk to networks and producers, ask to view programs at a site or conference room, send for and study videos of successful business TV. The following sections describe different kinds of business TV, how they've evolved, and provide examples of successful projects.

Different Kinds of Business TV

Satellite Updates. Traditionally, attending seminars was the standard way to update career knowledge in any field. Then, seminar audiotapes provided many of the advantages of being there, then videotapes offered far more. But a DBS seminar provides still more benefits because it's instant, can be taped, and is a fraction of the cost for everyone to attend the on-site seminar.

The U.S. Army Logistics Management College (ALMC) now trains officers at their home bases, via a national business TV network, at one-quarter the previous cost. National Technological University, one of the highest-rated postgraduate engineering schools, trains almost all its students by satellite at sites where they work. Hospitals first built up seminar video libraries and then subscribed to DBS seminars to update doctors, surgeons, and staff in many areas.

Customer Education. To Texas Instruments (TI), customer education is the key. It organizes free "satellite symposiums," which are vast global meetings covering areas of intense interest in which TI is pioneering new developments. These bring together world-recognized authorities (including TI experts), who discuss a subject in depth. Al Bond was the video manager in charge of the project. He reported:

> Our symposia on artificial intelligence and computer-aided systems engineering are global. We ran a seminar on artificial intelligence worldwide to 65,000 people at one time, with two-way communication. We presented some of the greatest authorities in the world who explained and then answered questions. We do this regularly. We use business TV to reach customers and prospects as well as staff. We organize training sessions. We want our programs to be educational experiences. We want you, the customer, to learn about this technology and design it into your business. So when you need the hardware, perhaps you'll think of the people who taught you how to use it.
>
> We introduce new products. It's a great door-opener for our sales force. We have case histories of traced success. We communicate directly with our customers and inform our entire sales force about a new development within an hour. It's tremendous.

TI's success has inspired many adaptations, including one for Converse, Inc.

The Converse Basketball Clinics.   Larry Holman is an entrepreneurial adman. From the TI series, Larry got the idea to swap advice in the sports and hobbies fields, in exchange for providing product loyalty. Questions would be called into the program through special toll-free telephone circuits. He named his business "TeleClinic." His first application was for a basketball shoe manufacturer, Converse, Inc. For them, Larry developed and is the producer of "Converse TeleClinic," a big hit.

Larry says that the key to the concept came from the Converse stable of professional basketball players and college coaches, all of whom were stars to basketball enthusiasts. These pros were already endorsing Converse products and making featured appearances for them. Now they could give advice on a national scale.

The first Converse TeleClinic used DBS and was conceived and produced in about six weeks. The second one still was DBS but this time had the benefit of nine months of promotion. Some cable systems "cherry-picked" the satellite feed at the request of local coaches and with the blessing of TeleClinic. The Learning Channel (TLC), which has a wide audience, rebroadcast the entire Converse TeleClinic to cable systems, prompting a deluge of viewer requests for videotapes.

The third year, the TeleClinic program consisted of ten of the greatest basketball coaches of the past decade giving advice on improving every aspect of one's performance. TLC took over cable distribution. Invitations to cherry-pick the program out of TLC's regular schedule went to each cable system in the United States. TLC was able to place promotion for the event in cable guides and other widely distributed publications. That year, there was an audience of between 25 to 50 million—mostly viewers on cable. Roger Morningstar, from Converse, Inc., says, "For the huge audience and goodwill gained, our two-hour basketball TeleClinic cost us less than we would have paid for a 30-second commercial during a Final Four game on the same weekend."

The fourth year, TLC ran the Converse Basketball TeleClinic in primetime. Although it became an all-cable event, TeleClinic started as a one-shot, small-scale business TV investment via DBS. Larry Holman advises:

> The foundation of all sales and marketing is information. Companies have more information about their products than their clients or prospects, but until recently the best TV had to offer was commercials or tokenism. Both are poor, insufficient processes for communicating good information in substantial chunks.

A Vital Information Link. Merrill Lynch uses its DBS network to help brokers help clients by providing up-to-the-minute news or research reports which may affect investment decisions. Merrill Lynch often introduces new products to the field on its business TV network. Merrill Lynch has spent over $1 million on just one DBS TV special event that was viewed by 50,000 Merrill Lynch customers. After this event, Merrill Lynch hosted a seminar on the latest tax changes to select groups of its customers gathered in its branch offices. Over the next month, approximately 30 percent of the attenders made investments. Marilyn Reed, Merrill Lynch vice president and manager of its DBS video network, said, "We did a study of offices that had the DBS teleconferencing exposure versus those that had none. We found that those viewing DBS programs felt that DBS had helped them increase their knowledge of production information, marketing strategies and product support."

In one controlled test, branch offices on the network achieved 30 to 40 percent higher sales than those who got the information by conventional means. Sales results like these convinced management to expand the network to over 400 sites.

Business after business has experienced similar business TV success. When Hewlett-Packard Company first used a telecast conference to announce a new product, it cut its product introduction costs substantially. The very first broadcast of the Xerox Education Network (XEN)—a private television network that uses the latest satellite technology—facilitated a large sale of Xerox copiers and duplicators which amounted to over $2 million.

On another occasion, Xerox Engineering Systems (XES) in one day launched eight complex new products. A week before the introduction, XES delivered (via XEN) two detailed product training telecasts with one-way video and two-way audio to its sales force. At the end of each of the eight product segments, viewers were given tests to see what they had learned. The result: The sales force had a basic understanding of the products and were ready to write orders the moment the new products were announced publicly.

Iacocca via Satellite.   For Chrysler Corporation, Hughes Aircraft Systems built a giant DBS network linking Chrysler headquarters with more than 5000 auto dealership and corporate sites in North America. The network consists of a central communications hub at Chrysler headquarters at Highland Park, Michigan, and remote terminals at Chrysler/Plymouth, Dodge/Dodge Truck, and Jeep/Eagle dealerships. Chrysler's new model launch became its new DBS network's first big assignment. Three satellite transponders delivered simultaneous feeds from the three respective Chrysler divisions to customers invited to the dealerships. It was the biggest DBS production to date.

The 23-minute TV program turned the new cars into stars and was co-hosted by star sportscaster Bob Costas and Olympic skating star Dorothy Hamill. The biggest star of the show was Lee Iacocca, who delivered a special message direct from corporate headquarters. After the show, dealer salespeople followed up by contacting both attendees and nonattendees via postcards and by phone. Responses were tracked according to various kinds of information, including the impact on sales and whether special incentives paid off.

The Chrysler DBS network continues to orient its dealers to Chrysler's latest marketing efforts. Tom McAlear, director of Marketing for the corporation, says:

> We have 5000 dealers. While our field reps call on each of these dealers periodically, it is physically impossible for us here at Detroit to be in real contact with each individual dealer every time we launch a marketing program. We do meet with the associations or the association presidents. But with our satellite TV network, we can reach everybody—our dealers and our field staff—instantly with the same message at the same time.

Within hours after new marketing programs are approved, Chrysler can have its dealers briefed with an explanation of how the new program works and the visuals that can be used in the program. Not to be outdone, General Motors is linking its 9700 U.S. dealers through the world's largest private satellite network.

Retailer Co-op Ad Network. Most ComputerLand dealers are franchised. Contracts require that each franchise maintain high standards and top-grade, technically proficient service people. Service and salespeople of all ComputerLand outlets must be trained continually regarding new products and product upgrades.

ComputerLand became interested in business TV, but its dealers were not willing to invest in it heavily. Al Maggio, ComputerLand's Television Production manager, found the solution:

> We talked with some of the big hardware and software vendors in the industry. They agreed a network was a good idea, but said they certainly weren't willing to pay for it. Next, we thought about a subscription operation. We considered charging our franchisees about $500 per month.
>
> We prepared a presentation for a group of our franchisees, and we produced a video conference. They loved it, they thought it was a wonderful idea, but they said they certainly would not pay $500 a month for it. We went back to the drawing board and came up with a more tempting proposal for franchisees and vendors. Enough agreed to get started.

The result became ComputerLand Learning TV (CLTV), a DBS network with 440 sites at stores. ComputerLand pays for the network equipment and overhead cost. The stores each pay a small fee for the system. Each vendor pays production costs of, or supplies program material for, a 20- to 30- minute program concerning its products.

Education is key to CLTV's strategy. CLTV fully trains franchise personnel. The two-way employee network airs before and after closing time each day in each store—to educate each salesperson and to answer any questions about a product. It saves stores the expense of sending personnel to seminars.

Two-way seminars also aid customers in the use of equipment they bought. Vendors train both customers and staff, plus update them on the latest models, peripherals, and software. Stores get add-on sales and upgrade old customers to more sophisticated product. Vendors run special programs to introduce new products. Two-way seminars are run for prospects during store hours. Stores telemarket for three weeks before each seminar to bring likely customers into the store.

CLTV helps ComputerLand management orient its salespeople and to get more sales from bigger business firms. ComputerLand does this by installing dishes in the offices or plants of customers who buy certain minimums and trains their personnel via CLTV.

There are marketing benefits to CLTV. Vendors offer ComputerLand store personnel incentives to sell specific items. Marketing Vice President Al Maggio explains:

> NEC-IS, the printer company, offered a two-week paid vacation for two in Hawaii when they showed our sales force a new printer. We got 225 calls from the 100 stores on the line.
>
> Oki'data (another printer company) formerly ran off-site seminars. To attend on average cost $1500 per person. Oki'data asked on our CLTV for registrations for a free CLTV two-way seminar and got 250 responses. This saved the stores $375,000.

Vendors now save the cost of sending personnel to conduct seminars at stores. They educate stores, customers, and prospects to their lines via CLTV. Stores, customers, and ComputerLand all save.

View and Buy by Satellite.   If you sell to big retail chains whose buyers use DBS networks, your firm's participation may increase your sales. Sears Roebuck and others have expanded the use of their own DBS networks to display new merchandise to buyers and managers.

The first year after J C Penney launched its DBS network, it saved $5 million in its buyers' travel costs. William R. Howell, chairman of J C Penney, said:

> DBS has altered forever the way we do business. We use an exclusive J C Penney direct broadcast television network between our buyers and our store management. Currently 812 stores are equipped to receive the broadcasts. The system provides one-way video and two-way audio, so that questions and comments from the stores can be addressed during the broadcast.
>
> With this new technology, buying procedures that used to take weeks have now been cut to days and sometimes even hours. The SONY Still Image System allows the transmission of highly detailed color pictures between Dallas and each of our overseas offices in only four minutes. Any can then be put on our DBS network.
>
> The result has greatly enhanced our response to new trends, reduced turnaround times, and increased the flexibility of those involved in the buying process. And of course, the system lets stores tailor merchandise purchases to local preferences.

Prior to DBS, the buyers would commit in the wholesale market for what they thought the stores would want. The stores would order from the buyers what they thought they could sell. When these two independent decisions didn't match, the result was unwanted merchandise creating large wholesale markdowns.

Now, the buyers show their recommended assortments over DBS, and stores determine the amount they plan to sell. Buyers make the wholesale commitment based on store orders. As a result, wholesale markdowns have been virtually eliminated.

More recently, we've set up research centers at selected stores in 16 major markets across the country. Consumer panels are invited into the centers to view a live satellite broadcast or videotape featuring samples of our new items.

The consumers are carefully screened in advance to assure right demographics. If children's merchandise is being tested, the panel might be restricted to mothers and their children, age 6 to 12. This prescreening results in highly reliable data.

While viewing the samples, the consumers are asked if they would buy, probably would buy, or not consider buying. They answer on PCs and their responses are electronically transmitted to Dallas, analyzed, and summarized in a market research report that takes 2 to 3 days, instead of the usual 3 to 4 weeks required by focus groups or mall interviews.

This allows our corporate buyers to edit and improve the selection of merchandise, based on direct consumer input, prior to the direct broadcast to store merchandisers. In effect, we're determining consumer preferences in advance, before merchandise commitments are made.

DBS Creates an Industry

Superior Live Stock Auction, Inc., sells entirely by TV auctions direct by satellite. Each auction is usually at the Superior office and studio in Fort Worth, Texas, or Brush, Colorado. The auctions (a combination of live auction and a super video) are usually conducted on Saturday mornings with no cattle present. Instead, camera crews go to the sellers' ranches and videotape the cattle offered.

At the studio, the auctioneer and an audience of cattle buyers start the bidding process. But previously registered viewers also may bid by phone. So that all phone bidders can get through, Superior leases 25 telephone lines.

Superior auctioneers are among the best in the world. And their camera crews are trained to come up with shots from every angle desired by the world's shrewdest cattle buyers. Tape editors select the very best of these shots. So, as the prize cattle prance down the runway, the camera zooms in so close it shows (to trained eyes) each desired feature and any possible flaw.

Prospective buyers are first sent by mail a printed catalog with detailed descriptions of each lot sold. An hour before the auction, there is a DBS preview. Also, a two-hour DBS preview runs in prime-time Thursday evening. This amounts to a video catalog, giving detailed, audio description of each lot as it is shown. Bidders can videotape it and review it carefully.

Superior Auction, Inc., holds sales 26 times a year with as many as 1000 buyers registered for each, and has sold as many as 110,000 cattle in a single auction. Devon Bailey, associate professor of economics at Utah State University, stated in a *New York Times* interview that Utah feeder cattle received 50 cents to a dollar more per hundred pounds when sold by video—as much as 1 percent higher than average. He believes the "video cattle" got higher prices because more buyers bid.

More than 300 Superior representatives work with the diverse buyers, each equipped with a satellite dish and bidding by phone. There are over 80 additional satellite auction room sites, each with a dish for buyers who don't have one. Superior gets a 2-percent auction fee and gives two-thirds of it to the local representative working with each buyer. Superior promotes the auctions with radio spots and trade publications. Local representatives advertise in local farm media. Spots on each TV auction promote the next one.

Buyers or sellers no longer need to spend time and money to travel to auctions. And continuing Superior promotions entice more ranchers to offer cattle for DBS auction and more buyers to attend the DBS auction. It's a hit show. Agricultural manufacturers buy commercial spots that run even before the preview begins.

Superior President Jim Odle comments:

> We are the prime describing tool of auction cattle. Last year we made, via 26 DBS auctions, about two-thirds of all DBS cattle sales. We see an unbounded future in video cattle auctions.
>
> Our sales volume is just about 1 percent of all cattle auctions. We think we can do 15 percent. We sell a lot of Canadian and Mexican cattle, and we get bids from other parts of the world. We want to increase all this.

Satellite Real Estate Auctions

Superior President Jim Odle got the idea for real estate auctions by satellite and formed a separate partnership with a leading real estate auction executive. They then set up local partnerships with top commercial real estate firms in other cities, such as Moore & Co., the biggest commercial real estate firm in Denver.

They bought satellite time for five auctions in the first year. They advertised in *The Wall Street Journal* and other media. Individual properties auctioned off range from the hundreds of thousands to several million dollars. Jim Odle began to run TV satellite auctions for homes. Jim says:

> We did two real estate auctions via satellite TV for Farm Credit Services. We sold 25 agri-related properties—farms and ranches—for over $2 million. This was 110 percent over appraised value. We sold another 28 for 105 percent over appraised value. These were Philips Petroleum properties which went for $1.4 million.

Jim feels that many kinds of auctions can be profitably run by satellite. In Japan, Aucnet, Inc., broadcasts direct by satellite televised automobile auctions to 2000 locations. New kinds keep starting.

Sharing the Cost

One way to share DBS costs is to sponsor an event with others in your field. Shared sponsorship of business TV events in many fields is often pioneered by trade associations. The program's production facilities, uplinks, and meeting rooms with downlinks can all be rented on a one-shot basis. Another way is to create or sponsor programming on industry and professional networks.

There are DBS networks just for lawyers, doctors, bankers, computer system executives, accountants, law enforcement officers, automobile dealers—and for an increasing number of other fields. Not all carry ads, but some do, and more will. If available, the least expensive way to reach any of these DBS groups is to sponsor a message of 30 seconds to several minutes on a DBS network program that closely fits your product.

New Strategies for Ads on DBS Programs

Doug Widner studies and writes about business TV's successes and supervises the production of some of the greatest. Doug has some advice for any firm considering advertising with or on a DBS program that's also paid for by a subscriber:

> Americans are used to doses of blatant advertising only when the surrounding program is free. Make them pay for programming, and they'll be sensitive about ads. DBS networks which consider or accept commercials protect their subscribers much as an association does. Each is the gatekeeper and can set the rules.
>
> To get acceptance for your business TV commercial and to make it effective, the key is to exercise tact. Make no sudden move, and avoid hard sell. Instead educate, inform, service, and help your customers.

Now consider Carl Westcott's Automotive Satellite Television Network. ASTN reaches 3800 car dealerships with daily programs targeted to sales, management, and service personnel. It's a subscription service that trains dealer sales forces. One subscriber, Howell Buick Mazda in Rocky Mountain, North Carolina, reported their closing ratio jumped from 22 to 43 percent due to ASTN.

It's not always easy to be welcomed as a DBS network program advertiser. But it can be very worthwhile to persuade the right network for your product to accept your message, because business TV targets VIPs. For example, on the Hospital Satellite Network, programs sponsored by a major supplier have reached as many as one-third of the registered plastic surgeons in the country. Doug Widner reports:

> DePuy Prosthetic Products, Inc., makes prosthetic hips and sponsored a DBS video conference in which a well-known orthopedic surgeon conducted a live hip replacement. Orthopedic surgeons throughout the country watched the procedure and questioned the starring physician through a telephone hookup to the operating room. DePuy's message was a factual description and demonstration of variations of its prosthesis. It was a natural addition but also amounted to powerful demonstration marketing and image advertising targeted precisely to prosthesis buyers.

Another Business TV Network

Bankers TV Network has signed up several hundred sites which service 1100 large and small bank branches. The network provides 20 hours of programming a month and charges $500 a month subscription fee to each site, $25 for each hour of programming. But often a site is used by a number of branches of the subscribing bank. Since a typical program has an audience of 5 to 15 people at one site, the cost comes down to less than $5 per person per hour.

The network offers a half-hour news and information program and "reg" programs (latest government rulings on banking) plus special program topics. There are live question-and-answer periods by phones for interaction between the audiences and speakers. Handouts and reference materials are provided. Sometimes there's a two-hour or more symposium on a subject. Jennifer Joffrey of BTN says, "Our programming makes learning the various aspects of banking easier and simpler because of our constant injection of visual aids and learning games to help grasp each concept."

The BTVN format includes several benefits available to the DBS business TV medium. A bank can tape programs and create a library of tapes for additional training situations. In addition to employee educations, the network runs seminars to help business prospects that are or could be big depositors. And Bankers TV Network accepts institutional advertising from companies which sell products and services to banks.

The Evolution of Business TV

The use of DBS business TV by a company can start in a simple way and evolve. It might start with programming to more effectively train your personnel and then gradually develop and expand to include sales training. The next step might be to orient your dealers and distributors as to your marketing efforts. From employee education, it's natural to expand to customer education. Next might come new-product launch announcements, then special screenings for top customers in conjunction with your salespeople.

As business TV continues to grow, opportunities for smaller and more diverse businesses to jump in and profit will increase. Keep studying the field and the best ways for your company to exploit it.

Help Source Guide

1. *ADM Productions* has video and film production facilities and a corporate services program: creative, technical, administrative, computer graphics, live satellite communications. Broadcasts from ADM NY area or specified site and

downlinks to any number of points across USA or beyond: 40 Seaview Blvd., Port Washington, NY 11050. (516) 484-6900.

2. *AT&T Global Business Video Services,* offers a *free* information kit: Room 31A80, 55 Corporate Dr., Bridgewater, NJ 08807. (800) Video-Go.

3. The *Business Television Directory* (annual) is available from Warren Publishing. Lists programming networks, programming services, and private networks: 2115 Ward Court, N.W., Washington, D.C. 20037. (202) 872-9200.

4. *EDS Video Services* handles all technical management for various business TV networks and offers a *free* information kit on how to start, shortcuts, mistakes to avoid: 3490 Piedmont Rd., Atlanta, GA 30305. (404) 262-1555.

5. *The National Business Communications Network* (NBCN) provides a *free* information kit on how to set up a business TV network: 708 Third Ave. (25th floor), NY, NY 10017-4102. (212) 351-2700.

6. *Private Satellite Network, Inc.* (PSN) offers two *free* booklets: *The Business Television Handbook* and *The Special Event Broadcast Handbook.* Contact the director of marketing: 215 Lexington Ave., NY, NY 10010. (212) 696-9476/9468.

7. *Satellite Media Tours* is part of Media Link's Video PR Network, a series of preset satellite inteviews of company spokesperson/TV station personalities in the United States and the world. The interviewers speak from one location but are electronically whisked station to station for on-air one-on-one discussions. A 16-page SMT how-to, case studies handbook is available for $9.95 from Media Link Video Broadcasting Corp.: 708 Third Ave., NY, NY 10017. (212) 682-8300.

8. *United States Satellite Broadcasting Company, Inc.,* offers a *free* information kit on how to start your own network: 3415 University Ave., St. Paul, MN 55414. (612) 645-4500.

9. *Widner Productions* provides an excellent booklet by top expert Doug Widner, "50 Do's and Dont's of BTV Programming" for $5.99: P.O. Box 280, Lexington, KY 40584-0280. (606) 231-0910.

28

Other Profitable Forms of Electronic Marketing

No single volume can cover every single form of electronic media comprehensively. But there are a half-dozen or so other methods of electronic marketing which we'll outline for your consideration. Let's begin with a medium that is universally available, is effective for presentations and many offers, and is simple and low-cost to test—audiotapes.

Audio Marketing

Pete Silver advised on audiotape marketing in his article "A Cassette May Be the Ultimate Brochure," in the July 1990, *Home Office Computing* (HOC) magazine:

> What would it be worth to you to sit with a sales prospect for 20 minutes on his or her way to work? How about $1.50? That's about what it costs to create an audiocassette to mail to your qualified prospects. Imagine...no ringing telephone, no secretary to interrupt. Just you and the prospect.
>
> What can a cassette do that a brochure can't? It can capture your

voice and enthusiasm for your product or service. Prospects can hear your clients telling how satisfied they are. It can't be skimmed as easily as a brochure. It's economical for only 100 copies.

A successful audio brochure offers useful information and makes the listener want to hear more. But nobody benefits if your tape can't get past the mail room or secretary. Here are some tips to package your cassette so that it lands on your prospect's tape deck:

- Make the title convincing.

- Put a value on it of $5 or $10. Print it on the package.

- Include a signed, tiny memo, not a printed brochure.

- Mail it first-class.

Audiocassettes convince as nothing else can. If you don't think you're talented enough in the voice department, hire a news announcer or radio personality from your local radio station. For recording a 20-minute tape, you might pay $25 to $50...a lot less than typesetting a brochure! Duplication is inexpensive...about 85 cents apiece, labeled and boxed. Have a longer message? A one-hour tape is about 90 cents.

Toivo Maki is owner of Intermedia Communications & Entertainment Support Services of Riverside, California. After reading Pete, he wrote HOC, warning its readers:

> Before you click your home audiocassette on "record," note this. Although only fractionally as difficult and costly as video production, audio does entail up-front costs that can significantly add to the per-unit total. Duplication, labeling, and voice talent aren't the only things to worry about.
>
> Design and printing of labels and packaging require the same professional look and production steps of any printed marketing item. Production costs like master tape, duplicating master, scripting, rehearsal, script editing and other on-the-clock fees can add up.
>
> What can look attractive as a $1.50-a-shot promotion piece can add up—costing more like $4 or $5 once you factor in all the things necessary to make the tape stand out and get the right person to listen to it.

Here is Pete's rebuttal of Toivo as he told it to me:

> Toivo Maki refers to costs from a service bureau or for tapes produced in-house by larger companies. My labels are simply generated on a dot-matrix printer for two cents each on special label forms available. There are no graphics and there is no printing. In the 85 cents, I include all costs of packaging.

I then talked to Toivo. He broke down his costs per cassette in the mail based on a hundred (totaling $6.33 each) and on a thousand ($1.425 each). He mails first-class in a padded envelope, which together, he says, can be well over a dollar more in the mail.

To a direct marketer these are test costs. In big volume, a promotional audiocassette's cost in the mail can be *lower* even than Pete estimates, but it's higher than print alone. Many successfully combine use of tapes with full, direct-mail kits.

Cassettes are great to precede a salesperson or as a leave-behind. They are often affixed to a store package. Cassettes are particularly effective for:

- Sampling an audio product
- Including audio testimonials
- Education and motivation
- New student recruiting
- Fund-raising messages
- Premiums with orders

Success Can Be Natural

The Phone Works is an imaginative, innovative creator of phone programs. It markets its phone programs on cassette by simulating a radio mystery show, complete with sound effects and excerpts from its most successful interactive phone promotions.

The biggest producer of promotional flexible records (sound sheets) and of audiotape cassettes is EvaTone Inc. It has distributed millions of sound tapes and audiocassettes to sample and advertise its services. Time-Warner Inc. profitably sampled on sound sheets and audiocassettes millions of excerpts from albums, from swing to rock.

Political candidates have successfully sent personal appeals for money on millions of sound sheets or cassettes. Richard J. Capalbo, president and CEO of Van Eck Securities Corp. of New York City, says:

> I used audiotapes early in my business life. They're ideal in markets where people commute or drive a lot. They're not good in New York City where people don't use cars. They also don't have the smash impact of radio or the prestige of video. They don't give that big smash impact. But they're good in certain markets.

Considering Audio

Audiotapes are not glamorous or impressive. Some people respond more to what they see in print than to what they hear. Even in big volume audiotapes cost more than the cheapest print alone. Success requires a strong, special reason for use of the human voice. Only the right products with the right presentation and right voice have a chance. The offer must have a strong appeal to the special groups targeted. The price and margin must be high enough so that the percentage of response required is not too high. Offers via videotape are often best used supported by or to support print or other electronic media. Try audio for one of these situations:

- If you or someone in your organization has a natural ability to convince, persuade, inspire by phone
- If you have a name spokesperson to tape a longer, more powerful message to enhance your shorter ads and commercials
- As a taped version of a successful seminar
- A personal message from your CEO to your dealers, representatives, sales force, or stockholders as part of a multimedia package
- A sample of music, or music instruction; a language course; a cassette course for anything, or an audio book
- Testimonials from customers which come across with great credibility
- An audio documentary of an event or a profile of an organization through interviews with key executives, customers, vendors, and experts

Nightingale-Conant creates and sells audiocassettes and videocassettes of some of the most successful business inspiration talks of all time, particularly for salespeople. It has sent out various sampler audiocassettes by the millions to inspire purchasers. Maybe you will find a way just as successful.

Vending Becomes Marketing

Vending machines arrived a century before electronic kiosks and are now entering the kiosk age. Herb Jamic, vending consultant, explains:

> Ninety percent of currently manufactured, electronic vending machines have capabilities to handle more logic to serve more products

and offer more choices and expand control. They can store memory capable of being retrieved with a hand-held device. We now want daily retrieval of data, to search all equipment, maintain inventory control, and audit. Data control leads to computer systems. Data conversion is a necessary part of vending. We want new applications for more sales and profits.

New vending opportunities via electronic marketing are unlimited for four reasons:

1. Exciting new food products, aided by refrigeration and microwave ovens, can break price barriers.
2. Money-changers and debit cards raise average sale. EM upgrades can add new ways to cross-sell.
3. Present operators can trade up to or go beyond traditional blue-collar to more upscale markets.
4. A new universe of products can be sold by entirely new vending machine operators and marketers.

Big food companies are supplying more products for vending machines. French fry vending machines, for example, have been successfully market-tested and are being adapted to other potato products and poultry forms such as chicken nuggets. Another frozen-items vending machine sells everything from French fries to TV dinners. It may soon sell any broad appeal, single-serving, casserole-type food.

Rowe International Inc., is the largest U.S. vending machine maker; 90 percent of all snack and beverage machines now built by Rowe are equipped with a bill adapter which accepts $5 and $10 bills. Ed Weiler, marketing manager of Rowe, says, "Virtually no vending machine is made now without electronic support. Sales productivity per machine has been dramatically increased, perhaps two to three times in the last two decades."

Robert J. Muller, the executive vice president of Crane Co., New York, and CEO of Crane National Vendors, states:

The computer opened up a whole new way of doing things in our industry. Computer technology reshaped the way vending machines operate. People want variety, good taste, and fast delivery. New vending equipment generations have been designed to respond to varied consumer demands. As an example, our new Hot Drink Center offers eight product selections that can be ordered in a choice of a small or large cup in 750 different ways. Product choices can include regular and decaf coffee ground fresh from whole beans, fresh-brewed cappuccino and expresso, international coffees, tea, hot chocolate, soups, and even artificial sweetener.

The backbone of this tremendous degree of flexibility is the microprocessor which is used to interpret the instructions supplied to it by the custom software in order to tell the other parts of the equipment what they should do. Electronic technology has also helped vending equipment play a more interactive role with both the user and the operator.

Customer communications are made through a vacuum fluorescent display. Messages include an up-to-the-moment credit status, product selection made, advice to make another selection and to use exact change, the all-important "thank you" following purchase, and even custom scrolling messages.

Both Crane National Vending and Rowe have vending machines with the capability of adding an LCD screen and to become interactive. After 5:30 p.m., each machine automatically reduces the prices of sandwiches 15 percent in order to sell them before they get stale. Ed Weiler, sales vice president of Rowe, says, "Cross-selling just started. A candy machine offers a second or third product to a purchaser. A general merchandise machine may tempt by a special offer like a sandwich *and* a candy bar for the usual sandwich price. This is brand-new and will be popular."

Robert Muller says:

> Equipment merchandising capability can be maximized through use of promotion and pricing features. Each product sold can be vended at a unique price. A "winner" promotion mode can be employed to deliver free product at predetermined purchase intervals. The equipment also offers time of day and/or week events where selected products can be vended at varying rates of discount all the way to free of charge. It automatically turns the desired feature on and off for the length of time specified by the operator.
>
> Computer electronics have also simplified life for the equipment operator. To aid the process of accounting, routing, and inventory control, the internal memory tracks unit and dollar sales down to the individual product selection. Results can be output to a hand-held printer or even be directly delivered to a host computer at a headquarters site via a modem.

Rowe Vice President Ed Weiler says "I see a vending kiosk with a control brain in back of the equipment and in front a debit card aperture, credit card slot, a menu touch-screen, and all the interactive features needed."

Vending is a mature industry and is overwhelmingly now blue-collar-based, selling to an income-shrinking group. Standards for kiosk-feature vending machines are still being settled so that each can talk to another. Sturdy, old, cheap, nonelectric machines keep making profits decades after amortization and delay this further. A machine sells for $4500 or so. Each new electronic kiosk feature adds to the price and causes price resistance.

Should you consider electronic vending? Don't jump into electronic vending unless you know the field or study it with care. Those in vending should study kiosks and vice versa. Success may come from entrepreneurs in each field joining efforts. Those outside vending may have the audacity to overcome vending shibboleths. Each vending expert I've talked to sees certain specific promising areas.

In addition to checking the Help Source Guide at the end of this chapter, phone manufacturers and get from them their lists of operators. Ask for their locations and buy from these vending machines. Then ask the location owner: Which are most popular? What is the average sale? What are the newest successes? What bugs are there, if any? Look for chances to sell present or new products to operators or to be an operator yourself. Test one location, then several, and expand gradually.

Audioconferencing

Although the conference phone call has been used for decades, entirely via phone lines, now with speaker phones it's a new way to close and help close major sales. The salesperson can call in company top brass and important experts outside the company. Audioconferencing can be a major meeting by phone and at many locations. The three major phone companies all use digital equipment and fiber optics for audioconferencing and have excellent sound quality.

Consultant Virginia Ostendorf says that audioconferencing (AC):

- Is suitable for small, medium, or large groups
- Is available anywhere in urban or rural areas in the United States, or abroad
- Reaches attendees in their offices or at any phone
- Is good for last-minute information
- Is the lowest-cost form of teleconferencing
- Needs no travel, plus no one need be "on-camera"
- Is easily convened in multiple sessions if needed
- Provides interaction among all parties

Virginia says, "There is no better way to reach an international audience than AC, and at a phenomenally low cost. It can be done simultaneously in many languages, with a translator cutting in for each one."

Dean Meyer, CEO and founder of N. Dean Meyer and Associates, Inc., of Ridgefield, Connecticut, consultants in management of the IS organization, coined the name "Teleforum" for his audioconferencing business. For nine years it has been a steady profit center, marketing arm, and core part of his enterprise.

Each Teleforum is usually for 8 to 15 clients and at 8 to 20 sites. Average attendance per site is 10 people. Dean charges $3400 for five 2-hour sessions for one site and less for each additional site. This means $34 an hour training cost per person and less for multiple sites.

Dean says,

> There is good synergy between consulting and audioconferencing. We sell both Teleforum and consulting at once. Half of Teleforum customers were consulting clients; 20 percent of consulting clients start as Teleforum sponsors.
>
> About 15 percent of our consulting fees come from Teleforum clients. This has added up to about 25 to 30 projects, ranging in fees from $10,000 to over $100,000. Teleforum is also the way I stay on the leading edge, the way I keep up with management.

But, Dean is unique. He is a popular and highly paid consultant, personnel trainer, and speaker. He has stature and writes major articles in leading journals. The need for the updating he gives never ends for any client. He is a perfectionist at putting on each Teleforum.

Dean explains:

> Audioconferencing is not easy to set up. We pay great attention to selection of speakers and moderators and to logistics. It's not ad hoc. It must be carefully planned.
>
> Our meetings are highly interactive, much more than a videoconference. This is partly due to the way I interview. Whether I introduce and question speakers or am my own guest speaker and expert, I get attendees to ask and bring up points. I make it a true meeting.

For example, for the Teleforum series on PCs, Dean secured Bill Machrone, editor-in-chief and publishing director of *PC Magazine*, as the moderator. Dean is a showman, an entrepreneur, and marketer. Dean integrates audioconferencing, audiotapes, direct mail, and telephone marketing to promote his own consulting and publishing activities.

Dean wants to make an impact on the industry more than he wants to make profits. He is his own PR person. Many of Teleforum's inquiries come from his frequent appearances and speeches at meetings and his articles in media.

Audioconferencing as a Free Service

Piero Melchiorri is president of Logical Communications in East Norwalk, Connecticut. Part of his business is creating audio conferences for top pharmaceutical companies to inform physicians about new developments. Piero explains:

> Years ago, pharmaceutical companies began to be convinced that it was to a company's advantage to train physicians, believing that doctors who feel comfortable about a field will be more receptive toward your product. G. D. Searles was the first company to use this learning system. It took a while, but most companies adopted this concept.
>
> These programs ended up as an integral part of the efforts of the marketing department. Meetings and teleconferences educate. They should not be a hard sell. The initial step is to interest physicians in the disease and product category.
>
> Our clients don't use audioconferencing as a presentation format at the end of which physicians buy. Our programs update and educate physicians to recent findings about disease and disease management. To our clients, benefits are indirect and gradual.
>
> We deal with the marketing department, but what we do is not promotion. It is education. For a program, we look for what will attract an audience. The topic is crucial. You need a topic about which doctors are concerned and a speaker they respect. The wrong subject will be a bust, as will the wrong speaker.
>
> Ninety-five percent of audioconferencing programs for physicians are free to them. All our meetings are hospital-based. We've done thousands. Attendance at one site varies from 2 or 3 physicians in an office to 200 people in an auditorium. The maximum number of sites have been 85.
>
> Our average meeting reaches about 200 people. We do three a day, 50 or 60 a month, for eight months a year. We reach over 12,000 people a month and about 100,000 a year—30,000 to 40,000 are the same physicians. About 30,000 doctors like audioconferencing enough to attend three or four sessions a year.
>
> Sixty to 70 percent of AC meetings have some sort of associated printed material at sites; 80 percent of our audioconferences have some visual support at the hospital (usually slides).

AC Marketing Applications

Audioconferencing can train a sales force and orient it to a company's latest advertising. It can introduce new products, new services, and promotions to field sales representatives. AC can be used for press conferences. It's ideal for discussions between national headquarters and dealers or franchise owners. Sometimes, business meetings are small and specialized. They can be seminars with prospects and customers. Valerie Thomas, of Conference Calls USA, says:

> When we run audioconferencing training seminars, we train 20 to 40 people at each location. For all clients, our average number of locations reached ranges from 8 to 15. The biggest number was over 400 locations.
>
> Hoffman-LaRoche reached over 1200 people in three audioconferences, one each day for three successive days. They were introducing a new drug product and had just gotten FDA approval to release it. They needed fast action to orient their sales force and dealers.

There are three kinds of audioconferences:

1. *Dial-Out Conference.*   To obtain the most attendance, conference coordinators contact conferees at the appointed time. For this long-distance rate and conferencing service combined costs range from 35 cents to 50 cents a minute per location plus any setup charges.

2. *Dial-In Conference ("Meet-Me").*   Conferees call the conference number at the agreed time. This may obtain less attendance but costs less. Combined long-distance rates and conferencing service typically cost between 10 cents to 25 cents a minute per location.

3. *Dial-In 800 Conference ("Meet-Me 800").*   Conferees call in to your conference 800 number at the appointed time. This may obtain more conferees than a "meet-me" conference while also getting more interested and qualified attendees than the first method. Combined costs are about 44 cents a minute per location.

Any type of audioconferencing usually involves setup charges for each location to staff conference coordinators admitting attendees to your conference. These coordinators are accessible to your conference director at any time during your conference.

Your company can arrange any audioconference itself. If your firm has experience in videoconferencing and uses it enough, the do-it-yourself rate may cost the least. Otherwise it is safest and often cheaper to deal with a conference service, including one owned by the phone companies. Often the same services handle audio- and videoconferencing. Check several phone companies and conference services for latest rates.

Videoconferencing

Videoconferencing offers a smash impact far beyond audioconferencing. It allows for a broad range of visual support, from 35-millimeter slides to computer graphics and video. Videoconferencing based on fiber-optic telephone lines can cost less than comparable direct-by-satellite (DBS) programs to transmit—and no satellite dishes are required. But for more than around five sites, DBS can be cheaper.

Videoconferencing is often used to close large sales and often replaces or reduces the travel expense to make these big deals. Sometimes a conference is between a company and key suppliers.

The average conference starts with two sites, and then expands to multisites. The typical conference involves six sites. To use multiple sites effectively, management must be fairly sophisticated, and in-house staff must have extensive training. Some companies have their own networks and equipment.

The Videoconference Facilities Room

For in-house videoconferencing, there are three cost components:

1. *The codec.* "Codecs" (digital coding and decoding equipment) code TV signals into digital computer bytes and then compress them by removing 99 percent of the information (such as background which is the same frame after frame). A codec is needed for each location. When you look at TV, you are seeing the equivalent of 90 megabytes per second. The codec compresses this to T-1, which is 1.5 megabytes per second. The top compression is T-1. But some customers use ½ T1 and others ¼ T1. Sprint can run at any speed under T1. Conferencing via fiber offers full-motion video. The codec gives visual quality not quite as good as a TV set. Graphics are closer to the quality on your PC screen, but quality is rapidly rising and the cost dramatically dropping.

2. *The conference system.* The conference system can include a codec plus cameras, usually with two monitors in a conference room. One you look at. The second shows what you are sending. The conference

room has audio and video equipment, so you don't use the phone. PCs can be hooked up and spreadsheets can be interactive.

3. *Fiber-optic transmission.* In remote places where there is no phone company digital service, private microwave may be used, but this is negligible. There are also other transmission means.

Videoconference systems may have a computer and monitor at each end. There may be a VCR at each site, a CD video player, or both. These can show a sophisticated full-color, action video. The computer system can add, using floppy disks, PC graphics including charts, graphs, drawings, or CADCAM (computer-aided design/computer-aided manufacturing) drawings all sent by modem. Besides video visuals, voice, fax, and computer networking can supply immediacy and interactivity. If a CD-ROM drive is added, a CD-ROM disc can be used in any of the many ways described in Chapter 22.

Some companies supply equipment and video conference specialists to help users choose equipment and services. Some specialists will take responsibility for customer education and seminar programs. Some present seminars.

Public Videoconference Rooms

Each public videoconference facility is equipped for meetings and is linked to other conference rooms in other locations. AT&T, MCI, and Sprint and independent organizations operate conference rooms that are usually available 24 hours a day, 7 days a week. You can rent several or many, each small or large, for one meeting or for a series of meetings. Sprint public room rentals average $150 per half hour. A dedicated T1 line from your facility to a public videoconference network is needed. Digital access cross-connect switches (DACS) join customer T1 lines to the network.

On Sprint Meeting-Channel, transmission rates are based on 384 kilobits (kbps), recommended by Sprint as a compromise between price and quality. Sprint has two U.S. network packages, west and east of the Mississippi. Within either area, Sprint charges $90 for a half hour for two-way interactive video between two sites. For multipoint transmissions (up to five locations) the cost is $180. When transmission crosses the Mississippi, the cost is $35 for point-to-point conferences and $270 for multipoint up to five locations. Sprint's maximum videoconferencing capacity is seven sites. For higher-quality graphics and video, higher transmission speeds can be used at higher costs. For lower transmission speeds quality drops, but so do costs. For overseas conferences, foreign carrier companies charge for return transmissions.

Costs are dropping fast. They will soon drop much faster with a video expansion board which slips into any PC that has the new modem connected to the phone. Enthusiasts say the combination will soon cost little more than a fax machine, and that videoconferencing will soon become as universal as fax.

Caution! People like to meet face to face. Videoconferencing will probably supplement and reduce but not replace sales travel. Marketing success case histories are still largely lacking.

Considering Videoconferencing

Large and small companies already profitably promote via videoconferencing in more situations. As the capabilities of videoconferencing grow and its costs drop, it will become possible to reach far more locations and will become so cheap that point-to-point can be a form of telemarketing.

Elliot Gold (who edited Chapter 27) is also the founder of Elliot Gold's Telespan, a newsletter bulletin on teleconferencing. He gave crucial help in editing the previous portions of this chapter on audioconferencing and videoconferencing. This excellent information source and others with latest information to get started in the field are listed in this chapter's Help Source Guide. Study the field, test on a small scale, but be ready for the sudden opportunity to employ audio- and videoconferencing to get big, profitable traced sales.

Electronic Targeted Magazines

On November 26, 1990, *Time* put my name on the front cover of my copy. In fact, it put each subscriber's name on the front cover of his or her copy. *Time*'s message to me was, "Hey, Cecil C. Hoge, don't miss our interesting story on the junk mail explosion!" It was done by sophisticated ink-jet printing and computer programs.

With selective binding, magazines are entering the electronic marketing arena. By matching individual subscriber characteristics while the magazine is still being bound, publishers can deliver different ads and editorials to different readers.

Prodigy ran a 4-page insert in *Time, Money,* and *Sports Illustrated* magazines with a personalized call-to-action card. The message addressed the subscriber by name, offered a premium for attending a Prodigy demonstration, and gave the address of the nearest participating retailers that handled Prodigy software. *Time*'s computer program measures the distance of each subscriber's home from the dealers for any advertised product and selects the closest one.

Bruce Judson, *Time*. Inc. Magazine's director of marketing, says, "A direct-response issue has been tested and proven successful. The day is here when magazine advertisements can be as personalized as direct mail."

It is possible to combine portions of up to three *Time* Inc. magazines into one customized publication—such as one-third *Time,* one-third *People,* and one-third *Sports Illustrated*—using specially targeted ads for each publication. An advertiser can print personalized messages for the recipient, along with an already filled-out response card. *Sports Illustrated for Kids* has run a personalized comic strip. *Newsweek* and others have personalized editions.

The magazine that started this electronic marketing revolution in print is *The Farm Journal,* which goes to 800,000 decision makers on big farms that account for 90 percent of U.S. agricultural production. *The Farm Journal*'s database includes what crops individual subscribers grow and what chemicals each uses. A marketer can aim its ads at more than 800,000 subscribers by name, with special copy for each. An individualized ad costs an advertiser from 35 to 60 percent more.

Other Innovations in Electronic Marketing

Targeted Piggyback Catalogs.   Laura Ashley had never mailed its *Mother & Child* catalog on its own when it obtained 200,000 active buyers from the catalog simply by selective binding it as an add-on to its regular catalog. Only a minority of Laura Ashley's general catalog customers got the piggyback edition, but those that did were precisely targeted. Outside names demographically suited to *Mother & Child* were also mailed the combined catalog. The catalog features matching women's and children's clothing. The extra postage of mailing the piggyback costs less than 25 percent of mailing *Mother & Child* solo.

Laptop and Notebook PCs.   Sales forces of many complex products and services have briefcase computers and modems. Now, salespeople and sales managers have really begun to get interested in notebook computers, which many feel are the first practical units for their purposes.

Pocket Computers.   Some hand-held computer models are programmed, battery-powered, and have 256K memory. They can scan barcodes to check stock for a retailer or jobber, work out an order, and modem it in, more cheaply and faster than the mail. The largest maker of such units is Telxon of Akron, Ohio.

Summary

Many more new electronic forms can be used profitably—too many to cover here. But I hope that the experiences of marketers in using each form of electronic marketing covered in this book, and what I describe about each form, will help you better investigate other new electronic media—and convert them to your own marketing success.

Help Source Guide

1. *AT&T AccuNet* is an audioconference and teleconference service offering a *free* information kit with rates, features, four service regions: 444 Jericho Turnpike, Huntington, NY 11743. (800) 232-1234.

2. *AT&T Skynet VideoConference Service* can be contacted for information at 51 Peachtree St., Atlanta, GA 30303. (404) 810-5807.

3. *Conference-Call USA* offers a *free* information kit; also ask about an audio-conference on audioconferencing: 5515 Security Ln., Suite 1109, Rockville, MD 20852. (800) 272-5563. (301) 816-9100.

4. *Elliot Gold's Telespan: A Pace Bulleting on Teleconferencing* is $247 for 40 issues a year from TeleSpan Publishing Corp.: P.O. Box 6250, 50 W. Palm Street, Altadena, CA 91001. (818) 797-5482.

5. *Eva-Tone Soundsheets, Inc.* provides soundsheets, cassettes, a *free Cassette Talk* newsletter and a *free* soundtrack, "Hear How Easy It Is to Create a Sound-track": P.O. Box 7020, Clearwater, FL 34618. (800) EVATONE (382-8663).

6. *The International Teleconferencing Association* (ITCA) sponsors an annual meeting and exposition and *free* newsletter: 1150 Connecticut Ave. N.W., Suite 1050, Washington, DC 20036. (202) 833-2549.

7. *Virginia A. Ostendorf, Inc.* provides a catalog of books on video and audio teleconferencing such as *Create Outstanding Videoconferences* by Eric Craven and Doug Widner: P.O. Box 2896, Littleton, CO 80161-2986. (303) 797-3131.

8. *Silver, Inc.* offers a *free* audiotape, "How to Attract More Clients without Advertising"—excerpts from three audiotapes about audiotape marketing, all by Pete Silver: 9066 South West, 112 Court, Miami, FL 33176-1171. (800) 745-8377.

9. *Sprint Marketing Division* offers a *free* information kit on audioconferencing, rates, case histories: 1240 Sunrise Valley Drive, Reston, VA 22096. (703) 689-5073.

10. *Sprint Video Group* offers a *free* information kit on fiber-optic videoconferencing, rates in the United States, worldwide: 1815 Century Blvd., Atlanta, GA 30334. (800) 669-1235 or (404) 859-8650.

11. *Teleconference* magazine is published by Applied Business Telecommunications, Inc., which also publishes *TeleConf* newsletter. *Free* sample issues of each are available: Box 5106, San Ramon, CA 94583. (415) 820-5563.

29

Electronic Customer Service

Among the fastest ways to increase sales is to improve your product's usefulness. Sometimes this amounts to simply answering questions better—telling your customers what they need to know to buy or use your products. It is now easier and less expensive to deliver customer service electronically (while often creating additional profitable sales), and it keeps your customer happier and more loyal.

Many of today's products and services are more complex than ever. Unfortunately, written manuals typically intimidate at best and often are frustratingly incoherent. The results are predictable. Many products lie underused or gather dust in closets, because purchasers don't know how to operate them. To make matters worse, your own employees are apt to be less informed about your company's products and less inclined to help customers.

Customers Lost by Phone

Why lose any of your loyal customers who call your company with a complaint? Or those who simply call for specific information? Many of these customers like your product quality and phone only to get answers to simple questions. They start by asking who is the proper person to talk to. Why let mishandling by one person, a voice system, or both lose them? Your losses don't stop there. Research indicates an unhappy customer will tell nine or ten people about it.

Moreover, smart customers are getting tougher. They want reasons that products cost more and they want fast answers when something doesn't work. Great products with superior features are perceived as useless unless people easily know how to enjoy the benefits. Customer education is often needed before they buy, before they use, and as they continue to use your products. For many of today's demanding customers, if you don't teach them, you lose them.

In Chapters 8 and 9, I quoted author and consultant Richard Bencin on telemarketing. In the next five paragraphs I will try to distill what Richard Bencin taught me about saving customers. Customer loyalty grows in direct relation to the degree of benefit derived from your products and services. The more they buy accessories and upgrade to your latest improved, bigger, or more deluxe models, the more likely they are to boast about your product and service. Their expectancy also rises and their affection can quickly turn to wrath, if they feel that they have been let down or crossed. Few new prospects are as valuable as angry customers who are reaching for the phone, about to leave you. Their calls represent your last chance at saving them as customers. Make handling each call count.

Most customers who vow never to buy your products again won't bother to tell you why but will tell many others. Make your employees feel that their jobs depend on pleasing such people.

Each of us is an angry customer at some time. Handle each on the phone as you would like to be dealt with. Listening takes less time than to argue. Cooperating and helping solves the problem and wins back lost customers. Do your homework. Find out what your firm did wrong. Tell the customer what you will do to remedy the problem. Never put a complaint aside. Always phone back fast, with the remedy.

Rage can become satisfaction. Never get mad, says Richard Bencin, even at illogical, wrong, and angry customers. Avoid an adversarial conversation. Speak quietly even as the customer raises his or her voice. Sympathize, identify with the customer's problem, and never infer the customer is misstating a complaint. Don't blame others, acknowledge your fault, and apologize completely, without reservations. Ask for the full story and listen. If it rambles, sum up all that you've heard. Be clear and ask if your summary is correct. Do this until you have all the facts.

Describe what "we"—he or she and you—must do to get satisfaction, and ask for his or her agreement. Give immediate action. Take your losses, if necessary, right away. Decide if you're up against a hopeless crank or a crook. If so, give up and leave it to the lawyers. Rarely will this happen. Have a post mortem with your staff on each lost customer.

Here are some simple steps to take:

- Set up forms and procedures to handle customer complaints.

- Develop customer-service representatives and "answer-center" personnel who are intelligent, interested, and sympathetic.
- Properly train the personnel to know the products they service.
- Computer-assist them with ample, precise information.

The General Electric Model

When General Electric devoted itself to top-quality consumer products and customer service, it decided to support these objectives by providing customers with personal, expert advice by phone. It is called The GE Answer Center.

GE found that an 800 number is considered to be a personal, direct means of communicating with a large company. Consumers said that it was faster, less trouble, and more pleasant than writing or visiting the service department. Each caller is handled as though sitting across the desk. The representative gives personal attention to the caller, answering each question completely and in a friendly way.

This is backed by a vast computer database available via PC screen. GE's database includes over 1 million answers to questions that might be asked about 1100 procedures for about 120 different GE product lines and 8500 models. The database is constantly updated to assure accuracy.

Most GE Answer Center representatives have a college degree. They participate in five weeks of training plus 100 hours of additional training throughout the year. Almost any question asked by phone can be quickly handled by an answer stored in the GE mainframe computer. The agent retrieves the answer on the PC screen while talking and immediately responds to the caller asking the question.

Callers may want to know what to buy for a specific purpose, where to buy it, and how to use it; or they may want to find out where to get service for a product or how to repair it themselves. Each call to GE is answered by a consumer specialist—over 80 percent of the calls are concluded by the same consumer specialist. If repair questions are complex, the call is transferred to product specialists. They can call up on the screen data such as parts listings, diagrams of circuits, and other product information including those for older GE models.

Selecting and Training Staff

The wrong people answering complaints can harm you. GE looks for understanding agents who are:

- Even-tempered, intelligent, and enthusiastic
- Personable, empathetic, and self-motivated
- Effective listeners
- Sympathetic, knowledgeable, and professional

Many are hired based on the recommendation of the present staff, and about 20 percent come from other GE departments.

The first thing an agent does is to identify the kind of person who is calling. Callers are divided into seven types:

1. Direct and natural
2. Pleasant and outgoing
3. Insecure and anxious
4. Confused and uncertain
5. Angry and belligerent
6. In an emergency and panicked
7. Skeptical, cynical

A GE agent is taught to respond to different customer types and to identify, within the first 15 seconds of the call, the response that fits. The response personalities that are matched up with the seven caller types listed above are:

1. Efficient, confident, and pleasantly professional
2. Equally pleasant, outgoing, friendly, some small talk
3. Nurturing parent, reassuring, optimistic, cheerful
4. Patient, caring, clarifying
5. Listening with empathy, responding with positive understanding, following through with professional action
6. Equal sense of urgency in dialogue and action plan
7. Reassuring, knowledgeable, proexpert response

Agents are trained in role-playing sessions so they can use these response personalities with push-button ease. Agents are prepared for irate callers. If someone uses profanity, the person is told quietly that GE can help but that the conversation will be continued only if the caller avoids using profane language.

Answering the Right Questions

Can your staff answer these questions? Only 15 percent of GE Answer Center calls are complaints, and 90 percent of them are taken care of at the time of first calls. These questions are divided roughly into three categories: A third are about product use and care after purchase. A third are about service—where to get it, how to diagnose the problems, and "do-it-yourself" questions. And another third are prepurchase inquiries. The Center offers, and sends to anyone interested, information on whatever GE product is desired. Some calls ask about incentive offers, financing options, and warranties, as well as the updated facts about product features and accessories. Computers give the agent, who tells the consumer the name, address, and phone number of the nearest dealer. The Center provides about a million referrals a year to dealers. Consumers are given dealer locations within their zip code areas. The Center solves customers' problems directly and makes customers happier, which saves dealers and distributors the bother while freeing them to create more business.

In addition to giving customer service, GE employees pass along the most frequent comments to their marketing, advertising, and product development departments. The subject of every call is recorded on the computer and analyzed. These departments then determine what people want. These data have a very real effect on the kind of new products that are developed.

For example, *The New York Times* reported that GE removed the switch hook on its one-piece phone when consumers said they were disconnecting calls with their chins. Other GE consumer complaints have resulted in easier-to-use VCRs that were redesigned with bigger knobs, more automatic fine tuning, and an easier-to-read VCR care book.

Research found that 95 percent of the surveyed people who called the GE center were satisfied, and that a satisfied customer will tell at least five friends. GE states that it receives millions of word-of-mouth recommendations, each year, from its telephone service center.

Turning Complaints into Profits

Here's how the GE Answer Center attained a profit-center status:

1. The Center made people like GE more after their calls than before.
2. The Center increased sales as a result of calls handled in the year.
3. The Center got GE a bigger market share than if it had no service.

4. The Center reduced the cost of warranties by providing service over the phone, saving service personnel from going to the home or office.

5. The Center created productivity and quality improvements for GE.

Do you get inquiries from businesses? GE has long been considered a consumer-oriented company, but today nearly 90 percent of GE sales come from technical, industrial, professional, and business buyers. GE has such a variety of products that even employees don't have a good understanding of that diversity. To give business customers easy access and understanding of GE's scope of business products, GE set up a GE Business Information Center (GEBIC) in Albany, NY. GEBIC focuses entirely on inquiries for industrial, technical, and commercial products and services. Its phone number is 800-626-2004.

Calls are handled by a staff including program directors and support people. Questions regarding any of GE's 13 different businesses and their thousands of products, services, and resources are handled by the program directors. They are backed by a computerized database of GE products and services, field sales contacts, and regional distributors. GEBIC even gives information about its discontinued product lines. They can refer a customer to another company if GE no longer makes a particular product. Over 3000 industrial and technical experts scattered through GE and its sales channels answer questions referred to them by GEBIC.

Helping customers makes the difference. GEBIC's focus on customer needs and linking those callers to someone who can help also includes providing product literature, putting buyers in contact with distributors, locating critical parts, and making suggestions that can save customers time and money. In some way, every call placed to it is either a new sales lead or an opportunity to serve GE customers or prospects. Callers are business or industrial managers, buyers, or specifiers with questions about GE products.

GE promotes GEBIC internally and to prospects and customers. GE places ads and listings in more than 200 trade magazines, buying guides, and directories, as well as some 1000 telephone directories. Each caller is also asked: "Where did you learn about the Business Information Center?" Forty-three percent are referred by other GE divisions, 22 percent called GEBIC before, 78 percent are first-time callers from the industrial marketplace.

Catalogers can learn much about customer service. N. Powell Taylor, retired manager of the GE Answer Center, believes that catalogs do not pay enough attention to customers and that any major catalog company must have this sort of center, or risk losing customers. An independent survey conducted by William J. Spaide, a management consultant to the direct-marketing industry, confirms this opinion. Spaide surveyed big-name catalogs and rated each for the handling of telephone inquiries based on:

1. Waiting time
2. Knowledge of stock status
3. Product knowledge
4. Whether operators offered any form of upsell or cross-sell
5. Quality of the operator—how he or she came across

Overall ratings for customer service for equally famous catalogs varied greatly—from excellent to poor. Spaide warns that a poor rating can be the first sign of a coming decline in sales and profits.

Other Customer Service Models

The Complaint Doctor. Dr. Jon Anton is manager of the Customer Response Information Systems Department of Tarp Information Systems, Inc. The business of Tarp is complaints. Dr. Anton makes these observations about complaints:

- Frustrated "noncomplainers"—dissatisfied customers who never contact you but are unhappy with your products or service—often "bad-mouth" your firm to one person after another.
- Neither they nor the people they talk to about you intend to do any business with you. Yet you don't know it.
- Getting a new customer costs five-to-ten times as much as keeping an existing customer, which can be accomplished through a properly organized customer service and information center.

Dr. Anton suggests that you establish:

1. An 800 number for questions and complaints and publicize it
2. A staff who can find the answers quickly and solve problems for unhappy customers
3. A phone-oriented computer system that assists your staff to find problems, track solutions, and access the information that is needed.

4. System reports and measures that detect trends in customer dissatisfaction to prevent catastrophes and help to rectify situations which cause problems

3M.   3M found that a service center can solve many problems by telephone just by telling a customer what to do. 3M offers a toll-free service line for customer equipment problems. Thirty percent of all incoming service calls are taken care of within a few minutes, and 3M saves the expense and equipment downtime cost of sending a service technician.

Clairol Cuts Costs, Increases Satisfaction.   Clairol used to get quite a lot of letters, all of which had to be answered. The typical letter didn't contain enough information to respond conclusively, so Clairol answered with a letter asking more questions. Only when the consumer wrote again answering these follow-up questions could the company give the customer the proper information. This process became extremely expensive.

Then Clairol installed a toll-free service number. Immediately, they were able to take care of people much more satisfactorily. Letter volume dropped sharply as phone activity went up. In one conversation, the Clairol service person answering usually finds out exactly what was wrong and very often gives the answer on the phone. The service number also made more people happy faster and built more future business for Clairol.

Clairol next decided to answer questions about hair coloring *before* people make the decision to color their hair. Clairol first provided this service marketing through electronic kiosks, as we described in Chapter 26. Now Clairol's "Hair Coloring Advice Hotline" gives information by phone about hair coloring to people who call after seeing its ads.

Whirlpool.   Whirlpool Corp. started its "Cool Line" in 1967 when AT&T first offered 800 numbers. Among the many benefits generated from this service is Whirlpool's new "Quiet Wash" dishwasher inspired by "Cool Line" complaints about noisy dishwashers.

Harry Newton is editor of *Inbound-Outbound*, a telemarketing trade magazine. He has said: "In high-tech marketing, your success swings directly on your customer support. If word gets out that you're not answering customers' questions, your sales will plummet."

Not all customer service phone lines are free. Compaq's customer service line charges a fee, but general questions about Compaq products are answered free at another number.

WordPerfect's Phone Support. WordPerfect currently provides the biggest customer support system in the computer software field. Approximately 850 people handle over 17,000 in-bound calls a day, 24 hours a day weekdays. Forty-one support groups each handle a specialty. Voice systems guide callers to the desired group and a live voice. Every effort is made to answer any WordPerfect question. PC beginners are told with simple words how to do any step not understood. And anyone who has problems after an explanation can call back again and again.

This customer support system is a research goldmine for Word-Perfect. Any criticism, suggestion, or desire is listened to and sent to the proper department. This feedback has helped programmers eliminate bugs and design new features and has led to marketing WordPerfect in new ways. WordPerfect also has encouraged its own customers to help service others by starting a computer bulletin board, The WordPerfect Customer Support BBS for registered owners of recent versions.

How much service can you afford? Lack of service, bad service, or overspending on service each threaten your company's survival. Toll-free service lines and even paid phone lines staffed by skilled personnel can become very expensive to maintain. The need is to improve service *and* cut costs.

Service by phone costs much less than a visit. An answer center at one location costs less than calls handled at many locations by people whose main work it interrupts. Using automated voice systems can greatly reduce costs if properly designed. These voice systems can answer most service questions quickly and can even expand your range of customer services while slashing your in-office costs.

Far West Federal Bank. Far West Federal Bank of Portland, Oregon, was receiving about 60,000 phone inquiries a month. Although the bank didn't want to hire any more operators, call volume continued to rise. Instead, Far West installed a voice system, which answered over 15 percent of incoming customer service calls.

When Far West greatly expanded the number of its checking account customers, incoming customer service phone inquiries jumped. With the voice system in place, new checking account customers could find out current balances, the last few checks paid, and interest earned; how to stop payment, order statements, or find out interest rates on other deposit accounts or on loans. Customers liked it. Far West's voice system handling cost per call to a system representative was $1.25 versus $0.05 by the voice system.

Montgomery Ward's Payback.   At its credit centers, Montgomery Ward was overwhelmed by 80,000 calls a week about customer balances and payments. Customer service operators were under great pressure, and frustrating waits for customers led to over 20 percent of calls kept on hold being abandoned. Ward had to either add more operators or automate. Ward chose the latter route.

In one week in its Fullerton, California, credit center, Ward received 42,000 calls through the voice system. Answers to customers' most-asked questions were all input on computer. The voice system took the first 12 incoming calls, allowing 12 terminals (costing between $30 to $70 a month) to be eliminated in each credit center. Ward's voice system paid for itself in six months, satisfied more customers, and delivered big savings thereafter.

Mervyn's.   Mervyn's of Hayward, California, operates 203 specialty stores and is a division of Dayton-Hudson Corp. Mervyn's first tested a voice system to speed up its customer service in the credit department and then expanded its functions one at a time. Bruce Watson is director of Telecommunications and Technology at Mervyn's. He said:

> Telephone holding time on credit was a sore spot. We looked for an alternative to hiring more people because the business is cyclical, and we weren't always staffed at the right time. Before Christmas, InfoBot (the phone system) handles up to 30,000 calls a week—20 percent of all calls coming in to the credit department. It cost less than $120,000. Maintenance is $1.75 an hour.

The InfoBot voice system helped Mervyn's operate with 12 fewer people in its Credit Department. Terrance Sculley, credit manager, said:

> It's been a terrific aid for our customer service and productivity. In our telephone lines, it's the equivalent of 28 operators.

Jordan Marsh's Three-Month Payback.   Jordan Marsh, the New England retailer, uses two voice systems to respond to 250 to 400 routine customer credit inquiries a day. James Prior, General Credit Manager, said:

> We were not able to hire enough people to handle the phone calls. The $40,000 unit paid for itself in three months by eliminating irate calls from customers who had trouble reaching an operator. About 30 percent of credit inquiries are handled by the machine.

Wachovia Bank. Wachovia Bank of North Carolina looked at voice systems for years until it found that lower equipment costs and bigger projected savings made the systems practical. Wachovia's system handles routine transactions out of 222 branches—85 percent by pushbutton and 15 percent by rotary phone. In one month, as many customers called as expected in six months. In five months, the bank had more than 1 million calls, most from a core of heavy users. Vice president Gaylon Howe says, "Over a period of years we can reduce the number of people in the bank's various branches by over 40 people, close to $1 million a year of savings."

Wachovia has added transaction services such as transfers, stop-payment requests, and statements to its voice systems. In addition, the same service is now being offered by Wachovia Bank of Georgia, which has 139 offices.

The Wachovia system was installed by Intervoice, Inc. The other firms referred to above used a voice system line made by Syntellect, Inc. Many other fine voice systems are made by a number of companies which also have exciting case histories of savings.

Voice systems can be disastrous if improperly installed, if they're unable to handle the call volume, or if they are poor in quality. Watch out for a new model with bugs or shoddy equipment from an extreme price-cutter. Check out your source, thoroughly orient your employees, and provide careful explanations to your customers.

Upscale customers sometimes resist. Bullocks of Los Angeles, for example, tried a voice system but didn't find it successful enough to continue; 90 percent of callers still wanted to talk to a human operator.

Once they get the knack of it, many people *prefer* to call a voice system to get the immediately desired information or a call back from the *right* person. Voice systems can perform many unique and much appreciated services. For example, calls pour into a utilities company during a power outage. Most such callers formerly got a busy signal but can now get a voice system which tells them which areas are out and when service should be restored. In short, calls get through and people get instant information they need badly. Few of them talk to a live operator at all.

Self-Service Bulletin Boards. On I&E computer networks such as Prodigy and CompuServe, special interest groups (SIGs) devoted to mutual aid for PC hardware, peripheral, and software owners are popular. Users help each other. Most SIGs are subsidized by manufacturers, because SIGs are a low-cost and excellent way to help customers. CompuServe has nearly a hundred SIG forums on various makes and models. These forums are often the best way to get the latest, in-depth information on PCs.

In Chapter 18, I reported on Scott Watson and his FreeSoft Company, which distributes White Knight and other software created by Scott. He says:

> User groups have been absolutely key to our success. BBSs made user groups have a wider audience. Bulletin boards help distribution. A person logs in and asks or answers a question. A discussion starts and soon they reach a consensus. One says he has a problem with a communications program. Three or four say they have been very happy with White Knight. We get a customer.
>
> We have a forum on GEnie run out of the house of one employee. It offers technical support and has tremendous traffic. It's a neat way to update. There's no out-of-pocket cost to us, but it takes the full time of one employee. User groups have been absolutely key to our success. BBSs give user groups a wide audience.

EDI.   The American Association of Railroads has an EDI software program to help U.S. auto manufacturers track delivery of parts which are en route. It also does this for Japanese car manufacturers for U.S. deliveries of cars and parts. The American Trucking Association also offers the same service.

Microsoft's Many Electronic Services.   Microsoft Corp. of Redmond, Washington, offers a variety of free electronic support for each of a number of service situations:

- Thirteen forums on CompuServe each give free help, information, and advice on specific Microsoft products but do involve connect time charges for CompuServe.

- For seven Microsoft products, live startup and installation support is given free on a special number each, 6 a.m. to 6 p.m., Monday through Friday but not on some holidays. Just pay the phone company charge.

- A number of different Microsoft products have their own number you can call via a touchtone phone to get free automated answers to the most commonly asked technical support questions. You can do this any time seven days a week, 24 hours a day, including holidays. Just pay the phone company charge.

- You can read free each word of any answer given by phone. Each answer (and additional technical information for MS-DOS 5.0) can be requested and sent via fax—seven days a week, 24 hours a day, including holidays. Just pay the phone company charge.

- For technical information on eight Microsoft product areas, there's a free Microsoft download service. Information is updated monthly. Customers use their own modems and terminal software.

- There's access to free support for all Microsoft products for hearing-impaired users—6 a.m. to 6 p.m., Monday to Friday. Access requires a special TDD modem.

Microsoft also offers a number of support services for those who desire more intensive or continuing help and are willing to pay for it. Subscription packages range from $750 to $15,000. Those paying for such support range from hobbyist software developers to professional developers to software dealers to medium-size and big corporate accounts.

Chrysler. Chrysler's computer network connects 6000 of its U.S. and Canadian dealers. One program guides mechanics in the repair of cars. Another program gets information from mechanics about cars brought in for repair and sends it over the network to Chrysler's mainframe computers. At Chrysler's headquarters, these data become part of a performance data bank to help designers create better cars.

Avis. Avis puts terminals on its shuttle buses that transport customers from the airport terminal to the Avis location. When a customer boards the Avis bus, he or she gives the driver key information. When the bus reaches the Avis location, the customer can be dropped off at his or her car and find a completed rental agreement waiting on the seat.

When Avis customers return a car, an Avis representative, with a hand-held computer linked to the Avis computer network, meets them at the parking lot. By entering only three pieces of information, the representative completes the rental transaction and gives the customer a receipt from a portable printer. The transaction can be completed often before customers have removed their luggage from the vehicle's trunk.

A free, automatic checkout is available at many hotels and motels exactly as if ordering a movie. A wake-up service can be ordered and room service and reservations for room and car at the next city. Guests can review their hotel bills anytime, day or night, by simply pushing buttons on the TV set in their rooms. Some hotels have video check-in systems similar to ATM machines. Travelers insert a credit card into a slot, put in their information, and pick up the key.

Kiosk Turns On Home or Office Phone. Some phone companies now have a method by which a part-time resident can turn the telephone service off or on electronically. There's no need to phone the telephone company or to wait in line for a service person to come and install the equipment.

Instead customers simply insert a credit card into a phone company electronic kiosk in town and indicate that they want the service restored. The machine checks if the bills are paid and, if so, makes all the arrangements. It's no more complicated than turning on an electric light.

Brooklyn Union Gas uses interactive kiosks as a service to people who are moving their business or into a home in the area. An application to get power from the utility can be filled out on the kiosk. The same kiosk also answers commonly asked customer questions—from how to pay the bill to safety tips about a home, office, or factory.

Blue Cross of Western Pennsylvania places kiosks in drug stores so that when patients come in to get medicine, they can also phone and enter claims. It's much faster for a customer, attracts business for the drug store, and costs Blue Cross far less.

Self-Teaching Products. Electronic manuals built into products help ensure customer satisfaction, thereby increasing the likelihood that customers will buy more from the same marketer. The Nintendo Piano Teaching System, for example, combines a 49-key electronic piano keyboard with special software. This software teaches the user how to play the piano and read music through a series of on-screen tutorials, video games, and computer-generated tunes. It is the first musical instrument to train the user how to play it.

Many of these applications are developed by big companies. But how can you start or improve your customer service in a small way? Start by improving the way your firm handles customer phone calls. If you now already have a customer service program, can it be improved? Does it cost too much?

Many Service Possibilities

You can start to improve customer service by instilling a new attitude and approach to one person—and then to others, one by one. You can set up a call center to handle inquiries and complaints. You can later try a simple voice system in house or via a service. If the system doesn't please customers in new ways and doesn't save money to cover part or all its cost, you can cancel the project. You can start in one area, one office, or one department. You can offer service to answer questions by phone, by fax, by modem, or by all three.

If you succeed in electronic marketing in any form described in this book, you can add a use for customer service at least extra cost. You may start with a customer service and then add electronic marketing. Or you may just share the costs to start. The Help Source Guide for each chapter can help you start or improve customer service in the field covered.

Service, savings, and marketing are intertwined. Service gives long-term benefits while savings pay for it. Marketing creates the profit. All three can be accomplished together, whichever the major thrust and however it starts. Different departments and divisions can pool budgets and share benefits. The biggest advantage may be the information you get from those who call as you tell them what they need to know.

Develop a few key questions that let you handle each call fast, yet allow you to get free marketing research and product development advice. Include questions about customers' preferences and thank them for their answers. With your answers, *teach* them more about your products and get them more involved. Whatever they call about, ask them about their future buying plans and if they would like to be called and when.

Customer service can start as a free product or service support function and, if it is valued, can gradually be limited to a warranty period. Customers and prospects may then be willing to pay you to give them the same phone support. The phone company or an electronic service bureau information service or your firm can bill for the service. Perhaps you can even go beyond selling information about your product to selling information about your product's field—whether it's for an interest, hobby, business, or profession.

You may choose to become an electronic publisher for profit *instead* of ever giving phone support. Or teach, as a separate venture, how to profit from a field of interest or how to get into the field or simply demonstrate the hobby. In the same way, as you sell the information you create desire for your product. By asking for an order for the information first, then for the product, you can up-sell and cross-sell as you follow up.

The electronic media described in this book can all be used for customer service as well as for marketing. Customer service is an essential part of marketing. As always, use the medium or combination of media best suited to you. Chapter 30 explains ways to integrate and enhance electronic and print media.

Help Source Guide

1. *Business by Phone, Inc.*, provides customer service training products, a service catalog, an audiocassette, "How to Manage Your Telephone for Bigger Profits," and "Servicing You Proactively," six audiotapes: 5301 S. 144th St., Omaha, NE 68137. (800) 326-7721.

2. For conference call service, *"Training-by-Phone"* audio conferences train how to present and gain greatest benefits, services to customers. Choose fax training broadcasts, audiographics, videoconference training: P.O. Box 835, New Providence, NJ 07974. (800) 272-5663.

3. *The Customer Service Institute* provides video and audio phone training packages, film, books, in-house seminars, workshops: 1010 Wayne Ave., Silver Spring, MD 20910-9931. (301) 585-0730.

4. *Customer Response and Information Systems, 1991,* is a fine book by J. Anton, T. R. Bennett, and R. Widdows, from Tarp Information Systems, Inc., who offers a *free* information kit: Suite 100, 1700 17th St., NW, Washington, D.C. 20009. (301) 546-2223.

5. *The GE Business Information Center* offers a *free* information kit, "How to Set Up and Organize a Business Customer, Phone-Service Center": One Winners Circle, Suite 200, Albany, NY 12205. (518) 438-2525.

6. *The GE Service Center* offers a *free* information kit on "How to Set Up and Organize a Consumer Customer, Phone-Service Center": 9500 Williamsburg Plaza, Louisville, KY 40222. (502) 423-4501.

7. *How to Use the Telephone More Effectively* (114 pages), Barron's Press, 1991, written by Madeline Bodin (editor of *Inbound/Outbound* magazine), provides needed service suggestions for department heads, other middle managers. Begins where customer service books end: 50 Wireless Blvd., Hauppauge, NY 11788. (516) 434-3311.

8. *Inbound/Outbound* magazine can be read in any business library. Look for special articles on customer service. Buy special issues, then subscribe: 12 W. 21st St., NY, NY 10011. (212) 206-6660.

9. *The Incoming Calls Management Institute* focuses on how to set up and manage incoming call centers and offers a free copy of *Customer Service Newsletter.* P.O. Box 6177, Annapolis, MD 21401. (800) 672-6177.

10. *IPC Trade Shows, Inc.* sponsors a call center annual show with new-technology exhibits, training seminars to help set up and operate customer service centers. Ask about video- or audiotapes of talks: P.O. Box 42382, Houston, TX 77242. (800) 777-4442.

11. *Muldoon Management* offers *free* the "Catalog Service Do's and Dont's" by expert Katie Muldoon: 300 Park Ave., South, 7th Fl., NY, NY 10010-5313. (212) 979-7200.

12. *Syntellect Inc.* offers a *free* information kit on InfoBot audiotext system for service purposes, case histories of successful use, big savings, product descriptions, costs: 15810 N. 28th Ave., Phoenix, AZ 85023. (602) 264-5900.

13. *Total Customer Service: The Ultimate Weapon,* by W. H. Davidow and Bro Uttal, Harper & Row, provides case histories that trace sales increases from improved service. Available at libraries or bookstores or at 10 E. 53d St., NY, NY 10022. (212) 207-7000.

30
The Integration of EM into All Marketing

Each form of electronic media can present a sales story in a special way. Each may have its own role in your overall marketing plan and its own way to enhance other media. For best results, each form of electronic and print media must be integrated into a cohesive, cost-effective marketing campaign, with the whole far exceeding the sum of its parts. This chapter will show you how others have done it so you can too. TV support advertising, for example, has repeatedly demonstrated its ability to increase total response from mailings by adding enough increased response to more than justify its additional cost. Before TV support ads, radio support ads successfully pioneered this method.

A German media study of 43 brands confirms the power of integration. It showed that when print and TV are used together, the brand awareness index rises much more rapidly than for the same expenditures for print or TV alone. In the Netherlands, Italy, Canada, and Great Britain, other studies have revealed similar findings.

Adding magazine ads to a TV ad campaign worked even better than adding TV to print. The Lintas ad agency reported:

> Print can lead people to perceive the TV commercial in new ways and can also convey new information that is not in the TV commercial. The result of adding print to a TV campaign is a richer, more complete communication.

Now more than ever, the failure to integrate and enhance electronic media with print advertising, by using every practical and applicable medium, amounts to throwing away a percentage of each dollar spent in advertising. Susan Bahr, when head of New Media at Young & Rubicam, said:

> Media are becoming complex. All communications are. We look for ways to talk directly to people, and in more meaningful ways. It's a challenge to advertisers to learn different ways to use the new media, to use interactive methods and integrate them all.
>
> The art of advertising is how to manage all this. If on TV you use image advertising in 30 seconds, you can supplement this with videos for special events and go to whatever length you need, maybe a half-hour.
>
> Thus, you can use different packages, different lengths in direct mail, newspapers, TV and in videos. You need the mix of the quick/short image repetition constantly repeated. And at the same time, you need the longer formats to tell the story you can't possibly tell on the short image spots.

A business may advertise to business firms on TV or radio, get inquiries by phone, and send reproductions of catalog pages by fax. The business may advertise on a computer network, get inquiries by modem, and answer them by mail. It may also produce a 10-minute touch-screen kiosk demonstration of its product or service and offer to mail a 30-minute video demonstration in more detail. The firm may also give a demonstration on a BBS and offer to send by mail a giant catalog on a CD-ROM disc.

Almost every case history mentioned in this book integrates one electronic medium with another, and with publications, direct mail, catalogs, or salespeople, often in ingenious ways. In many instances, the degree of integration went beyond the space allowed for description.

Some advantages of media integration include the following:

- Integrated media enhance each medium's impact, for more results per dollar spent.
- Integration unifies your entire campaign into a seamless whole.
- Integration can gradually build into a continuous chain of promotion.
- Integration can add instant action to image advertising.
- Integration helps trace results and the accountability of components.

Electronic sales staff training can be combined with the entire marketing campaign's orientation along with each electronic enhancement.

At the same time, the sales force can be instructed so as to get maximum sales from each component of the campaign. Simultaneously, electronic service and sales efforts can be integrated. Customers and prospects who contact the company for information or help can be informed of the latest products, appropriate add-ons, and incentives to purchase anything that specially fits the caller.

Some of integration's disadvantages include the following:

- Combining more media costs more.

- Picking media, conceiving and producing all these ads is more difficult.

- If poorly executed, integration can cause clutter, confusion, and bad advertising.

- If poorly conceived or agreed upon just to be "fashionable," the results often are subjective, unscientific efforts that eat up time and neglect measurement.

As word gets out about the success of any new electronic form (or of a new application of one), marketers often rush to use it in their campaigns. Sometimes it's a last-minute addition to an agency or marketing department's presentation to management. It may sound good but be overpriced or not right for the purpose. Disaster stories abound about "free" media offered as an inducement to purchase or as part of a combination buy—with little understanding of how to use it by either the seller or the buyer.

Should *you* integrate your marketing? Decidedly yes, but make sure you do it *correctly!* If you use more than one medium, and mention one in the other, you already integrate media to some degree. If you use one medium profitably, you almost certainly can profitably use others. If you use each medium alone, you usually should integrate their use together to the fullest extent possible. How do we do this?

The biggest integrate best. Large marketers have the widest and biggest distribution networks, the most extensive promotion and public relations capabilities. Plus they enjoy the expertise of top-notch ad agencies, consultants, and specialists in the newest electronic media. In short, large marketers have the most to weave together and the biggest need to do so. They must think in terms of campaigns, not ads and multimedia, not stand-alone media.

At any one time, Chrysler Corp. uses many forms of electronic media for its appropriate car lines, models, and makes, and integrates each form into an overall campaign. Chrysler was the first on CNN. It has been a pioneer outbound-phone marketer and a long-time user of an 800 number. Chrysler's Jeep has run spots on rental videos, while its other divisions have used computer disks. It's a big broadcast TV advertiser, but these buys are integrated with cable. Tom McAlear, director of marketing for the corporation, says:

> We buy a lot of cable sports, news, arts, and information. We buy motor sports. We buy MTV. We realize that the quality of audience of broadcast TV has dropped, that the audience of cable is increasing, and that cable has very good demographics.
>
> We get something else from cable: frequency—a good many repeats of the same commercials or series of commercials to the same audience. High expense of network TV means that we buy big gobs of audience, with much less repetition of our message to that audience.
>
> Frequency of cable enhances the effectiveness of our TV advertising. And on cable TV we get the more elusive viewer, the more affluent one whom we want to reach.
>
> We sell on the basis of lifestyle. Our average car sells for $14,000. We need to reach people who can afford that. We don't buy CPM. We buy many specialized programs on arts and entertainment to get quality circulation.

Electronic media help Chrysler integrate all its national advertising, from promotion to prospects in the showroom to the "couch potatoes" in the home. For many years, Chrysler has used videodiscs in its showrooms. These interactive programs entice car prospects to call up the information desired about the car they are interested in. Videos are also sent to Chrysler prospects. Tom McAlear says:

> We have an internal TV network. We beam down from the satellite just to connect our own house network to talk to our own people. We will also go to the educational TV channel and organize a video sales meeting. We're always trying something. We experiment.

Chrysler's largest direct-mail promotion promoted a satellite screening of its new line: Two mailings totaling 26 million pieces that cost over $10 million went out within weeks before the screening. The first mail piece sold the features of the new cars. The second invited recipients to a Chrysler Corporation private screening by satellite at the nearest dealer.

To prequalify those who accepted, potential buyers were asked to indicate (on the back of the invitation) the type of vehicle they were interested in purchasing and the make of their trade-in vehicle. Five thousand Chrysler U.S. dealerships (80 percent) participated in the program.

On average, 150 couples attended each dealer's screening. Some bought on the spot. But most sales were made later by salesperson follow-up.

The smallest can integrate. Team play multiplies the effectiveness of each player. However, a new medium (or "player") often starts without being seen by the coach and may be unknown even to some star players on the marketing team. A new medium often debuts in the bush leagues, or sometimes in the street, by opportunistic beginners just learning the game. A start-up or small firm may discover new uses for one medium on a stand-alone basis and then latch on to another in the same way. But media used together in the right way creates a consistently winning and profitable team.

Media teamwork or integration does not necessarily require a big budget. Inch ads and classified ads often reach more people per dollar spent than any other medium. If the ad's prime job is to pull response to an electronic medium, modest sizes can produce a very low cost per inquiry, while also allowing for follow-up messages that are as long as necessary.

Separately, sometimes neither tiny ads nor electronic media are apt to be profitable, although the combination of tiny ad and low-cost electronic follow-up can be very profitable. And because small business owners see the results, it's easier for them to measure, enhance, and integrate each additional marketing element than for a huge, complex company.

Integration is hardest for those in between. Marketers who are neither big nor small often find it difficult to integrate. Marketing and other management resources are stretched thin, allowing little time to investigate, develop, watch, and measure the results of each marketing step. How about your firm?

Nothing better illustrates both the enhancements of an electronic medium and the advantages of integrating media than the sales force itself—once you think of it as a marketing medium. Ways to electronically enhance and integrate a single salesperson or the biggest sales force are available to anyone. Anyone in sales who is not using these new tools is at a competitive disadvantage. Compare the following sales situation with what your firm does now.

The Electronically Enhanced Sales Force

Sales forces are now commonly trained via DBS, by video and audio, floppy disks, and via online computers and a host of other multimedia methods. Obviously, the coordination of all these electronic media is critical. Here's how book representatives use electronic media to get more sales.

A big marketing problem in book publishing is the placement of appropriate books in the optimum quantities in stores when an author is interviewed on TV or radio. Each sales representative is instructed to notify his or her biggest customers by fax or E-mail of the author's tour schedule. For a store chain like B. Dalton which has many stores in many markets, it's the sales representative's job to get the chain to notify all the store managers well in advance in a city on the tour schedule. Next, the representative sends by fax or E-mail a signed letter announcing the news to every other book outlet in the tour city, typically three weeks before the media event. The representative follows up by phone both before and after the promotional events, at which times title inventories are checked and reorders obtained. If sales are particularly strong, the representative may make personal visits to important accounts.

Many sales representatives use a call-waiting service to take a second call, while placing the first account on hold. Remote call-forwarding makes it easy and cheap for customers and prospects to call from anywhere at local rates. Autodialing reduces time to only one or two digits to reach important customers. Voice mail or fax announcements are made to accounts in a city the salesperson plans to visit. On the way, the salesperson confirms appointments by cellular phone from a car and phones the office to listen to the latest voice mail.

The fax is used for many purposes. From letters to contract proposals to engineering drawings to copies of catalog pages or ads, salespeople use fax to keep in close touch with their customers and their boss.

Sales forces selling complex products are using a never-ending succession of briefcase, notebook, and hand-held computers that continually become smaller, lighter, faster, and more powerful. Faster, smaller, cheaper modems connect them to the office or other computer sites. Multisensor capabilities are proliferating. For instance, the IBM Audio-Visual Connection card allows a salesperson to develop a complete presentation using audio, visual, data, and text, compress it ten times, and send it by modem.

Computer programs are also becoming more responsive. Many salespeople dial into their company computer and feed in the details of a complex proposal. The computer then calculates the costs involved, adds the markup, and spits out the price to quote. A Pepperidge Farm delivery/salesperson uses a hand-held terminal to input what was delivered to the store and then prints an invoice. At the end of each business day, the salesperson connects her or his terminal to a modem and sends delivery information via the AT&T network to Pepperidge headquarters. From there, daily deliveries are transmitted to the billing department and an order for fresh products is transmitted to the appropriate baking facility.

Integrating Sales and Advertising, Telemarketers and the Sales Force

Printed material helps convince sales prospects; when a contract is forwarded, a phone call can then explain and help take away the fear of small-print clauses. The final closure can occur by phone, a personal sales call, or by an appointment at a sales office or an event. The selling process is intertwined with national and local advertising, trade shows and trade magazine ads, PR and promotions. All produce leads that salespeople close.

A chain of promotional efforts in a variety of media may prove most effective to consummate sales. At each step those less interested drop out. Those remaining may want more answers to different questions. Electronic media can be programmed to answer those questions when they're asked. For example, the following three-step approach can produce quick sales. Just combine any medium with an audiotext response channel and additional messages with the sales force as the final "closer." Anyone inquiring can be electronically referred to the appropriate salesperson.

In Chapters 8 and 9 we described how much more productive telemarketers and the sales force are when their efforts are coordinated. IBM uses telemarketers for "commodity" items that are accepted and frequently ordered and uses the sales force to launch new products. The telemarketers work on smaller transactions and the sales force on bigger ones.

The telemarketers get leads for the sales force for transactions needing demonstration. The sales force turns over to telemarketers the accepting and solicitation of repeat orders for computer supplies and certain peripheral products and software. Both efforts are integrated with advertising, trade shows, targeted direct mail, and public relations. Smaller companies often use commission representatives on bigger accounts in bigger cities, and telemarketers on smaller, out-of-the-way accounts. There can be more enhancement.

Richard Bencin, a top telemarketing expert, is a great believer in the integration of telemarketing, direct mail, video brochures, and a sales representative. He calls it "telefocus" marketing. Bencin says: "By priming the prospect with a video brochure in advance of a sales call, that prospect is mentally prepared for the sales representative's call."

The same effect may also be realized with a computer disk. Sometimes, by coordinating a succession of marketing contacts—a video or disk, phone and mail—the sales force's efforts may be greatly reduced or even dropped. Typically, the telemarketing component of the integrated campaign must be expanded and enhanced in other ways.

Integrating All Direct Marketing

Murray Roman pioneered the telemarketing medium and launched the first telephone marketing firm to make over 100 million calls. His son, Ernan Roman, pioneered integrated direct marketing (IDM), starting with telephone and direct mail. Ernan cites many examples, among which is the following, where IDM in many combinations for clients of Ernan Roman Direct Marketing (ERDM), and for others, pulled more results than when direct marketing media are used separately.

> CitiCorp, for a home equity loan product and against a "mail only" control, tested an IDM combination of print, mail, plus inbound and outbound calls. The IDM test not only increased the number of new accounts by 15 percent but decreased marketing costs by 71 percent.

Direct mail can also be combined with telemarketing and audio conferencing. Dean Meyer Associates sell computer consultation and audioconferencing. Dean says:

> We use direct mail to get leads but have never closed a single sponsor by direct mail. We close by phone. If we qualify an inquiry by phone, we send them a free tape of a previous conference as a demo and then phone back to close.

Ernan Roman reports how Hewlett-Packard (H-P), working with ERDM, implemented an IDM approach to improve lead quantity and quality. The goal was to get more CEOs, CFOs, and VPs of finance and MIS to attend any of the four sessions of an audio conference:

> H-P used a 7-step IDM registration process developed by ERDM which included, on a time schedule, initial direct mail producing

800# and BRC response—outbound telemarketing, a confirmation letter and a briefing package—then two confirmation calls and a follow-up letter.

The registration rate was 163 percent of forecast; qualified leads were 222 percent of forecast; 12.5 percent of the mailed universe registered for the conferences; 61 percent of registrants attended with an average of 3.5 from each company. All stayed on the line the entire conference. The H-P sales force viewed the participants as high-quality leads of a senior level of decision maker previously inaccessible to them.

IDM-Enhanced TV

Direct marketers prefer two-minute TV commercials, but this time length can be difficult to place on the air during desirable times of the day. A 30-second direct-response commercial can be placed much more easily. Although 30-second spots typically can pull a phone inquiry, they can't usually complete a sale. One solution is to weave the rest of the sales message into the telephone script. When the prospect responds by calling the 800 number, a live salesperson can add sales points for about three minutes or so—time enough also to up-sell and cross-sell. Audiotext can also be the follow-up medium. For example, Weichert Realtors of Morristown, New Jersey, features a toll-free number. Once you provide a little interaction, including a down payment figure, the audiotext program calculates and states the monthly mortgage expense.

Electronic media have not and will not replace print. But electronic media are changing the ways in which print can be most profitably used. Integrating print with electronic media marketing leads to far better results than either one alone. Use print to get people to call an audiotext gateway, to fax response, to use EM kiosks, dial computer bulletin boards, or whatever other electronic media tool is appropriate. In certain business-to-business selling situations, the immediacy of the fax can be profitably combined by prominent mention within any size ad, even classifieds. The immediately returned fax delivery of one to several pages of additional sales material can clinch the sale while the prospect is hot.

The *Literary Guild Magazine* book club member magazine prominently features a 900 number. Members pay to hear a big-name author read short excerpts from his or her latest best-seller via a recorded message. Each 11-minute recorded message begins with a "hello" from 10 best-selling authors such as Judith Krantz, Danielle Steele, and Michael Korda, and reminds callers that they can participate in special offers not available in the magazine. The message also refers to promotions on various pages of the magazine. Members just press a button to make a purchase.

The recorded message changes every 21 days to coincide with new issues of the magazine. Callers must use a touchtone phone to participate. The system captures the caller's 11-digit account number, plus a 1-digit control to specify the magazine edition where a special promotion ran. The cost is 50 cents for one minute and 50 cents a minute thereafter. The average call is 3 minutes and 42 seconds. The Literary Guild phone program 900 conversion to sales averaged 10 to 15 percent during the first 21 days of the offer.

The Nexis division of Mead Data Central inserted 210,000 disks bound into *Forbes* magazine. Results have proven successful enough for both Nexis and *Forbes* to expand their programs. Chapter 16 explained how CitiCorp used integrated techniques to promote its business-to-business financial services. The best integrated marketing formula can require several attempts, but persistence pays off. You'll recall how CitiCorp slashed selling costs by 90 percent after first trying to combine direct mail with computer disk demonstrations and then online demonstrations combined with closure by telephone marketing instead of personal sales visits.

Catalog and Phone Combined

Lee Van Vechten, a top catalog and telemarketing authority, preaches:

> Catalogs have, literally, one brief shot. Catalogs cannot talk. Telemarketing as a new-business tool often fails because of its expense. Telemarketing in conjunction with catalog mailings is often very successful because of its added credibility. Confidence has been established; there is a reason for the call.

Spiegel gets 93 percent of its catalog business by phone. The J. C. Penney catalog gets and makes over 100 million phone calls a year and does over 98 percent of its business by phone. J. C. Penney's catalog features its 800 number every several pages, often in big type. The Sears catalog gets over 95 percent of its business by phone.

As I've explained in previous chapters, electronic catalogs in various media thus far have often proven to be more useful as support media or supplemental promotion rather than as a primary selling tool. There are exceptions, of course, and these should be studied closely. Video catalogs can be appropriate to show action and for demonstrations. Floppy disk catalogs and marketplaces are best when presenting limited amounts of text and graphics and where frequent updating is helpful. Online catalogs and marketplaces are best for smaller amounts of description to be viewed or downloaded at one time and for last-minute updating of price, items, or inventory status. CD-ROM catalogs and marketplaces can contain more pictures, graphics, color, far more items, and much more text.

In general, video cocatalogs and floppy disk cocatalogs each work hand in hand with print catalogs to make both media more profitable. Even CD-ROM catalogs are usually supported by print. And some print catalogs are supplemented by audiotape.

When the QVC shopping TV network launched a print catalog, it used its on-air personalities as models in the QVC catalogs. In turn, QVC print catalogs feature TV program guides, previews of items for sale on QVC, and stories about show hosts. Response rates of 4 to 8 percent are reported.

Multimedia Integration

With 50 to 65 percent of all cable pay-per-view purchases triggered by seeing "barker" channels (those that scroll what's playing on the system) and other cross-channel promotions, it's evident that multimedia integration can be powerful. United Artists owns radio stations, movie theaters, and cable systems. In areas where all three operate, they integrate promotion. Each medium sells the others. They cross-market radio and theater and cable. Via cable, on radio, and on the theater screen, they sell cable subscriptions. Radio commercials sell listeners to watch UA cable and see movies at UA theaters. And UA cable sells viewers to go UA theaters and to listen to UA radio.

Michael Horne, another multimedia operator, offers advertisers this integrated package:

1. Commercials on his *Cable Radio Network*

2. Use of cents-off coupons

3. Coupon mailing to cable homes, with cable program

4. Hourly commercial mentions on cable

Hearst offers integrated media packages, custom-designed for the products of each advertiser. For an advertiser's campaign in Hearst shelter magazines, Hearst included an in-store custom-decorating video, using editorial material and talent from the magazines. Marketers now routinely ask for and get such deals from various types of media.

Enhanced, Integrated PR

More kinds of public relations are available via electronic media than via print. Don't overlook any, and integrate each into your plan. Big companies use PR very effectively to introduce products. Often, PR produces more inquiries than all advertising combined and then increases the response from advertising. PR can pull phone calls, fax, and modem requests. When a CEO speaks to stockholders, the message can often be repackaged to be appropriate and powerful persuasion to your sales force, dealer network, or to the world. A little PR for a small company can help it start to become big.

Texas Instruments' Voice Chip.   Texas Instruments ran a four-page insert in *BusinessWeek* (*BW*) to tell the story of its voice chip. To demonstrate it, TI affixed a talking chip module just a little larger than a credit card to selected copies of *BW*'s corporate elite edition of 140,000 subscribers. Over each module was a sticker labeled "Lift and Listen." Anyone who did heard a digitized male voice say in 15 seconds these 41 words:

> I am the talking chip, one of Texas Instruments' MegaChip technologies which is changing the way the world lives, works, and plays. Through such innovations, TI can help creative companies like yours win the race to market with products that excel.

Ed Morett, then director of communications of TI, says:

> Development, production, and distribution of the talking ad had to be both cost- *and* expertise-driven, which meant that we went to several parts of the world in order to execute the project.
> The 41 words were recorded in Los Angeles, software was enhanced in Dallas, and the semiconductor wafer was fabricated in Lubbock, TX. The wafers were tested and separated into individual chips in the Philippines. Assembly of the speech module took place in The People's Republic of China, while printing of the insert occurred simultaneously in Los Angeles.
> The assembly of the module into the 6-panel insert took place in Tijuana, Mexico, after which the inserts were shipped to binderies in Arkansas and Virginia. 140,000 copies of *BusinessWeek* with inserts bound-in were delivered to selected readers in the Northeast and Western U.S. and 76,000 copies to Europe and Asia.

The completed insert cost about $4 and increased the CPM for the four pages from about $200 to about $4000, or about 20 times. Out of TI's total cost of over $900,000, about $864,000 was for the chip. But the difference in impact changed the usual rules of reach and frequency.

Integration of TI's Entire Campaign.   While this ad appeared only once, it was not a "one-shot" promotion but part of TI's four-year MegaChip Technologies campaign that appeared in *BusinessWeek, The Wall Street Journal,* and *Electronic Business.* TI's target audience included corporate officers and policy-level executives within original equipment manufacturing firms. TI had three objectives:

1. Develop a demonstration for TI's new threshold in speech synthesis technology. This featured a 50-percent lower chip cost than previous designs; a flat dimensional form; high-quality speech, music, and sound effects; and durability to survive magazine insertion.
2. Create a new market development opportunity for TI's solid-state speech synthesis business.
3. Broaden awareness of TI's MegaChip Technologies to help customers get to market faster with more competitive products.

A Major Media Event
Ed Morett tells the story:

> PR about the ad far surpassed the reach that we achieved with the ad itself. Major newspaper features included *Wall Street Journal, The New York Times, Newsday, USA Today, Boston Globe, Los Angeles Times,* and *The Christian Science Monitor.*
> An AP newswire story was picked up in 27 major US dailies. There was extensive radio coverage, with the chip itself put on the air. Feature stories appeared in 8 electronic publications. Features appeared in *Ad Age, AdWeek* and *Publishing and Production Executive.*
> All this happened although the talking ad appeared on the day of the San Francisco earthquake...which did lose us most of the TV coverage we expected. International media exposure in Europe and the Far East was equally successful. I would put the global value of the publicity the project received in excess of $2 million.
> A Starch Reader Impression study indicated a positive overall response by more than 7 of 10 readers. Verbatim comments included "great idea" and "amazed to hear the ad talk." TI was regarded as an "innovative company" and a "leader in its field."
> We received well over 2000 phone inquiries from the ad, about 30 percent from advertisers and 70 percent for other applications.

AT&T was the first advertiser to complete a project—a talking direct mail piece promoting their WATS line services. And we are currently negotiating contracts for millions of chips over the next couple of years. Since the project, talking chip sales have multiplied several times until production has hit top capacity.

Judging EM Enhancement

What should you consider in judging any electronic media enhancement? A TI chip seems a natural for a toy marketer with a cartoon character. But in a mass circulation magazine, a chip enhancement multiplies the cost of a page ad over 400 times and even more for a smaller ad. At current prices, it's very unlikely to produce enough extra sales. However, via a 900 number, one $4 chip might be used for thousands or hundreds of thousands of calls. A minute and a half of speech can be put on one chip. The offer might attract calls at a profit, with free advertising thrown in. While cost prohibits its use on a package, it could be highly profitable added to an in-store display.

Any electronic media enhancement can only work if the use fits, the presentation is perfected, and the price is right. Even then, if the electronic promotion is done on its own, the benefit to your company will be far more limited than if it is integrated throughout the entire marketing campaign. However, none of the new electronic media discussed in this book should be embraced by *your* marketing team without ample investigation and stand-alone testing and measurement of its sales results.

Which EM Enhancement Fits

Your type of business, its organization and distribution network, plus your marketing and creative objectives will dictate which electronic media warrant your attention. Other considerations include your product, product line, or service; your marketing plan and strategy; your target audience; your offer, copy, and presentation; and where are the best electronic links in your selling chain. This takes a comprehensive knowledge of your business.

What are the strengths and weaknesses of your firm and product line? What is its history, and the history of your competition? Past focus group summaries and other research and statistical analysis reports may give you many answers. What is the concept behind your marketing and your present campaign theme? What media are most successful for you? What are the limitations of each? What EM enhancement can best overcome these constraints?

The ability to integrate media starts with making the right selection—the right marriage of media capabilities to marketing needs. You also must keep up with the newest EM forms and their successes and failures, especially involving companies similar to yours.

Let's review what electronic media can do best:

- Reach more people at one time.

- Offer more frequency than any other media. Cheaper EM supplies frequency that can help qualify the use of other, more expensive EM.

- Sell in seconds or offer instantly more detailed information than any other media.

- Offer information instantly when wanted, to anyone who wants it.

- Reach any ethnic, professional, business, or other special market—even the blind or the deaf.

- Teach the use of your product and give instant help at any time. This builds customer friendship, loyalty, and recommendations.

- Demonstrate product benefits in ways no other media can.

- Save people cost, as it sells, in ways no other media can.

- Instantly refer customers to your nearest dealers or connect them instantly with your dealers, salespeople, or other offices.

- Stage a spokesperson, even a different one for each ethnic group or special market, to offer your product.

- Auction items instantly, conduct an instant sweepstakes, answer inquiries, take orders, and be an electronic catalog.

- Raise funds in a flash. Supply cents-off coupons at once. Create and distribute more PR than any other media.

- Create an instant profile center with product or service information. They pay you as you sell and service them.

The Spectrum of EM Forms

Some new forms of electronic media are potentially universal. Others act as electronic "magnet" media—by attracting specialized groups from broad segments into narrow niches. Instant-action electronic media close sales for dealers, salespeople, or the company itself. "Forward pass" electronic media qualify and pass on prospects to the next selling step. Some electronic media combine a number of these features. Although the "eye and ear" appeal of TV is usually more effective than radio's sole ear appeal, radio can offer more frequency for the same money than TV. Print, radio, or TV can tell the beginning of your story and produce inquiries for more detailed information. This can be followed up by letter or phone; by an audio- or videotape, a floppy disk, or CD-ROM disc; or by a salesperson.

There is an electronic medium with the capability to remedy almost any of your marketing problems. And many of these electronic media can and will become important tools in the increasingly difficult task of reaching your marketing objectives. But keeping up with the proliferation of EM is not easy.

EM is more personal than print. Electronic friend-making, via a spokesperson, can be more personal and warmer than via print. It can start a relationship between seller and prospect. The same spokesperson can give a short message by TV or radio and deliver a far longer appeal in a video. Different spokespeople can talk on different audiocassettes, even in different languages, each in his or her own way.

Electronic service information help is more personal, faster, and lower-cost for you. With a 900 number, service can become a profit center. Electronic testimonials, from real people, can be more compelling than their print counterparts. Entirely new uses for a product, new benefits, and new reasons for using it come across on EM as news, in a very personal way.

Each EM form must earn its keep. As in all media buying, in order to know if EM works, you must track results. EM often has built-in self measurements such as computerized running totals of inquiries, percentage of sales conversion from inquiries, dollars of sales, and ad cost per dollar of sales. Telemarketing, audiotext, kiosks, and many electronic media forms usually have software capable of keeping track. For certain ways of using many of these media forms, cooperation by people is needed but often lacking. Dealers can measure, but often don't. The national marketer often can trace local sales from those inquiries produced nationally but often doesn't. In this way, smaller marketers usually can watch more closely and react more quickly than the big marketers.

Does your sales force or dealer network follow up on the leads you send them? Do you know your sales versus lead cost? Be scientific. Set up tests to determine what inquiry and sales action your electronic media marketing can produce at what cost. Compile results of exactly what your EM does for you. Calculate the effectiveness of any EM enhancement you use and study the results. If they don't measure up, either modify your approach or drop the medium.

Integrating EM Most Profitably

The following are some guides for how to integrate EM most profitably:

1. Research ways EM integrates with other media.
2. Find out how media integration increases marketing effectiveness.
3. Study how companies like yours integrate EM.

Keep investigating the Help Guide sources listed while you keep up with EM's rich variety. Take notes on EM media by listing what each can do. On your own or with a team, compare and select the best EM for your purpose. Then select the EM enhancement that's right for you. Test only the most logical and lowest cost forms first. Be sure to orient your sales force, your distributors, your dealers, and your dealer sales force as to how you are using it. And whatever EM you use, integrate it with your other marketing.

Help Source Guide

1. *Applied Telematics Inc.* provides a service to connect an inquiry to your office or 800 number to nearest dealer and offers a *free* information kit: 487 Devon Park Dr., Wayne, PA 19087. (215) 687-3701.

2. *Richard L. Bencin & Associates* offers a *free* article, "Team Selling: A Successful Synergy of Direct Marketing, Telemarketing and Field Sales": 8553 Timber Trail, Brecksville, OH 44141. (216) 526-6726.

3. Ernan Roman's *Integrated Direct Marketing: Techniques and Strategies for Success,* McGraw-Hill, Inc., 1988, provides case studies from AT&T and IBM—how to integrate the mix, media and field sales and is a much-praised work: 13311 Monterey Ave., Blue Ridge Summit, PA 17904. (800) 722-4726.

4. *"Strategies in Interactive Video"* (and how best to integrate it will all media) is a *free* report by John J. Pollack: 207 Bridge St., Dedham, MA 02026. (617) 329-5273.

Index

Applications of electronic marketing (EM):
  airline, air-freight division, 147
  broker:
    real estate, 134
    stock, 162, 181
  catalog:
    appliance, 305
    computer books, 312
    online, 303–315
    by phone, music boxes, 161
    print, 181
    voice system, financial-information, 161
  condominiums, developer of, 201
  dental equipment exporter, 148
  frequent-flyer programs, 159
  home office, 5
  life insurance company, 258
  manufacturers, 166
    boat, 160
    camera film, 237
    computers, repeat orders, 135
    diapers, 169
    fashion, 281
    greeting cards, 239
    pet food, 237
    pharmaceuticals, 166
    potato chips, 166
    sewing thread, commercial, 148
    soap, 239
    tennis balls, 240
  moonlighter, 6
  publisher:
    book, 310
    financial information, 255
  retailer, 57–59, 61–62
    tackle shop, 167
  retailer, chain:
    supermarkets, 135
  services:
    courier, air, 159
    800 directory, 267

Applications of electronic marketing (EM),
    services (Cont.):
    food service, 148
    instant cash, 135
    liquor delivery, worldwide, 134
    referrals to doctors, 135
    sales medium, for travel agents, 165,
      180, 294–295
    theater ticket agency, 148
    vacation-travel packager, 195
  small business, 3
  wholesaler:
    auto parts, 313
    books, 313
    cut flowers, 148
Audience measurement:
  and market research, 33–34
  and quantitative and qualitative re-
    search, 36
  and sales measurement, 31–33
  and single-source data, 34–36
    for radio, 116–117
  computer help, broadcast TV, 37
    cable TV, 37–38, 55, 68–69
    radio, 38
  free help, 39
  media:
    broadcast TV (BTV), 27–31, 55
    cable TV, 37, 38, 75–76
    radio, 112, 116
  rating reports, 29
  ratings, 29
  terms, 39
Audience trends:
  in broadcast TV, 51, 52, 54
  change in, 3
  radio, 110–112

Bulletin board systems (BBSs), super,
    275–276, 284–287

Bulletin board systems (BBSs), super
(*Cont.*):
America Online, 300
Bix, 299
CompuServe, 290–292
GEnie, 299
Main Street, 300
Prodigy, 293–298

Cable-classified (*see* Media)
Careers, most affected by electronic marketing (EM), 2–3
Case histories (Mini- and Micro-):
American Airlines online reservation
system, 324–325, 326
auctions:
Superior Livestock Auction, 417–419
book club:
Literary Guild, 465–466
broker:
Fidelity Corporation, stocks, 163
catalog:
Hammacher-Schlemmer, appliances,
305, 308, 311
Heath, appliance kits, 306, 307, 308,
309, 310–311
Quill Corporation, business catalog,
181
Sixty-Eight Thousand, Inc., com-
puter/write supplies, 271–272
Spiegel, large-size fashions, 211–213
discount marketplace, online:
CUC International, 319, 321–322, 326–327
distributor, 313–315
Camfour, firearms, 313–315
education:
Kansas City Art Institute, 207–208
financial services:
Citibank, 253–255
Far West Federal Bank, 447
Howard Bank, 395
Merrill-Lynch, 413
Mid-State Savings and Loan, 163
Wachovia Bank, 449
importer:
Marco Polo by Milani, Ltd., 208–209,
229–231
manufacturer:
Amiga computers, 198–199

Case histories (Mini- and Micro-), manu-
facturer (*Cont.*):
Apple computers, 199–200, 224–225
Benjamin Moore paints, 372
Buick, 256, 264, 265, 266
Chrysler, 414–415, 459–461
Clairol, 398–399, 446
Clarion, cosmetics, 379–381
Converse, shoes, basketball clinics,
412–413
Crane National Vendors, 427, 428
Dell Computer, 131–134
DePuy Prosthetic Process, 420
Ford, 264, 265, 266
General Electric, consumer appli-
ances, 441–444
General Electric, technical, profes-
sional, business products, 444
Hewlett Packard, computer peripher-
als, 413–414, 464–465
ITT, Bell & Gossett, 268
Levi Jeans, 371–372
Lincon-Mercury, cars, 256–257
Roger Hong Foods, Chinese season-
ing, 383
Software Developers Company, 181
SoloFlex, exercise equipment, 193
Texas Instruments, computer-aided
systems engineering, 411–412
Texas Instruments, voice chips,
468–470
Weyerhauser, lumber, 372–373
White Knight Software, shareware,
284–285, 450
Wood Mizer, sawmills, 210–211,
225–228
WordPerfect, computer software, 447
Xerox, copiers, 414
marketplace, CD-ROM, 338–339
furniture, 340–341
mannequins, 339–340
marketplaces, online:
AutoInfo, salvage, 319–320
BUCNET, yacht, 317, 320–321, 323, 328
CUC International, discounted prod-
ucts, 319
FASTFINDER, industrial fasteners,
321, 323
Inventory Locator Service (ILS), air-
craft parts, 321, 326

Case histories (Mini- and Micro-), market-
        places, online (*Cont.*):
    PUBNET, book publishers, 321–322
    publisher, magazine:
        Soap Talk, subscriptions, 168
        Sports Illustrated, subscriptions for, 168
        Technology Marketing, ad sales of,
            146–147
    restaurant chain:
        McDonalds, 114–116
    retail chain:
        Computer Land, 415–416
        Farmers and Builders Supply, 114
        J. C. Penney, 416–417
        J. C. Penney, men's clothes, 281
        Jordan Marsh, department stores, 448
        Jr. Food, convenience stores, 117
        Mervyn's, specialty stores, 448
        Montgomery Ward, 448
        SuperValue Stores, 281
        Tom Haynes's Tackle Shop, 167
        Vann's Appliances, 57–59
        Walden Books, 307–308, 310, 311
    retailer:
        Chrysler dealer, 201
        Kogut Florist & Nurseryman, 76–78
        P. C. Flowers, 295–297
    service:
        HoteleCopy, fax kiosk, 396
        Laser Travel Network, travel agen-
            cies, sale and service, 368–369
        Mead Data Central, Nexus News
            Plus, 257
        PIC, health information and ad net-
            work, 386
        Rosenbluth Travel, 294–295
        Safe Harbor's Travel (agency), 165
        Teleforum, audio conferencing,
            430–431
Compact Disk Interactive, (CD-I), 356
Creating and producing:
    computer disk, interactive ads, 252
        Hypercard, 270–271
    interactive catalogs, 251–253, 270
    copywriting, 24–25, 91–93
    creative research, 25
    faxmail message, 182
    message length, broadcast TV, 48
    radio commercial, 105–107
    sponsored telemedia message, 162–164

Creating and producing (*Cont.*):
    storyboards, 92
    telemarketing script, 150
    telemedia program, 164–165
    TV commercial, 83–100
        cost, 96–97
        do-it-yourself, 86–88
        low cost, 88–90, 94
        medium-to-higher cost, 94–97
        production decisions, 86
        production house, selection of, 97–100
    TV photo-ad, 87
    video, 193–194, 221–232
Customer Service, 22, 439–455
    bulletin board system, 449–450
    computer network, 451
    800 phone number, 129
    fax, 450–451
    kiosk, 452
    personal phone, 447
    product-support, bulletin board system
        (BBS), 286
    various services, 451–453
    voice system, 447–449

Digital Video Interactive (DVI), 355
Direct marketing, 303–315
    media, 41–42

Electronic data interchange (EDI) (*see*
        Modem marketing, EDI)
Electronic mail (E-Mail), 277–278
Electronic targeting, of magazines, 435–436
Enhancement of:
    print catalog by phone, 181, 466
    sales meetings, 196
    salesforce, 195, 461–463
    store display, 197
    telemarketing, 119
    TV by live telemarketer, 465
    TV by voice system, 465–466

Failures, what they teach, 4–5
    kiosks, 368–370
Finance:
    bank, "electronic funds transfer sys-
        tem," 255

Finance (*Cont.*):
  credit rating services, on CD-ROM, demo sampler, 255

Guidance:
  for advertising agencies, 17–19
    specializing in interactive computer discs, 255–256, 257
  consultants, 16
    audio conferencing, 429–433
    catalog, 466
    customer service, telephone, 445–446
    interactive discs, 257
    kiosk presentations, 348–353, 357–358
    online media, 306, 312
    telemarketing, 440–441
    vending, 426
    video, 201–203
    video production, 231
  magazines, inbound-outbound, telemarketing, 446
  research experts, 41
  video conferencing, newsletter bulletin, 435

In-store TV and radio networks, 385–386
Integration and enhancement, of media and marketing, 457–473
  any medium and faxback, instant and later, 182
  any medium-phone-fax, 183
  audiotex referral to nearest dealer, 160
  bulletin board system (BBS), support and on-screen ads, 268
  co-media and support media, 42–43
  computer disk, magazine bind-in, 257
  direct mail and three electronic media, 253–255
  800 phone numbers, 119, 123–126
  electronic "bingo cards," 183–184
  fax and phone number:
    on leave-behind, 182
    on letterhead, 182
    on trade show handout, 182
  kinds of, 1–2, 61–62
  literature by electronic multichoice, 183
  multimedia integration, 467–468
  print and TV, 457

Integration and enhancement, of media and marketing, print and TV (*Cont.*):
  research, effectiveness of, 457
  sales, and advertising, 463
  talking ads, 159–160
  talking ads on hold, 160–161
  telemarketers and the sales force, 463–464
  various combinations of, 458, 460–461
  various media, 42–43
  video and phone, 214–215
  video brochures and other media, 197
  video catalog and print catalog, 205, 207
  videos and sales meetings, 195–196

Market research:
  companies, 19–20
  do-it-yourself, 7–8, 21–23
  free, 21
  qualitative, 35
  quantitative, 36
  report forms for, 21
  target marketing, 23
Marketing campaign procedures:
  internal, 12
  organizing, 12
  outside, 12–13
  plan, 23
  pre-campaign analysis, 7–8
    TV, 48–49, 191–193
  roll-out expansion, 215–218
  targeting via database marketing, 23
    via outbound telemarketing, 142–143, 212
  testing, 24, 50
    audiotext, 170, 213–214
    radio, 109
Media, selection and negotiation:
  before beginning, 40
  broadcast TV, 45–63
    basics, 48–50
    local, 59–60
    low-power (LPTV), 61–62
    networks, 52–53
    networks, unwired, 61
    spot, 54–57, 61
  cable TV, 65–81
    local, 73–79

Media, selection and negotiation, cable TV (*Cont.*):
   local, photo-classified, 79–80
   networks, 68–73
   photo-classified, 79–80
   spot, 73–76
   commercials in movie theaters, 244
   custom-created, sponsored video, 237
   Direct Broadcast Satellite (DBS), business television, 407–422
   networks, 419–421
   seminars, 411–413
   magazines, electronically targeted, 435–436
   radio, spot and local, 107–108, 110–114
   telemedia, sponsored, 161–166, 169–170
   tracing and measuring sales, 31–33
   video media, 233–245
   video-movie sponsorship, 233–238
   videos as premiums, 238
     direct marketing, 31
     store promotions, 31, 32
Methods:
   audio conferencing, 429–433
   audio marketing, 423–426
   audiotex, 155–173
     automated phone-ordering, 159
     beginning, 155–157
     computer disc, interactive brochures, 247–273
     computer disc, interactive catalogs, 261–273
     computers, as interactive displays, 385
     900 phone numbers, 166–167, 171
     talking ads, 159–160
     talking ads on hold, 160–170
     voice mail, 158–159
   catalogs, CD-ROM, 331–338
     autoparts, 332
     CAD/CAM, 333
     cost, 337–338
     creating, 335
     jet parts, 333
     marketing uses, 331
     new CD-ROM sales method, 333–334
     service bureau, 336–337
   catalogs, electronically targeted, piggyback, 436
   catalogs on computer disk, 261–273

Methods (*Cont.*):
   Direct Broadcast Satellite, networks, 419–421
   Direct Broadcast Satellite, seminars, 411–413
   in-flight video, 243
   online marketplaces, 317–328
     setting up, 326–327
   outbound telemarketing, 137–153
     beginning and expanding, 139–143, 148
     cold calls, 144–148
     scripts, 149–150
   retail marketing machines, 361–375
     Automatic Teller Machines (ATMs), 364, 395
     kiosks, 363, 368–374, 403
   vending machines, 426–429
   video brochures, 189–204
     creating, 189, 191–193, 200–201
     uses of, 190, 195
   video catalogs, 205–220
     creating, 205–207, 209–210
     testing and expanding marketing, 213–219
   video conferencing, 433–435

Online marketplaces (*see* Methods)

People meter, the (*see* Audience measurement)
Produce-it-yourself, 13–15, 270–271
Product demonstration, 210
   via video cassette recorder (VCR), 197–198, 383
Production houses, 13, 90–91, 97–99
   audio conferencing, 429–433
   interactive discs, 268–269
   kiosk programs, 348–353, 357–358
   video, 228–229
Production in-house:
   produce-it-yourself projects, 13–15
Promotions:
   instant-sweepstakes by phone, 169
   media cross-promotions by phone, 169
   media fun-polls by phone, 169
   radio stations, 114

Promotions (*Cont.*):
  recipes by phone, 169
Publicity and public relations:
  enhanced, integrated PR, 468
  instant-phone, fan club, 169
  news releases, fax, 181
  online PR, 283
  video releases, 196–197

Radio commercial, 105–107
Research, 19–22

Sales communication, 277
  sales meetings, 195
  sales training, 195
Sales measurement (*see* Media, selection
  and negotiation)

Service bureaus, 15, 171, 184
  fax, 184
  telemarketing inbound/outbound,
    126–129, 152–153
Service, in-house:
  serve yourself, 16
Shareware, 284–286
Small businesses:
  home office, 5–6
  moonlighting, 6

Talking displays, 384

Video Cassette Recorder (VCR) networks,
  in-store, 383–384
Video conferencing, 433–435
Video walls, 387–388

About the Author

Cecil C. Hoge, Sr. is widely hailed as one of the nation's direct mail pioneers and marketing innovators. He is president of Harrison-Hoge Industries, a Port Jefferson, New York–based marketing firm, where his day-to-day responsibilities keep him at the cutting edge of all the latest electronic marketing techniques. He is the best-selling author of *Mail Order Moonlighting*, which has sold more than 100,000 copies.